s Published in Cooperation with
tional Food Policy Research Institute:

Change and Rural Poverty: Variations on a Theme by Dharm
hn W. Mellor and Gunvant M. Desai

nce for Agricultural Development: Issues and Experience
ter B. R. Hazell, Carlos Pomareda, and Alberto Valdés

Food Production in Sub-Saharan Africa
hn W. Mellor, Christopher L. Delgado, and Malcolm J. Blackie

AGRICULTURAL PRICE
FOR DEVELOPING COU

Agricultural Price Policy
for Developing Countries

edited by
JOHN W. MELLOR and RAISUDDIN AHMED

Published for the International Food Policy Research Institute
THE JOHNS HOPKINS UNIVERSITY PRESS
Baltimore and London

Second printing, 1989

The Johns Hopkins University Press
701 West 40th Street
Baltimore, Maryland 21211
The Johns Hopkins Press Ltd., London

The paper used in this publication meets the minimum requirements of American National
Standard for Information Sciences—Permanence of Paper for Printed Library Materials,
ANSI Z39.48-1984.

Library of Congress Cataloging-in-Publication Data

Agricultural price policy for developing countries / edited by John W. Mellor and
  Raisuddin Ahmed.
     p.   cm.
"Published for the International Food Policy Research Institute."
Bibliography: p.
Includes index.
ISBN 0-8018-3586-0 (alk. paper)
    1. Food prices—Government policy—Developing countries. 2. Agricultural
prices—Government policy—Developing countries. I. Mellor, John Williams,
1928–   . II. Ahmed, Raisuddin, 1932–
HD9018.D44A367   1988
338.1'8'091724—dc19   87-26862
                                                                       CIP

Contents

Tables and Figures

Tables

Figures

Preface

The weight of agricultural prices in political debate, their searing importance to the poor, and their common association with unusually low agricultural output levels often lead to policies that focus directly on prices at
the expense of other underlying economic relations. In contrast, our objective is to focus explicitly on agricultural price policy in the context of economic growth and, more specifically, of technological change.

In the recent past, and in some cases even now, developing countries
have followed foreign trade, exchange rate, and domestic policies which
have so grossly distorted agricultural prices as to call for a singleminded
focus on removing those gross distortions. We note such circumstances
and their causes but look beyond "once-and-for-all" price adjustments to
the process of technological change and the institutional changes that go,
pari passu, with technological change. Agricultural price policy is important to those processes, and it is that interaction to which we constantly
return.

Although our subject is agricultural price policy, we give particular attention to food crops produced for domestic consumption. Demand for
export crops is largely determined outside the country. Domestic price policy for export products is, for the most part, limited to exchange rate determination and domestic prices as they affect supply. In contrast, for nearly
all developing countries both supply and demand for food crops are substantially determined by domestic forces and are influenced by national
policy. Further, the role of food crops as the primary item of expenditure
by wage earners gives these crops a special importance in employment-
oriented strategies of growth.

The importance of agricultural price policies to development motivated
the International Food Policy Research Institute to undertake the research, the papers, and the discussions that generated this book. The
papers were prepared by the senior research staff of the International

Food Policy Research Institute in the course of their in-depth research programs.

Analysis of agricultural price policy is a never-ending task. Objectives, instruments, and consequences constantly move in seemingly unpredictable patterns. Hence this book "stops the action" so that we can examine relationships at a particular time. Emphasis is given to the complexity of the issues. In some chapters, this is best brought out by exposition of the relationships themselves, with only modest reference to illustrative data. Other chapters are strongly empirical and deal with particular situations in order to show interactions. The purpose throughout is to inform practical policymaking.

Policymakers and their advisors, staff economists, and expatriate professionals who may conduct dialogue on price policies with national governments thus constitute the primary audience for this book. Today's students constitute our secondary audience. Consistent with this objective, the book focuses on applied problems of developing countries rather than on the abstraction of economic relations and measurement emphasized in standard texts on price policy.

Research on policy issues is not useful if it does not concurrently deal with the policy process itself. Hence, the International Food Policy Research Institute invited a group of senior government officials from developing countries to hear such details of our research findings as we thought would be useful to them, and to give us their reactions to our attempts to generalize in a meaningful and appropriate manner. With the help of Swiss Development Cooperation, the meeting was convened at Belmont Estate, in Maryland, for three days of intensive discussions with eminent intellectuals, ministers, permanent secretaries, and directors from ministries of planning, finance, and agriculture and from central banks. All participants were major actors in agricultural price policy determination. It was an extraordinarily stimulating interchange, and we are grateful for their participation. We are especially grateful to Rolf Wilhelm and Marco Ferroni, of Swiss Development Cooperation, for facilitating the meeting and for the active participation of Mr. Ferroni. These outside participants are listed in the Appendix to this volume.

Papers were developed for the Belmont seminar, but those papers served only as the starting point for the discussions there; the chapters of this book were written in light of the seminar discussions. We have retained the specifics of cases and examples which our colleagues from policy positions found most valuable and have been cautious about generalization in this complex area. We are grateful to all our colleagues for their continuous work on these papers and especially to Michael Lipton, who shared with all of us extraordinarily detailed critiques of each chapter.

Particular thanks are due to Robert Bordonaro and Laurie Goldberg, for the management of the workshop; to Irene Pereira, for her coordination of the work and for the typing; and to Andrew Bernard, for checking the bibliographic references and reading the manuscripts for omissions and errors. The staff of IFPRI's Information Services Department, as usual, deserves thanks for bringing the book to fruition.

Finally, we thank Wayne Dexter for his invaluable assistance in shortening the final text and improving its clarity and uniformity.

AGRICULTURAL PRICE POLICY
FOR DEVELOPING COUNTRIES

1

INTRODUCTION
Agricultural Price Policy—
the Context and the Approach

RAISUDDIN AHMED and JOHN W. MELLOR

Determination of agricultural prices is intensely political because of its profound influence on equity, income distribution, consumption, production, and economic development. Thus agricultural price policy occupies a major place in political debate, the deliberations of government bureaucracies, and the decisions made by consumers and producers. This is so in both high-income countries, where food and agriculture represent a small part of aggregate income but are still important in consumption and politics, and in low-income countries, where they are central to the political and economic processes.

The bulk of adjustment to food supply shortfalls in low-income countries is borne by low-income people through drastic reduction in their intake of basic nutrients. Since the poor spend essentially all their income on food, a rise in food prices causes an almost equivalent reduction in their income. Richer people, who spend a smaller proportion of their income on food, can maintain their food consumption even when food prices rise substantially. In India, for example, a typical person in the poorest one-fifth of households reduces food consumption by ten times as much when food prices rise as does a typical member of the "richest twentieth" of households (Mellor 1978). A 10 percent reduction in the aggregate supply of food results, via increased prices, in a 37 percent reduction in food consumption by the 20 percent of the population with lowest income. Given the initially low level of consumption of this group, such a cut means that famine conditions are present (Mellor and Gavian 1987). Thus, governments in developing countries do not leave provision of adequate food supplies to the vagaries of weather or the market. It follows, of course, that government intrusion into the market to deal effectively with extreme circumstances may persist into more normal periods, with unfavorable effects on efficiency.

Governments are generally aware of the role of agricultural prices in distributing income between farm and nonfarm sectors, among geographical regions, and among income classes. In developing countries, where the urban population, particularly public employees and the military, may exert a disproportionate political influence, food pricing is likely to be used to benefit the urban constituency at the expense of farmers. In these circumstances, government is particularly likely not to understand the requisites of technological change in agriculture. As a result, enforcement of low agricultural prices tends to go hand in hand with neglect of the modernization of agriculture. As such political systems mature, however, particularly as they become more democratic, the increasing political power of the rural population may bring a reversal of this price policy. Problems of excessive subsidies and stock-building, which keep prices to producers above international levels, may then replace excessive government expenditure on subsidies to urban consumers that keep prices below international levels. In either case, the fiscal costs tend to become unmanageable.

The small, family-size farms that dominate the agriculture of most developing countries are responsive to price as well as to other economic forces. Consequently, agricultural prices play a role in achieving efficient allocation of a country's resources within agriculture, between agriculture and non-agriculture, and between domestic production and imports. Changes in prices that affect relative profitability may occur through market forces, in which case the farmer's response may increase efficiency. However, they may result from government manipulation of exchange rates, trade regimes, and public expenditure. In that case, what is an efficient response for farmers may reduce the efficiency of the national economy.

Four caveats concerning price responsiveness are in order. First, markets in developing countries are particularly imperfect. Farmers may be reluctant to risk their own food supplies by switching to nonfood crops. Second, farmers are often severely constrained in their ability to respond to price changes by fixed land area (e.g., Asia) or by extremely low productivity of labor (e.g., Africa). It is for this reason that we emphasize the interaction between price policy and technological change that may increase land and labor productivity. Third, for price policy alone to increase production presumes that farmers can increase input use and obtain a favorable output response independent of other actions by government. If they cannot, increased prices will only transfer income to producers, with little effect on output. Finally, when agricultural output is increased by prices higher than international prices, a cost is paid in less employment, as domestic wages are pushed above those of other low-income countries by the higher cost of food.

Governments have limited power to maintain food prices that are substantially at variance with the forces of supply and demand. This is because food production is so diffused throughout the economy and the macro aggregates in the food sector are so large. If domestic demand is greater than supply at a government-imposed price, an unofficial market is likely to develop that will divert more and more supplies away from the low-price market until the official market effectively ceases to operate. Of course, the efficiency of the unofficial market may be low. Perhaps more important, if imports are used to reduce food prices below international levels, both the subsidies and the foreign exchange requirements will soon become so large as to bring pressure on government to change policies.

These considerations apply particularly to developing countries. Developed countries can be more successful in manipulating food prices because agriculture is a smaller part of their economies and thus is more easily supported by other sectors. Developing countries with massive oil revenues or ample foreign assistance can, of course, maintain agricultural price distortions much longer than those without such resources.

While maintaining prices at sharp variance with the balance of supply and demand may be difficult, non-price policies of developing countries have a major effect on the levels of both supply and demand and thus may alter prices markedly. If the bulk of the capital of a country is coopted by the public sector for large-scale industry or capital-intensive import substitution, employment growth and hence the demand for food will be sharply constrained. That facilitates a low food price policy. In practice, overvalued exchange rates are associated with such an investment and employment policy. Thus the slow growth in effective demand for food commonly associated with exchange rate overvaluation makes it feasible to maintain relatively low agricultural prices. Broader consideration of development strategy as it affects agricultural prices is discussed in the concluding chapter.

The extraordinary complexity of agricultural price policy arises from the immense magnitude of the economic forces involved, the large fluctuations in agricultural prices and their profound implications for the distribution of income and power, the small size of production and consumption units for food in low-income countries, their wide geographical dispersion, and the peculiar limitations imposed by land and other natural factors. Governments decide on the appropriate level of agricultural prices and their range of fluctuations in the context of changing economic circumstances, political configurations, and national goals.

If prices are not at an appropriate level or within a desired range, governments design policy instruments to change them. The choices are large, the limits manifold. The choice of objectives and instruments involves considerations that necessarily range far beyond the initial objective. Thus, governments must build substantial institutions with well-trained people to develop an effective price policy, a point stressed in most of the chapters in this book.

The context within which agricultural price policy is analyzed in this book includes the elements discussed above—its political nature, its important allocative role, the limits to countering underlying supply and demand forces, the opportunities to change supply and demand through non-price factors, and complexity. The elements, each vital to agricultural price determination, considered in the remaining five parts of this book are the international environment, domestic market interventions, production response and technology, consumer welfare, and policies for agricultural growth.

In a world of extensive economic and political interdependence among nations, it is essential to analyze the international environment within which domestic policy is determined and carried out. The rapid changes in that environment have important implications for national agricultural price policy.

In chapter 2 Leonardo Paulino documents the increasing dependence of developing countries on imports of basic food staples. Cereal exports of developed countries from 1960–65 to 1978–82 grew 74 percent faster than those of developing countries. Conversely, imports of developing countries grew 43 percent faster than those of developed countries.

Developing countries that expand food production most rapidly also generally expand food imports (Bachman and Paulino 1979). This means that the dynamics of agricultural growth, as discussed in the concluding chapter, are associated with employment growth that causes demand for food to outpace even a rapid growth in supply (Mellor and Johnston 1984). Similarly it shows a potential to maintain upward pressure on domestic food prices through rapid growth in domestic demand.

Demand for cereals for feed is the most dynamic element in global cereal trade. In the period 1962–82 that demand grew about 50 percent faster in developing countries than demand for cereals for food. In developed countries, essentially all the growth in demand for cereals is for feed.

The trends suggest for the future a steady growth in net food imports into developing countries and in food exports from developed countries, accompanied by considerable fluctuation in stocks and prices. Thus developing countries can plan in a favorable environment for employment growth, with the expectation that internationally available food supplies need not be a constraint if domestic production shortfalls occur.

In chapter 3 Peter Hazell points out that within these trends the food policies of developing countries have been adopted in an environment of increasingly volatile prices in international markets. Markets have become less stable at a time when developing countries have become increasingly dependent on them for food imports.

Structural shifts in demand, changes in U.S. storage policies, and increased production variability for both exporting and importing countries are the main sources of increased price variability in world cereal markets. Because of the openness of the markets of exporting countries, price variability in the domestic markets of the United States, Canada, and Argentina has been similar to that in world markets. In contrast, domestic policies reduced variability in EEC countries, Japan, and most developing countries, and it is ironic that thereby they increased the turbulence in world prices. For most developing countries there is at best low correlation between movements in domestic prices and international prices. The absolute variability in domestic cereal prices in these countries was only one-half to one-third of the world price variability during the 1970s. Careful attention to stocking policy and reserves of foreign exchange can markedly reduce fluctuations in domestic prices. The special lending facility installed in the International Monetary Fund to preserve national capacity to finance imports of cereals in periods of unusually heavy requirements is an innovation favorable to such stability. While it has been relatively dormant, properly developed and utilized it can be an important assurance of food security in an increasingly unstable international environment.

The importance of international markets is a recurring theme in the six chapters of this book dealing with issues related to interventions in domestic food markets. Raisuddin Ahmed, in chapter 4, starts with the position that developing countries should try to obtain the advantages in efficiency of trade at international prices. He then discusses the many practical difficulties in relating domestic prices to international prices, including the extreme volatility of international prices, the lack of comparability of grades, the problems in determining the real exchange rate, and the high marketing and transport costs so common in developing countries. He suggests that domestic prices be set with reference to, but not necessarily precisely at, international prices and that a moving average be used to smooth out the immense fluctuations in international prices. He suggests pricing rules that avoid additional transaction costs in the market and increased price spreads. He notes that private trade generally operates more efficiently than the public sector, and that major savings can be made if the public objectives of price policy can be achieved without dislodging the private sector.

Since resources for achieving price policy objectives are very limited, governments often must choose between investments that will achieve increased productivity—the longer-run price policy objective—and measures that may reduce productivity but will achieve at least some goals immediately. As an example of the former, comparative data for Asia and Africa illustrate the large opportunities in Africa for obtaining lower consumer prices and higher producer prices through judicious public sector investment in market infrastructure, particularly in transport.

Government stock policy, discussed by Ammar Siamwalla in chapter 5, is basic to any government effort to minimize price fluctuations. The operational requirements are illustrated by a successful public stocking system. Siamwalla examines issues related to year-to-year, seasonal, and working stocks, considers the relationship between private and public stocks, and measures the fiscal burden of storage cost and the optimal level of stocks.

Public intervention in foodgrain markets in Indonesia has successfully stabilized prices and supply at a cost which is a minuscule part of the Indonesian budget. A well-defined operation, using price rather than quantity as the policy target and backed by resources that are used only when necessary, can make a program successful. Even then, such programs tend to act as partial substitutes for private trade and involve an indirect credit subsidy not reflected in the budget.

The potential costs in the risks of farming are large for both farmers and society at large. In chapter 6, Peter Hazell reviews the many types of risks and the devices for reducing them. Improved market information services, credit programs, and specialized types of insurance are useful but tend to be poorly developed in low-income countries. Whether price stabilization programs reduce income risk or not depends on a variety of circumstances. Costs of generalized types of crop insurance usually are well above the level of benefits.

In chapter 7 Alberto Valdés and Ammar Siamwalla discuss the effects on agriculture of policies meant to favor growth of the nonagricultural sector. They show that trade regime and exchange rate policies operate at the expense of exportables and import-competing products in agriculture. A policy that protects industry raises the cost of importables like fertilizers, pesticides, and machinery used in agriculture. In addition, these policies have a large unrecognized but significantly discriminating effect against agricultural exports. In Colombia, for example, a uniform import tariff of 20 percent represents an implicit tax of 18 percent on exports.

Since the burden of policies protecting nonagricultural sectors falls so heavily on agriculture, the question arises as to whether they are consistent with a sound development strategy. Chapter 16 deals broadly with this question, while chapter 7 examines the arguments favoring the nonagricultural sector and concludes that these arguments apply at least as well to agriculture and hence are not a case for favoring the nonagricultural sector. The chapter carries this argument to its logical conclusion by arguing strongly for international prices as the reference point for domestic price policy. Other chapters discuss the need to modify the first-best position that is invoked by pragmatic considerations. Chapter 7 is an important antidote to the still-popular emphasis in many developing countries on industrial development policies that are strongly deleterious to agriculture. Preventing the real exchange rate from becoming overvalued is emphasized as a key policy requirement for protecting agriculture from discrimination.

The complexities of public intervention in agricultural price determination are examined in case studies of China and India, which have developed unusually broad price policies. Bruce Stone's chapter on China traces the changing objectives of agricultural price policy as the political situation changes. Public intervention grows in crisis years but is not easily reduced in normal years. He highlights the complementarity between changes in price policy and other production-related policies, as does Gunvant Desai, in chapter 12. In China the reversal of price policies unfavorable to agriculture was matched by major policy changes regarding institutional relations, input availability, and capital investment. More recently the investment programs have been cut back, suggesting, in the framework of chapter 12, that the pace of technological change will slow.

J. S. Sarma's study of India (chapter 9) highlights the tensions between producers' incentives and consumers' welfare and the complex policies that attempt to reconcile the two. He points out the rationales for various policies and the way in which they were set forth and accepted for India. He emphasizes the high levels of administrative skills and organizational capacities required for effective public intervention in agricultural prices.

Since the focus of this book is on agricultural prices in the context of economic development, the four chapters which make up part III deal with the extent to which production will change with change in prices, the relation of prices to the pace of technological change, and the relation of technology and prices to the increased use of purchased inputs. The first of these chapters is conceptual and emphasizes the interaction of technical change and capital accumulation. It then establishes the role of relative prices in capital accumulation and their production effect. The second chapter provides empirical evidence as to the effect of technological change on cost of production and supply response to price. The third and fourth chapters take a close look at the role and pricing of purchased inputs and credit.

In his conceptualizing chapter, Yair Mundlak places agricultural prices squarely in the context of technological change and establishes that aggregate agricultural supply responds little to price without technological change. Production response to prices is expected to be markedly inelastic in the short run and much more elastic in the long run. Mundlak notes that short-run price changes have a large transitory component, so that it is not efficient to attempt to relate long-run aggregate supply to them. This implies that smoothing price fluctuations for the benefit of consumers will have little distorting effect on aggregate production.

Prices affect production through their effect on resource allocation.

When the implementation of new techniques is constrained by capital availability, increasing capital use in agriculture in response to an increase in price will be conducive to such implementation and thereby will increase output over and above the direct effect of resource allocation. Availability of new techniques at farm level is, however, a critical condition for a large increase in output in response to an increase in price.

Two other elements implicit in Mundlak's discussion deserve to be stressed. First, misallocation of agricultural investment is most likely to be due to insufficient attention by government to key elements of technological change, such as research, input delivery systems, and infrastructure. In that case there will be tension between taxing agriculture in the short run to obtain the revenues for necessary investment and reallocating government resources. Second, developing countries are far behind in technology and typically are lagging in the development of support systems for agricultural growth. Much progress can be made by developing these systems.

The forces of technological change, such as public expenditure on agricultural research, may be responsive to prices in the long run. However, viewing these long-run forces only as a supply response to price tends to understate the importance of technological and institutional policies required to exploit the potential for growth. Because of the time required to obtain adjustment through price policies, it is generally more efficient to attempt to predict long-run constraints to technological change and to deal with them explicitly. In the developing countries of Asia and Africa the time required for prices alone to induce the technological innovation and institutional development that would increase production could be decades rather than years.

The chapter by Ranade, Jha, and Delgado illustrates the two major points critical to the role of price policy in economic development. First, the effect of a reduction in the cost of production resulting from technological change in agriculture normally has a far greater effect on incentives than a price change. Second, the responsiveness of supply to price increases with technological change and modernization of agriculture. These two points underline the importance of seeing price policy in the context of technological change and the necessity for a range of public policies to bring about a steady stream of cost-reducing technologies.

Studies in West Africa and in the Punjab in India show the positive effect of agricultural innovations on the return to land and management, the internal restructuring of input use, and increasing price responsiveness. That technology increases the responsiveness of supply to price, in addition to shifting the supply schedule, is an extremely important finding.

The possibility that price may take a subsidiary position relative to other forces of growth is discussed by Gunvant Desai (chapter 12) and by Mark Rosegrant and Ammar Siamwalla (chapter 13). For them, fertilizer price and interest rate subsidies are much less important than policies to assure adequate supply at the time and in the form desired by farmers. In the case of fertilizer, Desai shows clearly that developing countries operate in a situation of gross disequilibrium. In general, it still would pay farmers to use much more fertilizer than they now do. The disequilibrium arises from such factors as poor distribution channels and lack of technical knowledge. In these circumstances, effective price policy must take into account these non-price factors.

Similarly, the productivity of credit is determined by access to it, availability of technology, and institutional factors, rather than by interest rates. The greatest impact of a credit program is in making credit available. The independent effect of interest rate reduction is relatively small. This illustrates a major point made in chapter 10: the pace of technological change is regulated by the pace of capital accumulation. Chapter 13 shows that traditional credit systems are adequate in a static technological environment, but that with technological change the pace of acceptance is much more rapid if credit is financed from outside the local economy.

Thus, a powerful empirical case is made for institutional credit. This implies that many governments could reduce their cost of credit subsidy by raising interest rates, if such rates are below market rates, without increasing the risk of default or slowing of production growth. In general, a high level of subsidy to financial institutions acts as a substitute for management development and prevents banks from competing effectively in agricultural credit markets. As is the case for fertilizer, subsidy in the early stage of credit markets could be instrumental in the development of financial institutions if it is directed to institutional development, including management skills.

Perhaps few people would object to high price incentives to food producers were it not for the fact that high food prices adversely affect consumers as much as or more than they benefit producers. Two chapters cover pertinent issues in this conflict between producers and consumers. Chapter 14 by Per Pinstrup-Andersen analyzes the short- and long-run problems and solutions involved in consumer food subsidies. Food prices dramatically affect the real income of the poor. However, a general policy of inexpensive food may well cause severe disincentives to production increases. These disincentives may be direct, in the form of lower farm prices, or indirect, in the form of reduced public expenditure on essential public services for agriculture. It is thus desirable to develop mechanisms for targeting benefits to those with lowest income. In doing so, attention must be paid to the tradeoff between administrative costs and leakage of benefits to high-income consumers. If a target group is too large and the program is not properly managed, it can be very costly and can create severe obstacles to growth in other sectors, as in the case of Egypt.

The food aid mechanism is traditionally used for resource transfer from food-surplus developed countries to food-deficit developing countries. Its effect on production of foodgrains in recipient nations remains widely controversial. In chapter 15 Joachim von Braun and Barbara Huddleston dispute the widely held belief that food aid necessarily discourages domestic production through price disincentives to farmers and induces laxity in institutional development by government. The disincentive effect of food aid has seldom been proved significant empirically. Most striking is the rapid growth of agricultural production achieved by major food aid recipients. The key is to use food aid in a manner that increases effective demand commensurate with the added food. To achieve this result, the food aid must reach low-income people.

In the concluding chapter, price policy issues are placed in the context of an underlying development strategy. In the generalized strategy, the relative roles of prices, technology, capital, and labor are related in a manner consistent with increasing the demand for labor while encouraging the augmentation of capital necessary for growth in per capita income and employment.

Inexpensive food facilitates application of labor-intensive techniques and capital accumulation in nonagricultural sectors. An integral part of the strategy is to utilize technological progress in agriculture to sustain the incentives for increasing food production in the face of inexpensive food. This provides the context for management of price policy issues related to price stabilization, equity, price setting for individual commodities and inputs, direct intervention in markets, technological diffusion, and macroeconomic instruments, including trade, fiscal, monetary, and exchange rate policies.

In the context of development strategy, particular emphasis is given to the price effects of the dynamics of unequal shift in supply and demand. It is noted that upward shifts for both supply and demand create a favorable circumstance for growth at the same time that either rising or falling output prices send a strong signal of increasing disequilibrium.

Two major concluding points are emphasized. First, the laggard side of the demand-supply equation is to be emphasized whenever a disequilibrium indicates the need for corrective policy. Second, because of complex and lengthy lags in response, such a policy has a better chance of succeeding if it can be anticipated than if it is launched at the peak of disequilibrium. That means that the ability to predict approaching price disequilibrium and to respond with supply and demand actions that are not price-oriented is a critical element of an effective public price policy.

I

THE INTERNATIONAL ENVIRONMENT FOR NATIONAL PRICE POLICIES

2

Trends in Cereal Supply, Demand, Trade, and Stocks

LEONARDO A. PAULINO

Forces underlying commodity trade, capital movement, technology transfer, and political cooperation contribute to increased interdependence among nations. The policies of a country are influenced by the international policy environment, which represents the collective national policies of other countries. Thus, depending on the policy area, countries affect one another in varying degrees. This chapter discusses the past, present, and emerging global conditions of the supply and demand for cereals, an important element of agriculture and trade in this international environment.[1] These global conditions constitute a crucial part of the framework of agricultural policies of developing countries. A global backdrop is provided here for the chapters that address domestic aspects of price policies.

Adjusting global cereal supply to demand is a dynamic process that has to deal with fluctuations in production in both importing and exporting countries, changing patterns of domestic utilization, shifts in national production and trade policies, and other factors both economic and political. The growth of cereal production in developing countries has been much more rapid than population growth, but demand has grown even faster than production.[2] As a result, net cereal imports of developing countries have shown a steep upward trend.

PRODUCTION

Between 1961–65 and 1976–80, world cereal production increased by about 100 million metric tons every three years. Annual increments averaged 19 million metric tons in the developed countries and 15 million in the developing countries (including China). Developing countries, which con-

---

1. Based on 1976–80 data, cereals account for nearly 90 percent of the world's major food staples production and about 95 percent of their volume in world trade.
2. Unless otherwise stated, the term "developing countries" refers to these countries as a group.

tain three-fourths of the world's population, contributed less than half of the total world cereal production in the late 1970s. On a per capita basis, estimated output for developed countries was more than three times that for developing countries.

Growth of world cereal production, excluding China, averaged 2.8 percent a year during 1961–80 for both developed and developing country groups (table 2.1). Meanwhile annual growth rates of population were 1.0 percent for developed countries, 2.5 percent for developing countries, and 1.9 percent for the total. Thus while cereal production growth rate was 2.8 times the population growth rate for developed countries, it was only 12 percent greater than the population growth rate in developing countries.

It is notable that in the period 1961–80 the average annual percentage variations from trend of world cereal production were far larger in the developed countries, 4.5 percent, than in the developing countries, 2.5 percent. These greater fluctuations in developed countries may be caused in part by adjustments in their production and trade policies to volatile conditions in the world grain trade. Most developing countries, which are largely net importers, can more easily insulate their domestic production from external conditions and thereby smooth domestic production.

Production growth rates slowed significantly for both country groups from the levels of the 1960s, at the height of the green revolution, down through the 1970s. Compared to the growth during 1961–70, the average annual rate of increase of world cereal output fell 30 percent during 1971–80, with a drop of 40 percent for developed economies and only 10 percent for developing countries. The slowdown of the growth of cereal production in the developed economies occurred largely in the U.S.S.R. and Eastern Europe, where the annual growth rate declined from 4.0 percent in 1961–70 to only 1.2 percent in 1971–80. In the rest of the developed countries there was an 18 percent decline in the production growth rate. Consistent with that, world cereal output rose every year in the 1960s except 1965, but alternated between increases and decreases during 1971–80 except for two successive increments in the mid-1970s (fig. 2.1). Nevertheless, production was farthest above trend in 1971, 1973, and 1978, when it exceeded trend estimates by more than 4 percent.

Output performance during the second half of the 1960s clearly reflected the initial impact of the green revolution in Asia. Figure 2.1 also shows that world cereal output was significantly below trend in 1961, 1965, 1975, and 1980. During these two decades, simultaneous production declines in developed and developing countries occurred only in 1972 and 1977. Both groups showed increases in eight of the observed years, with total production increasing 8 percent or more in five of those years.

Practically all of production growth in developed countries is attributable to rising yields, while expansion of area has been a relatively impor-

Table 2.1 Growth trends of world cereal production, 1961-80, 1961-70, and 1971-80

	Annual growth rate of cereal production[b]		
Country group[a]	1961-80	1961-70	1971-80
	(percent)		
Developed countries	2.8	3.2	1.9
Developing countries	2.8	3.1	2.8
World total	2.8	3.2	2.2

Sources: Basic data from FAO production tapes, 1975, 1979, 1980; China (Taiwan Executive Yuan) 1982.

[a] Following the FAO classification of countries. Excludes China, whose production levels in the early 1960s were abnormally low on account of disruptions during the period. Use of data for the People's Republic of China would tend to exaggerate output trends for developing countries and the world as a whole. The country's cereal production data indicate average annual growth rates of 4.0 percent, 5.4 percent, and 3.9 percent in 1961-80, 1961-70, and 1971-80, respectively.

[b] The measures of annual growth rates were derived from the fitted semi-logarithmic equation $Y = e^{a+bt}$ to time-series data on cereal production, where Y represents production, t number of years from the base period of the series, and b the annual rate of change in the logarithm of Y.

tant factor in developing countries. But, as agricultural research systems mature in developing countries and the land frontier recedes, that contrast is becoming less. Thus, in the period 1961-80, about 90 percent of production growth in developed countries is explained by yield increases and only 10 percent by area; in contrast, for developing countries those proportions were 65 percent and 35 percent, respectively. But developing countries raised the proportion of production increases explained by yield from 50 percent during 1961-70 to 70 percent in 1971-80. That evolution can be expected to continue.

CONSUMPTION

While the production growth rate in the past two decades has been similar in developed and developing countries, there is a sharp contrast in their consumption trends.[3] It is that contrast which provides the dynamics of the major changes in trade to be discussed below and the possible favorable environment for agricultural investment in developing countries.

Cereal consumption between 1961-65 and 1976-80 expanded at 3.2 percent a year in developing countries and 2.5 percent a year in developed countries (table 2.2). Relative to their respective rates of production growth, consumption was 14 percent faster in developing countries and 11

---

3. Consumption here refers to total domestic utilization.

Figure 2.1 Actual world cereal production and trend estimates, 1961–82

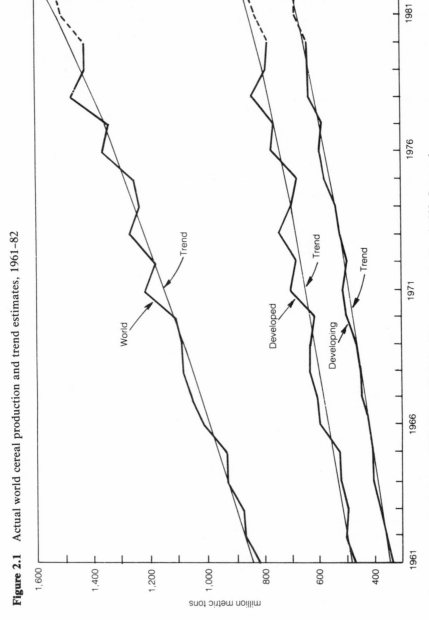

Sources: FAO production tapes 1975, 1979, 1980; China (Taiwan Executive Yuan) 1982; Stone n.d.
Note: Broken line indicates data not included in the analysis.

Table 2.2 Trends in world consumption of cereals, 1961–65 to 1978–82

Country group[a]	Relative distribution of cereal consumption among uses									Average annual rate of consumption growth, 1961–65 to 1978–82		
	1961–65			1978–82								
	Food	Feed[b]	Other uses	Food	Feed[b]	Other uses				Total	Food	Feed[b]
	(percent)											
Developed countries	25	60	15	18	68	14				2.4	0.5	3.0
Developing countries	66	17	17	64	21	15				3.3	3.0	4.7
World total	39	45	16	36	49	15				2.7	2.2	3.3

Source: FAO 1985.
[a]Following the FAO classification of countries. Excludes China.
[b]Estimates include cereal bran and cake.

percent slower in developed countries. The contrast is much sharper if the Soviet bloc is excluded from the estimates for developed countries, in which case the consumption growth rate of the group is 29 percent slower than production growth. The Soviet bloc has a comparable production growth rate to other developed countries, but with its lower per capita income there is much more scope for increased per capita consumption.

The dynamics of consumption are brought out more clearly by separating food and feed uses of cereals. In developed countries growth in food use is negligible, at 0.4 percent. It is only because of the growth in feed use at 3.4 percent a year that overall consumption grows. During 1978–82 feed use accounted for about two-thirds of cereal consumption in the developed economies, compared to one-fifth in developing countries (fig. 2.2). And we can see from the behavior of the highest-income countries that even their livestock consumption and hence feed use will also stop growing. It is clear why developed countries have been able to provide rapidly increasing exports of cereals to developing countries. Their production grows moderately fast through yield increases from cost-decreasing technological change, and demand grows hardly at all.

The feed story is also dynamic for developing countries. Growing at 1.5 times the rate of food use, the use of cereals for animal feed almost doubled from the early 1960s to the late 1970s. One of the major changes in the

Figure 2.2   World cereal utilization, 1978–82

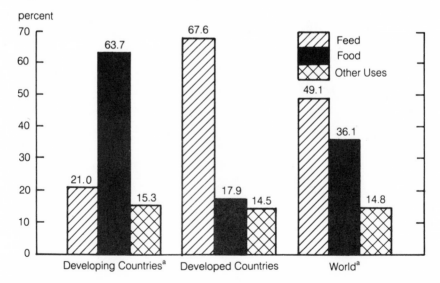

Source: FAO 1985.
[a]Excluding China.

world cereals scene is the rapid growth in demand for feed in developing countries and the growth of the base of feed use from what began as a negligible quantity to a significant portion of total cereal consumption. Thus rapid growth in per capita incomes in developing countries is favorable to rapid growth in demand for cereals.

TRADE

The dynamics of differing supply and demand forces in developed and developing countries is reflected in the rapid growth of cereals trade with flows from developed to developing countries, a particularly striking aspect of the global scene.

World trade in cereals during 1978–82 averaged about 220 million metric tons annually (table 2.3). This was equivalent to about 14 percent of the average yearly cereal production in the period. Developed countries accounted for more than 85 percent of exports and 60 percent of imports. Average yearly exports of Third World countries were less than 30 million metric tons; imports were about 90 million metric tons (China accounted for 1.3 million metric tons of these exports and 16.8 million metric tons of imports). Based on trade estimates for these country groups, the net flow of grains from the developed economies to developing countries in 1978–82 was about 60 million tons a year, or more than one-fourth of the total moved by trade.

From 1961–65 to 1978–82, cereal exports of developed countries rose 2.5 times. This was equivalent to a rate of growth of 5.5 percent a year. The annual rate of increase in their grain imports was 4.6 percent. In the developing economies, grain imports increased at nearly twice the rate of exports. Net cereal imports by the developing countries rose 8 percent a year in this period.

Net imports of developing countries rose from 3.6 percent of cereal consumption during 1961–65 to 6.6 percent in 1976–80 and, based on later consumption data, to 7.4 percent during 1978–82. Cereal food aid to low-income countries, particularly those in Africa, has been a significant part of this net flow from the developed economies, although it dropped 30 percent from 1961–63 to 1981 (Huddleston 1984). The bulk of the increase in developing country imports has been on commercial account.

Examination of trade data of developing countries grouped by their 1980 per capita incomes indicates a tendency for an exception to the relationship between growing food imports and production for those countries belonging to the $250–$500 range. This group of countries has shown a tendency to become increasingly self-sufficient and is projected to have net exports in the future. This unexpected performance may occur because the group happens to include countries with poor employment growth policies.

Table 2.3 Trends of world cereal trade, 1961–65 to 1978–82

	1961–65 Average			1978–82 Average			Annual growth rate, 1961–65 to 1978–82	
Country group[a]	Exports	Imports	Net exports	Exports	Imports	Net exports	Exports	Imports
	(million metric tons)			(million metric tons)			(percent)	
Developed countries	77.3	59.8	17.5	191.9	129.5	62.4	5.5	4.6
Developing countries	18.6	33.4	−14.8	31.0	90.2	−59.3	3.0	6.0
World total	95.9	93.2	(2.6)[b]	222.9	219.8	(3.1)[b]	—	—

Source: FAO 1985.

Note: Data include trade in cereal bran and cake. For the 5-year averages of quantities traded, parts may not add to totals due to rounding.

[a]Following the FAO classification of countries.

[b]The statistical discrepancy between global export and import volumes results from traded quantities in transit and from lagged reporting of import data and other data-gathering problems.

Alternatively, it may be a function of their stage of development, when livestock consumption has not yet become large enough to affect demand significantly, and development generally is at too rudimentary a stage for rapid employment growth. In either case, with further development these countries can be expected to shift to rapid import growth behavior.

It is particularly important to note that, as a group, the developing countries that have done well in food production have tended to increase net imports. Likewise, the higher-income countries and the countries with faster overall growth rate tend to increase net imports. All these elements are interrelated. Countries that accelerate food production growth tend to do well in other elements of development as well, and so overall growth rates and employment growth rates are faster. There is also a causal link between agricultural growth and employment growth. This is an important set of relationships in looking ahead because they suggest that when developing countries succeed in agricultural growth, net imports of basic food staples tend to increase.

STOCKS

Indicators of the mid-year levels of world cereal stock in the period 1961–82 fluctuated widely from a minimum of 135 million metric tons in 1975 to a maximum of about 221 million metric tons in 1969 and 1979 (fig. 2.3).[4] The minimum and maximum levels of reported stocks were, respectively, 25 percent below and 23 percent above the average during 1961–65. Yearly stock averaged about 198 million metric tons during 1961–71 and 162 million metric tons during 1972–82. For the whole 1961–82 period, annual cereal stocks averaged about 180 million metric tons. These stock levels represented 22 percent of world production (excluding China) in the earlier decade and 14 percent in the later decade.

Cereal stocks rise and fall with annual grain output, thus serving as a buffer to production fluctuations. During 1961–82, annual grain stocks decreased nine times from the previous year, dropping by as much as 20 percent or more below the 1961–65 average in 1966, 1973, 1975, and 1976. Grain stocks were lowest in 1975, when the estimated level was only three-fourths of the 1961–65 average. As may be expected, cereal stocks rose following good production years. This occurred in 1967, 1972, 1977, and 1979, when gains in annual output of the preceding years exceeded 8 percent. In other years, however, this relation between stocks and production

4. Limitations of data on stocks are expected to result in underestimates. The reported figures mostly represent those held by the public sector and large private sector holdings. However, assuming consistent reporting procedures and generally unchanged proportions of reported and unreported quantities over the years, their trends can reasonably be taken to reflect those of grain stocks as a whole.

Figure 2.3   World cereal stock levels, 1961–85

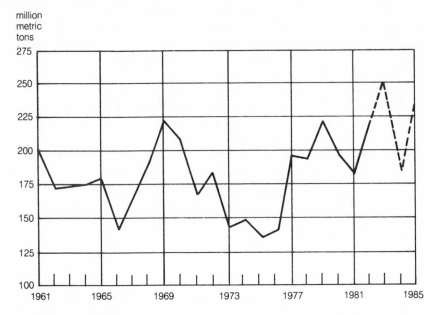

million
metric
tons

Source: USDA 1986.
Notes: Stock levels are those at end of marketing year (mid-calendar year). Data are based on an aggregate of various local marketing years. People's Republic of China and parts of Eastern Europe are excluded. *Broken line* indicates data not included in the analysis.

was weaker. The relatively high levels of grain stocks in the late 1960s were associated with the production growth spurred by the green revolution in developing countries. The accumulations during the late 1970s were associated with the increases in cereal output that followed the high prices during the "world food cisis" in 1973 and 1974. (Later data show that in the mid-1980s, stocks again rose to very high levels, probably associated with major problems of structural adjustment, which particularly slowed growth in food consumption.)

Cereal stocks were apparently more effective in reducing the market impact of variations in total grain production in the 1960s than in the 1970s. The annual changes in world cereal production during 1961–70 did not lead to major price changes in the world market, as did those in 1971–80. The output decrease in 1965 caused a noticeable drawdown of cereal stocks but was less than those of the mid-1970s, when stocks fell to their record low and prices rose to their highest level since 1960. With the accumulation of cereal stocks in the late 1970s, prices remained low and seemed little affected by the changes in output. The data suggest that the relatively lower level of cereal stocks during the 1970s than the previous decade was likely a major factor in the instability of grain prices in that period. Without cereal stocks as buffer, a decline of 3 percent in average world cereal production could mean a decline of 20 percent in the average volume of world cereal trade.

Most of the world's cereal stocks are held by the developed economies, especially the major grain exporters. However, many grain importers, especially the developing countries, view the concentration of stocks in a few exporting countries with concern and are alarmed when the exporters take measures to reduce cereal production.[5]

PRICES

Over the very long run cereal prices have shown little trend one way or the other (Martin and Brokken 1983). There have been several substantial periods of decline in real prices and several periods of increase. There has been a tendency for superior cereals, e.g., wheat, to decline relative to inferior cereals, e.g., maize, reflecting in part the growing relative importance of livestock feed in cereal use. In the short run, however, cereal prices have fluctuated violently.

Grain prices were relatively stable in the 1960s (fig. 2.4). Annual price changes were less than 5 percent between 1962 and 1969, except for a 7 percent increase in 1966, when cereal stocks dipped due to a slight decline in world production in the previous year. Output and stock holdings rose in the late 1960s. In the 1970s, global grain demand increased steadily, but significant changes in production and stocks led to wide price fluctuations. During the food crisis years, the price index rose to 197 in 1973 and to its peak of 216 in 1974. The extraordinary rise in grain prices in these two years played a role in the rapid growth of output in the late 1970s that resulted in larger than average stock holdings and the sharp decline in prices. Cereal stock levels in 1982 were about 20 percent above and prices, in real terms, more than 30 percent below their 1961-65 averages.

The major swings in grain prices in the 1970s were largely compensating. The 1961-80 price trend declined only slightly, largely because of low prices beginning in 1977. The difference of just a few years in the period analyzed makes a substantial difference to the perception about trend. Thus, a simple linear trend equation fitted to the price indices in table 2.4 would show an average annual rate of change in the real prices of cereals of 1.1 percent during 1961-75, −1.3 percent for 1961-80, and −1.6 percent for 1961-82. This simply shows that the fluctuations are very largely relative to whatever trend exists. Although the 1973 and 1974 prices were un-

5. International Wheat Council 1983.

Figure 2.4   Index of world cereal prices, 1961–85

1977-79 = 100

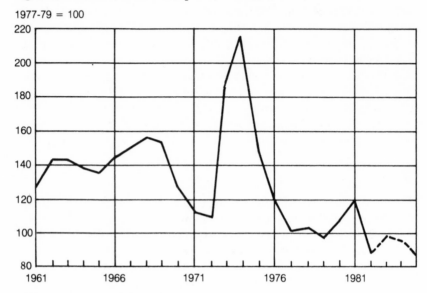

Source: World Bank 1984a.
Note: Broken line indicates data not included in the analysis.

Table 2.4 Index of world cereal prices, 1961–85 (1977–79 = 100)

Year	Price index[a]	Year	Price index[a]	Year	Price index[a]	Year	Price index[a]
1961	128	1968	156	1975	148	1982	88
1962	143	1969	153	1976	119	1983	98
1963	143	1970	126	1977	101	1984	95[b]
1964	138	1971	112	1978	103	1985	85[b]
1965	135	1972	109	1979	97		
1966	144	1973	187	1980	107		
1967	150	1974	216	1981	119		

Source: World Bank 1984a.
[a] Calculated from prices in constant dollars, which include those of rice, wheat, maize, and sorghum.
[b] Preliminary.

usually high for the two-decade period, they were not spectacular when viewed in the long term. Martin and Brokken (1983) analyzed real cereal prices for more than a hundred years ending in 1981 and found that 1973 and 1974 levels were exceeded 19 times in corn and 33 times in wheat. A World Bank study sees gains in cereal prices for the coming decade, especially those of wheat and coarse grains (World Bank 1985).

CONCLUSION

Agricultural development in developing countries is a long-term proposition requiring large public investment in the rural sector and major commitment with respect to development strategy. As will be brought out in chapters 4 and 7, resource productivity will be higher if advantage is taken of international trade with consequent adjustment of domestic production according to international prices. What does our analysis of global cereal trends tell us about longer-term price relationships as a basis for public investment decisions in agriculture? Only a few points are clear.

First, developing countries in general can be expected to face rapidly increasing net imports of cereals. Because demand for food tends to increase more than domestic production as a result of development processes, increases in their net import position seem inevitable. That provides a relatively favorable domestic price environment for developing countries that are net importers, as they price above international prices by their transfer costs. The developing country exporters, however, must compete in a market in which developed countries are generating increasing exports. At best, that will be a competitive environment requiring attention to reducing costs and taking maximum advantage of low-cost food to foster rapid growth in employment-increasing types of production.

Second, international prices are likely to be highly unstable, reflecting increasingly unstable production and a reluctance of the major exporters to hold larger stocks. Thus, at any given point in time, it will be difficult to judge the likely average international price. This also means that food security will be costly to achieve whether by domestic stock, domestic supplies, or foreign exchange. (One will note in chapter 5, however, the discussion of the success of Indonesia in ensuring food security in the face of an unstable global situation and at modest cost.)

Third, in view of the strong growth in demand in developing countries, it is reasonable to expect pressure for real food prices to rise. With their production resources and greater adaptability to changes in output policy, developed country exporters can be expected to provide most of the response to this market demand. Thus exportable supplies will also grow rapidly over time. As only a small proportion of total food production moves in international trade, it is unreasonable to attempt to predict reliably the trend of cereal prices. But that should also warn us against trying to predict trend from sharp short-term movements one way or another.

Fourth, the market adjustment process for world grains involves various interacting forces, both economic and political, which affect world supply and demand. These include changes in output policies of the major exporting countries and in trade decisions of large grain importers, such as the U.S.S.R., that can alter market conditions considerably. The implications of these forces for the ability of developing countries to import cereals at prices they can afford can be very significant, particularly at a time when many countries have foreign exchange difficulties.

Finally, special concern needs to be given to the food situation of the world's poor and undernourished, as both developing and developed economies adjust their agricultural and trade policies to market changes. It is in the interest of developed countries as major exporters to use food aid to increase future markets. Food aid programs that increase consumption of low-income people beyond what they could otherwise afford is in line with those interests and facilitates development, food security for the poor, and long-term prices that favor more resources devoted to agriculture than would otherwise be the case.

3

Changing Patterns of Variability in Cereal Prices and Production

PETER B. R. HAZELL

The substantial growth in world cereal production of the past two and one-half decades has been accompanied by a widening band of variability around the trend. Although each trough in production has been consistently higher than in all previous downturns, the probability that aggregate production can fall substantially below trend has increased since the 1960s.

Increased variability in world cereal production implies even larger-than-average increases for many countries. To secure their consumption and to moderate domestic price fluctuations, these countries may need to stockpile more grains or depend more on world markets. However, storing food is expensive, and world markets have become more risky as variability in world cereal production increases.

Increased variability in national cereal production tends to destabilize national income, particularly in poorer countries where agriculture is the predominant sector. This effect will be reinforced if a country's cereal production is positively correlated with fluctuations in world prices. Its effects on the welfare of farmers and poor consumers is less predictable, however, depending on such factors as the way in which domestic production and prices are correlated, the possibilities of substitution between commodities, especially in demand arising from government intervention policies, and so forth (see Sahn and von Braun 1985; Walker forthcoming; and chapter 6 of this volume).

Variability in world cereal prices also increased markedly in the 1970s. Structural shifts in demand and changes in U.S. storage policies were probably the main causes, but increased production variability and the domestic price policies of many industrialized countries were also important (Myers and Runge 1985; Blandford and Schwartz 1983; Josling 1980). By stabilizing prices for consumers, these countries essentially exported much of the variability in their domestic production. Since the volume of cereals traded in the world market is only about 15 percent of total production, a relatively small increase in production variability of major exporters can induce a much larger increase in world price variability.

The following analysis documents the changes in the variability of world cereal prices and production since the 1960s and, by use of a variance decomposition procedure, identifies the main components of the increase in production variability.

CHANGES IN THE VARIABILITY OF CEREAL PRICES

Using available data on farmgate cereal prices from selected countries,[1] price variability is measured in two time periods: 1961–71 and 1974–81. This partitioning usefully coincides with structural shifts that occurred in world cereal markets. The years 1972 and 1973, when major structural adjustments occurred in world and many domestic cereal markets, were omitted from the analysis. Their inclusion would have exaggerated the changes in variability that have since occurred.

Since all the price data obtained were in nominal (or current) prices, many of the series showed strong trends over time. These may arise from trends in real (deflated) prices as well as from general inflationary forces, and separating the two effects is difficult. Fortunately, for the purposes of this chapter, it is possible to avoid the thorny problem of constructing relevant price deflators and simply to detrend the data directly. It is only necessary to analyze fluctuations in prices around trend. Even if the data were deflated, it might still be necessary to detrend the resultant real prices.

Separate trend regressions were run for 1961–71 and 1974–81. In most cases linear equations gave excellent fits, but where nonlinearities were apparent, quadratic functions were used. The residuals, centered on the mean prices for each period, became the primary data for analysis.

Table 3.1 shows the changes in the variability of world prices and of domestic farmgate prices for selected countries. These countries represent a range of agricultural policy regimes as well as providing a broad geographical coverage. Price variability, as measured by the coefficient of variation, is much higher in world markets than in the domestic markets of most countries. The coefficients of variation of world cereal prices for the two periods increased 400 percent for wheat, 59 percent for rice, and 67 percent for maize. Patterns of increase were similar in the United States,

---

1. The data were obtained mostly from FAO sources. These are *Agricultural producer prices 1961–70*, the 1982 *Producer yearbook*, and the 1982 *Statistics on prices received by farmers*. Price data for India for the years 1961 to 1968 were obtained from various issues of *Agricultural prices in India*, published by the Ministry of Agriculture. The world prices used are as follows: *wheat*, U.S. No. 1 (No. 2 prior to 1974), soft red winter, f.o.b. Atlantic ports; *rice*, 5% broken, milled, f.o.b. Bangkok; *maize*, no. 2 yellow, f.o.b. Gulf ports. These prices are published by the World Bank in *Commodity trade and price trends* (1985).

Table 3.1 Changes in the coefficients of variation of world and national cereal prices, 1961-71 to 1974-81

	Wheat		Rice		Maize	
	1961-71	1974-81	1961-71	1974-81	1961-71	1974-81
World	4.05	20.50	17.76	28.16	7.37	12.35
France	3.02	2.41			2.51	4.27
U.S.	15.03	20.20	2.56	20.29	7.98	16.77
Mexico	2.92	5.47			7.60	10.03
India	9.89	7.20	22.36	11.10		
Japan	3.37	8.39	13.50	4.24		
Canada	7.37	20.06				
Turkey	2.67	25.48				
F. R. Germany	2.92	3.00				
U.K.	2.68	4.78				
Italy	2.53	3.43				
Pakistan	7.84	8.11				
Argentina	24.58	50.17			23.15	33.05
Brazil			13.75	18.69	5.04	26.07
Yugoslavia					18.07	14.00
Kenya					10.91	10.00
Burma			2.54	0.66		
Philippines			12.57	4.17		
Colombia			14.05	9.32		

Canada, and Argentina, which have grain markets relatively open to international trade. Many other countries were successful in using domestic policies to contain or reduce the variability of domestic farmgate prices, despite the increased turbulence in world markets. The EEC countries were particularly successful in this respect, as were Japan, India, Pakistan, Burma, the Philippines, Colombia, Kenya, and Yugoslavia.

Tables 3.2, 3.3, and 3.4 show the changes in inter-country price correlations for wheat, rice, and maize. Countries that maintain open grain markets for international trade would be expected to have positive price correlations with both the world price and domestic prices of other trading countries.

In fact, however, only Pakistan and Italy had statistically significant and positive correlations between their domestic wheat prices and the world wheat price during 1961-71. These correlations became negative in 1974-81, when only the United States and Canada had significant positive correlations with the world wheat price. Similarly, very few countries had statistically significant and positive correlations between their domestic rice or maize prices and the corresponding world prices, and there is no indication of any widespread shift toward more positive correlations between the two periods.

Table 3.2 Intercountry correlations between wheat prices, 1961–71 and 1974–81

	World	France	U.S.	Mexico	India	Japan	Canada	Turkey	F. R. Germany	U.K.	Italy	Pakistan
France												
1961–71	0.37	1.00										
1974–81	−0.29	1.00										
U.S.												
1961–71	0.22	0.81***	1.00									
1974–81	0.95***	−0.38	1.00									
Mexico												
1961–71	0.21	−0.78***	−0.67**	1.00								
1974–81	−0.49	0.53*	−0.31	1.00								
India												
1961–71	−0.19	0.41	0.25	−0.59**	1.00							
1974–81	0.50	0.29	0.60*	0.39	1.00							
Japan												
1961–71	0.00	0.10	0.14	−0.19	0.36	1.00						
1974–81	−0.59*	−0.39	−0.55*	−0.04	−0.58*	1.00						
Canada												
1961–71	0.38	0.26	0.40	0.11	0.05	0.32	1.00					
1974–81	0.97***	−0.46	0.97***	−0.46	0.50	−0.44	1.00					

	1	2	3	4	5	6	7	8	9	10	11	12	13
Turkey													
1961–71	−0.01	0.20	0.42	−0.09	−0.52*	−0.12	0.15	1.00					
1974–81	−0.58*	0.76**	−0.54*	0.73**	0.26	−0.19	−0.64**	1.00					
F. R. Germany													
1961–71	0.24	−0.33	−0.44*	0.60**	−0.36	−0.05	0.36	0.24	1.00				
1974–81	−0.42	0.60*	−0.50	0.21	−0.17	−0.38	−0.54*	0.73**	1.00				
U.K.													
1961–71	−0.13	0.17	0.03	−0.07	−0.27	−0.84***	−0.22	0.43*	0.13	1.00			
1974–81	−0.25	0.15	−0.46	−0.44	−0.47	0.41	−0.34	−0.15	−0.02	1.00			
Italy													
1961–71	0.64***	0.02	0.14	0.47*	−0.30	0.10	0.86***	0.13	0.57**	−0.19	1.00		
1974–81	0.24	0.50	0.07	−0.06	0.47	−0.14	0.16	0.18	−0.06	0.38	1.00		
Pakistan													
1961–71	0.54***	0.35	0.28	0.07	0.13	0.36	0.86***	0.09	0.57**	−0.23	0.81***	1.00	
1974–81	−0.69**	0.41	−0.53*	0.84***	−0.10	0.07	−0.68**	0.64**	0.43	−0.40	−0.44	1.00	
Argentina													
1961–71	0.37	0.62**	0.26	−0.43*	0.60**	0.28	0.20	−0.33	0.04	−0.18	0.08	0.56**	1.00
1974–81	−0.58*	0.86***	−0.54*	0.81**	0.23	−0.13	−0.68**	0.84***	0.49	0.05	0.18	0.70**	1.00

Note: ***, **, and * indicate correlation coefficients that are significantly different from zero (one-tail tests) at the 1%, 5%, and 10% confidence levels, respectively.

Table 3.3 Intercountry correlations between rice prices, 1961–71 and 1974–81

	World	U.S.	India	Japan	Brazil	Burma	Philippines
U.S.							
1961–71	−0.58**	1.00					
1974–81	0.55*	1.00					
India							
1961–71	−0.17	0.62**	1.00				
1974–81	0.70**	0.33	1.00				
Japan							
1961–71	0.67**	−0.69***	−0.67**	1.00			
1974–81	−0.02	−0.21	0.20	1.00			
Brazil							
1961–71	0.03	0.72***	0.52*	−0.40	1.00		
1974–81	−0.24	−0.07	0.26	0.23	1.00		
Burma							
1961–71	0.44	−0.22	0.29	0.41	−0.24	1.00	
1974–81	0.39	0.22	0.42	0.02	−0.54*	1.00	
Philippines							
1961–71	−0.40	0.18	−0.41	−0.03	0.13	−0.55**	1.00
1974–81	−0.44	−0.66**	0.16	0.30	0.60*	−0.38	1.00
Colombia							
1961–71	0.56**	−0.64**	−0.60**	0.94***	−0.45*	0.49*	0.04
1974–81	−0.04	−0.19	0.05	0.93***	0.06	−0.11	0.27

Note: ***, **, and * indicate correlation coefficients that are significantly different from zero (one-tail tests) at the 1%, 5%, and 10% confidence levels, respectively.

Table 3.4 Intercountry correlations between maize prices, 1961–71 and 1974–81

	World	France	U.S.	Mexico	Brazil	Argentina	Yugoslavia
France							
1961–71	0.63**	1.00					
1974–81	−0.24	1.00					
U.S.							
1961–71	0.59***	0.46*	1.00				
1974–81	0.80***	−0.30	1.00				
Mexico							
1961–71	0.33	0.21	−0.18	1.00			
1974–81	−0.21	0.06	−0.47	1.00			
Brazil							
1961–71	−0.25	−0.03	−0.06	−0.35	1.00		
1974–81	0.07	−0.19	−0.01	0.63**	1.00		
Argentina							
1961–71	−0.32	−0.60**	−0.30	0.14	0.00	1.00	
1974–81	−0.22	0.31	−0.71**	0.77**	0.26	1.00	
Yugoslavia							
1961–71	0.48	0.41	−0.16	0.27	0.03	−0.15	1.00
1974–81	−0.12	0.04	−0.62**	0.54*	0.13	0.90***	1.00
Kenya							
1961–71	0.21	−0.02	−0.23	0.23	0.34	0.31	0.69**
1974–81	−0.56*	−0.38	−0.63**	0.69**	0.47	0.45	0.37

Note: ***, **, and * indicate correlation coefficients that are significantly different from zero (one-tail tests) at the 1%, 5%, and 10% confidence levels, respectively.

There were more substantial changes in patterns of collinearity between prices of different crops than between prices of the same crop among countries (tables 3.5, 3.6, and 3.7). World prices became much more collinear between crops. The correlation between world maize and rice prices increased from −0.62 in 1961–71 to 0.79 in 1974–81. Similarly, the correlations between world rice and wheat prices increased from −0.13 to 0.82, and from 0.30 to 0.89 for maize and wheat. Not surprisingly, these changes were accompanied by increases in the correlations between the prices of different cereals among countries. The number of significant and positive price correlations between rice and corn increased from 7 in the first period to 15 in the second (table 3.5), while those between rice and wheat rose from 15 to 23 (table 3.6). There was little change in the number of significant and positive price correlations between maize and wheat (table 3.7).

CHANGES IN WORLD CEREAL PRODUCTION

Production variability for cereal crops is measured for 1960/61 to 1970/71 and 1971/72 to 1982/83.[2] This split:

(a) corresponds to speculated changes in yield variability that are possibly associated with the green revolution, usually regarded as occurring around 1970 in many developing countries;

(b) corresponds broadly with the dramatic increases in price variability in the early 1970s; and

(c) more pragmatically, gives roughly equal sample sizes from the available data.

Year-to-year fluctuations in areas sown and yields of each crop in each country reflect the separate influences of long-term and short-term sources of variation. By assuming an independent and deterministic long-term trend in each variable, the area and yield data for each crop and country were detrended by regression analysis. The residuals, centered on the mean areas or yields for each period, became the primary data for analysis.

Quadratic equations were chosen because they do not assume a deterministic part to any relation between the variance of the dependent variable and time. Also, unbiased and efficient estimates of the variances and

2. The production analysis in this chapter is limited to the major cereal crops of wheat, maize, rice, barley, millet, sorghum, oats, and a residual crop comprising rye and mixed cereals. Only cereals grown for grain are considered, and no distinction is made between grains utilized for human and for livestock consumption.

Data on the production and area sown of each crop by country were obtained from the U.S. Department of Agriculture for the period 1960/61 to 1982/83. For the purposes of this analysis, the 34 most important cereal-producing countries (excluding the People's Republic of China) were selected, and all other countries were combined into a single residual country.

Table 3.5 Intercountry correlations between maize and rice prices, 1961–71 and 1974–81

Rice price	Maize price							
	World	France	U.S.	Mexico	Brazil	Argentina	Yugoslavia	Kenya
World								
1961–71	−0.62**	−0.59**	−0.33	0.11	0.24	0.75***	−0.54**	−0.12
1974–81	0.79***	0.16	0.79***	−0.30	−0.24	−0.30	−0.29	−0.81***
U.S.								
1961–71	−0.07	0.00	−0.07	−0.65**	−0.15	−0.32	0.23	0.02
1974–81	0.43	−0.27	0.82***	−0.41	−0.13	−0.83***	−0.88***	−0.38
India								
1961–71	−0.29	−0.11	0.21	−0.97***	0.26	−0.28	−0.28	−0.42
1974–81	0.82***	−0.38	0.62**	0.18	0.14	0.04	0.12	−0.22
Japan								
1961–71	−0.26	−0.27	−0.25	0.61**	0.01	0.68**	0.00	0.32
1974–81	−0.34	0.21	−0.38	0.69**	0.02	0.55*	0.38	0.36
Brazil								
1961–71	−0.46*	−0.33	−0.47	−0.60**	0.00	0.19	−0.09	−0.03
1974–81	0.03	−0.34	0.00	0.72**	0.95***	0.27	0.16	0.59*
Burma								
1961–71	−0.45*	−0.44*	0.11	−0.27	0.27	0.29	−0.21	−0.10
1974–81	0.29	−0.41	0.34	−0.52*	−0.69**	−0.30	0.03	−0.36
Philippines								
1961–71	0.40	0.33	−0.41	0.35	0.05	−0.03	0.87***	0.71
1974–81	−0.06	−0.16	−0.53	0.82***	0.58***	0.84***	0.79***	0.69**
Colombia								
1961–71	−0.19	−0.31	−0.18	0.49*	0.20	0.65**	0.11	0.52*
1974–81	−0.37	0.41	−0.46	0.65**	−0.10	0.57*	0.30	0.32

Note: ***, **, and * indicate correlation coefficients that are significantly different from zero (one-tail tests) at the 1%, 5%, and 10% confidence levels, respectively.

Table 3.6 Intercountry correlations between rice and wheat prices, 1961–71 and 1974–81

Wheat price	Rice price							
	World	U.S.	India	Japan	Brazil	Burma	Philippines	Colombia
World								
1961–71	−0.13	0.08	−0.33	0.11	0.19	−0.46*	0.85***	0.70
1974–81	0.82***	0.65**	0.60*	−0.53*	−0.24	0.43	−0.48	−0.55*
France								
1961–71	0.47*	0.12	0.14	0.14	0.49*	0.01	−0.04	0.04
1974–81	0.00	−0.68**	0.08	0.29	0.20	−0.47	0.68**	0.39
U.S.								
1961–71	0.28	0.29	0.22	−0.11	0.47*	−0.02	0.01	−0.18
1974–81	0.78**	0.60*	0.71**	−0.41	−0.22	0.64**	−0.42	−0.50
Mexico								
1961–71	−0.59**	−0.16	−0.50*	0.01	−0.53**	−0.32	0.55**	0.06
1974–81	−0.16	−0.71**	0.22	0.70**	0.20	0.17	0.61*	0.53*
India								
1961–71	0.87***	−0.54**	−0.14	0.64**	−0.14	0.52*	−0.50*	0.63**
1974–81	0.72**	0.16	0.96***	0.32	0.15	0.41	0.23	0.21
Japan								
1961–71	0.17	0.09	0.13	0.35	−0.04	0.72**	−0.01	0.57**
1974–81	−0.40	0.10	−0.59*	0.44	−0.21	−0.04	−0.37	0.49

Canada								
1961-71	-0.16	-0.04	-0.49*	0.23	-0.30	-0.14	0.36	0.30
1974-81	0.81***	0.75**	0.63**	-0.43	-0.21	0.54*	-0.57*	-0.49
Turkey								
1961-71	-0.39	0.36	0.44*	-0.57**	0.10	-0.05	0.03	-0.58**
1974-81	-0.34	-0.66**	0.15	0.56*	0.66**	-0.47	0.92***	0.49
F. R. Germany								
1961-71	-0.38	-0.37	-0.41	0.06	-0.62**	-0.18	0.36	0.20
1974-81	-0.53*	-0.59*	-0.17	-0.11	0.68***	-0.75**	0.80***	-0.11
U.K.								
1961-71	-0.08	-0.08	0.05	-0.30	-0.01	-0.42*	-0.25	-0.53**
1974-81	-0.18	0.09	-0.55*	-0.04	-0.34	-0.47	-0.14	0.32
Italy								
1961-71	-0.45*	0.03	-0.55**	0.04	-0.26	-0.47*	0.73***	0.15
1974-81	0.63**	0.26	0.36	0.33	0.06	-0.33	-0.02	0.48
Pakistan								
1961-71	0.04	-0.25	-0.54**	0.39	-0.28	-0.10	0.46*	0.50*
1974-81	-0.56*	-0.89***	-0.22	0.39	0.21	-0.02	0.57*	0.22
Argentina								
1961-71	0.72***	-0.40	-0.37	0.66**	0.15	0.12	0.11	0.66**
1974-81	-0.28	-0.84***	0.01	0.54*	0.15	-0.23	0.79**	0.58*

Note: ***, **, and * indicate correlation coefficients that are significantly different from zero (one-tail tests) at the 1%, 5%, and 10% confidence levels, respectively.

Table 3.7 Intercountry correlations between maize and wheat prices, 1961–71 and 1974–81

Wheat price	Maize price							
	World	France	U.S.	Mexico	Brazil	Argentina	Yugoslavia	Kenya
World								
1961–71	0.30	0.41	−0.26	0.23	0.28	0.17	0.70***	0.69***
1974–81	0.89***	−0.22	0.92***	−0.59*	−0.18	−0.59*	−0.45	−0.76**
France								
1961–71	−0.17	−0.21	−0.03	−0.27	0.15	0.58**	−0.15	0.11
1974–81	0.06	0.56*	−0.44	0.61*	0.31	0.87***	0.70**	0.08
U.S.								
1961–71	−0.12	−0.32	−0.15	−0.29	0.13	0.28	−0.05	0.05
1974–81	0.87***	−0.41	0.89***	−0.56*	−0.24	−0.56*	−0.32	−0.65**
Mexico								
1961–71	0.53**	0.56**	−0.01	0.60**	−0.23	−0.48*	0.62**	0.24
1974–81	−0.21	0.05	−0.53*	0.59*	0.08	0.81***	0.88***	0.34
India								
1961–71	−0.56**	−0.52*	−0.10	0.03	0.45*	0.57**	−0.55**	0.04
1974–81	0.76**	−0.17	0.47	0.24	0.04	0.23	0.29	−0.27
Japan								
1961–71	−0.27	−0.48*	−0.08	−0.26	0.39	0.36	0.26	0.55**
1974–81	−0.82***	0.23	−0.40	0.00	−0.33	−0.16	−0.31	0.27

Canada								
1961–71	0.53**	0.06	0.19*	−0.38	−0.07	0.14	0.47*	0.61**
1974–81	0.82***	−0.33	0.96***	−0.60*	−0.22	−0.69**	−0.53*	−0.70**
Turkey								
1961–71	0.52*	0.21	0.42	−0.35	−0.22	−0.24	0.20	−0.27
1974–81	−0.17	0.09	−0.55*	0.93***	0.63**	0.90**	0.76**	0.62*
F. R. Germany								
1961–71	0.85***	0.46*	0.50*	0.42*	−0.10	−0.05	0.44*	0.34
1974–81	−0.13	−0.01	−0.44	0.60*	0.81***	0.56*	0.48	0.56*
U.K.								
1961–71	0.36	0.44*	0.43*	0.08	−0.50*	−0.18	−0.36	−0.68**
1974–81	−0.34	0.58**	−0.31	0.00	−0.25	0.00	−0.31	0.02
Italy								
1961–71	0.71***	0.34	0.09	0.46*	−0.03	−0.06	0.73***	0.74***
1974–81	0.38	0.61*	0.27	0.31	0.10	0.19	−0.14	−0.38
Pakistan								
1961–71	0.53**	0.00	0.15	0.39	0.07	0.46*	0.47*	0.75***
1974–81	−0.51*	0.02	−0.73***	0.43	0.17	0.71**	0.83***	0.48
Argentina								
1961–71	−0.22	−0.43*	−0.27	0.19	0.19	0.94***	−0.09	0.45*
1974–81	−0.23	0.34	−0.73**	0.70**	0.14	0.99***	0.91***	0.39

Note: ***, **, and * indicate correlation coefficients that are significantly different from zero (one-tail tests) at the 1%, 5%, and 10% confidence levels, respectively.

covariances of the detrended variables are easily obtained from the variance-covariance matrix of the residuals.

For more reliable estimates of long-term trends, the regressions were fitted to the full-time series in each country. The assumption of a homoscedastic error term is not appropriate when both periods are combined in this way, so a generalized least squares estimation procedure was used (Hazell 1984). The residuals were subsequently divided into two periods and their period means adjusted to zero before centering on the mean areas and yields for each period.

Estimates of detrended production for each country were obtained from the relevant products of the detrended area and yield series. When calculated this way, the means of these production series typically differ by less than 1 percent from the means of corresponding original data.

Table 3.8 shows the changes in world cereal production from 1960/61 to 1970/71 and 1971/72 to 1982/83.[3] Total world cereal production increased 37 percent, or 305 million tons, with wheat and maize accounting for one third each. Rice accounted for 12 percent of the total increase, barley 18 percent, and sorghum and millets for the rest. Production of oats and other cereals (rye and mixed cereals) declined moderately.

The coefficient of variation of total world cereal production rose from 2.8 percent to 3.4 percent between the two periods, an increase of 22 percent. The variance of total cereal production increased 178 percent. The F ratio of 2.78 is significant at the 10 percent confidence level. Both area and yield variability also increased, although only the F ratio for yields is statistically significant at the 10 percent level.

A useful policy measure of the increase in production instability is the probability that production will fall 5 percent or more below trend in each year (Valdés and Konandreas 1981).

A difficulty in calculating these probabilities is that the distribution of possible production outcomes for individual years is not known; there is only a single observation for each year. However, from the detrending procedure used, estimates of the variance of production around trend are available for each of the two periods. By assuming that the variance of production remains constant for all years within a period, the average probabilities can be obtained.[4] This probability was 3.5 percent for 1960/61 to 1970/71 and increased to 6.8 percent for 1971/72 to 1982/83.

---

3. The People's Republic of China is excluded from all calculations because of the extraordinary disruption of production in the early 1960s and subsequent periods.

4. Let detrended production in year t be denoted by $\hat{Q}_t = \bar{Q} + e_t$ where $\bar{Q}$ is the period mean and e_t is the deviation from the mean that year. Then the probability of a shortfall of 5 percent or more below trend is derived from $\Pr\{\bar{Q} + e_t \leq 0.95\,\bar{Q}\} = \Pr\{e_t/\sigma_e \leq -0.05\,\bar{Q}/\sigma_e\}$, where σ_e is the standard deviation of e_t. Assuming e_t is approximately normally distributed, the desired probability can be obtained from tables for the cumulative normal distribution.

Table 3.8 Changes in the mean and variability of world cereal production, 1960/61-1970/71 to 1971/72-1982/83[a]

Cereal	Average production			Coefficient of variation of production			F ratios		
	First period	Second period	Change	First period	Second period	Change	Production	Area sown	Yield
	(metric tons)			(percent)					
Wheat	253,454	352,982	39.3	5.46	4.83	−11.5	1.52	0.34**	1.64
Maize	210,074	317,303	51.0	3.29	4.41	34.0	4.08**	1.65	4.17**
Rice	119,971	155,031	29.2	3.97	3.80	−4.3	1.52	2.45*	0.88
Barley	95,283	150,997	58.5	4.81	7.50	55.9	6.18***	3.13**	3.28**
Millets	19,705	21,381	8.5	7.78	7.66	−1.5	1.14	2.22	0.69
Sorghum	40,159	53,386	32.9	4.75	5.70	20.0	2.55*	1.08	2.10
Oats	49,033	47,595	−2.9	11.30	5.35	−52.6	0.21***	0.07***	4.42**
Other cereals	41,404	35,231	−14.9	4.57	9.33	104.2	2.95**	0.36*	3.61**
Total cereals	829,087	1,133,908	36.8	2.76	3.06	21.7	2.78*	2.22	2.69*

Note: ***, **, and * indicate statistically significant F ratios (one-tail tests) at the 1%, 5%, and 10% confidence levels, respectively. The first period is from 1960/61 to 1970/71; the second period is from 1971/72 to 1982/83.
[a]Does not include China.

Table 3.8 also shows that the sizeable increases in world wheat and rice production were not accompanied by a significant increase in variability. In fact, the coefficients of variation declined from 5.5 to 4.8 percent for wheat and from 4.0 to 3.8 percent for rice. Production variability increased substantially for maize, barley, and other cereals but declined for oats.

There is little observable relationship between a country's performance in increasing cereal production and the changes in production variability (table 3.9). The correlation across countries between the percentage change in average production and the change in the coefficient of variation of production is in fact -0.15. This is not significantly different from zero at the 10 percent confidence level.

How robust are these results? The question is particularly relevant since there were only eleven years in the first period and twelve in the second. There is a danger that extreme years may determine the results, depending in which period they are assigned.

Ten-year moving averages for the mean and, after (in this case) linear detrending, the standard deviation and the coefficient of variation of production were calculated, and the results are reported in table 3.10.

Absolute variability around the trend has increased quite consistently over the years, so our previous result is not due to the particular periods chosen. The coefficient of variation has also trended upward in a similar manner, though it peaked in the early 1980s and there has been a modest gain in relative stability since then. The probability of a 5 percent shortfall below trend in world cereal production followed a similar pattern and has diminished a little since the early 1980s. But the probability of a shortfall is still much higher than in the 1960s.

METHOD OF FURTHER ANALYSIS

To analyze the components of change in the mean and variance of world cereal production, a variance decomposition procedure is used, as reported in Hazell (1982, 1984). There are four sources of change in average production. Two parts arise from changes in the mean yield and mean area. These "pure" effects arise even if there are no other sources of change. There is also an interaction effect between changes in the mean yield and the mean area, and a further effect arises from changes in the covariability of areas and yields.

The variance of total cereal production consists of the sum of the following four types of production variances and covariances: individual crop variances within countries, intercrop covariances within countries; intercountry covariances within crop; and covariances between different crops in different countries. The change in each of these production variances and covariances can be further decomposed into the following ten parts: change in mean yields, change in mean areas, change in yield variances and covariances, change in area variances and covariances, change in area-yield covariances, interaction between changes in mean yields and mean areas, interaction between changes in mean areas and yield variances, interaction between changes in mean yields and area variances, interaction between changes in mean areas and yields and changes in area-yield covariances and change in the residual (Hazell 1984).

The first five sources of change are "pure" effects, the next four are interaction effects which occur because of simultaneous changes in all the constituent parts, and the last term is a higher-order term which is typically small and of little importance.

COMPONENTS OF CHANGE IN WORLD CEREAL PRODUCTION

Increases in mean yields account for 72 percent of the increase in world cereal production, and area expansion accounts for 22 percent (table 3.11). Yield improvements were even more important in expanding the production of wheat and were more important than area expansion in increasing the production of maize, rice, and millet. Area increases were more important for barley.

Table 3.12 shows the results from the decomposition of the change in the variance of world cereal production. The rows in the lower half of this table correspond to four groups of production variances and covariances delineated. The first six columns correspond to six of the ten sources of change for a production variance and covariance listed above, while the seventh is the total of the four types of interaction terms. All entries in the table are expressed as a percent of the change in the variance of total cereal production; hence rows and columns sum to 100 percent.

The row sums in table 3.12 show that 34 percent of the increase in the variance of world cereal production is attributable to increases in the production variances of individual crops within countries. Wheat, maize, and barley account for nearly all of this increase. The remaining 66 percent is due to increases in production covariances, and of these the most important are between crops, both within and between countries. Changes in intercountry covariances within crops turn out to be only 5 percent of the total variance increase.

The dominance of the production covariances arises for two reasons. First, they are far more numerous; for each r variances in the equations used, there are $r^2 - r$ covariances. Second, unless there are changing pat-

Table 3.9 Changes in the mean and variability of total cereal production by major countries, 1960/61–1970/71 to 1971/72–1982/83

Country	Average production (thousand metric tons)			Coefficient of variation of production (percent)			F ratios			Probability of 5% shortfall below trend	
	First period	Second period	Change	First period	Second period	Change	Production	Area sown	Yield	First period	Second period
1. U.S.	181,982	265,022	45.6	6.83	6.64	−2.8	1.97	1.24	8.23***	23.3	22.6
2. U.S.S.R.	138,436	180,952	30.7	12.16	14.26	17.3	2.35*	1.28	1.69	34.1	36.3
3. India	74,753	104,000	39.1	7.65	5.42	−29.2	0.97	0.65	0.92	25.8	17.9
4. Canada	29,991	40,033	33.5	17.07	10.66	−37.6	0.69	0.22***	0.44*	38.6	31.9
5. France	27,456	41,085	49.6	6.01	9.19	52.9	5.26***	1.58	4.30**	20.3	29.5
6. Indonesia	13,464	20,341	51.1	6.09	5.15	−15.4	1.62	0.74	2.89*	20.6	16.6
7. Brazil	16,500	26,149	58.5	5.19	8.87	70.9	7.25***	4.30**	2.47*	16.9	28.8
8. Argentina	17,186	23,764	38.3	11.80	14.04	19.0	2.72*	1.04	2.12	33.7	35.9
9. Mexico	10,487	15,571	48.5	7.03	11.10	57.9	5.58***	3.99**	3.40**	23.9	32.6
10. Turkey	12,932	18,363	42.0	7.06	9.71	37.5	3.80**	3.98**	3.45**	23.9	30.2
11. Australia	12,618	17,445	38.2	19.54	23.15	18.5	2.66*	1.65	1.67	39.7	41.3
12. Thailand	8,555	13,255	54.9	7.82	8.40	7.4	2.76*	3.00**	2.01	26.1	27.4
13. F.R. Germany	16,030	22,211	38.6	9.13	5.96	−34.7	0.82	3.24**	0.59	29.1	20.1
14. Bangladesh	10,544	12,861	22.0	7.21	5.03	−30.2	0.72	0.20***	1.05	24.5	16.1
15. Poland	8,373	13,135	56.9	9.21	9.29	1.0	2.52*	0.12***	4.00**	29.5	29.8

16. Romania	11,602	17,360	49.6	10.87	9.87	−9.2	1.83	0.80	2.17	32.3	30.5
17. U.K.	12,442	16,754	34.7	8.73	8.34	−4.5	1.66	0.33**	1.77	28.4	27.4
18. Italy	14,219	16,680	17.3	3.44	5.68	65.1	3.72**	5.50***	0.66	7.4	18.9
19. Pakistan	7,668	13,179	71.9	10.23	3.15	−69.2	0.28**	0.44*	0.27**	31.2	5.6
20. South Africa	7,499	11,999	60.0	20.37	19.69	−3.3	2.40*	2.63*	1.99	40.1	40.1
21. Yugoslavia	11,397	15,069	32.2	9.98	5.18	−48.1	0.47	0.74	0.57	30.9	16.9
22. Burma	4,933	6,537	32.6	9.88	7.68	−22.3	1.06	0.45	1.77	30.5	25.8
23. Japan	14,565	11,393	−21.8	6.01	9.31	54.9	1.45	4.27**	1.58	20.3	29.5
24. Vietnam	6,011	7,326	21.9	8.99	5.59	−37.8	0.58	1.26	0.41*	28.8	18.7
25. Hungary	7,342	12,115	65.0	10.08	6.05	−40.0	0.98	0.35**	1.39	39.9	20.3
26. Spain	9,291	13,676	47.2	8.09	13.86	71.3	6.37***	0.68	7.73***	26.2	35.9
27. Philippines	4,295	7,005	63.1	5.51	5.43	−1.5	2.56*	6.87***	0.77	18.1	16.1
28. Nigeria	7,793	8,491	9.0	11.68	5.05	−56.7	0.22***	0.16***	0.14***	33.4	25.5
29. Czechoslovakia	6,189	9,688	56.5	11.73	7.54	−35.7	1.01	0.07***	1.62	33.4	25.5
30. German D.R.	4,606	7,147	55.2	11.29	6.40	−43.3	0.78	1.18	0.65	33.0	21.8
31. Iran	4,955	6,508	31.3	8.29	9.24	11.4	2.15	1.00	3.88**	27.4	29.5
32. Bulgaria	5,429	7,706	41.9	10.27	7.47	−27.3	1.05	3.55**	0.72	31.2	25.1
33. South Korea	5,266	6,227	18.3	5.97	10.77	80.4	4.02**	0.96	7.76***	20.1	32.3
34. Egypt	5,789	7,109	22.8	4.95	2.67	−46.1	0.44**	0.23**	0.37*	15.6	3.1
35. Rest of world[a]	98,481	117,747	19.6	3.19	2.80	−12.2	1.10	0.47	0.75	5.9	3.8
36. Total world[a]	829,087	1,133,908	36.8	2.76	3.36	21.7	2.78*	2.22	2.69*	3.5	6.8

Note: ***, **, and * indicate statistically significant *F* ratios (one-tail tests) at the 1%, 5%, and 10% confidence levels, respectively.
[a]Does not include China.

Table 3.10 Variability of world cereal production around linear trend for
different periods[a]

Decade beginning	Average production	Standard deviation	Coefficient of variation	Probability of 5% shortfall below trend
	(million metric tons)			
1960/61	819	24.3	0.030	4.65
1961/62	837	20.7	0.025	2.17
1962/63	867	22.4	0.026	2.62
1963/64	890	24.1	0.027	3.22
1964/65	923	26.8	0.030	4.18
1965/66	946	31.2	0.034	6.55
1966/67	972	32.5	0.034	6.68
1967/68	1,001	34.3	0.035	7.21
1968/69	1,026	34.4	0.035	6.81
1969/70	1,057	40.0	0.037	9.01
1970/71	1,081	40.0	0.037	8.85
1971/72	1,108	40.1	0.036	8.38
1972/73	1,132	39.5	0.035	7.64
1973/74	1,159	38.5	0.033	6.68

[a] Does not include China.

terns of correlation, the sum of the production covariances should increase
at about the same rate as the sum of the production variances.[5]

The part of the increase in the variance of total cereal production attributable to intercrop production covariances within countries increased proportionally more than the part due to the sum of the crop variances within
countries. The F ratio was 42 percent larger. Similarly, the F ratio for the
part of the variance increase due to production covariances between different crops in different countries was 86 percent larger. For these larger F
ratios to have arisen, there must have been a loss in offsetting patterns of
variation in production among crops within and between countries.

The column sums in table 3.12 show that 96 percent of the increase in
the variance of world cereal production is directly attributable to changes
in the variances and covariances of crop yields. Changes in yield variances
within countries account for one-quarter of this increase, and most of this
is attributable to increased yield variances for wheat and maize.

For most crops, increased yield variances account for the lion's share of
their contribution to the variance of total cereal production. For example,
when summed over countries, the increased production variances for

5. If x and y are random variables with variances σ_x^2 and σ_y^2, and if ρ is the correlation
coefficient, then $\text{cov}(x, y) = \rho\sigma_x\sigma_y$. Assuming ρ is fixed, then the covariance will increase at a
rate equal to the square root of the product of the rates of increase in the variances.

Table 3.11 Disaggregation of the components of change in the average of world cereal production, 1960/61–1970/71 to 1971/72–1982/83[a] (percent)

	Wheat	Maize	Rice	Barley	Millets	Sorghum	Oats	Other cereals	Total cereals
Change in mean yields	80.93	64.21	60.62	39.52	63.64	45.63	−528.09	−179.99	72.40
Change in mean areas	14.94	28.61	33.64	49.11	44.76	44.42	534.84	220.53	22.36
Change in area-yield covariances	0.19	0.09	−0.02	0.45	2.96	0.20	15.21	−1.08	0.14
Change in interaction term	3.95	7.08	5.77	10.93	−11.36	9.76	78.05	60.54	5.10
Contribution of crop to change in mean production of total cereals	32.65	35.18	11.50	18.28	0.55	4.34	−0.47	−2.03	100.00

[a]Does not include China.

Table 3.12 Disaggregation of the components of change in the variance of world cereal production, 1960/61-1970/71 to 1971/72-1982/83[a]

Variance Component	Source of change							Row sums
	Change in mean yields	Change in mean areas	Change in yield variances and covariances	Change in area variances and covariances	Change in area-yield covariances	Change in interaction terms	Change in residual	
Crop Variances								
Wheat	2.06	−2.38	5.27	−0.57	3.57	−0.49	0.15	7.61
Maize	6.67	1.94	17.16	−6.15	−5.01	−1.54	0.73	13.80
Rice	0.11	0.25	0.45	0.12	0.16	0.13	0.05	1.26
Barley	0.43	2.30	1.87	0.86	1.37	4.67	0.96	12.46
Millet	0.01	−0.01	0.04	0.01	0.06	−0.02	0.00	0.07
Sorghum	0.19	0.07	0.57	−0.23	0.12	0.07	−0.05	0.74
Oats	0.83	0.27	0.11	−1.25	−0.54	−1.06	−0.19	−1.85
Other	0.14	−0.15	0.00	−0.14	0.29	−0.77	0.06	0.36
Sum crop variances within countries	10.44	2.28	26.40	−7.36	0.01	0.99	1.70	34.45
Intercrop covariances within countries	0.97	4.48	36.68	−0.94	−9.38	1.89	1.65	35.35
Intercountry covariances within crops	0.09	1.61	11.49	−3.61	−4.40	−0.98	0.49	4.70
Covariances between different crops in different countries	2.75	0.85	21.36	19.13	−28.51	6.43	3.55	25.50
Column sums	14.24	9.22	95.93	7.22	−42.28	8.33	7.40	100.00

[a] Does not include China.

wheat account for 7.61 percent of the increase in the variance of total cereal production. Of this, 69.3 percent is due to increased yield variances. Yield variance shares for other crops are: maize, 124 percent, rice, 36 percent, millet, 57 percent, sorghum, 77 percent, and total cereals, 77 percent.

Changes in yield covariances are more important than changes in yield variances for the variability of world cereal production. However, part of the increase in the yield covariances is itself a direct consequence of increased yield variances. Part of it may also be due to changing correlations between crops and regions. To separate these effects it is useful to pursue the decomposition one step further.

Using the same kind of decomposition procedure as before, the change in a yield covariance between two periods can be decomposed into three terms (Hazell 1984): changes in yield variances alone, autonomous changes in the yield correlation, and the interaction between these terms.

For the world, only 6 percent of the 69.5 percent increase in the variance of total cereal production arising from changes in yield covariances is directly attributable to changes in yield variances. About 52 percent of the increase is attributable to changes in yield correlations alone, and the remaining 42 percent is due to interaction effects. The predominant correlation increases are between the yields of different crops in different countries. Increases in the intercrop yield covariances within countries were nearly all attributable to increased yield variances.

Table 3.12 also shows that changes in area-yield covariances reduced the variance of total world cereal production by 42 percent. Virtually all of this reduction can be attributed to a decline in area-yield correlations, the most important of which were between crop yields in one country with the sown areas of the same or different crops in other countries.

DISCUSSION

This analysis has identified three major components in the change in the variability of world cereal production since the 1960s: increased yield variances, an increase in correlations between the yields of different crops, and a decline in area-yield correlations, particularly between the crop yields in one country with the sown areas of the same or different crops in other countries. Additional research will be required to determine why these changes have occurred, but a number of hypotheses can be offered.

Given the importance of improved seed and fertilizer-intensive technologies in increasing yields in many countries, it is tempting to conclude that the increased yield variability is a direct consequence of the improved technologies. Indeed, under controlled (especially field trial) conditions, modern varieties typically have higher mean yields and variances than unimproved varieties. But their coefficients of variation are either lower or about the same. Recent evidence is available for winter wheat in the Great Plains of the United States (Peterson et al. forthcoming), and winter wheat and spring barley in Bavaria (Fischbeck forthcoming). Similar results seem to hold in farmer-managed trials, as shown for upland rice in the Philippines (Flinn and Garrity forthcoming) and for wheat and rice in India (Mruthyunjaya and Jha 1985). CIMMYT varieties of wheat and maize also seem to be more stable than available alternatives under experimental conditions when their performance across contrasting sites (environments) is compared (Pfeiffer and Braun 1985; Pham, Waddington, and Crossa 1985).

Apart from their greater absolute variability, there are a number of other reasons why modern varieties may have contributed to the greater variability observed in aggregate time series data for nations.

First, some of the early modern varieties associated with the international agricultural research centers proved to be susceptible to particular pests and diseases. Because of their high yields, these varieties were widely adopted in a very short time, and when pest and disease outbreaks occurred, these had a sizeable negative impact on farm and aggregate yields. This problem has been contained in recent years by the availability of a greater range of modern varieties, many of which have a wider range of resistance to pests and diseases (Coffman and Hargrove forthcoming; Duvick forthcoming; Holden 1985).

Second, modern varieties are more responsive to modern inputs. Some modern varieties seem to perform about as well as traditional varieties in poorer environments or under low input conditions, but their yields are much higher under favorable conditions and with greater application of inputs (Pfeiffer and Braun 1985; Pham, Waddington, and Crossa 1985). Consequently, if farmers adjust input use from year to year in response to changes in price signals, or in response to limited supplies of inputs, this may induce a much higher degree of yield variability in modern varieties. Such behaviorally induced yield variability may have become an important factor in some countries, and particularly in developing countries, where the greatly increased demand for the inputs that accompanied the green revolution outstripped the possibilities for adequate and timely supplies, given limited infrastructure and foreign exchange shortages (Jain, Dagg, and Taylor 1985). The problem may also have been aggravated by the sharp increases in the cost of fertilizers and other agrichemicals that accompanied the oil crises of the 1970s and by an increase in the variability of cereal prices in world markets.

A third reason why aggregate yields may have become more variable with the introduction of modern varieties is an increase in correlations among yields between regions (Hazell 1984; Walker forthcoming a). This again may be due to variations in input use, since farmers in the same or adjacent regions are likely to face the same prices and input shortages, thereby making similar adjustments in their use of inputs. The increased correlations may also be a consequence of the widespread adoption of relatively few varieties. As more farmers grow the same varieties, their yields may be becoming more synchronized because of a common susceptibility to the same kinds of pest, disease, and weather conditions.

Yields may also have become more variable because the production of some crops has expanded into more marginal and high-risk areas. The latter consideration has been particularly important in such countries as Brazil and Australia. While weather is an important factor in determining base-line levels of yield variability, Carter and Parry (1985) conclude that there is no indication that recent changes in cereal yield variability can be ascribed to climatic change. If anything, weather in some areas may have become less variable, e.g., in the cornbelt of the United States.

The broad increase in yield correlations among crops, both within and between countries, is likely associated with the broad increase in the correlations between cereal prices since the early 1970s. It is, however, difficult to determine whether greater correlation among cereal prices is due to changes in demand, such as increased substitution, or whether it in turn is a consequence of the more correlated yields. In either case, the effect could have been accentuated by the concurrent increase in the use of fertilizers and irrigation water. Farmers in more countries are increasingly responsive to price signals, and greater covariability in world prices would lead to greater and more synchronized variations in water and fertilizer application rates across crops and countries.

These factors may also explain the broad reduction in area-yield correlations between crops and countries. If price ratios in many countries move simultaneously in favor of particular cereals, not only might the land area allocated to these crops increase, but fertilizer and other yield-increasing inputs might be diverted from other crops.[6] This would lead to an observed negative relationship between the area sown to favored crops and the yield of the less favored crops. The effect could become quite pronounced if price ratios among crops fluctuate and as the use of fertilizers increases with improved varieties.

CONCLUSIONS

World cereals prices have become more variable since the early 1970s, which has led to corresponding increases in the variability of domestic

---

6. Even though the prices of different cereals have become more closely correlated, they still do not move in perfect unison. Thus there is still scope for changes in relative prices to favor one crop over another.

farmgate prices in some of the major cereal-exporting countries. However, many countries have successfully buffered their domestic prices from the increased volatility of world markets, and some have even been able to reduce the variability of domestic prices.

There is a surprising lack of collinearity between domestic and world cereal prices in many countries. Countries that buffer their domestic market prices apparently also shield their farmers from directional changes in world market prices. There does not appear to have been any significant change in these patterns of collinearity since the early 1970s.

On the other hand, a dramatic increase in the collinearity of world cereal prices between crops has been reflected in an increase in the correlation of domestic farmgate prices between crops, both within and among countries.

The growth in world cereal production from 1960/61 to 1982/83, largely due to improved yields, was accompanied by a more than proportional increase in the standard deviation of production. Increases in yield variances and a simultaneous loss in offsetting patterns of variation in yields between crops and countries were the overwhelming sources of the increase in production variability. More research is required before firm conclusions can be drawn about the cause of these changes in yields. An important factor may have been that the increased use of improved seed and fertilizer-intensive technologies since the 1960s has led to more variable and synchronized patterns of input use across crops and regions in response to changing prices. This effect may have been amplified by the sharp increase in the variability of world cereal prices since the early 1970s, and particularly by the increase in price correlations between crops. It does not appear that any inherently higher sensitivity of new technologies to environmental stress has been a significant cause.

Continued high levels of variability in world cereal prices seem likely. The United States is unlikely to return to its stockpiling policies of earlier years, and cereal imports by the U.S.S.R. remain unpredictable. World prices will also be affected by the levels of production variability now established. These factors, together with a continuing trend towards more input-intensive technologies, suggest that world cereal production and prices are likely to continue to become more variable in the years ahead.

II

DOMESTIC MARKET INTERVENTION

4

Pricing Principles and Public Intervention in Domestic Markets

RAISUDDIN AHMED

Public intervention in foodgrain markets is pervasive in most developing countries. Governments procure foodgrains from farmers, import and export, distribute to consumers, set procurement and distribution prices, strive to maintain floor and ceiling prices in markets, and regulate private trade. In doing so they often alter the structure of incentives in the markets. Current debate on market intervention, however, has resulted in a trend towards liberalization of control and regulation in markets of many countries. An important issue is whether or not undesirable changes in incentives can be minimized through improved operation of public and private markets or whether alternative policies for ensuring higher incentives to producers and lower prices to consumers can be devised through, for example, infrastructural development.

In order to explore these questions, it is necessary to examine two sets of issues relating to pricing. The first set concerns the average level of price and the criteria that constitute the basis for targeting this average in pricing policy. The second set relates to the mechanisms of interventions in domestic markets and their implications for spatial and intertemporal price differences in relation to the average price and the efficiency in distribution of commodities from producers to consumers.

CRITERIA FOR PRICING

Most countries with mixed economies take a pragmatic approach and adopt a mix of cost of production, parity with various sorts of domestic prices, and, occasionally, world prices as guides for fixing producer prices (see chapter 9). However, because growth of the economy and hence efficiency is of primary concern, world price as a reference for domestic price determination is considered by many economists to be an appropriate base from which to discuss price interventions.

The World Price Criterion

Conceptually, world price, correctly identified and measured, provides the appropriate measure of opportunity cost of resources used in production of a tradeable commodity and therefore is also its optimal price. This means that if domestic price is lower than world price, the nation will gain by raising domestic price and selling the excess supply in the world market. If the domestic price is higher than world price, the country can gain by imports which will lower domestic price, divert resources from the commodity concerned to another with a comparative advantage, and thus increase total production in the national economy. This is the logic of world price as a pricing guide. The logic applies mainly to countries whose share of the world market is too small to affect the level of world price. Large countries with monopolistic or near-monopolistic market share and influence on world prices should rely on marginal export revenue or import cost. Such countries (of which there are few) generally are more price setters than price takers in the world market, even though they have to consider potential competition from others in order to protect market share in the long run.

Simple formulations of the world price criteria and the nominal and the effective protection coefficients generally used in empirical investigations (World Bank 1986b; Scandizzo and Bruce 1980; Squire, Little, and Durdag 1979) are presented in note 1 below. In real world applications, there is a general question of how exactly a country can adopt these formulas. Should the domestic nominal price be set *equal to* border price, as equation (1) in note 1 enunciates, or should the border price be adopted only as a *reference point* so that fixation of domestic price is guided by it as well as other pragmatic considerations?

In a sense, equation (2) in the note is an example of one of many types of modifications necessary for using world price as a reference for fixation of domestic price. This equation provides for netting out subsidy and taxes

1. Among various formulations of the pricing principles, the following formulas are generally employed in comparing domestic with world prices and assessing the extent of disincentives to farm producers:

$$\text{NPC}_j = P_j^d / P_j^w V \tag{1}$$

$$\text{EPC}_j = (P_j^d - \Sigma a_{ij} * P_i^d)/(P_j^w - \Sigma a_{ij} * P_i^w) * V \tag{2}$$

$$\frac{P_1^d}{P_2^d} = \frac{P_1^w}{P_2^w}; \quad \frac{P_2^d}{P_n^d} = \frac{P_2^w}{P_n^w}; \quad \frac{P_1^d}{P_n^d} = \frac{P_1^w}{P_n^w} \quad (\text{for } j = 1, 2, n) \ldots \tag{3}$$

where NPC is Nominal Protection Coefficient, EPC the Effective Protection Coefficient, j the jth output, a_{ij} the ith tradeable input coefficient to the jth output, P the price, d domestic price in domestic currency, w world ("border") price in foreign currency, and V the exchange rate. Border price includes appropriate transportation costs, as explained in the text. NPC is the ratio of the domestic price to its border price. EPC measures the effects of protection measures not only on traded outputs but also on traded inputs, i.e., the ratio of value added expressed in domestic market prices to value added expressed in border prices.

from price and thus is more relevant for countries with a high incidence of input subsidy. This procedure also permits taking into account an import price higher than the freely quoted world price for inputs like fertilizer, which is often the case with imports under concessionary arrangements.

For example, Bangladesh spent about 14 percent of its budget allocation to agriculture (TK 1,426 million) on fertilizer subsidy in 1983–84. The price of imported fertilizers under concessionary arrangements was 15 to 25 percent higher than the free market world price. The subsidy on irrigation was almost equal to that on fertilizer (Bangladesh 1985). Similarly, India spent about Rs 5,053 million on fertilizer subsidy, Rs 4,785 million on irrigation subsidy, and about Rs 7,261 million on other categories of subsidy related to rural development in 1980–81 (Subbarao 1984). Consideration of input subsidy in the pricing of products is not an endorsement of the economic rationales of the subsidy policy. Subsidy is treated as given at the time of formulation of product prices. In fact, the general view is that input subsidy, except under special circumstances, is an inefficient policy instrument for accelerating agricultural development (Mellor 1976; Shalit and Binswanger 1984).

In a multi-commodity context, say, for example, two agricultural products and one nonagricultural product with prices P_1, P_2, and P_n, we have a more complicated problem of pricing at hand than the one-commodity case. If prices of all tradeable commodities are to be set equal to their border prices, as would be the case in a perfectly open economy, absolute prices as well as price ratios in the domestic market will equal corresponding prices and price ratios in the world market. If, however, there is a compulsion to keep a certain price (say P_1) below its border price (P_1^w), as is often the case with food, then the pricing rule of equating price ratios between domestic and world markets following equation (3) in the note would produce a different set of implications. The pricing rule in this instance, assuming that the exchange rate is applicable uniformly across all commodities, will result in a relative disadvantage of the other two commodities (P_2 and P_n) in the domestic market even though P_2 and P_n were initially equal to their border prices. Obviously, the principle of maintaining parity in price ratios between domestic and world markets may extend distortion and intervention in one commodity to other commodities as well. (See Ahmed [1981] for the problem of parity in jute and rice price ratios in Bangladesh.) Therefore, application of the principle that seeks to equate domestic with world prices across all tradeable products can perhaps be a reality only in a completely free market economy. Considerations for poverty and income distribution are often very serious and real. These forces may impell governments to keep prices at variance with world prices or to prevent the operation of the free market. Thus, world price can serve as an approximate yardstick, albeit a significant one, in pricing, but actual pricing may deviate from the yardstick to an extent determined by the severity of various constraints.

Technical Problems and Suggested Solutions

The first problem associated with the use of world prices involves an exchange rate of domestic vis-à-vis foreign currencies, as stipulated in equations (1) and (2). This exchange rate (V) should reflect the real opportunity cost of foreign currencies. But most exchange rates in developing countries are considered to be overvalued (World Bank 1986b). Some estimates of differences in domestic and world prices of cereals in a few selected countries, following equation (1), are presented in table 4.1. Overvaluation of the exchange rate explains a large part of these differences. At official exchange rates the price differences are small, except for rice in India and Tanzania.

Because most developing countries maintain a strict control on the exchange rate, with limited flexibility for the rate to reflect market forces, it is necessary that a country's central bank monitor the real exchange rate of its currency and make this information available to all other public agencies concerned with commodity pricing on a regular basis. (Chapter 7 provides considerable detail on this question.) However, monitoring the real exchange rate is not the basic problem. The basic problem rests with the ability or willingness of a country to make fundamental adjustments in its macroeconomic policies in order to sustain a stable real exchange rate. This problem is covered to an extent in chapter 7 and more fully in chapter 16 in the context of growth strategy.

The second problem that motivates governments to avoid world prices and insulate the domestic from the international market is the high degree of instability in world prices. Chapters 2 and especially 3 clarify the extent of this problem. Fluctuation in the prices of rice and other cereals is sharper than for wheat because of the underdeveloped nature of international markets for rice and other cereals (Siamwalla and Haykin 1983). Along with this instability in world prices, fluctuation of exchange rates themselves adds greatly to the potential instability in the domestic market. Few developing countries could afford to import such high world price instability into their domestic markets, particularly in foodgrains, and, as chapter 3 shows clearly, few countries do. In the determination of domestic price, using world price as a reference, an average world price can be employed to overcome the instability problem. If the fluctuations in world prices are random without any underlying trend, a simple average price would be a good guide. If the fluctuations in world prices are accompanied by an underlying time trend, a moving average could be a reasonable indicator of world prices for the purpose of guiding domestic price determination. Actual world price in any year could be higher or lower than average.

Table 4.1 Comparison of domestic and world prices of foodgrains, selected
countries, average 1978–80

Country	Commodity	Ratio of domestic to world price at official exchange rate	Ratio of domestic to world price at shadow exchange rate
India	Rice	0.72	0.62
	Wheat	0.80	0.68
Bangladesh	Rice	0.85	0.61
Indonesia	Rice	0.84	0.70
Tanzania	Rice	0.69	0.43
	Maize	0.86	0.54
	Wheat	0.98	0.61
Kenya	Maize	0.80	0.65
Nigeria	Rice	1.20	0.71
	Maize	1.15	0.78

Sources: World Bank agricultural sector reports, various countries; Jansen 1980.
Note: The price comparison is based on the border price at wholesale level. Tanzania's prices are official prices, and others are open-market prices. Since 1978–80 world prices for foodgrains have fallen sharply so that domestic prices at official exchange rates are now closer to world prices than in the past; in fact, rice prices in Bangladesh were slightly higher than world prices in 1985–86.

A supplementary stabilization fund and stocking provisions may be required for such policies to be operationally feasible.

The third problem relates to the status of a country with respect to trade. The formula commonly used for empirical studies, referred to in note 1, does not specify whether the world price (P_j^w) is an export or an import parity price. If a country is a consistent importer, the import parity border price, for comparison with the farmgate domestic price, would be c.i.f. price plus transportation cost up to retail price level minus transportation cost from farmgate to retail level. If a country is a consistent exporter, the export parity border price would be f.o.b. price in the competitive world market, and the comparable domestic price would be farmgate price plus transportation and other costs up to f.o.b. level in the country concerned. It is clear from this procedure that the effects of marketing costs, including shipping costs, are subsumed under the border price.

Moreover, the decision as to whether a commodity is to be priced on an export parity or an import parity basis is not often straightforward. Developing countries with small deficits or surpluses in foodgrain production are numerous (table 4.2), and for them the choice of which pricing route to follow is a difficult one. Export parity and import parity prices in maize in most African countries differ by 40 to 125 percent (World Bank 1983a).

Before starting to export rice, the Philippines was, according to conventional analysis, paying a rice price to its farmers 20 to 25 percent lower

Table 4.2 Degree of self-sufficiency in foodgrains, developing countries, 1976–80

Country	Self-sufficiency ratio[a]	Country	Self-sufficiency ratio[a]
Thailand	168.3	Burkina Faso	91.5
Gambia	143.7	Sierra Leone	91.2
Zimbabwe	118.5	Mali	91.0
Niger	109.0	Bangladesh	90.0
Nepal	101.4	Vietnam	89.3
Sudan	100.9	Nicaragua	89.1
India	100.4	Ghana	88.4
Pakistan	100.0	Guatemala	88.1
Chad	99.3	Angola	87.7
Malawi	98.6	Mexico	87.5
Kenya	97.5	Ivory Coast	86.0
Tanzania	97.4	Mozambique	85.9
Senegal	96.2	Zambia	84.3
Philippines	95.2	El Salvador	81.3
Ethiopia	95.0	Bolivia	80.4
Indonesia	93.9	Morocco	72.2
Zaire	93.4	Sri Lanka	66.2
Cameroon	92.8	Tunisia	61.2
Nigeria	92.7	Malaysia	54.2
Brazil	91.5	Algeria	47.8

Source: Paulino 1986.
[a] Domestic production/total consumption × 100.

than the world price on an import parity basis. But the Philippines soon found that it could not export rice without a subsidy. That subsidy was reported to be P 90 million (P 8 = U.S.$1) from 1977 to 1979, equivalent to about 28 percent of export price (Unnevehr 1983).

When Bangladesh, a consistent importer of rice, faced a temporary surplus in 1981, it attempted to export 20,000 tons to Guinea, only to find the export price 65 to 70 percent of the regular price of its own rice imports. India, with a current stock level of 20 to 25 million tons of foodgrains, has reportedly been facing a situation where it cannot export grains commercially without a large subsidy.

Differences in quality are one of the reasons for the wide gap in export and import parity prices. A dramatic example is the case of white maize in the African domestic market and yellow maize in the world market. Grading and packaging a commodity for the world market is certainly different than for the domestic market. These facts indicate not only the necessity of carefully considering differences in quality when comparing prices but also the problems involved in using import or export parity prices as guides to pricing.

Whether a country should adopt export or import parity prices should be decided at the initial stage of a pricing exercise on the basis of a careful examination of its pace of increase in domestic production and the nature of its trade gap. In general, countries at the threshold of self-sufficiency—probably with a shortfall in domestic production of around 5 percent of domestic demand and with a growth rate in production equal to or above population growth—should use the average of export parity and import parity prices. This approach reduces the chance of unusual variability in prices resulting from the wide gap between export and import parity prices. Use of simple or moving averages to overcome the problem of fluctuation would imply an averaging of the respective simple or moving average export and import parity prices. For consistent importers and exporters, import parity or export parity prices should be used.

Domestic prices (P_j and P_i), production coefficients (a_{ij}), and the exchange rate (V) are all averages—one average value for each variable for a whole country. In reality, values of these variables vary widely, and the validity of assuming that these mean values represent true measures depends on how well the marketing system operates and is integrated and how good the statistical systems are that process such data. A recent study shows that the variability of indicators measuring farm level incentives, estimated on the basis of formulas similar to equations (1) and (2), was very high in Niger and Upper Volta (McIntire and Delgado 1983). The findings on sorghum, millet, maize, and groundnut indicate that the standard deviations of the measures of NPC and EPC are substantially larger than the means in most cases. This is a reflection of enormous variability in prices and marketing margins among geographically dispersed farmers.

One can expect this to be the case in all countries but more so in developing countries. Use of national averages, whether of price, supply, demand, or marketing margin, is unavoidable in price policy analysis. But the income distribution, efficiency, and political implications of the variability underlying such averages are real and must be the subject of analysis. In practice, such variability may be reflected in a weighted average price and a variety of prices for various segmented markets. In any case the problem is serious and thus far unresolved.

Finally, the predictability of the medium- and long-term trends of world prices is extremely poor. For example, the World Bank projected rice price for 1982, made on the basis of information available through 1978 (World Bank, 1980), was off the mark by about 100 percent. The Bank 1985 projected world rice price reported in 1980 had to be brought down by 64 percent in its 1984 document (World Bank 1984b) on the basis of additional information gained from 1979 through 1983. Even with that adjustment, the actual prices in the world market differ from this latest projection by about 38 percent. Such is the magnitude of this forecasting problem!

Application of the world price criterion in a rigid manner is virtually impossible when long- and medium-term resource allocation issues are involved, as, for example, in the question of the low priority given to irrigation development in the light of the current low prices of rice in world markets. There is no way to know whether this deemphasis on irrigation development today will not look like a misallocation of resources in the context of tomorrow's market prices. No solution to this problem, through development of forecasting effort and technique, appears in sight. The unpredictability of world price is a formidable argument against the use of world price as a pricing guide. But the existence of options in the world market is not washed out by the condition of unpredictability. The point is that world price is only a rough guide that can neither be rigidly followed nor completely abandoned in national pricing policies.

Cost of Production as a Pricing Criterion

The simple rationale behind the cost of production principle is that farmers ought to receive a fair return on their outlays. In this sense, the cost of production criterion is oriented toward safeguarding the gains of private producers, while the world price criterion is concerned with social profitability. Cost of production is a widely accepted criterion in both developed and developing countries. Generally, the average cost of producing a unit of output, rather than the marginal cost, is used as a reference point in fixing producer prices. This is not an issue because the difference between the two costs is insignificant for most crops. There are several other problems in using cost of production as a guide. First, the cost of specialized resources (e.g., land) is demand-determined and therefore is affected by product price. Accommodation of this cost in the fixing of price involves circularity. Every time the product price is raised, the cost of these resources will also rise and the administered price will have to be raised. Of course the argument is of much less practical relevance in the context of developing countries because of the larger share of family labor in the agricultural cost of production there. A similar argument is also made against inclusion of "rent" in the cost of production. Second, because of uncertainty, the cost that determines producer decisions is a subjective opportunity cost that cannot be measured objectively. Third, since differences in costs among farmers and regions is very high, the choice of groups and regions whose cost is to be fully covered by the administered price will be arbitrary (Pasour 1980; Krishna 1982). An arbitrary choice of a cost estimate may generate enormous problems of interregional or intergroup income distribution. Moreover, the production conditions in agriculture, as dictated by factor and product market imperfections, make the cost estimates deviate more widely from their true opportunity costs than would be expected in case of industrial production. Thus, fixing prices on the basis of cost of production is even less likely to approach optimality in agriculture than in industry.

Although arguments against the cost of production as a principle for fixing agricultural prices are real, use of the principle persists because it provides a basis for discussion between groups representing producers and other interests involved in the political economy of price fixing. It is of course true that the criterion is seldom applied consistently enough to protect the relative profitability of agriculture vis-à-vis non-agriculture.

Professional economists in governments of developing countries have proposed various solutions to minimize the nonoptimality associated with these problems (see chapter 9). A number of alternative estimates of cost of production have been prompted by questions concerning the opportunity cost of family labor, valuation of such labor at market prices, and the measurement of rent and its inclusion in the estimates. These improvements in the estimation of cost of production have sought to bridge the gap between private and social costs that exist in conventional estimation of cost of production. Despite the deficiencies, when farm income is a consideration, cost of production becomes a relevant criterion, in addition to world price, in pricing decisions.

The statistics on cost of production and procurement prices for foodgrains in India for 1955–80 indicate that cost of production was perhaps not a firm guide for procurement price. Procurement price of foodgrains (wheat) was generally 20 to 30 percent lower than the average cost of production from 1955 through 1965 and about 20 to 50 percent higher from 1965 through 1980 (Krishna and Chibber 1983). This divergence resulted more from technological influences than from any abrupt rise in procurement price during the green revolution. New technology in wheat reduced average cost of production per unit of output while the procurement price did not move, *pari passu*, with cost of production. This of course is a reflection of an accelerated rate of incentives that Indian policy extended to farmers for diffusion of technology in the second period compared to the first (Kahlon and Tyagi 1983).

The relation between cost of production and technological progress underscores further the need for monitoring cost of production, even though it may not be a precise guide for determination of producer price. New technology substantially changes the factoral terms of trade for agriculture—that is, the returns to the factors of production, including labor. It is important that price policy be made in full cognizance of such dynamic forces. They are important to influence distribution but may even be harbingers of future changes in world prices as new technologies diffuse broadly. Information on cost of production is required in designing policies to accelerate diffusion of technology. A precipitous decline in prices caused by the initial success of a new technology may arrest its spread before it reaches its full potential (Mellor 1969). Moreover, compulsions to pass on some of the benefits from technological progress to consumers through a lower market price is often quite great. Managing these two sets of forces then becomes a balancing act for policymakers. They cannot succeed in this attempt without information on the extent of reduction in cost of production caused by a new technology and the dynamics of this cost structure under technologically progressive conditions (chapter 11 goes into this issue in detail).

Forces Underlying Issue Price

Strictly speaking, an issue price represents a sale price at publicly controlled shops for distribution of subsidized foods. But a policy-targeted ceiling price in markets can be meaningfully treated as an issue price designed to benefit consumers. The level of issue price is generally a result of many interacting forces rather than clearly formulated criteria.

Issue price originated from pricing at ration shops organized in a few selected cities of south Asia during World War II. Issue prices were set at the levels of the market prices that prevailed immediately before the inflationary trend of prices induced by the war expenditures (Knight 1954). Since the end of the war, the rationing system has been extended to most urban areas and to some rural areas of south Asian countries. Rapid urbanization and industrialization have brought along with them a number of evolutionary forces that have fashioned the process by which the issue price has been determined at public foodshops.

First, the recipients of public foods have emerged as a politically vocal and powerful group which no government seeking political stability can ignore, as shown in table 4.3. It is clear that the urban population, government employees, industrial workers, and urban-like rural population receive the lion's share of ration foodgrains.

Second, as the quantity of subsidized food and the budgetary burden of subsidy has increased, demand for scarce public resources for investment has been mounting. This has also generated pressure in governments to reduce the food subsidy by increasing issue prices.

The levels of the issue price generally prevailing in developing countries reflect these opposing forces. Very often, trade unions of industrial and city workers and government employees demand a lower issue price as a part of wage settlements. On the other hand, multinational donors and finance ministries of government occasionally raise the question of food subsidy and propose higher issue prices of foodgrains. The balance of the two forces has generally been helpful for price stability. Issue price seldom fluctuates as widely as market price, and therefore shields against price instability for ration recipients. It is stability in prices, supply, and real income of consumers that has made the food subsidy system so important

Table 4.3 Public distribution of foodgrains under various categories, Bangladesh, 1973–83

Category	Average quantity, 1973–76	Average share, 1973–76	Average quantity, 1977–82	Average share, 1977–82
	(thousand tons)	(percent)	(thousand tons)	(percent)
Food for work (rural)	150	8.4	300	15.0
Open market sale	no[b]	no[b]	150	7.5
Rationing	*1,570*	*87.4*	*1,506*	*75.0*
Statutory (urban)	460	25.6	365	18.2
Modified (50% rural, 50% towns)	640	35.7	310	15.4
Priority group (urban)[a]	105	5.8	336	16.7
Gov't employees (urban)	180	10.0	260	13.0
Large industries (urban)	75	4.2	120	6.0
Flour mills (urban)	110	6.1	115	5.7
Relief	75	4.2	50	2.5
Total	*1,795*	*100.0*	*2,006*	*100.0*

Sources: Ahmed 1979; Hossain 1984.
[a] Police, army, paramilitary, hospitals, hostels.
[b] Not in operation.

an issue to urban consumers, and any effort to reform or remove food subsidy has always been resisted by these urban beneficiaries.

DOMESTIC MARKETS AND PUBLIC INTERVENTIONS

So far the discussion has centered on an average price for a commodity, but generally there are as many prices as there are markets in an economy. An average can be misleading unless the interrelationship among components of the average is clearly recognized. For example, suppose that the price of a good in the lean season is 100 and the price in the harvest season is 50. The average of 75 is the same as if the lean season price were 80 and harvest season price 70. But the two situations are drastically different. A producer usually selling in harvest season would receive only 67 percent of the average price in the first situation and 93 percent in the second.

The interrelationship among prices of various markets are founded on marketing functions and their associated costs. In the case of spatially separate markets, transportation cost, including profit and transaction costs, if any, account for price differences. In the case of seasonally separated markets, the price differences are explained by storage cost, including traders' profit and transaction costs, if any. The extent of traders' profit, transaction costs, and the rapidity in transmittal of prices between markets generally depend on competitiveness in markets.

In the context of public policies in foodgrain marketing the most relevant questions are whether markets perform these functions most efficiently (that is, at minimum cost) and whether public actions in markets hinder or help efficiency. Unlike undeveloped markets for new products (for example, modern agricultural inputs), market failures (i.e., absence of market) in foodgrains are less common, though occasional disruptions occur due to natural extremes or wars. Market failures may be infrequent, but market imperfections are not uncommon. They imply inadequate competition in the market resulting from difficult entry conditions, such as unequal access to capital and information, inadequate size of market for an economically viable competition, natural factors, etc. These imperfections are generally reflected in the difference between the price paid by consumers and that received by producers, including profit. The marketing margin in an imperfect market is likely to be higher than that in a competitive market because of abnormal profit. Marketing margins can also be high, even in a competitive market, because of a high real marketing cost. For example, marketing cost for transportation is higher in places with developed than with underdeveloped infrastructures. A distinction between these two types of costs—cost related to genuine functions (e.g., transport, storage, processing, etc.) and cost related to market imperfections—has to be recognized in order to focus public action on appropriate correctives.

Spatial Price Margins

A comparison of Asian and African markets dramatizes the effects of infrastructural development and public intervention on market efficiency (table 4.4). Even though the estimates are based on weak price information, particularly from African countries, the rough order of magnitudes is instructive. Marketing margins in African countries shown in the table are more than twice those in Asian countries. Farmers in these African countries receive only 35 to 50 percent of the price of foodgrains paid by final users. In contrast, farmers in the Asian countries selected receive about 75 to 90 percent. This difference is not due to additional processing and packaging services, as is generally the case in developed economies. The spreads in interregional prices are also much wider in African than Asian countries.

The implication for producers and consumers of policies designed to reduce high marketing margins can be clarified by an example. If the price

Table 4.4 Regional and producer-consumer price spreads, selected countries of Asia and Africa, various years, 1975–80

Country	Commodity	Weights (by production)	Regional spread[a]	Weighted average	Producer-consumer price spread[b]	Weighted average
Nigeria	Maize	14	35.60		54.5	
	Rice	6	72.89	46.1	57.0	58.9
	Sorghum	80	45.92		59.8	
Malawi	Maize	79.5	21.86	31.2	48.2	49.6
	Rice	20.5	68.20		55.1	
	Sorghum					
Tanzania	Maize	76.0	25.70		38.2	
	Rice	9.8	61.27	30.6	56.6	41.4
	Sorghum	14.2	35.47		48.1	
Kenya	Maize		30.0	30.0	42.0	42.0
Sudan	Sorghum	91.9	48.2	48.5	61.2	61.2
	Wheat	8.1	52.1			
Indonesia	Rice		71.9	71.9	84.0	84.0
India	Rice	54	69.8		82.0	
	Wheat	38	65.9	68.0	79.5	81.0
	Sorghum	8.0	63.5		80.0	
Bangladesh	Rice		75.0	75.0	79.0	79.0
Philippines	Rice	70	82.7		87.0	82.4
	Maize	30	64.2	77.3	71.5	

Source: Ahmed and Rustagi 1985.
[a] Lowest price/highest price × 100.
[b] Producer price/terminal price × 100.

spread between producers and consumers in Kenya and Malawi could be reduced to the levels of India and Bangladesh, it would imply an increase in the African producer prices of 30 to 50 percent, depending on demand and supply elasticities of foodgrains, and a decline in consumer prices of 9 to 17 percent. A 30 to 50 percent permanent shift in real prices would be an extremely powerful incentive for farmers. Furthermore, it would benefit consumers too.

The data outlined in table 4.4 raise questions as to why the differences in spatial marketing among the countries are so high and how much of these differences are due to market imperfections and to cost differentials. Empirical studies have frequently demonstrated that foodgrain markets unencumbered by distortive public interventions work competitively, with no significant degree of abnormal profit. Competitiveness is generally greater in Asian markets than in West or East Africa, while West African markets are more competitive than East African (Lele 1971; Cummings 1967; Mears 1981; Jones 1970; Whetham 1972; Schmidt 1979). These regions also differ rather substantially in interference in markets. Poor design and clumsy implementation of intervention are generally the causes of market inefficiency.

Infrastructures play a critical role in mobility of people, goods, and information and in realizing the potential production from land. These factors positively contribute to growth and efficiency of markets. The difference in infrastructural development between Asia and Africa is glaring. Most African countries have 15 to 30 persons per square kilometer, compared to 500 to 900 persons in Asian countries. By 1978, African countries had 0.01 to 0.11 kilometers of road network per kilometer of area, compared to 0.4 to 0.5 in Asian countries. Moreover, only about 10 percent of the roads in African countries are paved, compared to around 35 percent in Asia (International Road Federation 1980). Asian countries are equally better off in railways, water transport, and rural electrification. They also have more modes of transport than African countries. The backwardness of infrastructures in Africa is compounded by urban dependence on imported wheat and rice rather than domestically produced coarse grains and by a much sharper dualism in farm organizations. Due to underdeveloped infrastructures, search and information costs in African markets are, perhaps, many times greater than in Asian markets.

The net effect of all these factors is synthesized in the study on which table 4.4 is based. It showed that roughly 9 percent of the average total difference in marketing margin between Asian and African countries is explained by differential taxes, 40 percent by differential transportation costs, and 24 percent by differential extents of profit. The remaining 27 percent is attributed to residual factors representing transaction costs that could be traced to effects of haphazard public interventions.

Interventions and Spatial Prices

Administratively determined, a single procurement price throughout a country is a common rule in the procurement programs of developing countries. Besides being an administrative convenience, a uniform price is rationalized by considerations such as regional equity, sense of national unity, and compensation for backward infrastructures. The effect of panterritorial price will differ with different models of procurement. The Asian model generally allows private trade to operate side by side with public procurement, whereas the African model is usually a public monopoly. If private trade is operative with a panterritorial price and producers are free to sell to anybody, the quantity a government parastatal can purchase will depend on procurement price relative to market price. Procurement price cannot be set above the market price everywhere, as the result would be to eliminate private trade entirely if budgetary, administrative, and physical storage resources were not a constraint. Even if the procurement price is below the country or statewide average market price, procurement could be substantial. Producers in remote and infrastructurally backward areas will find the procurement price more profitable than market prices, while those nearer to the main consuming centers may find the market price more profitable. In this situation, public procurement will be limited to outlying production centers. Thus, 78 percent of the procurement of rice in Bangladesh is limited to 4 outlying districts of Denajpur, Sylhet, Rajshahi, and Rangpur. A similar pattern is also discerned from a study in Tanzania. This study shows that 80 to 85 percent of total procurements of maize in 1979/80 through 1981/82 were concentrated in five out of the twenty producing regions of the country (Suzuki and Bernard 1987). Most of these five regions are remote and isolated regions with difficult infrastructures.

This model of procurement tends to reduce interregional spreads in market prices—the higher the procurement price relative to market price, the lower the interregional price gap. But a higher procurement price also implies an increasing substitution of public for private trade. Private trade finds working in remote areas no longer profitable and leaves such areas to public agencies. If the market has some degree of imperfection implying a higher than normal profit, relatively efficient traders will accept a cut in profit and stay in trading and inefficient ones will be eliminated. Then the substitution effect will be small. These effects, however, will depend also on the quantities procured. Very often, countries with budgetary constraints set quantity rather than market price as policy targets. Targeting market price rather than quantity of procurement tends to result in more uniformity in spatial prices. Subsidy to producers through this type of procurement is in effect a compensation for infrastructural backwardness.

Compulsory procurement (also called levy) is a special mechanism by which farmers, traders, and millers are legally obligated to sell a part of their produce to government at a lower than market price. This instrument was particularly common in India, Bangladesh, and Pakistan, mainly to supply the public distribution system, during the sixties, when the food shortage in South Asia was more critical than at present. The practice was criticized by some as an indirect tax on farmers but was strongly supported by others. Several studies have convincingly proved that the levy does not impose any disincentive effect on producers under a special condition (Dantwala 1967; Mellor 1968b; Hayami, Subbarao, and Otsuka 1982). If the procured foodgrains are distributed through the subsidy system to the poorer section of the population, the weighted average price received by the farmers would be at least equal to or higher than it would be without a levy. This is because the elasticity of demand for foodgrains of the poor is higher than the price response (supply elasticity) in production. Farmers get a lower price for the levy quantity but a higher price for remaining sales in the free market.

Restriction on movement of a commodity has perhaps a much wider implication for prices than levy. When movement between deficit and surplus regions is prohibited, the price is expected to go up in the deficit area and fall in the surplus area. Thus movement restrictions have the potential for widening the gap between interregional prices and also produce a few other distortions in the economy. Such restrictions serve two immediate purposes: a) under scarcity conditions they prevent more prosperous areas from pulling so much food from low-income rural regions as to cause famine; b) by depressing the price in surplus-producing areas they facilitate procurement for public distribution.

Movement restrictions stimulate corrupt practices, and interregional smuggling may become rampant. A marketing study on maize in Kenya produced interesting estimates of the social costs of these distortions. Besides imposing the transaction costs directly on traders, which were equivalent to about 7 percent of price, movement restrictions induced inefficient use of the transportation system (Schmidt 1979). Traders attempted to move goods in buses and matatas rather than in trucks to avoid detection by police, increasing marketing cost and price spread.

The public procurement of India, Bangladesh, Pakistan, Indonesia, and the Philippines allows private trade to operate. In most of these countries, public procurement covers 20 to 50 percent of marketed foodgrains. Indonesia has been particularly successful in reducing the interregional price spread (measured as an index of the highest to the lowest prices) from 150 in the mid-fifties to 115 in the mid-seventies (Mears 1981). Chapter 5 elaborates on this system.

The other model of intervention is represented by cases where private trade is banned through public monopoly. The bans being of limited effectiveness in practice, procurement depends very much on the level of procurement price, budgetary resources, and the logistical capability of the government. Few governments with a mixed economy can muster adequate financial, administrative, and logistical resources to conduct a monopoly of public marketing in foodgrains without causing severe disincentives to producers. There are three reasons why this is so.

First, a limited and inflexible budgetary resource may lead to setting procurement price at a lower level than is otherwise appropriate. Recourse to deficit financing in order to overcome budget constraint has often resulted in sharper increases in nonagricultural than in agricultural prices. Such effects, even though widespread, are recorded in marketing and price policy studies only in an indirect manner (Ahmed 1979, 1981; Chopra 1984; Schmidt 1979).

Second, the cost of marketing increases rather dramatically as the government expands its marketing logistics to cover most farmers, even in remote areas. This is particularly true of countries with poor infrastructures. Thus, a study on Malawai indicates that during the seventies, as the number of purchasing centers in small-scale production areas increased, the cost of procurement per unit of marketing went up at about twice the rate of inflation (Kydd and Christiansen 1982). Similar evidence was found in other studies (Kenya 1982; World Bank 1983b; Lele 1984a). A large share of the increased costs has ultimately been shifted to producers through a lower procurement price. Such escalations in costs are unlikely in private trade. For example, where a public truck is often utilized to carry even a few kilograms of goods, a private system will find diverse modes of cheaper transport for such small-scale operations.

Third, when farmers must sell to designated public purchasing centers, they incur additional transaction costs. The government officials in charge of such centers have the power to accept or reject a consignment on the grounds of quality or some other pretext, a power which can easily be turned to their own financial benefit. The result is that the effective procurement price for farmers is lower than the declared one by the amount of such extortion (Schmidt 1979).

Finally, a parallel or black market is bound to coexist with public monopoly in a situation of financial and administrative constraints. It is not uncommon for prices in a parallel market to be two to three times higher than the publicly fixed price (Lele 1984a). In one sense, the parallel market is a natural consequence of an unrealistic public monopoly; it provides an alternative market to both producers and consumers. But it cannot have an impact equivalent to that of a competitive market because its illegal nature results in a risk premium as a markup to the "free price."

Public procurement with panterritorial pricing and inflexibility in quality control has additional implications. Panterritorial pricing tends to stimulate production but limits the scope for regional specialization. It penalizes production of the same crops in regions nearest to the market. It may also mislocate production of high-value (less bulky) crops, but the evidence is scarce (Kaberuka 1984). Panterritorial pricing has been modified in many countries by adding a transport bonus, which varies with distance, to the procurement price.

Procurement on a one-grade basis (FAQ or fair average quality) definitely discourages production of better-quality products. Such effects on demand for African export products were reported to be significant (Lele 1984a). A study on Philippine rice production and its competitiveness in world rice markets also found that government's pricing policy on the basis of average quality created disincentives in the production of quality rice (Unnevehr 1984). Elaborate quality control is not practical in a public system, particularly one with a weak administration. Losses in public go-downs due to purchase of grains with high moisture contents are occasionally detected and are purported to be high (Kaberuka 1984).

There are numerous other problems with public procurement, particularly the mode of payment, which is complex where no banking facilities are nearby. Farmers generally do not like payment by check, which sometimes takes months to cash. On the other hand, handling of a large amount of cash by low-ranking officials has been found to create opportunities for numerous irregularities and corruptions.

Intertemporal Price Margins

The separation of spatial from intertemporal distribution of foodgrains is an analytical convenience. Most often, the people who trade in spatial and in wholesale markets also hold stocks for profit. The function of storage is to minimize seasonal fluctuations in supply, prices, and consumption. Public policies are generally concerned with intra- and interyear fluctuations. The discussion here is limited to intrayear or seasonal fluctuations; annual and, to a certain extent, seasonal fluctuations are analyzed in chapter 5.

The distinction between seasonal and annual variation in supply and prices arises partly from the difference in frequency of harvests. If a country harvests foodgrains in more than one season (for example, summer, autumn, and winter rice crops in Bangladesh, India, and Sri Lanka), then the seasonal pattern will generally show more than one trough and peak in prices. On the other hand, if a country has only one harvest in a year, there will normally be a trough just after the harvest and then a gradual rise to a peak just before the next year's harvest. The differences between troughs and peaks will normally be smaller in the former than in the latter case.

Agroclimatic factors and agricultural technology exert a substantial influence on seasonality. Two or more crops of the high-yielding varieties of rice can be grown in a year where conditions are appropriate. This helps reduce seasonal fluctuations. On the other hand, new varieties of wheat grown only in winter may accentuate seasonality. Irrigation and water control facilities, if developed extensively, can also minimize weather-induced fluctuations in production and prices.

Although some smoothing in fluctuation of prices and supply can be achieved through adjustments in the production process, storage is perhaps the principal instrument. Private traders buy foodgrains at the harvest season for sale during the period of peak prices in order to make a profit. This action results in a smoother seasonal price pattern. The decisions of such traders on the amount of grain to buy during harvest time is influenced by the price at harvest, expected changes in price during the following peak season, and storage cost, including interest on capital. In most countries, actions of private trade generally affect seasonal markets, whereas public storage function is principally geared to control of annual fluctuations. Nevertheless, the expectation of private traders about future prices is influenced by public actions in markets. Erratic public stock management would be expected to cause a sharper fluctuation in prices than would a consistently stable intervention policy.

Estimates of seasonal fluctuation in foodgrain prices for the Asian and African countries listed in table 4.4 are presented in table 4.5. Although seasonal price changes are also wider in African than in Asian countries, they are smaller than the differences in either regional prices or the producer-consumer price margins. One reason for the wider seasonal spread in African prices compared to Asia may be that crops in Asia are harvested in two to three seasons while Africa is primarily limited to one harvest. Moreover, real cost of storage may also be larger in Africa than in Asia.

Interventions and Seasonal Prices

While procurement policy is meant to raise harvest season prices, public distribution policy, particularly open-market sale, is meant to prevent a rise in price above a ceiling during a period of lean supply. Public rationing is primarily a mechanism for supporting consumption the year round, but

Table 4.5 Spreads in seasonal prices in selected countries, various years, 1975–80

Country	Commodity	Seasonal price spreads[a]	Weighted average price spread
Nigeria	Maize	70	
	Rice	68	71
	Sorghum	72	
Malawi	Maize	55	56
	Rice	60	
Tanzania	Maize	51	
	Rice	56	51
	Sorghum	50	
Kenya	Maize	49	49
Sudan	Sorghum	51	53
	Wheat	71	
Indonesia	Rice	87	87
India	Rice	81	80
	Wheat	78	
Bangladesh	Rice	74	74
Philippines	Rice	82	81
	Corn	78	

Source: table 4.4
[a] Lowest price as percent of highest price.

in practice it is used more in lean periods than in harvest season and is more effective in urban than rural areas. Offtake from rationing is chiefly determined by the difference between ration and market prices and the ration quota. Thus, the demand for ration foodgrains becomes higher in the lean than in the harvest season. Ration offtake has an indirect effect on market price. At given levels of production, import, and income, the market price can be raised or lowered by decreasing or increasing the proportions of public stock allocated for rationing and open-market sales (Ahmed 1979; Prabha 1982). The income effect of rationing tends to increase market price, but the substitution effect tends to decrease it. The net effect results in some decline in market price. Open-market sale has no immediate income effect and therefore is more price-depressing than rationing.

These relations indicate that public distribution, whether through rationing or open-market sales, has implications for average market price in general and lean season price in particular. If procurement and distribution are not managed in a planned manner with clear objectives, the difference between lean and harvest season prices may either be narrowed sharply or may remain wider than desirable. While stability in prices is desirable for the welfare of consumers and producers and for political stability, such action may limit private storage activity, with potentially high public costs. Experiences in Bangladesh and Indonesia provide empirical evidences of these effects. With approximately the same size and cost of public marketing, the Indonesian system, operating on carefully targeted ceiling and floor prices, has a better record than Bangladesh, where quantity is the basis of operation of the system. In Bangladesh, seasonal fluctuation (difference of highest and lowest amplitudes) in market prices (normalized for trend) was reduced only slightly, from about 50 percent during 1975–79 to around 40 percent during 1979–83, partly by operation of public distribution in a somewhat improved manner (Montgomery 1983; Ahmed 1979). Indonesia has a better record in this respect. A specialized organization, BULOG (National Logistics Agency), has systematically set procurement and ceiling prices so that seasonal price variation has been held to 15 percent (Mears 1981). This contrasts sharply with the fluctuations of about 40 to 60 percent before BULOG came into operation. In both countries the roles of private stores (including on-farm storage) have diminished, more so in Indonesia than Bangladesh. Occasionally, foodgrain prices in main consuming centers of Indonesia (urban areas) have been pushed below rural levels (Timmer 1976).

Budgetary and financial obligations of a government running public marketing programs in foodgrains are large. For example, the Indian foodgrain system under public management during 1978–80 involved a budgetary subsidy equivalent to Rs 6–7 billion (in that period U.S.$1 = Rs

9) (Chopra 1984). The subsidy was 8 to 12 percent of total public expenditure in Bangladesh during the mid-seventies (Ahmed 1979), and may have declined only slightly in recent years. Obviously, a balance between the degree of price stability and the cost of public marketing is required. An integrated approach and an improved management are critical ingredients for minimizing the cost of a given objective.

Generally, government budgets and financial rules are not flexible enough for a marketing operation intended to stabilize prices. There is almost always a gap between the time when financial commitments are made to parastatals and harvest of the crop. Deviation of harvests from the expected volumes can render the best financial planning ineffective. Therefore, financial inflexibility and fluctuation in the harvest could cause unusual dips in harvest season prices in good production years, particularly when private trade is ineffective or inoperative. Uncertainty about the scale of the public marketing operation generates uncertainty among private traders. Thus, the objective of price stability may be vitiated by budgetary constraints.

An Integrated Approach to Stabilization

An approach that integrates spatial, seasonal, and average prices in a unified framework is necessary for public price policy. A reduction in seasonal and regional price spread is generally desirable. But if this objective is carried too far, with substitution for private trade as a result, the social costs are too great. The social cost may be high not only because of higher marketing costs in public compared to private trade, but also because of the effect of public trade in limiting the opportunity for investment of surplus by farm households. This adverse impact of public trade on investment opportunities in rural areas generally encourages conspicuous consumption (e.g, expenditures on social ceremony), stimulates demand for land purchases, and discourages savings among rich rural households (Ahmed and Hossain forthcoming).

Therefore, an approach to price stabilization that limits public intervention to management of unusually wide fluctuations of prices is required. This approach consists of two interlinked steps in price analysis. In the first step, the annual average price has to be determined, as discussed earlier. The second step is the analysis of seasonal (as well as regional) prices. In the case of seasonal price, a band around the annual average price is formulated in real terms on the basis of a real interest rate that allows private trade a normal rate of profit. Both abnormal and subnormal profit is thus reduced or eliminated. These real prices are then transformed in nominal terms by applying an inflation factor. Public intervention is activated when the price fluctuation goes beyond the band. In this approach, price target rather than quantity target becomes the operating rule for public agencies (see Ahmed and Bernard [forthcoming] for details of this procedure). In application of the framework for Bangladesh, the seasonal price band was found to range from 97.1 to 123.5 around an average of 110, including an inflation factor of 10 percent for recent years. This approach limits public interventions to situations with high irregular factors in price fluctuations. The administrative structure for operating such a system has to be flexible, with a greater degree of dependence on private agents for procurement and sale of foodgrains in the countryside.

Market Integration and Price Transmission

Markets are integrated only if their prices do not behave independently. The pace at which price signals are transmitted between producers and consumers is conditioned by the degree of market integration. Market integration has a weighty implication for analysis of price policy issues. Price policy analysis depends on aggregate supply and demand schedules which are valid only if markets are integrated. Independent markets must be modeled in a disaggregated manner. Moreover, if markets are not integrated or are integrated very weakly, a change in a macro policy may not be completely transmitted to individual producing and consuming units. Unfortunately, this aspect of pricing and marketing policies has not been extensively studied empirically. Precise analytical techniques have yet to be perfected to examine market integration (Delgado 1986). Carefully conducted empirical studies as well as firsthand knowledge of markets do, however, indicate that foodgrain markets are generally well integrated (Lele 1971), though to a greater degree in Asian countries than in African countries.

When countries devalue their currencies, the local currency price of a commodity at the export market increases by the full proportion of devaluation if the foreign price does not change. In a competitive market, assuming that the marketing margin bears a proportionate relation to farmgate price, a 10 percent increase in price at export point would be expected to lead to a 10 percent increase in farmgate price. For the exchange rate change to be reflected at farmgate, however, a time lag may be involved. Therefore, it is appropriate to look into the short- and long-run effects of such changes. A recent study of rice and jute in Bangladesh and cotton and sorghum in the Sudan measured farmgate prices after one month of devaluations and related the prices to changes in the exchange rate. With a devaluation of the exchange rate by 50 percent, the jute price at farmgate appears to go up by 31 percent. With the same devaluation, the rice price at farmgate goes up only 7.5 percent. For sorghum and cotton, the principal export crops of the Sudan, farmgate prices appear to be sensitive to changes in the exchange rate, but again, only about 45–55 percent of a change in the exchange rate is transmitted to farmers (Ahmed and Rustagi 1985).

Results were similar in another study (Scandizzo 1984), which also indicated that the transmittal of prices in African countries was extremely distorted compared to Asia. This empirical evidence points to the potential of market fragmentation arising from public policies in trade and infrastructural underdevelopment.

INSTITUTIONAL DEVELOPMENT FOR PRICE AND MARKET ANALYSIS

Materials presented in the foregoing sections provide a clear indication that pricing and market intervention policies involve complex interrelationships with immense consequences for economic efficiency. Developing countries generally intervene in agricultural markets without sufficient analysis of problems, policy instruments, and their consequences. So long as positive price policy is a rule rather than an exception, analytical input from specialized institutions is necessary to minimize the risk of wasteful intervention (Lele 1977).

Few countries have an institutional setup like that of the agricultural prices commissions in India and Pakistan. To make these institutions function effectively, however, it is critical that they be staffed by persons trained in price and policy analysis with easy assess to policymakers at the highest level. A number of lessons can be derived from the prices commissions operating in south Asian countries.[2]

First, statistics required for price analysis usually cannot be readily pulled out of published documents in useable form. A prices commission can maintain and develop the data sets required. The operations of the agricultural prices commissions in India and Pakistan indicate that a number of criteria determine administered prices that satisfy multiple objectives and constraints. For example, the Agricultural Prices Commission in Pakistan arrives at the recommended level of procurement price for rice and wheat on the basis of cost of production, world price, target production and stock position, and market price. Market price enters into pricing consideration partly because of consumers who depend primarily on the free market for supply. Because of the multiplicity of complex considerations, the scope of arbitrary decisions is large, and the Prices Commission can play its designated role of minimizing this scope only by applying systematic logic. Even when the policy goal is to reduce public intervention in

2. The comments which follow are based on the author's discussions with the Chairman of the Agricultural Prices Commission of India and the Member of the Agricultural Prices Commission of Pakistan, as well as his own experience in Bangladesh.

markets, it is necessary for the goal to be spelled out clearly and the transition to be smooth. A prices commission can perform this monitoring task.

The second lesson is that an agricultural prices commission should play a coordinating role. Fixing support prices for individual crops without regard to prices of other products is a common practice in developing countries. This practice can be attributed in part to an organizational structure in which a particular government department is entrusted with or interested in a particular crop. When interproduct price relatives are changed by changing support price of one product, farmers switch resources between products. This can cause considerable loss in employment and agricultural production. Employment loss in substitution of rice for labor-intensive jute in Bangladesh is a classic example of this phenomenon (Ahmed 1981). An agricultural prices commission, if institutionally linked to the process of macroeconomic policy formulation, can play a potentially powerful role in protecting the interests of farmers, which are so often overlooked in exchange rate, fiscal, and monetary policymaking.

Certain governmental behaviors are quite common in developing countries. They promulgate regulations requiring licensing of traders before entering a trade, restrict holding of stocks beyond a certain limit, occasionally designate certain areas as out of bounds for traders (for example, the trade ban in five-mile border belts of Bangladesh), and limit certain trade only for cooperatives. These measures are generally rationalized on grounds of reducing hoarding, speculation, and smuggling, and encouragement of cooperative enterprises. These rationales are founded more on popular belief than systematic analysis, and an institutional body for price and marketing analyses can play a useful role here.

CONCLUSIONS

A country pursuing a positive price policy and intervening in markets can do the job better by adopting proper principles for determining domestic producer and consumer prices and implementing them with consistent and well-designed measures of intervention. The principle of cost of production, widely used in developing countries, is not a socially optimal guide for determination of producer price. However, it is a useful basis for discussion in the political process of determining prices that involves both social and private gains and monitoring technological transformation in agriculture. Use of world prices, complex and imprecise as they are, as a reference for producer prices is socially optimal in the sense that the principle is consistent with the maximization of growth potential. Setting domestic price in reference to world price does not mean setting it at par with world price. Instead, it implies an alignment of the domestic toward the world price trend so that the impact of world price fluctuations can be minimized and short-run constraints associated with the principle can be accommodated through selective interventions. These interventions are primarily related to price stabilization and consumer subsidy.

The extent of consumer subsidy depends on the level of subsidized price and the coverage of the subsidy program. The level of subsidized price is determined by a complex set of factors involving political and humanitarian considerations. But a low consumer price is likely to involve a high subsidy and an implicit taxation on producers through a reduced producer price. Similarly, coverage of a subsidy program has to be restricted to target groups to keep the subsidy down. After all, the subsidy implies a lost opportunity for investment, perhaps in infrastructural development. If such a dual mechanism, involving markets as well as special subsidy programs, is not effective because of widespread poverty and political infeasibility, a low producer price in markets becomes unavoidable. The critical factor, however, is avoidance of the instability that occasionally causes a spurt in food prices. If instability can be contained, the pressure for food subsidy will be minimal and the subsidy can be kept down and even eliminated as the economy grows and the incidence of absolute poverty diminishes. Such fine-tuned management of producer and consumer prices depends, of course, on an institutionalized analytical input in policy formulation.

Governments use various forms of direct and indirect interventions in the domestic market to maintain higher producer and lower consumer prices in a stable manner. Often these measures are undertaken without a correct appreciation of the functions of the domestic market. Implementation of a measure may also falter because of inadequate skilled administrative and professional management and infrastructural facilities. In such a case, instead of spatial and intertemporal price spreads being narrower, these faulty measures tend to impose additional transaction costs in the market and widen the price spread. Transmittal of price signals in the market channel get blurred. This is particularly evident in Africa.

The longer-run solution to this problem lies in infrastructural development and correction of market imperfections. Market imperfection can be corrected by development of financial institutions, creation of institutions for gathering market information, standardization of grades and weights, strengthening of the legal framework for enforcement of contracts, and minimization of uncertainty arising from haphazard public intervention and natural factors. Infrastructural development contributes crucially, albeit indirectly, to the growth of market institutions and the elimination of imperfections. Achievement of long-run goals, particularly in Africa, may have to be gradual. Introduction of unencumbered private trade (or elimination of public monopoly) should be given a priority. This should be followed by liberalization of regulatory measures (for example, movement restriction, licensing, etc.) and adoption of positive measures for improving the structure and conduct of markets. Public marketing should be limited to certain strategically important areas such as management of security stocks and supporting prices, if necessary, in infrastructurally backward areas and for accelerating diffusion of a technology in its initial stages. Determining when and where such support measures are necessary should be based on case-by-case analyses of price variability. Price rather than quantity should be the target for price stabilization.

5

Public Stock Management

AMMAR SIAMWALLA

Governments in developing countries have traditionally played a dominant role in foodgrain supply management. The problems and issues raised by this intervention have been analyzed in a number of studies made during the last decade.

An understanding of the role that stocks can play for a commodity can be obtained from the following simple identity between aggregate supply and demand:

$$S_{t-1} + P_t + M_t = S_t + C_t, \tag{1}$$

where S_t is stock, both public and private, at the end of period t, P_t is domestic production during period t, M_t is net imports during t (negative if the commodity is exported), and C_t is domestic consumption and wastage.

Identity (1) can be converted to

$$C_t - P_t = M_t - \Delta S_t, \tag{2}$$

where ΔS_t is increase in stocks during t (or $S_t - S_{t-1}$). Equation (2) says essentially that the gap between consumption and production can be met either by imports or by a drawdown of stocks (negative ΔS_t), and conversely, when production exceeds consumption, the excess can either be exported or put in storage (positive ΔS_t).

This simple identity shows that trade and storage issues are closely interrelated. Both can be used to plug the gap between domestic consumption and production. The two have to be considered together.

While changes in stocks are sometimes required to plug the gap, these changes are subject to limitations as the time of storage becomes longer. Continual increases or decreases in stocks become less possible as stocks rise to a very high level or sink to zero. Consequently, the relationship between trade and storage will be examined in the context of three time frames:

(a) storage to even out consumption in the face of *year-to-year* fluctuations in harvest;

(b) storage to even out consumption within any given year, given the seasonality of production flow in agricultural commodities; and

(c) precautionary storage (or working stocks) to cope with sudden surges in demand and supply for a given commodity.

In the longest time frame, year to year, trade and storage are close substitutes. For many developing countries, and for most commodities, reliance on international trade is almost certainly the better route to attain supply security. Exceptions are rice and white maize, among the major food staples, for which there are special problems in the international market. An important distinction that will emerge is between countries that are regular importers or exporters of grains and those that are close to self-sufficiency. The greater freedom to vary the volume of trade makes the problems of the former much easier to handle.

Trade clearly plays a sharply reduced role in the intermediate time frame (seasonal storage). Even here there is some possibility of economizing by a proper timing of trade flows.

Trade and storage complement each other in the shortest time frame. If a country is to rely on trade, adequate working stocks are essential.

YEAR-TO-YEAR STORAGE

As a consequence of the 1973/74 crisis in the international grain markets, there has been considerable discussion of ways to avert another. Individual developing countries are seeking ways to cope with price fluctuations in these markets as well as with fluctuations in their own production. An expanded public storage capability is sometimes recommended.

Analytical work at IFPRI and elsewhere has shown that, with few exceptions, countries that are regular importers or exporters of grains would do better to rely on trade volume adjustments to cope with fluctuations in their domestic harvests than to hold domestic buffer stocks. Thus, Reutlinger and Bigman (1981), employing a simulation model where the parameters and variable values approximate Indian conditions (including a domestic subsidy program), show that a strategy of rising imports to compensate for domestic fluctuations in production without holding inter-year buffer stocks could save approximately $450 million in fiscal costs. A similar study by Amanda Te (1982) for the Philippines indicates similar savings. In both cases the saving in fiscal costs is largely at the expense of a reduced income for farmers. In all cases analyzed, the studied country as a whole gained from the savings in storage costs, which were generally conservatively estimated. However, the savings were much smaller. In the "Indian" case the aggregate economy gained only $87 million.

The central message of these studies is that for an individual country, costs to the government of holding large volumes of domestic stocks to cope with possible harvest shortfalls can be quite high. However, there are some caveats and exceptions to this central message which may be important to individual countries.

The first point is that most of these studies concentrated on wheat, for which a very large world market exists. Reliance on such a market is not so risky because the requirements of each individual country can always be met, though perhaps at a higher price. At no time, even in 1973 and 1974, was wheat completely unavailable at any price. The same cannot be said for other cereals such as rice or white maize (Siamwalla and Haykin 1983). In these cases, if the size of the individual country's import demand is large relative to the total volume of international trade, some domestic storage will be necessary. Also, as supplies in world markets are not large and transactions generally take considerable time, a larger volume of working stocks or longer-range import planning is essential.

Where substitute crops are available, shortfalls in one type of cereal may be made up for by another. Many Asian countries (Sri Lanka, Indonesia, the Philippines) have expanded their consumption of wheat enormously since World War II. One consequence has been that at times of shortfalls in production of rice, wheat can be imported in its place. Where a multiplicity of cereals are domestically consumed and produced, such substitution is also possible, although there are at times dangers that a politically unacceptable short-term shift in income distribution may take place.

Even for a commodity such as wheat, supply security may be threatened by the lack of foreign exchange to finance imports. For this reason, IFPRI has been an early proponent of an IMF food facility which would finance large expansions in the food import bill should the need arise (Adams 1983). Since the funds available for this purpose are still quite modest, the threat has not entirely disappeared. However, one has to be very careful not to jump from this observation to the conclusion that domestic buffer stocks are necessary to help a country meet a food crisis due to lack of foreign exchange, particularly if it is a regular grain importer even in good harvest years. Such a country would have to expend foreign exchange to keep its imports large enough to build up its grain reserves even in years when its harvests are high. If, on the other hand, it did not accumulate the grain reserves and reduced its imports instead, the foreign exchange thus saved could be kept as a reserve to finance food imports in adverse years. To hold these foreign exchange reserves, even if they yield low returns, would be economically preferable to holding a stockpile of grain that has a positive carrying cost which can be covered only if the price rises. It is not advisable for a developing country to take speculative positions in the world grain market, which is what importing grain for storage against the prospect of a rising price implies, unless its information on the market is as reliable as that of the multinational grain companies and other speculators with whom it will be competing.

Of course, there is no reason why a developing country importer should not enter the futures market as a hedger. If the political and administrative structure allows little flexibility in adjusting the budgetary and foreign exchange allocations to sharp movements in world prices, the importing agency may wish to cover its planned grain purchase by buying futures in that commodity at about the time it gets its allocation. If such an action is permitted by the controlling agencies (for example, the finance or planning ministries), it must be formalized and administered in a way that prevents the importing agency from speculating in the world market.

A different problem faces a country which produces more than it consumes in some years and less in other years. In good years, its domestic market clearing price may be somewhat above the f.o.b. (export parity) price and in bad years below the c.i.f. price. In this case, domestic storage may well be a viable alternative, particularly if the gap between the low and high prices is wide enough to cover the expected storage cost. McIntire (1981) has shown that for many land-locked Sahelian countries with poor transport facilities, reliance on the world market is not a viable alternative. Some domestic storage capacity is essential for supply security.

Even in such instances, however, it is not necessary to exclude the possibilities of trade. A model by Krishna and Chibber (1983), which reflects a more complex set of policy objectives, shows that the accumulation of substantial stocks of wheat by the Indian government has been very costly. These stocks could have been disposed of and future shortfalls met, if necessary, through smaller imports than the massive purchases of the mid-1960s. In fact, the worst case projection envisages an import of a little more than a million tons in a few years.

SEASONAL STORAGE

Trade clearly plays less of a role in seasonal storage than in the year-to-year case. Public policy in this area has been guided by the perception that, if this storage function is left entirely in the hands of the private sector, farmers will receive less for their grain at harvest time than consumers pay at a later stage in the marketing year, sometimes considerably less. This implies that farmers do not receive sufficient incentive to produce. There are also equity and nutritional implications. It is presumed that income is transferred from the poor farmers and consumers to the better-off traders, and that already vulnerable groups consume less food during the lean season.

Research in different countries shows that, on the average, the return to holders of grain stocks just compensates them for the costs of storage, with relatively little left over for profit (Lele 1971; Mears and Anden 1972; Goldman 1974; Tubpun 1974), although there is an opposite finding in Farouk (1970). The statistical procedure used to establish this fact involves averaging the rates of price increase over different years. This is consistent with the observed fact that traders can and do "make a killing" because of abrupt changes in prices during a particular marketing year.

The implication of this finding is that because the actual seasonal price spread reflects real resource costs and there is no "slack" in the form of monopoly profit in the system, any public intervention would, over the long run, cost the treasury money. For this reason, if private traders are to be persuaded to lower the price spread, some form of subsidy has to be given to their storage activity. Since storage of food grains is typically spread over the whole country, this is probably the most efficient method. However, administration of the subsidy is usually quite difficult, and the government usually finds it more convenient to take over the storage function. As stronger and stronger attempts are made to squeeze the price spread, the government finds that it has to take over more and more of the storage function. An example from Indonesia indicates the extent of this burden on the government.

Government rice price policy in Indonesia has concentrated on maintaining a floor price for paddy and a ceiling price for rice. The agency charged with these twin tasks is the National Logistics Agency (BULOG). Between 1975 and 1984, BULOG has unfailingly achieved both price targets. The burden on the government arises from the attempt to squeeze the floor and ceiling prices together. To take a concrete example, in the marketing year from June 1979 to May 1980, the price increase from the lowest month to the highest was only 13 percent. This was not an atypical year—in some other years, the seasonal price spread was even less. For comparison, it is conservatively estimated that the interest component of equivalent private storage cost alone can reach 36 percent per annum (Mears 1981).

Table 5.1 shows a calculation of the implicit subsidy channeled by BULOG as a result of the government intertemporal price policy. The assumption is that without the subsidy the government will maintain the *average* price for the marketing year at the same level as attained with the subsidy, but will allow the variations within the year to reflect actual storage cost. This alternative price path is shown in column 2 of table 5.1. The figures in column 3 show the difference between the actual and alternative price path and indicate a subsidy to producers if it is positive and to con-

Table 5.1 Calculation of implicit subsidy on storage, Indonesia, 1979/80

Month	Actual price	Price without subsidy	Difference (1) − (2)	Net BULOG operation (sale− purchase+)	Total subsidy (3) × (4)
	(1) (rp/kg)	(2) (rp/kg)	(3) (rp/kg)	(4) (tons)	(5) (million rupees)
April 1979	156.61	146.67	9.94	31,528	313.4
May 1979	165.56	151.86	13.70	67,276	921.7
June 1979	172.45	157.24	15.22	22,947	349.2
July 1979	178.37	162.78	15.59	−4,356	−67.9
August 1979	180.89	168.52	12.37	1,766	21.8
September 1979	181.64	174.44	7.20	1,831	13.2
October 1979	181.78	180.87	0.91	−5,129	−4.7
November 1979	182.65	187.19	−4.50	−4,069	18.3
December 1979	185.01	193.73	−8.72	−2,172	18.9
January 1980	185.96	200.48	−14.52	−1,989	28.9
February 1980	187.54	207.47	−19.93	1,248	−24.9
March 1980	187.60	214.68	−27.08	−45,993[a]	1,245.5
Carryover	(187.60)	(214.68)	−27.08	−62,888	1,703.0
Total subsidy					4,536.4

Sources: Data in columns 1 and 4 are from Parhusip 1984, tables 16, 27, and 28; storage cost data used in calculation of column 2 are from table 7.7 of Mears 1981. The interest rate used is 36 percent per year.

[a] The figures here do not show the net operation in this month, as BULOG was then already engaged in buying the new year's crop, which came somewhat earlier. It is equal to the month's gross distribution, assuming that BULOG disposes of the old rice before it sells the new rice.

sumers if negative. Column 4 then shows the net operation of BULOG for domestic rice—BULOG simultaneously distributes imported rice, which had been much larger in volume until 1981. If it is a net seller at a time when the figure in column 3 is negative, it is selling at less than the price it should be getting if it is to cover storage cost. If it is buying at a time when the figure in column 3 is positive, it is paying out too much and not making a sufficient provision for the storage cost. Multiplication of columns 3 and 4, with the appropriate signs tacked on, yield the implicit subsidy.

The calculation shows that the total subsidy on storage cost was on the order of Rs 4.5 billion, which at the then prevailing exchange rate was equivalent to only $7.2 million and represented a minuscule proportion of the Indonesian budget. Domestic procurement in 1979/80 was small and expanded five- or six-fold in the following years. But even with the higher levels of procurement, it is unlikely that the storage subsidy exerted a large drain on Indonesian resources.

This particular feature of Indonesian rice price policy has to be judged a success. Without it price swings would have been at least 40 percent per annum in nominal terms, or about 20 percent in real terms at the inflation rate then current. This would have had considerable impact on nutrition and incentives to producers. Before any attempt is made to generalize from this example, it is important to bring out a few features that probably make this case unique.

(a) The main reason why the total implicit subsidy on storage was so small is that BULOG operated on a fraction of the marketed surplus, which was a fraction of total production. As the gap between the floor and ceiling prices became smaller, the extent of the intervention had to increase. This has been going on in Indonesia, albeit at a manageable pace, so that BULOG's market operations now extend down to the district level (Mears 1981). A large jump in BULOG's storage burden will occur if the seasonal price spread is pushed too low, for then farmers can obtain a de facto credit subsidy by selling at harvest time all the rice, including that which they are storing for later consumption, and then repurchasing it later, meanwhile enjoying the yield on the cash obtained from the earlier sale. There are thus limits to the extent to which public operations can lessen seasonal price spreads.

(b) BULOG is a highly efficient organization. Its operations are relatively free of excessive waste although, significantly, as the storage period has lengthened the waste has increased somewhat (Mears 1981). Also, BULOG's operation has been sensitive to rice quality variations, although not as much as in a system dominated by the private sector such as Thailand's. The result has been that there is now less deterioration in the quality of Indonesian rice than is usual in a public-sector-oriented system.

(c) BULOG's procurement is fully backed by access to unlimited credit from the central bank and its ceiling price maintenance is backed by unquestioned access to foreign exchange, so that its imports have always arrived in time to combat price pressures. BULOG has built up a sophisticated market intelligence system so that its operations have been well-timed and generally effective.

This last point is crucial. It has made it possible for the Indonesian government to follow a price target rather than a quantity target (Mears 1981). The overriding consideration has been the maintenance of floor and ceiling prices. There have been no constraints on quantities bought and sold by BULOG to achieve these targets, in contrast to the practice in many other countries, where limits are set on funds allocated to the food grain agency to procure grain and perhaps also on the amount of foreign exchange allocated for imports. These limitations automatically set a quantity target. If these allocations have a large "slack," there is little problem. More usually, however, they are binding constraints on the agency's operations. As the allocations near exhaustion, private traders are able to anticipate the price movements away from the targets. The agency's operations then can be defeated by speculative attacks.

Ironically, while ceilings appear attractive as a means of financial control, they may be costlier and more wasteful than the type of open-ended commitment that the Indonesian government has given to BULOG.

A market intelligence system and sophisticated import purchase operations are also important ingredients in BULOG's success. When they are inadequate, as they were in the 1960s for BULOG and the National Grains Authority (as it then was called) in the Philippines, insufficient or untimely imports can lead to increased seasonal price spreads (Bouis 1983). Countries that rely on imports face risks of delays and interruptions, but the proper method of dealing with them is to increase working stocks.

A well-run market intervention by the government to reduce the seasonal price spread need not be expensive and has nutritional and incentive benefits. To achieve the objective, however, an open-ended commitment to purchase or import, but with clear and realistically formulated *price* targets, is essential.

WORKING STOCKS

When a government agency is continually intervening in markets, it has to be able to cope with unexpected deviations of demand or supply. And when it depends on supplies from abroad, it must also be able to cope with delays and interruptions in imports. The way to cope with these problems is to maintain an adequate level of working stocks. More accurately, the stock level which will trigger an import order (the minimum reorder level) must be set to minimize the probability of a "stockout." Rules of thumb are sometimes used to calculate this level, though formal models are available. The data required are the means and variances of the monthly outflow and the order time, which is the difference between the date of reorder and the date the grain shipment arrives at the warehouse ready for distribution (Rachman, Sakrani, and Yogana 1984). Unfortunately, each of these variables differs considerably from country to country, depending on the institutional framework and the decisionmaking capabilities of the government and its employees. However, sufficient data should be available to allow calculation of these values.

A minimum reorder level is clearly relevant only for countries which import. If the government is determined to be self-sufficient, the relevant concept is the planned level of carryover stocks at the end of the marketing year. This level is also a necessary factor in consideration of price policy. If no import is contemplated, the price must be set so as to clear the domestic market and yield the planned level of carryover stocks. Once the price level is settled on, procurement and withdrawals from the public system will automatically determine the stock level through the marketing year. Without imports the government has no instrument left to meet the stock target. It is essential, therefore, that no government foreclose the possibility of importing foodgrain. A minimum reorder level should be set to trigger a decision to import.

A second requirement is that the government should follow a price target rather than a quantity target system. As discussed earlier, the latter is vulnerable to speculative attacks which could result in a very high outflow from public storage. One of the ingredients in the calculation of minimum reorder level is the variations in the monthly outflow. A vulnerable system will have very high, possibly infinite, variance. In such cases either there would be no minimum reorder level or it would be so high as to be irrelevant.

We conclude that trade and working stocks are closely complementary. Without trade, the level of working stocks is no longer a policy variable at the disposal of the government. Conversely, trade without adequate working stocks is a highly risky enterprise.

PUBLIC AND PRIVATE STORAGE

The discussion above outlines a rational mode of storage operation for a public agency trying to maintain a particular price structure. Its main policy instruments are public storage and, to a lesser extent, publicly controlled levels of imports. The interaction between public and private storage was not considered. In equation (2) above, no distinction was made between public and private stocks. Either could plug the the gap between production and consumption. In theory, they appear to be perfect substitutes.

Public agencies are, however, troubled by private stocks, particularly when they move in a direction opposite to that which the agencies wish them to move. The possibility of speculative movements by private traders implies that at any given time the public agency will have to carry larger stocks to maintain prices than would otherwise be the case. Speculators can and will frustrate the work of a public agency charged with the task of maintaining price stability if their price expectations differ from the government's. As stockholding in grain is probably the private action most difficult for any government to control, many price policies have come to grief as a result of speculation.

Since it is impractical to control private storage, the public agency must pursue a credible price policy that leads stockholders or potential stockholders to expect prices in the future to move in line with what the government projects. This implies that the public agency can command sufficient resources for it to engage in market operations that will bring prices into line with what the government projects. As the Indonesian case shows, these resources need not always be utilized. Consequently, even though the resources available on call may be very large, their costs need not be high.

The credibility of government policy also depends on the period of time during which a particular policy is to be followed. A relatively short commitment on prices is more feasible and therefore more credible, as the Indonesian example has shown. Even here, however, there are some problems. Speculation concerning the movement of the publicly set prices in the next period may frustrate the government objectives during the current period. Thus the government cannot allow movements in price from one period to the next to be so high as to induce speculative storage in the first period (Siamwalla 1986). If a price change is forced by excessively volatile conditions, such as rapid inflation, a disastrous harvest, or devaluation, it is extremely difficult for the government to pursue a realistic price policy, and it will have to expend a great deal of resources to maintain credibility.

If government price policy is so constrained by the need to maintain credibility with private traders, a valid question is: why not turn over all functions of storage to private traders? It has been claimed that if markets are competitive, private traders will make the best use of information to forecast the future and will engage in storage to the extent that will maximize economic efficiency.

While internal grain markets in many countries approximate the competitive model, many others, particularly in South Asia, are pressured into large-scale storage by dual markets in which the government supplies foodgrains at prices below those in the open market. If prices in government outlets are stickier than in the open markets, the public storage authorities will have to contend not only with harvest fluctuations but also with large swings in demand as consumers switch back and forth between the public outlets and the open market. The possibility of such swings significantly increases the pressure on the public authorities to hold stocks large enough to reduce the probability of a "stockout" (Krishna and Chibber 1983).

Another impetus for large-scale storage activity by public authorities is their monopoly on foreign trade operations, which are usually forced by a scarcity of foreign exchange. Since expected import levels are a major influence on present price, and since the import agencies have an informational advantage, it is not surprising that they become involved in storage. In some countries they also became involved in price support operations, as imports began to play a declining role. These agencies also continue to engage in storage but now have mostly domestic rather than imported grain in stock.

As long as foreign trade in grains is subject to quantitative restrictions, public authorities cannot disengage themselves from the storage function.

Once the main impetus to storage comes from domestic supplies and the need to shore up farm prices, storage becomes an adjunct of the price support policy and may, in many instances, almost totally supplant private storage. The whole program may also become quite costly. The problems that Indonesia is now facing as it has attained the food self-sufficiency target since 1984 arise precisely for this reason.

THE FISCAL BURDEN OF STORAGE POLICIES

For countries which regularly rely on trade to balance their yearly gap between domestic production and consumption, the function of public storage is quite clear and can be conceptually separated out from other policy instruments. It is to reduce the seasonal price spread and, where trade is a public monopoly, to ensure against supply interruption. The costs of storage can, in principle, also be distinguished from other costs of public policy, for example, from import subsidy (if the domestic price level is set below the import parity), as the Indonesian policy of reducing seasonal price spreads indicates. If well run, such storage operations need not impose a large burden on the public treasury.

The difficulties of the partially self-sufficient countries are much greater. In most of these countries, storage is really carried out to achieve other policy targets, primarily those of domestic price policy. If the domestic price level is set by considerations other than the need to clear the domestic market, the logic of equation (2) forces storage operations to bear the entire brunt of adjustment in any given year, as foreign trade is precluded from playing any role. Over a longer period, it is not always possible to use domestic storage operations to sustain a given price level, even if that price level is calculated to balance demand and supply in the long run. When the stocks are close to zero, it is not possible to draw on them, and there will be an upward pressure on prices. The reverse case is not so stark, since governments may continue to accumulate stocks, as many countries in Asia did in the late 1970s. As stocks piled up and storage time increased, however, the fiscal burden grew because of increased interest costs and waste. Lags in the construction of storage facilities tended to exacerbate the waste problem. Added to these are extra costs induced by a public storage system such as cross-haulage. Adjusted for inflation, the costs per year can be at least 10 to 15 percent of the value of the grain stored. Developed countries such as Japan, the EEC, and the United States have had similar problems.

These cost pressures raise the question of what an optimal level of storage should be. This implies that for a government to reach an optimal storage target, it must either inject or withdraw grains from the market, which would cause prices to deviate from the level set by policy, or it must import or export grains. Price targeting and a self-sufficiency policy cannot be simultaneously attained.

If a price policy independent of demand and supply conditions is to be abandoned, the recommended procedure is for the foodgrain agency to compute a storage *rule* which sets the optimal carryover storage level at the end of the year as a function of total supply—that is, the sum of carryover stocks at the beginning of the year and the production in that year (Gardner 1979). The basic ingredients of this calculation are the demand and supply conditions expected over the next several years and storage costs. In essence, this procedure recognizes that the maintenance of a particular price level over a number of years is costly and that storage costs are a major component. Consequently, some price variability has to be accepted.

If the government is confident that the capital market and the domestic grain markets are sufficiently competitive, it can withdraw altogether from storage operations. Since no trade is envisaged, private storage will be automatically optimal under these conditions. Where the capital market is imperfect, the government may correct for this by making credit available to storers at a special subsidized rate. This will reduce the price variability without heavy government involvement in stock operations.

The tradeoff between domestic price stability and the level of stocks can be eased somewhat if foreign trade is allowed, particularly if the gap between the export parity (f.o.b.) and import parity (c.i.f.) prices is relatively small, say, less than 20 percent. In that case, trade will contribute significantly to grain price stability. As the gap between the two parities widens, the role of trade will gradually decline. But it will remain useful in extreme years when stocks are excessive and have to be disposed of or when they are very low and have to be supplemented by imported grain. It is quite unwise for a government to commit itself to a self-sufficiency policy under all circumstances, except perhaps when that country is potentially a very large actor in the world market.

Should it be decided that private storage should play a larger role, private foreign trade in grains should be freely allowed, subject only to a variable tax or subsidy that will bring the landed cost in line with domestic price targets. Alternatively, if the public monopoly on foreign trade is to be retained, its targets should be announced and its operations backed by access to adequate credit and foreign exchange.

CONCLUSION

Countries that are regular importers or exporters of grain need to engage in little year-to-year storage of grains. Varying trade volumes is a more effective means of achieving domestic price stability than storage. Within a given marketing year, imports can be timed to arrive during the lean season or exports during the post-harvest season. This will lessen the seasonal price spread. If private traders are discouraged from engaging in sufficient storage by the low spread, the public foodgrains agency may have to procure and store domestic grain. This need not be costly, provided the price target is well-defined and realistic.

The main function of public agencies in these countries should be to determine carefully the need for and level of working stocks and to establish a minimum reorder level that will assure adequate supplies.

Countries close to self-sufficiency usually acquire larger stocks than intended when they follow price policies dictated by considerations other than the balancing of domestic demand and supply. In such a circumstance, these countries must bear the higher storage costs, accept more price variability, or open up the foodgrain economy. The choice will depend on the policy objectives. Cost minimization objectives would tend to point toward a lessening of the government role in storage and a relaxation of its rules on trade.

6

Risk and Uncertainty in Domestic Production and Prices

PETER B. R. HAZELL

Agricultural production is typically a risky business. Farmers face a variety of price, yield, and resource risks which make their incomes unstable from year to year. In many cases farmers are also confronted by the risk of catastrophe. For example, crops may be totally destroyed by hurricane, fire, drought, pests, or diseases, and product prices may plummet because of structural adjustments in world markets.

The types and severity of the risks confronting farmers vary with the farming system and with the climatological, policy, and institutional setting. Nevertheless, agricultural risks seem to be prevalent throughout most of the world. They are particularly burdensome to small farmers in developing countries. There is also strong evidence that farmers are universally risk-averse (see Binswanger 1980) and that they seek to avoid risk through various managerial and institutional mechanisms. For example, they may diversify their crops, favor traditional farming techniques using less modern inputs, and enter into sharecropping arrangements.

The incidence of risk and risk-averse behavior in farming is important to policymakers for a number of reasons.

First, fluctuations in farm incomes, particularly the risk of catastrophic losses, may present difficult welfare problems for rural people. For the households operating small farms in developing countries, these losses can too easily translate into episodes of misery and malnutrition. They can also cause distress sales of farm assets, with deleterious consequences for recovery and long-term agricultural growth. Poorer farmers may even lose their land in catastrophic years because of indebtedness to local moneylenders. There are also important spillover effects on other rural households. Destroyed crops reduce employment opportunities for the landless, as does the substitution of family for hired labor in harvesting a lower output. A lower output also reduces sales by agricultural merchants and agroprocessors. Reduced farm incomes have negative multiplier effects on income and employment among the producers and traders of rural consumer goods and services. These adjustments may lead to sizeable income distribution effects in the short term.

Second, exposure to severe risks increases the likelihood that farmers will default on bank loans, particularly in years of natural catastrophe. The provisions of subsidized farm credit through agricultural development banks (ADBS) is a cornerstone in the development strategy of many countries. However, the performance and long-term viability of ADBS can be severely impaired by poor loan collection, particularly if many farmers default at the same time because of a common catastrophe. The problem is accentuated when ADBS deliberately target a generous share of their lending portfolio on small farmers, who are least able to withstand catastrophic losses without defaulting.

Third, farmers' efforts to avoid risks through management practices reduces the average returns to their resources. This not only reduces average farm incomes, with immediate welfare ramifications, but also leads to smaller supplies of the riskier agricultural commodities. If these are important food or export crops, curtailment of their production can affect consumers' welfare directly as well as reducing foreign exchange earnings. It also leads to a lower national income and to reduced long-term productive investments in agriculture.

Fourth, because of the time required for agricultural production, most farm inputs have to be allocated well before yields and product prices can be known. Farmers must allocate resources each year on the basis of their expectations about yields and prices. If these expectations are wrong, their resource allocations will be less than optimal. Such errors can be costly to national income. Typically they are also costly to farmers when their average incomes are compared to the incomes that could be achieved given perfect foresight.

For a given market, there is always a rational price expectation or forecast that utilizes all the available information to maximize the average income that farmers can realize in a competitive environment. If all farmers hold rational price expectations, competitive markets will be maximally efficient, given the existence of price and yield risks. However, gains in realized social welfare might still be attainable if price risks could be eliminated, for example, through buffer stock schemes or price supports. Even larger social gains will be possible if farmers do not initially plan on the basis of rational price expectations (Newbery and Stiglitz 1981; Scandizzo, Hazell, and Anderson 1983).

Fifth, yield variability leads to unstable supplies of agricultural commodities. The problem is accentuated when farmers adjust input use and the area they plant to different crops from year to year in response to changing expectations about uncertain prices and yields. Instability in national food production tends to increase domestic price variability, presenting food security problems for the poor and increasing uncertainty for farmers. Instability in export crop production leads to more volatile foreign exchange earnings, which can destabilize the national economy.

Given these concerns, there may be good grounds for government intervention to help farmers and consumers cope more efficiently with risk, to improve the efficiency of markets and aggregate resource allocation, and to curtail any risk-induced worsening of the distribution of rural income. Price policy can sometimes play an important part in achieving these goals.

POLICIES TO ASSIST FARMERS IN COPING WITH RISK

Risk-sharing arrangements can reduce the burden of risk for the individual farmer in two ways: one, by transferring the risk to other individuals or institutions who are better able or more willing to bear it; two, by pooling risks across regions, crops, or other sectors of the economy to take advantage of less than perfectly covariate risks. Efficient risk-pooling reduces the total risk burden to society and can sometimes prove beneficial to farmers, even if they have to pay the full cost of the risk-spreading mechanism.

Risk-sharing institutions are most widely available in developed countries. Farmers can borrow for production or consumption purposes to ease the transition from bad years to good. In most cases, they also have access to a variety of privately provided insurance against specific types of risks (such as fire, accident, or theft). They may even be able to trade in commodity futures markets. In developing countries these kinds of institutions are usually much more rudimentary, and may not be available at all for small farmers. Nevertheless, a range of informal risk-sharing arrangements have often evolved. These include share tenancy contracts, traditional moneylending, and risk-sharing within extended family networks. A major limitation to these arrangements is that the participants tend to come from the same region, or even the same village, and hence face much the same risks. Therefore, the arrangements do not pool risks as efficiently as they would if they spanned regions or broader sectors of the national economy, as do nationwide crop insurance or credit schemes.

Risk management interventions have proved costly to governments and have not always been effective. Before embarking on such interventions, it is desirable to have a clear understanding of what is to be achieved, for whom, and the alternatives available. I shall assume that the primary objective is to help stabilize farm incomes, particularly in disaster years. This objective might be justified on the grounds of welfare, improving efficiency in resource use, or increasing loan recovery rates for ADBs. Assisting farmers in this way will also help stabilize the incomes of some other rural households, such as the producers and traders of local consumer goods and services. However, it may do little to help landless workers or agricultural merchants and processors, since the demand for their services will still decline with farm production in bad years. If these groups are to be assisted, more direct types of intervention may be required such as emergency food rations or food-for-work programs.

Given the objective of stabilizing farm incomes, a government typically has a range of policy options, depending on the kinds of risk involved. It is important to begin by assessing the real sources of risk, since some risks can be reduced directly. For example, production variability arising from unreliable fertilizer deliveries can often be resolved by consistent import policies and improved transport, distribution, and storage systems. Likewise, some weather-related risk may be diminished through irrigation investments, which also contribute to increased production. Plant breeders might also be able to reduce some yield risks by selecting for lower sensitivity to environmental stress.

Many risks lie beyond direct government control and can only be offset by compensating farmers in years of low return. If price fluctuations are the primary cause of income fluctuations, price supports or price stabilization schemes may be the best approach. A well-functioning credit market can also help tide farmers over from poor to good years. Crop insurance works best when yield risks are the primary source of fluctuations in income, and particularly when there is the risk of catastrophic yield failure. However, to be effective, crop insurance schemes must be designed to provide protection for very specific types of risk, such as hail, the damage from which lies beyond the farmer's control and which can be objectively and cheaply assessed. Multiple risk crop insurance schemes have not proved effective and typically require substantial subsidies from the national exchequer (Hazell, Pomareda, and Valdés 1986).

If price and yield risks are both important in determining farm income, crop yield insurance can be effectively combined with price support or price stabilization schemes. In fact, if yields and prices initially move in compensating directions, yield insurance and price stabilization must be introduced together. Enacted separately, neither would have the desired compensatory effect on farm income.

POLICIES TO ALLEVIATE INSTABILITY IN NATIONAL FOOD SUPPLIES

Many countries have achieved impressive rates of growth in national foodgrain production in recent decades. Much of this growth can be attributed to new technologies and the increased use of modern inputs such as fertilizers. At the same time, the variability of national foodgrain production around trend has often increased (see chapter 3).

Despite such increased instability, there is no question that the growth in foodgrain production in most countries has been desirable for meeting the increase in domestic demand. However, increased domestic production variability is reflected in increased market and price instability, which, if not compensatory or offset by government intervention, may pose difficult problems for low-income people. It also increases the size of emergency food stocks that need to be held within countries to ensure that consumption does not fall precipitately below trend.

In chapter 3 we showed the importance of yield variability as a component of production variability and examined some of the links between the widespread adoption of the improved seed and fertilizer-based technologies and increases in yield variability. The yields of crops grown with the new technologies appear to have larger variances, but typically their coefficients of variation are lower than those of traditional technologies. However, because they require modern inputs, their yields may also be sensitive to year-to-year variations in input use arising from frequent price changes or from supply restrictions. Yields may also be more positively correlated across farms and regions with the new technologies (Hazell 1982, 1984).

If part of the increase in production instability is technological in origin, it can be asked whether the solution should be sought primarily through changing agricultural research priorities. There are two arguments against such an approach for developing countries. First, continued growth in foodgrain production is of paramount importance, and any tradeoff that might exist between breeding for growth and stability may prove costly. Second, there are other more important sources of increased variability in production which would not be affected by changing agricultural research priorities. In many cases instability may be caused by government policy, or it may be amenable to changes in government policy. For example, policies to provide more stable farm prices and fertilizer and electricity supplies could make a direct and useful contribution toward stabilizing cereal production in India (Hazell 1982). Increased irrigation investment can also contribute to greater stability (Mehra 1981).

Some of the problems for consumers posed by increasing instability can also be alleviated through appropriate policy interventions. Food supplies and prices can be stabilized through storage schemes and international trade. Emergency ration schemes and food-for-work programs can assist low-income people in disaster years. Interregional correlations in production can also be exploited to reduce aggregate production variability. This can be done by focusing producer incentives and public investments to increase production in regions with lower production variability or regions in which production is negatively or only weakly correlated with the production of other important regions.

Within this broader perspective, agricultural research can usefully contribute to limiting yield risks for farmers when the tradeoff against higher yields is low or when there are no public policies to permit farmers to diffuse their risks efficiently. Such reductions in yield variability for farmers may also help reduce variability in national foodgrain production, but not if they aggravate the problem of increasing interregional yield correlations. In terms of containing future increases in aggregate instability, greater attention should be given to containing the increasing yield correlations across farms and regions. If these are due to the narrowing of the genetic base that has accompanied the development of high-yielding varieties, the broadening of this base through more regionalized breeding and seed release programs should be given greater priority in agricultural research.

POLICIES TO PROMOTE MARKET EFFICIENCY

Policies that help farmers cope more efficiently with risk will also lead to more desirable resource allocations for national income and welfare. In particular, such policies should help increase the production of riskier crops toward more optimal levels as their risk costs are reduced.

Despite these adjustments, however, farmers are still likely to confront the difficult problem of forecasting yields and prices each year when committing their resources. As discussed earlier, forecast errors can lead to two types of losses in market and resource allocative efficiency. The first type arises when farmers do not hold rational price expectations, so that their forecast errors are larger than necessary. The second loss arises because even with rational expectations, forecast errors still occur. These could be eliminated if prices and yields were stabilized.

In competitive markets, the efficient price forecast for each farmer should take account of the correlation between price and his yield (Scandizzo, Hazell, and Anderson 1984, p. 16). Often this correlation is negative; the market price is inversely related to variations in farm yields. The rationale for considering this correlation is apparent if we consider a farmer who seeks to maximize the expected profit from his crop. Let p denote the product price, y the yield, and c the per hectare costs of production. Then in any given year profit per hectare w is: $w = py - c$.

If price and yield are both risky (we shall assume c is not), then the farmer must form an expectation about gross revenue py. In the absence of structural shifts in demand and supply, an unbiased prediction is the average of past gross revenues. This can be written mathematically as the expected value: $E(py) = E(p)E(y) + \text{Cov}(p, y)$. That is, the average gross revenue per hectare is the product of the average price and the average yield plus the covariance between price and yield.

If we divide this per hectare return by the average yield $E(y)$, the resultant measure of return per unit of output is comparable to a price forecast; it is defined in similar units, for example, dollars per ton. This price forecast, $P* = E(Py)/E(y)$, which we shall call the unit revenue forecast, embodies full information about the mean price, the mean yield, and the price-yield covariance. It is a rational forecast for the farmer, and as Hazell and Scandizzo (1977) have shown, in the absence of storage schemes it is also the price forecast which maximizes expected social welfare.

If prices and yields are negatively correlated, the unit revenue forecast will be less than the average price. In this case rational farmers will produce less of the commodity than calculations based on average prices would suggest, a point often overlooked by many economists and policymakers. The opposite will happen when the correlation is positive. Farmers should produce more of the commodity than calculations based on average prices would suggest. Note that these supply effects will arise even if farmers are risk-neutral. The correlation effect will be amplified if farmers are also risk-averse.

Using time series data from a wide range of countries, Scandizzo, Hazell, and Anderson (1984) provide some evidence that farmers in industrialized Western economies do take account of price and yield correlations but that farmers in developing countries and in the centrally planned economies do not. If these results are correct, then there is relatively greater scope for policy intervention to improve market efficiency in developing countries.

Given less than rational price forecasting behavior, the magnitude of market inefficiencies increases with the variability of yields. The inefficiency is also greater the more inelastic is the market demand. On the other hand, the more risk-averse farmers are, the less important it is to consider the correlation between prices and yields when forecasting prices.

Where markets are very inefficient, a government can choose between three basic policy approaches. First, production quotas could be imposed to limit the average output levels of risky crops to their socially desired norms. Second, market information services could be established or improved to help farmers forecast better. Third, the government could attempt to reduce or eliminate risks from the market through price stabilization schemes. Using a simulation model, Scandizzo, Hazell, and Anderson (1983) have shown that the social return from price stabilization is likely to be much less than the cost of stabilization where farmers plan on the basis of revenue expectations. Larger gains are possible where less appropriate price forecasting is pursued, but then the largest part of the social gain may more easily be attained through improved market information services (see also Newbery and Stiglitz, 1981).

CONCLUSIONS

Risk has significant effects on the welfare of farmers and low-income people. It can also lead to distortions in resource allocation that are costly to the national economy.

Governments may have an important role to play in reducing risk for farmers. Some public investments, such as irrigation, can reduce yield risks while also enlarging average production. This risk-reducing aspect may enhance the value of such investments in cost-benefit analysis. Risk-pooling schemes such as crop insurance can also reduce the cost of yield risk to farmers and allow them to allocate their resources more efficiently. But such schemes should only be implemented when their benefits are commensurate with their costs. Too many crop insurance schemes are heavily subsidized by governments.

Price risks are often as important as yield risks in agriculture. If prices are negatively correlated with yields, the correlation has a stabilizing effect on income over time, and policies that stabilize yields or prices alone would act to destabilize farm incomes. The appropriate intervention in this case is to stabilize both prices and yields or not to stabilize either. Where the correlation is zero or positive, stabilizing either prices or yields will suffice to help stabilize incomes.

Price stabilization schemes based on buffer stocks are likely to be too expensive in terms of the benefits they generate. More realistic policies to reduce price risks are minimum support prices. These can be achieved through deficiency payments or, where the commodity is traded internationally, through variable levies and tariffs (Siamwalla 1986).

An additional advantage of reducing price variability is that it helps farmers to forecast prices more accurately when committing their resources. However, market and resource allocative efficiency still depends on farmers' holding rational price expectations, such as the unit revenue forecast, so as to take account of any nonzero correlations between prices and yields. Where alternative and less efficient price forecasting prevails, significant improvements in resource productivity might be attained by introducing or improving market information services for farmers. Such programs might range from assistance to farmers in recording and calculating weighted averages of past revenues and yields to more elaborate intelligence services that provide timely and detailed information throughout the year on prices, weather, sown areas, and the like.

Finally, the government may also have an important role to play in protecting low-income people from fluctuating food prices. Again, buffer stock schemes to stabilize prices would seem to be too expensive. Emergency food stocks might prudently be carried as insurance against major catastrophes in production, but emergency ration schemes, food subsidies, and food-for-work programs can also be useful.

7

Foreign Trade Regime, Exchange Rate Policy, and the Structure of Incentives

ALBERTO VALDÉS and AMMAR SIAMWALLA

This chapter analyzes the combined effect of commercial policy and exchange rate management on relative prices affecting agriculture. But movements in price of traded products (relative to nontradables) result not only from adjustments in trade policy and the nominal exchange rate but also from the behavior of macroeconomic variables such as wages, capital movements, and fiscal and monetary accounts. Although not treated directly in this chapter, all these variables impinge on the final outcome. We shall omit here discussion of purely domestic policies and constraints that affect incentives to agriculture or major restrictions of movements within the borders of countries resulting from both policy and poor infrastructure.

WORLD PRICE AS A GUIDELINE

One of the many uses of prices is that they send a signal to farmers to arrange their cropping pattern and allocation of resources in the direction desired by the policymaker. If the policymaker's desire is to increase the efficiency of the economy, then clearly the price signal that is sent to the farmers has to bear some relationship to the social marginal benefits to the economy of producing a given commodity. We submit that for most small and medium-sized economies and for most commodities, social marginal benefit is measured by the world price, converted to domestic price at an appropriate exchange rate. Even when a country has some effect on the world price level, the world trading environment for the commodity in question will have to be taken into account in gauging the marginal benefit of producing it.

We do not claim that the price quoted in the world market for a commodity is a reflection of the world's opportunity cost of producing it. But for the national policymaker, the question is irrelevant. In general, of course, the world market for agricultural commodities is highly imperfect, there being a considerable layer of taxes and subsidies which ensure that world prices for a commodity do not reflect the world's opportunity cost. However, saying that the world market is imperfect is quite different from saying that it is arbitrary. If long-term investments are to be made to increase production of any commodity, a long-term forecast of the commodity price must be made. If prices are to be set for the coming crop, a short-term forecast is necessary. Major commodity exchanges are a source of such forecasts. These short-term and long-term forecasts are not error-free. How the risks arising out of these forecasts should be managed and what this management implies for price policies are discussed at the end of this chapter in the section on risks.

This brings us to the second objection, namely, that "the" world price for any given commodity is a pretty elusive number, in that it varies a great deal from month to month and indeed from day to day. Any attempt to use it for policy purposes thus runs immediately into practical trouble. Market instability makes this exercise difficult, but it is not conceptually unsound.

As a measure of social marginal benefit, world prices are signals that need to be sent to individual producers. Do the policymakers have to know the marginal cost of production in order to set the price? The answer is most certainly not, for it is the farmers who, aware of their cost of production, will adjust their cropping pattern and input use to match the signal sent by the policymakers. The present practice of many countries (developed and less developed) of collecting masses of data on cost of production from farmers, recomputing and refining them, and then sending the results back to the same farmers as a signal may serve some purposes (see chapters 4 and 9), but production efficiency cannot be one of them.[1]

In cases where fixed quantities of inputs such as credit and irrigation investment are to be directly allocated by the government, estimates of cost of production become essential. But they are merely components in feasibility or cost-benefit studies that are used in analyzing applications for loans or investments. In such cases, the notion of the cost of production is farm-specific or at least location-specific and therefore more meaningful

1. Many countries adopt cost of production as the basis for pricing on the grounds that they wish to ensure farmers a "fair" return on their inputs. The main problem with this approach is that it assumes that the "cost of production" is a prior concept independent of the level of prices. Actually, of course, many components of the cost of production are a function of the price that is to be set, most notably the rent on land, although other product-specific factors of production such as dairy cows and specialized equipment display the same characteristic. Even if land rent is to be excluded, the intensity of input use will be determined by the price and therefore will affect the costs. The cost of production is not a unique number which can be called upon to set a price level for any given commodity. It is a function of many variables, among which is the level of production desired (or achieved). But the level of production that is achievable is in turn a function of the price level. To use the "cost of production" as a means of setting the price level is indefensible.

than the aggregate measure normally used in setting price policies.

We stress our conception of the world price as a *measure* of the marginal social benefit of producing a given commodity. We are most certainly not recommending a direct translation of that price into the domestic price, that is, a commitment to free trade. There are circumstances when a divergence between the domestic price and the world price is called for.

One such case would be the presence of domestic (production) distortions, such as failure of private marginal cost of farmers to reflect the social marginal cost (for example, input subsidy by government, market imperfections). If this divergence between the private and social marginal cost cannot be corrected by a domestic tax-cum-subsidy policy, then some adjustment on the output price would become necessary (Kemp and Negishi 1969). Another case would be when nutritional objectives override efficiency concerns; in that case, the best means of achieving such objectives is to adjust *consumers'* prices to induce the required intake of food, without affecting producers' prices. Clearly such a divergence between consumers' and producers' prices will have fiscal implications. If government budget constraints preclude this method of meeting the nutritional need, then some adjustment of the world price after its conversion to domestic producers' prices is required.

If the objective is self-sufficiency in a commodity, then the price to be set is what will clear the domestic market. In such a situation, implementation of the price policy may well ignore world prices altogether. Evaluation of such a policy in terms of its social costs, however, will have to take the world price as the standard for the marginal social benefit of the policy.

Other seemingly more complex grounds for modifying the world price standard need detailed examination. One favors introduction of sector-specific biases in the price regime, in particular, a bias in favor of the industrial sector and against the agricultural sector. The reverse bias would seem more intelligible for some countries, as an attempt to correct biases against the rural sector in other allocations mediated by the public sector. This argument implies an activist trade policy. Another refers to the need to modify the exchange rate used in converting world prices to domestic prices to account for the various distortions brought about by a protective regime, large capital movements, or large foreign exchange earnings from some particular "booming" sector (for example, petroleum). Such an argument implies an active exchange rate policy. A third refers to the risks and uncertainties characteristic of world markets and the need to protect producers and consumers against such risks. The following will examine these arguments in turn.

SELECTIVITY IN PROTECTION

Some countries resist relying on international markets, partly because they dislike the income distribution implications and the feeling of a lack of control over economic events. At the other extreme there are those who oppose government intervention which results in semi-closed economies because they are skeptical of planners' ability to guide economic activities. In addressing the issue of trade strategy, which we define to mean settling on the optimal degree of "openness" of the economy to foreign trade, it is useful to present briefly a simple taxonomy of the rational motives for trade intervention with special references to agriculture.

Trade Taxes To Help Finance Government and as Balance of Payments Support

Export and import duties have traditionally been important in countries with a thin tax base, as the collection costs of alternative taxes are usually higher, particular in the poorest LDCs. Over time, these duties have become a less important source of revenue for governments in most countries. While the revenue motive would argue for a uniform across-the-board treatment for all items, in practice trade taxes in most countries have become extremely complicated and highly discriminatory in their impact on individual industries or activities. The protection motive has been superimposed on the revenue motive.

Many LDCs face balance of payments problems and resort to temporary tariff surcharges to overcome them. Unfortunately, as the BOP problem persists, sometimes as a result of inappropriate monetary and fiscal policies, these "temporary" surcharges become permanent features.

The Optimum Tariff Argument

The "optimum" tax argument for tariffs or export taxes is unquestionably valid. To implement this policy, good estimates of trade elasticities are required. In Thailand, after almost three decades of discussion on the optimum export tax on rice, there are still wide margins of differences in the estimates of the foreign elasticity of demand for rice. The same applies to similar estimates for Bangladesh's jute exports. One should not conclude, however, that the tax should be zero.

Policies To Reallocate Resources Away from Market Dictates

Two lines of argument urge protection, particularly for manufacturing industries. The first is that market forces, being impersonal and subject to constant shifts, have caused parts of the economy to bear large burdens of adjustment costs. It is thus incumbent on the government to reduce such costs by correctly anticipating the changes and promoting those industries (e.g., manufacturing in poor countries) that are destined to grow (the infant industry argument). The second argument objects to the solution dictated by market forces on the ground that the resulting income distribution, particularly to labor, may end up being "unsatisfactory," and hence some modification may be called for. We now examine each of these two lines of argument in detail.

We shall ignore the thorny issue of whether governments or markets can make better forecasts of the winning industries. But much of the arguments for planners to favor industry can be turned around to favor agriculture. For example, the basic assumption in much of the infant industry literature is that agriculture is technologically static, while industry is supposed to be dynamic. The experience of many poor countries' agriculture has demonstrated the fallacy of this assumption. If we then examine in particular the conventional arguments for the subsidization of infant industries, we can easily establish that they are as relevant to a dynamic agriculture.

The first argument is that infant industries are unable to obtain risk capital on account of the greater uncertainties and therefore have to be artificially provided an assured market by governmental measures such as protection or subsidies. The problem faced by farmers in obtaining credit because of their high risks even in traditional crops is well known. The risk is obviously even greater when a new crop and a new technology are involved.

In addition, there is the problem of externalities, which are probably even more acute in agriculture than in industry. When a new technology is introduced into a locality, the farmer who decides to adopt it first is generating a public good in the form of new knowledge and less uncertainty for his neighbors. The externality that the innovator has created cannot be captured by him, and therefore his incentive to innovate is not enough to maximize the social benefits.

The distributive argument can also be used to favor agriculture. In most instances, technological change has unequal impact among different farmers. In the new cereal technology for the poor countries involving high-yielding varieties, it is the irrigated areas that are helped. The increased supply induced by the new technology then acts to depress prices. This would absolutely lower the income of those farmers left out by the new technology if the crop were nontradable or the country were producing a significant proportion of the world output. A dramatic example is the case of Colombia, where upland rice farmers suffered a severe decline in income as a result of introducing new rice varieties which required good irrigation (Scobie and Posada 1978), or the Philippines, where the HYV revolution has led to questions concerning rice growing in marginal areas. The public policy implication of such changes, it is then suggested, is to cushion the effects of such income declines, particularly if the losers are poor to begin with. In the case of Colombia, the government did not respond in this way. By imposing an export ban, it displayed a preference for urban consumers' welfare over that of upland farmers.

Industrial protection is sometimes advocated on the grounds that it will lead to a net increase in the demand for labor. That protection may be given either in the form of tariffs that raise the prices of industrial goods or a "cheap food" policy that eventually results in a lower supply price of labor for the favored sector, or both. A variant of this argument is that imperfections in the urban labor market tend to raise labor costs above the social opportunity cost, and thus bias the economy away from industry; a corrective policy would have to be instituted in the output market to bring it back closer to the optimum.

Much of the theoretical work on protection and income distribution in rich countries has been motivated by the need to show that protection may stimulate the demand for labor (Stolper and Samuelson 1941). In contrast, much of the recent empirical work on protection in poor countries has shown the validity of the opposite view, that protection leads to a net decrease in the demand for labor (Little, Scitovsky, and Scott 1970; Krueger et al. 1981). These studies have focused almost exclusively on the impact on industry. Unfortunately, empirical work on the impact of protection on agriculture has been scarce. Nor do we have a clear picture as to whether industry is on the whole more or less labor-intensive than agriculture.

Policy Interventions To Deal with Economic Stability

It has been recognized in the debate on export orientation that the degree to which a country chooses to rely on foreign trade may relate to the instability of its export proceeds (MacBean 1966). Similarly, short-run instability in world food markets makes them appear to be unreliable guides for import planning and long-run domestic production planning. Thus, it is argued that it would be to the advantage of many LDCs to reduce their reliance on international markets by setting the domestic price of food staples somewhat higher than world prices to reduce imports and hence vulnerability to world price fluctuations. Trade instability is an issue which is addressed in more detail later in this chapter.

Trade Pessimism

Three interrelated arguments favor a closing up of the economy. First, it is argued that the terms of trade over the long run have been moving against the products of the poor countries. It follows that investment will tilt away from export goods (i.e., agricultural commodities) toward importables (i.e., manufactured goods). Government policies should, therefore, aim at speeding up this process.

Second, it is argued that if a country expands production of a particular agricultural commodity, it will find the overseas markets limited so that it can only sell at much reduced prices, that is, the marginal revenue from the extra output will be significantly below the initial world price. This argument applies *a fortiori* to the poor countries taken as a group. Prebisch (1959) has used it to advocate that they pursue a policy of industrialization through protection.

Finally, the market may be limited not by the nature of the final consumers' demand but by protectionist policies adopted by the rich country buyers against "excessive" imports (Valdés and Zietz 1980).

The extremely aggregative nature of these arguments is their chief attraction but also their main weakness. It is by no means clear that the real price of every tropical commodity has fallen. Much of the empirical evidence for a secular fall in the terms of trade is period-specific. Also, much of the discussion on price movements overlooks cost-reducing innovations. Rapid expansion of exports of new agricultural products has led to greater diversification in some countries. Examples are soybeans and frozen concentrated orange juice from Brazil, fresh fruits from Chile, and pineapples and tapioca pellets from Thailand. Thus, it is possible for a poor country to exploit the international economic environment, imperfect as it surely is. A more open trade strategy could lead to an increased diversification of exports, largely because it would enable the economy to be more flexible and thus better able to adapt to changing world conditions.

We concede that a number of very small economies with highly specialized resources are "condemned" to continue very specialized patterns of production and exports. While most of the strictures against reliance on trade apply to these countries, the sad fact is that any alternative strategy would entail a severe loss of income in most of these cases.[2]

Protection Against Dumping

Export subsidies in agricultural commodities are widespread phenomena practiced by many developed and some developing countries. The temptation for the domestic counterpart in importing countries to cry foul is irresistible. Some governments have succumbed to such arguments and raised countervailing barriers against subsidizing exporters.

Surely, to object to another country's providing subsidies to goods which one imports is pure mercantilism. The inconsistencies that one can run into become obvious when one considers the case of food aid, which is, after all, also a form of export subsidy. It seems that there is only one rational line of argument against export subsidies, including food aid. They

---

2. Despite almost two decades of serious attempts to shake loose from the dominance of sugar, the Cuban economy remains as exposed to the vicissitudes of the sugar market as ever.

are harmful to the importing country only if they are both temporary *and* strong enough to cripple the competing industry. In this view, the loss to the importers is the adjustment cost that is artificially imposed by the exporter's short-term subsidy policy. If the subsidy is expected to continue for a long time, it may be better for the importer to permit the demise of the domestic industry. Finally, if the food aid inflow is intended to offset a shortfall in production due to adverse weather, no permanent harm will be done to domestic agriculture.

Although the task thus facing policymakers in the importing country is in concept simple, it is in practice difficult. It requires being sensitive to other countries' policies, both present and future, and making decisions which are risky, given the inherent difficulties in forecasting. Unfortunately, we can see no means of skirting the issue. Cutting the Gordian knot and imposing a countervailing tariff automatically every time there is an export subsidy (as required, for example, by U.S. law) is just as risky a course of action as a decision to let the domestic industry die.

Compensating Agriculture for Protection to Other Industries

By now it is a well-accepted argument that protection to other sectors can penalize producers of exportables and of import-competing products in agriculture. A direct penalty of a policy which protects industry is to raise the cost of importable inputs such as fertilizers, machinery, and other materials used by rural producers;[3] an indirect and probably more important penalty is that it adversely affects incentives in agriculture because of its effect on the exchange rate. The exchange rate which balances the external account at the prevailing, presumed "higher" rate of protection to industry is below the rate at lower levels of protection. The final result is that the domestic prices of tradable products from agriculture are lower relative to (protected) tradables in industry and home goods in the economy. This drives up the prices of labor and other inputs to the rural sector relative to the output price, reducing profitability in the production of tradables in agriculture. Thus, protecting industry means disprotecting agriculture. A similar effect on the real exchange rate and the profitability of farming results from the booming oil and other mineral export sectors, the "Dutch disease," or heavy dependence on foreign assistance, and also reduces the profitability of farming through a similar effect on the real exchange rate.[4]

3. For example, many countries impose protection on packaging materials such as tinplate for cans or glass bottles. These can impose severe penalties on would-be agricultural exporters. Thus, the cost of the can to the Turkish tomato canner exceeds the total value of his canned tomato paste in the European community. Similarly, the cost of the tomato ketchup bottle in the Dominican Republic exceeds the export price of the bottled ketchup.

4. The full set of relationships among sectors and foreign exchange markets can only be captured in a framework which is of a general equilibrium nature. Fortunately, important theoretical and methodological advances in recent years have elucidated the nature and mag-

In view of this, it has been proposed that if a policy to remove protection in industry is not considered feasible, a second-best approach would be a form of tariff compensation assistance to rural producers of tradables.[5]

A three-sector approach with exportables, importables, and home goods[6] helps identify clearly which sector loses and which sector gains, and shows also that its resource allocation effects could end up being quite different from those originally intended, i.e., nominal protection (Sjaastad and Clements 1981). From the parameters estimated by Garcia for Colombia, most of whose exports are agricultural goods, it is calculated that a uniform tariff on imports of 20 percent, which is not high by LDC standards, represents an implicit tax on exports of 18 percent. If exports are taxed directly at a rate of 16 percent, as coffee exports in Colombia are, the total tax rate net of the exchange rate effect is considerably higher than 16 percent (Garcia 1981). Studies for Argentina, Chile, Colombia, Peru, the Philippines, and Uruguay show that the previous policy of import substitution of industrial goods in these countries implicitly taxed agricultural and nonagricultural exports. The discrimination against agricultural exports resulting from tariffs was enhanced in Colombia (before approximately 1976), where industrial exports have been subsidized while agricultural exports have not.

Since nontraditional exports usually have a high supply elasticity, a small tax on trade can substantially affect their volume and growth. As argued by Garcia for Colombia, protection increased the dependence of foreign exchange earnings in Colombia on a reduced number of primary products in which the country has a strong comparative advantage but low supply elasticity. To diversify and promote nontraditional exports, it is

---

nitude of some of the relationships involved. Bhagwati and Srinivasan; Dervis, de Melo, and Robinson; Sjaastad; Sjaastad and Clements; and Corden are major contributors in this area. They address the effects on the overall economy but pay little, if any, specific attention to agriculture. To our knowledge, the first empirical applications of such a framework with special reference to agriculture in developing countries are found in IFPRI's work by Garcia, Cavallo, and Mundlak.

5. This was, for example, the case in Australia, in a debate articulated initially by Gruen (1965). The argument of tariff compensation is implicit behind various forms of assistance to agriculture, such as subsidies on inputs and price supports.

6. Home goods (or nontraded goods) are those goods whose internal prices are not directly deduced from world prices plus tariffs. The price of nontraded goods and services becomes the reference point, a sector which to some extent is sheltered from trade. "True" protection, as described, for example, by Sjaastad, is the tariff-induced change in the internal price of traded relative to home goods, and the response of the price of home goods in terms of exportables is used to measure the tariff incidence (which Sjaastad refers to as the incidence parameter).

In this approach, the domestic sector is the residual sector, absorbing and spilling resources to the traded sectors as the relative price changes. The home goods sector in most developing countries is a large sector, including subsistence agriculture, and the value of its production is usually large.

necessary to reduce trade barriers against imports. If only the industrial sector is protected from import competition, which is usually the case in developing countries, much of the lost output on this trade regime will fall on nontraditional agricultural exports.

However, the incentives provided by policies on specific crops could partially or totally offset the disincentives from the more general policies. Before adjusting for overvaluation, this was the case for some food products in Colombia during the 1960s and 1970s, which were subject to quantitative restrictions on imports. However, when overvaluation of the peso is taken into account, net rates of protection in those products became negligible during the 1960s and became negative during the early 1970s.

The potential role of home goods in agriculture can be an important point to consider, depending on the country. The study in Colombia concluded that traditional food crops like cassava, potatoes, plantains, and beans behaved like home goods; resources released from exportables could go to the production of food. This analysis suggests that production from these nontraded crops was probably favored by the distortions introduced by commercial policies, presumably because the substitution possibilities in consumption between these home goods and importables was rather limited (Garcia 1981).

Thus, only part of the tariff is a tax on consumers of importables and protection to producers' import-competing activities. The rest is an implicit tax on producers of exportables and of import-competing activities with lower or no protection. This is often the case with food. It is also an implicit subsidy to consumers of exportables and of these importables.

An important message of such an approach is that "true" protection can differ significantly from nominal protection. Government policy controls nominal protection through commercial policy, but the incidence of trade policy on resource allocation will depend on "true" and not on nominal protection. The policy implication is that if it is not feasible to reduce industrial protection, then tariff protection on agricultural imports should be increased and subsidies on exports instituted.

EXCHANGE RATE ISSUES

While there are two major concepts of the exchange rate, namely, the nominal and the real, the latter can be further subdivided, depending on the deflators being employed.

The nominal exchange rate is an undeflated conversion factor between one currency and another. It corresponds to the exchange rate a government can announce or attempt to fix.

The equilibrium nominal exchange rate is that rate at which the demand and supply of foreign exchange (to finance both current and autonomous capital account transactions) are equal for a given set of trade taxes and subsidies. The purchasing power parity rate and the equilibrium nominal rate do not necessarily comprise an optimum exchange rate, nor do they correspond to the shadow price of foreign exchange that is used in evaluation of social projects.

In analyzing single activities, the concept of the nominal or effective exchange rate is important. It corresponds to the price of foreign exchange inclusive of all taxes imposed on its purchase.[7] Thus, in a given country, differences in the effective rate reflect differences in the level of protection or export taxes imposed on each activity. This measure is clearly commodity-specific, and thus it is more suited to the analysis of the differential impact of trade policy among traded goods.

In contrast, the real exchange rate is a single relative price, and stresses the differentiated impact of trade policy between traded and nontraded goods in the aggregates. The real rate represents the price of a basket of tradables relative to that of a basket of nontradables. As explained in Dervis, De Melo, and Robinson (1982), a given nominal devaluation is consistent with equivalent, smaller, or greater *real* devaluations, depending on the adjustment in the price of home goods (relative to the price of tradables) resulting from the nominal devaluation. Labor is the single most important market determining this relationship between nominal and real devaluation, as wages are the principal determinant of changes in the price of home goods.

Clearly, the real exchange rate is to be understood as a long-term signal for resource allocation between various sectors. As such, it has a policy significance which is somewhat removed from the day-to-day concerns of the central bank, whose task it is to manage the nominal exchange rate in the face of changing expectations, nominal price movements of the country's principal imports and exports, money supply, and international rates, among others. Of course, how successful the central bank is in its pursuit of its objective will affect the course of the real exchange rate, but this will not be our concern in this paper.

There are several proxies for this real rate, depending on the deflators chosen. Since the nominal rate is the ratio between two monies, two deflators are typically involved in measuring the real rate, one foreign currency (e.g., the dollar) and one for domestic currency (e.g., the peso). Theoretically, the most desirable deflators would have the weights of the dollar price index of goods reflecting the share of the traded commodities as they are traded by the home country, with the peso index being the index of the price of nontradable goods.

7. See Krueger et al. 1981; Dervis et al. 1982, chapter 6. This use of the effective exchange rate differs from the convention adopted by the IMF, which is a trade-weighted average of individual foreign exchange rates against different currencies.

A more commonly used proxy for the deflators is to use a general dollar deflator (for example, the U.S. GNP deflator) and a general peso deflator (for example, the home country GNP deflator). This is sometimes referred to as the purchasing power parity (PPP).

A government acts through changes in the nominal rate but with the intention of modifying the real rate. Both act simultaneously across all traded activities. But movements in the real rate result not only from adjustments in the nominal rate but also from the behavior of wages, as well as the capital account, and fiscal and monetary variables. They all impinge on the final outcome.

We believe most products in agriculture are tradables,[8] and thus the main force behind real exchange rate changes will be intersectoral resource flows, essentially of savings and labor, toward or away from the nontraded, nonagricultural sector.[9] Real exchange rates can move for autonomous reasons, for example, as a result of oil discovery or a drastic shift in terms of trade. They can also be influenced by policies on trade, fiscal policy, and capital movements (including reserve changes and foreign borrowing and assistance). These are only instruments by which the government can influence the real exchange rate.

Trade issues are best analyzed with a disaggregated version of the real exchange rate—the price of import-competing goods relative to nontraded goods and the price of exportables relative to nontraded goods. The imposition of, say, a uniform import tariff implies increasing the former and not the latter. This opens a wedge between the two relative prices, causing the former to move up and the latter to move down. Thus, even though an import tariff may be levied in order to raise the domestic price of an import-competing good, this price may increase by only a part of the tariff, whereas the other part of the tariff results in a fall for exportable goods.[10] If a country imports industrial goods and exports agricultural goods, a policy of industrial protection would then impose a burden not only on consumers of industrial goods but on agricultural producers. A method of calculating the relative incidence of import barriers on the price of consumers of import-competing goods and producers of agricultural goods has been applied to Colombia, Chile, Nigeria, Peru, and the Philippines (Valdés 1986).

Capital movements can heavily influence real exchange rates. Heavy overseas borrowing can lower the real exchange rate substantially, as happened in Argentina and Chile in the late 1970s and early 1980s. Conversely, large overseas investments may raise the real exchange rate. The

8. In some countries, particularly in rural areas in sub-Saharan Africa, nontraded food could represent a large fraction of total food.
9. For an example of Argentina, see Cavallo and Mundlak 1982.
10. Dornbusch 1974.

adverse effects of a booming export sector on the nonbooming tradable sectors (the "Dutch disease") can then be ameliorated by a conscious policy of real exchange rate management.[11] This can be achieved by any of the following policies: a) sterilization of foreign exchange receipts (e.g., accumulating foreign exchange reserves); b) retiring previously contracted foreign debt; and c) a conscious policy of overseas investment.

This last policy could be chosen as a result of a natural resource discovery. Even if profitable investment opportunities exist at the current relative prices, the decision to invest heavily may shift those costs and thus threaten the viability of the program. Such a situation would surely arise if the investment program were largely based on home-produced goods and services (for example, construction). In such cases not only would the profitability of the investment program be adversely affected, but the movement in the real exchange rate would begin to endanger the survival of many traditional tradable sectors as well, including agriculture. We believe that this is what happened in Nigeria (Oyejide 1986) and Mexico between 1979 and 1982. In both instances, the problem was compounded by the countries' decision to borrow on top of their high oil revenues. To put it another way, it would be better for the country to pace its domestic expenditure program over a longer period, consistent with its capacity to supply and absorb domestically produced capital goods.

Conversely, consider an economy that finds itself with continuous budget deficits, leading in turn to a chronic balance of payments problem. If the foreign deficit is met continually by foreign borrowings or assistance, the real exchange rate will drift to a level lower than what it would otherwise be. This would work against the entire tradable component of the agricultural sector, both exportable and import-competing.

If the balance of payments problem is tackled by quantitative import restrictions, or by explicit tariffs rather than by devaluation of the currency, the consequence for the exportable component of agriculture will be clearly adverse. The favorable impact on the import-competing component will depend on how far these restrictive policies are applied to imports.

The relevance of these considerations for agriculture is that, far from being unaffected by the developments in the other sectors, it is highly vulnerable to these changes and to various macroeconomic policies of the government. The linkage is not excessively mysterious but can be understood through the concept of the real exchange rate.

Estimating real exchange rate misalignment is difficult and imprecise, but it is important for governments to try to measure the implications of

11. An example other than the petroleum booms which is often cited is the impact that the coffee boom of 1975 had on the Colombian economy. In this case the boom resulted in an increase in the price of home goods, thus increasing the real exchange rate for noncoffee.

fiscal, monetary, trade, and wage policies on the RER. To do so, judgments must be made of optimal foreign capital flows, the size of the fiscal deficit, the coverage of home goods, and other issues, subjects which can be debated technically. While in no position to be precise, economists are able to make sufficiently accurate estimates to provide a useful guide to policy.

RISKS AND MARKET FAILURE

In a sophisticated market economy there are institutions that enable agents that face risks to rearrange and thus perhaps stabilize their consumption over different states of nature, just as the loan market enables them to do so over time (Hirschleifer and Riley 1979). In agriculture, when these risk markets do not exist farmers bear the full brunt of the price risks. If they are risk-averse, they will undertake action that sacrifices mean income for a reduced degree of fluctuation, that is, risk will lead to "under-investment" in risk-prone sectors. At the same time, there *may* be agents in the economy who are willing to accept an increased fluctuation if they are given some increase in mean income. The lack of a risk market means that this group and the farmers have the potential to, but cannot, engage in this exchange, which would increase their welfare. Farmers thus have to impose a risk premium, which is indistinguishable from a tax, on themselves. Therein lies the source of market failure.

A common presumption is that a more open economy is more specialized and therefore riskier. The evidence for this presumption is weak. In economies where a more open regime is introduced, the export composition has become more diversified. Examples are Thailand in the 1960s and Chile, Turkey, Spain, and Greece in the 1970s. We shall, however, ignore in this discussion the lessons of this important phenomenon and accept, for the sake of argument, the common presumption.

Externalities to Consumers

Brainard and Cooper (1968) have justified government action on the grounds that risks generate secondary risks, or externalities. They argue that the primary group (in this case, the farmers) affected by the risks does not shoulder the entire burden, but as the risks spread through the economy others come to be affected as well. As farmers do not bear these secondary risks, they do not take them into account, and may therefore overproduce exportables.

By thus passing risks from one sector to another, the market may have induced some involuntary risk-sharing between producers on the one hand and consumers on the other. While it is very unlikely that such an outcome is an optimal one, it is quite possible—indeed, likely—that in a community of risk-averse individuals, such involuntary risk-sharing would lead to a higher level of welfare than where there is no sharing. With incomplete markets, such spillovers constitute external economies rather than diseconomies (Newbery and Stiglitz 1981, chapter 25).

Nevertheless, policies that spread the primary risks facing farmers (assumed to be risk-averse) more systematically among all taxpayers may result in a higher level of welfare than would be attained as a by-product of the market movements outlined in the previous paragraph. We shall explore this possibility later.

Two groups other than producers are affected by the world price instability for agricultural commodities in a free-trade environment. These are the consumers of the traded commodities and the producers of nontraded goods (including the government), whose real incomes fluctuate with the prices and generally with the degree of prosperity in the traded-goods sector. Here and in what follows we examine the problems created by the risks imposed on these two groups as a result of the price fluctuations in traded agricultural goods.

The problem of the consumers' risks in the face of fluctuating agricultural (particularly food) prices is a complicated one. In one sense the risks can be considered minor or nonexistent because, unlike producers, consumers know the prices when they buy. The only limited risk they face arises from the timing of a purchase before consumption.

However, when the consuming household in a money economy contracts to supply factors of production, say, labor, it does so for given nominal wages, based on its expectations of the future course of nominal prices. In an economy where prices of major items in the budget, such as food, can lurch upward unexpectedly. there is necessarily a risk involved in negotiating such contracts unless some sort of indexation clauses are built into the contract. If workers are risk-averse, this additional risk element, which cannot be shifted out, would be another instance of market failure justifying some sort of government intervention.

Externalities to Nontraded and Government Sectors

In many poor countries export-oriented agriculture is a dominant sector. Changes in the revenues from such a large sector can spill over, through the familiar multiplier effects, into other sectors, causing the aggregate income of the country to fluctuate.

The fall in export sector revenues will first affect the nontraded sector. If real wages are flexible, the fall in demand in the nontraded sector should reduce its price relative to those tradables which have remained immune from the changes. In other words, the real exchange rate will rise, increasing production in the import-competing sector.

Where real wages are prevented from falling, relative prices will not move sufficiently, and unemployment may well be the consequence (Corden 1981). In this case, the risk originating in the traded sector creates external diseconomies, as the multiplier effect ensures that the impact to the economy from the foreign (exchange) fluctuations is magnified through the system. If the real wage rate is pegged so that significant unemployment remains even in a good year, some labor market policies are called for.

The desirability of the government's sharing some of these risks is a controversial matter, as two opposing views are held in the profession. The first is held by Brainard and Copper (1968) and by Jabara and Thompson (1980).[12] They believe that if the earnings from traded crops fluctuate to the extent that tax revenues are affected, an additional social cost is imposed by the export crop producers' decisions. In this view, the government is an economic agent and, like any other, is entitled to have its own preferences weighted in any social evaluation. It is generally assumed that its preference is risk-averse. The opposite view (Arrow 1971) is that in evaluating public projects, government should act as if it were risk-neutral. The risks of adopting any given project or policy would be spread over, and borne by, a large number of taxpayers who are, in effect, involuntary shareholders in the project.

This second analysis assumes that the project under consideration is small relative to the economy. Clearly, in a country where agriculture is a dominant sector, this assumption has to be modified, although we suspect that the direction of policy would be retained—namely, that the government should intervene to alleviate the price risks of crop producers by spreading the risk over the larger number of taxpayers. In other words, a move by the government to mediate a partial risk exchange, albeit a compulsory one, between producers and nonproducers can, in most cases, improve welfare.

What Is to Be Done?

The main thrust of our argument is that, starting from a free trade situation, the international price risks for the traded agricultural commodities of a country lead to certain distortions requiring corrective action by the government. But far from leading private agents to undertake decisions that overexpose the economy to risks, the economy loses considerable income because of these agents' real aversion to risks and because these risks cannot be shared with others through various institutions such as futures markets. The main corrective action that is required from the government, in the absence of such devices and futures markets, is for it to mediate in this sharing of risks. This would move the economy in a direction exactly

---

12. If one is to take their planner's utility function in its literal sense, rather than as a convenient computational device.

opposite of that sometimes proposed by those who assume that private producers are risk-neutral and the government risk-averse (Brainard and Cooper 1968; Jabara and Thompson 1980). We argue from the position that private producers are, in fact, risk-averse but that government should be risk-neutral. Without government action, risk-averse private agents will tend to avoid making full use of their comparative advantage, causing some loss to the economy (see also chapter 6 above). Government intervention would, however, generally entail an increased exposure to trade, relative to a situation when the government does not intervene at all.

One way the government can intervene is to institute a price insurance scheme (Siamwalla 1986). To make that scheme work, first, at the macroeconomic level, the government should arrange that at any point in time the nominal exchange rate should not stray too far out of line with movements in the domestic price level. A threat of major and abrupt changes in the nominal exchange rate would play havoc with the type of intervention that we propose. Such a policy implies that, at least for the period covered by the price insurance, the government is, in effect, attempting to hold the real exchange rate level.[13]

The second step is to forecast the mean world prices of the commodities to be insured, and then set the domestic prices at those levels—insulating domestic prices from movements in world prices by means of variable trade taxes and subsidies. Such variable trade taxes and subsidies clearly imply that the government budget will be quite unstable. This is the other side of the coin of the policy maintaining foreign exchange reserves. If the domestic prices of the commodities are completely stabilized, then when the world price for an exportable, say, moves strongly upward, bringing in a great deal of foreign exchange, the government will be taxing away precisely that extra amount of foreign exchange earnings. On the other hand, a subsidy would be paid when the world price drops. The variable trade tax/subsidy scheme can thus be called an automatic foreign exchange sterilization mechanism.

This particular policy package can thus bring a reduction of risk to the agents in the economy, the main cost being the foregone earnings (because of the high degree of liquidity needed) on the foreign exchange reserves, which can be considered as insurance reserve. It may be asked why the government has to hold such reserves, as farmers can be expected to hold

13. Note that we are assuming that generally basic changes in the *real* exchange rate, related as they are to movements in intersectoral productivity growths and preferences, are slow and are small within the period normally covered by the price insurance scheme below. In recent years, countries have experienced abrupt shifts in their real exchange rates arising from changes in petroleum prices or interest rates. How these major and sometimes abrupt changes should be worked into the economy is hotly disputed among economists. For some discussion see Van Wijnberger forthcoming.

their own reserves and peg their expenditures to their permanent rather than actual income and achieve the same result as the government reserves do (Knudsen and Parnes 1975). In the final analysis, the justification for government action arises from the imperfections of the rural capital market.

It is important that the procedure by which the insured price is set should be kept nondiscretionary. This scheme is designed specifically to cope with unexpected shifts in world prices within the production period. As such, it should incorporate as much unbiased information as possible about future world price trends.[14] Of course, the government may wish to implement a longer-term policy to protect or penalize the agricultural commodities covered by the scheme. If so, the procedure for doing so should be distinct and carried out prior to the setting of the insured price.

The capacities of developing countries to pursue these policy prescriptions will differ. They may choose to follow them in different degrees, but surely there can be no question as to the direction of policies. With free trade, farmers face the risk of price changes. Because the changes are exogenous, the risk is insurable. Such a policy as outlined above would provide that insurance and should be attempted even though the country may end up more exposed to trade as a consequence.

Risks of a Permanent Loss

The more serious worry that nags many policymakers when they contemplate the international environment is not the temporary losses that afflict their countrymen but the possibility of a permanent loss of economic wealth through shifts and changes occurring elsewhere (for example, Brazil's loss of natural rubber export markets). Unfortunately, very few general proposals can be laid out for such essentially uninsurable risks. Ex ante, the policy issue is whether the producers have themselves considered all the risks. Generally, producers of individual commodities are more exposed to these risks to their income than is the economy as a whole. If they remain in the same activity despite the risks, they presumably must be obtaining significantly higher returns from it than from alternative activities. It is then questionable what is to be gained by the economy as a whole if the government penalizes them or holds them back from this decision. The one instance where perhaps some intervention is justified is when multinationals, through their ability to diversify across borders—a step

14. We have assumed, along with Jabara and Thompson, that the price risks faced by the country are stationary in the sense that they are repetitive and nonautocorrelated. Where, as is normally the case, new information keeps flowing in which causes constant revisions to the price forecasts, a stubborn attachment to a previous forecast can become socially costly. Some modifications are necessary to the above scheme. Such a scheme is analyzed in detail by Siamwalla 1986.

unavailable to the other agents in the home country—make a major invest-ment in an economy, causing it to concentrate its resources on one or a few commodities.

Ex post, once it becomes known that a particular commodity is facing problems, then the public issue concerns the size of public expenditure on areas such as research, extension, irrigation, or credit that are specific to the commodity. It is assumed here that producers of the commodity are better attuned to movements in the world market than are governments and will begin to withdraw resources at a more appropriate speed than would most governments.

A second issue is how far the government should go in cushioning the impact of such an adverse movement. Obviously, when the affected groups are already earning lower incomes than most of the population, some cush-ioning is warranted. Aid to these individuals should be of a social welfare nature and should affect the structure of incentives as little as possible. Note, however, that if government repeatedly provides assistance to ail-ing industries so that it becomes expected, government is in effect provid-ing insurance for risky decisions, but it is an insurance with a moral haz-ard: the encouragement to make profitable but high-risk investments must be balanced against the inefficiency generated by these government interventions.

The National Security Argument

A common argument against relying on world price signals for decisions concerning domestic investment and production policies is the fear that if this procedure leads to a reliance on imports of foreign agricultural prod-ucts, particularly of food, then the country becomes vulnerable to an inter-ruption of that flow of imports. This interruption may be caused by any number of events, including labor strikes in the exporting countries, politi-cally motivated embargoes, and war. The last argument in particular has been used many times, and successfully, to silence critics.

The proponents of self-sufficiency on security grounds are in effect ad-vocating that capacity to produce certain commodities should be main-tained within the country even if it can be demonstrated that, in peace-time, that capacity is inefficient. The social cost (the dead weight loss) of maintaining this industry is as justifiable as any other defense expenditure. To our knowledge, there has been little attempt to measure this cost de-spite the widespread use of the argument.

Still less has there been any attempt to measure this cost against other equally effective alternatives. Thus, instead of maintaining, year in and year out, the capacity to produce these commodities, including the labor force and other inputs, it may well be more economical to have a strategic stockpile that would protect against, say, a one- or two-year interruption of imports. The briefer the interruption of food imports (say, as a result of a blockade), the more advantageous is storage compared to domestic production. On the other hand, the longer the interruption, the greater the extent to which production can be reorganized during the emergency. This trade-off between domestic production and storage, in the event of a blockade, was studied for Sweden (Gulbrandsen and Lindbeck 1973). Is a one- or two-year import requirement essential? Are there no substitute cereals available which can be used for human consumption during the critical period? These are questions that are amenable to analysis, although unfortunately economists have tended to shy away from the subject.

CONCLUDING COMMENTS

We have argued that for both policy analysis and policy design, the use of world prices as references is inevitable. This conclusion does not automatically imply endorsing a free trade policy. The use of world prices as references must be kept distinct from an advocacy of free trade. Three broad conclusions emerge from our examination of the issues of free trade versus protection and government intervention in trade and exchange rate.

First, discriminatory protection has generally worked against tradable agricultural goods. This is not only because varying tariffs across commodities single out industrial goods as the favored sector, thus raising the cost of inputs for agriculture, but also, perhaps more important, because it makes for the overvaluation of domestic currency compared to a more liberal trade regime. The discouragement to agricultural tradables is usually across the board, affecting import-competing commodities as well as export products. This penalty on agriculture is inherent and will last as long as industry is protected; it cannot be eliminated by better management in other areas of economic policy. Consequently, we have argued that, if fiscal requirements make a trade tax unavoidable, the tax rate should be uniform across commodities—it really does not matter whether the tax is levied on all exports or on all imports. Since even a uniform import or export tax ultimately discriminates against export activities, a low rate is clearly preferable to a high rate.

Second, since agriculture is such a dominant sector in most poor countries' economies, not only does it propagate its fluctuations to the other sectors, but also the converse: changes in the other sectors can have profound effects on it, particularly if those sectors produce traded goods. Even a promising development such as the discovery of petroleum resources, or a heavy influx of capital, can have a strongly adverse impact on agriculture. Consequently, the macroeconomic management of the economy (for example, on nominal exchange rates, interest rates, wages, international capital flows, and fiscal policy) is of the utmost importance to the agricultural sector. The key link, we suggest, is to be found in what happens to the real exchange rate. As a producer of traded goods, the agricultural sector is best served if the real value of the domestic currency is relatively low (high real exchange rate).

Third, we conclude that although risk is often cited as grounds for discarding the doctrine of comparative advantage, we find that in fact the risk aversion of private agents in a free trade environment tends in any case to move the economy away from that ideal, but that is a failure of the market to provide the insurance. Government intervention to share the risks within the economy more effectively is required to enable the economy to reap the full benefits of its trade opportunities. We propose, therefore, that the government institute a variable tax/subsidy scheme to reduce the fluctuations in the domestic price relative to those of the world price. If this generates a response among producers, then the exposure of the economy to trade would be larger than before, which we claim would cause the economy to be better off.

8

Relative Prices in the People's Republic of China: Rural Taxation through Public Monopsony

BRUCE STONE

A BRIEF CHRONOLOGY OF THE PRICE SETTING INSTITUTION

The government of the People's Republic of China has used agricultural price policies and other instruments which influence or determine relative prices in agriculture since the early 1950s. As the 1950s progressed, it became clear that price issues were sufficiently complex that a centralized independent organization was required expressly to supervise the establishment of appropriate prices and their periodic adjustment. Consequently, in July 1957, the National Price Commission was established. Although its operational development was arrested during the Great Leap Forward (1958-59) and the subsequent period of economic and administrational upheaval, the Commission was reestablished in 1963. With the advent of the Cultural Revolution era (1966-76), the Commission's relative autonomy was again impeached, to the extent that it ceased to exist as an independent organization, and a five-year program to correct the existing price structure was scrapped. It was not until the reform years following the period of economic chaos at the close of the Cultural Revolution that the current version of the National Price Commission, the State General Commodity Service Bureau, was reestablished. Of course, the Bureau cannot act without close consultation with the Ministry of Finance, the Ministry of Agriculture, and (until its abolition in 1982) the Ministry of Food. As in other socialist countries, pricing issues are so critical and political within government and throughout the nation at large that the Bureau's actions must normally be approved by the highest administrative organizations: in China, these are the State Council and the Central Committee of the Chinese Communist Party.

PRINCIPAL DIFFICULTIES IN APPLYING EFFECTIVE
PRICE POLICY

It should be clear from the above brief discussion that the relationship of the price setting organization to other government bodies whose constituencies are affected by price changes has been anything but constant. In fact, although "unified" quantity planning has been practiced for China's major sectors throughout most of the People's Republic era, the periods 1958–60 and 1966–76 seem to reflect relatively little effort to use prices to affect incentives and allocation of land, labor, and current inputs among alternative crops, whereas the remaining years (1949–57, 1961–65, and 1977–86) were typified by some serious effort to do so.[1]

Consequently, the choice of price changes as policy instruments has been sporadic, and redundant mechanisms have necessarily been developed for accomplishing goals which price changes are sometimes aimed at addressing. In the current period, characterized by a greater role for prices, these parallel mechanisms are still intact to varying extents. When there is poor coordination between the price-setting organization and related government bodies, price policy has sometimes been rendered ineffective by the operation of other instruments (such as acreage controls, tied subsidies, market restrictions, and preferential allocations of scarce producer goods and credit), resulting in inefficient expenditure of government resources.

Conversely, when a particularly critical target variable has become the subject of great concern at the highest levels, the entire arsenal of instruments has sometimes been directed at the goal of influencing it. Without proper coordination of the application of these instruments and with weak quantitative understanding of their differential impacts and of the underlying economic and environmental mechanisms, price adjustments have been made when the operation of more powerful direct instruments would have sufficed. This procedure wastes government resources and engenders other unnecessary and unproductive side effects.

But there is also a self-perpetuating difficulty associated with this "shotgun" approach to intervention. When the target variable is influenced in the proper direction, it is more difficult to isolate and estimate the differential impacts of the policy instruments. This touches on the more general problem of the inadequate understanding of the impacts of various instruments in China and the lack of explicit and effective research in the area, a

1. Even in periods characterized by relative attention to prices, the frequency of adjustment of prices has been generally inadequate. The history of price versus quantity control in Chinese planning and the theoretical superiority of relatively price-oriented rather than strictly quantity-oriented control in peasant agriculture has been developed in Lardy 1983a.

problem which is compounded by the blunting of standard warning signals such as spontaneous price movements owing to generalized price rigidity.

Figure 8.1 provides one example of these difficulties with respect to cotton purchases. Application of an impressive arsenal of instruments progressively accelerated cotton production in the late 1970s and early 1980s. Supply began to exceed demand by 1980, imports were cut, and stocks began to build. During the early 1980s, it was clear to decisionmakers that export potential was limited and domestic demand for low-grade cotton (comprising most of the output) was reaching plateaus, despite rising consumer income. Consequently, marginal prices for these low grades were gradually cut back toward the pre-acceleration level, since domestic industry not only was refusing to purchase larger quantities but also preferred to purchase higher-quality cotton to fill its existing requirements.

Government did not realize that it was not so much marginal prices that had been effective in accelerating cotton production but the availability in recent years of particularly high-yielding, low-grade cotton varieties, coupled with massive governmental fertilizer allocations in exchange for cotton sales and guarantees not only to purchase growers' output but to supply them with tradable goods, especially food, in return. Supply contin-

Figure 8.1   Index of shifting supply and demand constraints in the Chinese cotton sector

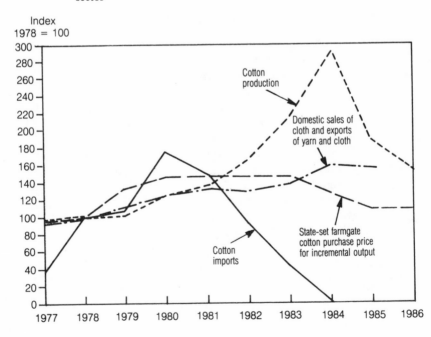

ued to accelerate despite falling prices, so that by the end of 1984 the government was storing more than 50 percent of the world's cotton stocks, which neither foreigners nor domestic industry wanted to purchase. The following year fertilizer allocations were cut back, and the government initiated a contract system for cotton procurement, arranging to purchase only 70 percent of the previous year's output. As government had been the near-monopoly purchaser of cotton for two decades, its refusal to guarantee purchase above contracted amounts had a major impact on output, which then fell even below the 70 percent mark. In addition, government purchasing organizations refused to buy two of the particularly popular high-yielding but low-grade cotton varieties (Zhongguo 1986; JPRS 1985a, 1985b, 1985c).

But the main problem of implementing effective price policy in China is that prices are expected to serve too many functions, allocative and distributional (Lardy 1983b). Specifically, procurement prices have been expected to serve in the difficult production planning effort. This by itself is a complex task. It involves reconciling the production goals with cost and incentive relationships among various interrelated activities and outputs within the agriculture and animal husbandry sector and affiliated sub-sectors, including industries using farm goods as inputs or supplying industrial inputs to agricultural production. In addition, however, procurement prices are expected to perform many of the functions of government tax and expenditure policy, that is, to effect broad allocation of resources among industry and agriculture, rural areas and urban areas, governments and individuals, and regions of the country.

Thus price rigidity in China arises not only out of a firm commitment to price stability arising from China's devasting experience with hyperinflation in the 1940s and rapid inflation in the early 1960s[2] but because price has been chosen as a means of controlling and simplifying allocation of resources among broad groups and sectors in China. The problems have been first, that the strategy of allocation has not been consistent with rapid balanced growth, and second, that the tendency toward price rigidity has played havoc with incentives and efficient allocation within sectors, a problem of growing severity with increased development and complexity of the economy.

Since 1979, China has been undertaking the tremendous task of price reform, attempting to realign prices throughout the economy for incentive purposes, as well as to reduce price rigidity *selectively* (substitute markets for dictated prices) so that prices can more efficiently perform their allocative function. Farmers are also allowed more decisionmaking power. The problem is that prices are now so far out of line with opportunity costs that

---

2. Xue Muqiao, Several questions on prices, *Renmin Ribao,* 28 January 1985, p. 5.

partial price reforms tend either to be ineffectual or to lead to unpredicted and unwanted consequences. But more comprehensive reforms also require major initiatives in tax and expenditure policy to avoid unwanted patterns of distribution. All of these shifts are taking place in an atmosphere of very imprecise knowledge.

In other words, Chinese policymakers have several tigers by the tail; as they reach to secure one that seems in danger of slipping away, they jeopardize their grip on the others. They can no longer hold all; letting one or two go seems even more dangerous; the only solution may lie in loosing them all at once, an unthinkable alternative. But to understand how China got to this point, it is necessary to review the broad history of prices over the past three decades, of course focusing on procurement prices and their role in serving broader short-term and long-term objectives.

PROCUREMENT QUOTAS, FARMGATE PRICES, AND FOODGRAIN PROCUREMENT HISTORY, 1950 TO THE MID-1970S

In 1954, the year after a grain crisis that resulted in the establishment of the state purchasing monopoly, compulsory grain deliveries were introduced because state procurement organs had again been unable to secure enough grain for urban areas, grain-deficit areas, the army, and planned exports. Another crisis in 1955 led to the assignment of a planned production quota to each unit of land. Fixed portions of these production quotas constituted required sales to the state (compulsory procurement quotas) at given low prices. But sales obligations did not end there. After retaining a provincially determined per capita quantity to meet the immediate food, feed, and seed needs of rural farms and households, and even after tax and compulsory quota obligations were met, 80 to 90 percent of all "surplus" grain was also to be sold to the state. Production and fixed purchase quotas were to be set for the period 1955–57 in "normal" years to avoid the powerful disincentive effect of increased output immediately resulting in higher quotas. After a fall in state procurement, an "abnormal" year was invoked, allowing compulsory sales to be increased beyond a legal restriction of 40 percent of extra output (over and above compulsory deliveries, tax, and "planned surplus"). Subsequently, the 40 percent limit was eliminated. Pressure to produce more and to deliver more grain to the state led to the abandonment of fixed quotas, but the system returned, even before 1962, during the agricultural disasters. Quotas were fixed for five years and, in some areas, ten years, although there is evidence that the limitations on quota reassignment were sometimes transgressed.

But if virtually all "surplus" grain had to be sold to the state at the same low price anyway, the disincentive effect on farmers was still powerful regardless of how infrequently the quotas were changed. This was not immediately appreciated by policymakers, but by 1960 a 10 percent price increment for "surplus" grain sales above a set amount of sales per team member was common practice in a number of Chinese procurement areas. Although ostensibly eliminated in 1962, the bonus for surplus deliveries was reintroduced in 1965 at a premium of 12 percent above quota prices. Between 1966 and 1970, quotas were increased but were fixed usually for three-year periods, and two kinds of incentives were instituted for surplus deliveries: half the surplus amounts earned 30 to 50 percent price premiums, while half received no price premiums but earned quantitatively specified rights to purchase certain industrial commodities. By 1970 several provinces had instituted across-the-board surplus price increments of 20 to 30 percent, and in 1971 they were established nationally at the 30 percent level (Tang and Stone 1980; Xiao 1983; Lardy 1983b; Zhongguo Shangyebu 1984).

The requirement of selling "surplus" grain to the state was institutionalized in the form of surplus quotas in the 1960s. Although basic compulsory quotas and the planned production quotas upon which they were based were set for a specific number of years, surplus quotas were subject to change annually and were fixed prior to planting in order to facilitate aggregate procurement planning and to ensure (to the extent possible) that additional fertilizers and other inputs would be delivered to those units trying for larger surpluses. Nevertheless, the delivery of surplus quotas, once set, became as obligatory as the basic compulsory quota. And the two-price system not only constituted regressive taxation but made farmers' tight financial planning even more subject to uncertainty, since it increased the financial impact of yield variations (Tang and Stone 1980; Lardy 1983b).

The land tax (normally payable in grain), the state grain monopoly, basic quotas, strict foodgrain acreage controls, surplus quotas, quota increases, and restrictions on nonagricultural activities were sequentially introduced by the state in order to ensure purchase of large quantities of staples at low prices for urban and army consumption, export and relief needs, and stockpiling plans. But these measures were not sufficient. Ill-conceived and badly-executed policy combined with disastrous weather in 1960 and 1961 to knock grain production back to the 1951 level. Thus China began importing between 3.7 and 8.1 million tons of grain annually, and continued to do so in almost every year through 1977. The age distribution of the rural population was changing in such a way that even though per capita grain consumption in 1977 was no lower than it was in 1956, the most basic rural needs were not satisfied at current production levels. Thus, despite so many policies aimed at increasing state purchases, the marketed ratio for foodgrains fell from an average of 28.0 percent (1952–60) to 20.5 percent (1961–70) to 17.5 percent (1971–80).[3]

With the marketed ratio declining, it became very important to restrict the state's demand for grain. An urban rationing system was instituted as early as the 1950s. Migration to urban areas was severely restricted. Exports were not allowed to grow, and inter-rural trade was limited so that any local surplus could more easily be siphoned off to the cities. The rural grain relief program remained undeveloped. Despite this parsimony, state grain needs increased.

The only alternative to increasing the already onerous import burden was more rapid growth in grain production. The proportion of sown area planted with foodgrains was increased, to the detriment of cotton, oilseeds, and other economic crops. Irrigation construction and a seed-breeding emphasis on early-maturing varieties combined to push up the multiple cropping index. The state also engaged in major reclamation efforts to open new lands for growing foodgrains, even to the point of transforming aquaculture areas into rice paddies and semi-arid and poor-soil herding economies into grain cultivation zones. Production and basic quotas were raised periodically, and surplus quotas were increased whenever possible. For an added incentive, preferential fertilizer and credit allocations and other governmentally administered privileges were awarded to units pledging and delivering increased grain supplies to the state (Tang and Stone 1980).

Foodgrain production in the early 1950s was preindustrial. Plowing was the only farm task that was even partly mechanized, and the machine-plowed area represented only 0.1 percent of all farmlands. Annual chemical fertilizer application averaged less than a kilogram per hectare. By 1975, foodgrain production had increased 74 percent over that of 1952, but in order to reach this higher level of output, chemical fertilizer application exceeded 50 kilograms (nutrient weight) per hectare, tractors were reported to plow 35 percent of China's cultivated areas, 23 percent benefited from power-, diesel-, or gasoline-driven irrigation equipment, and mechanization on a variety of other farm tasks had begun. So that farmers could pay for increased production costs, state grain purchase prices by 1978 had been increased by 66 percent since the mid-1950s, while reported sales

3. Tang and Stone 1980, Zhongguo 1983, pp. 389–90, 437–38. Alternatively, based on production years (1 April–31 March) rather than calendar years and slightly different coverage, the shares are 28.9 percent for 1952–60, 24.2 percent for 1961–70, and 21.0 percent for 1971–80 (Zhongguo 1983, p. 393). If resales to peasants are deducted, the net procurement proportion still declines from 20.0 percent (1952–60) to 17.2 percent (1961–70) to 14.9 percent (1971–80).

prices of industrial inputs to agriculture had been cut in half (Stone 1983b).

The interesting point of the Chinese experience in this respect is that the considerable price adjustments made were insufficient. Most of the farm-gate price increase through 1975 had occurred by 1963, and a considerable portion of the latter reflected market forces in the early 1950s, prior to the solidification of the state grain market monopoly. There was relatively lit-tle price increase during the period of greatest growth in production costs (1965–75). Purchase prices for wheat, rice, and corn remained virtually unchanged from 1966–77 on.

The results had serious implications for rural cooperation with the state and party administration and hence, ultimately, for the sustainability not only of low relative farmgate prices but of a host of policy activities which had become associated with rural oppression. By the mid-1970s the reports of production units that had increased output but had reaped little or no gain in per capita income were numerous. Among those particularly hard hit were units that had acceded to government pressure and concentrated all available resources on crop production, especially that of grain and cot-ton. The blame was placed on the large increase in input requirements (particularly fertilizers, water supply facilities, insecticides, and machin-ery) and on the quantity of labor applied per unit increase in output, as well as on insufficient cuts in prices of industrial inputs to agriculture and inadequate boosts in state procurement prices.

The results of an extensive 1978 survey in Hebei Province are particu-larly telling in this regard. Hebei is a major agricultural province in North China. It produced 5.4 percent of the nation's grain and 19.2 percent of its cotton in 1957 and had benefited considerably from tubewell construction since that date. But by 1979 its share of domestic grain production had not increased, and its proportion of cotton output had fallen to 5.2 percent of the national total. Among surveyed localities, gross agricultural revenues had risen 46 percent (1965–77), but nonlabor production expenses had risen 190 percent. The latter as a proportion of total product price rose from 26.5 percent (1965) to 40.2 percent (1977). Labor application per *mu* also rose (wheat, from 19.1 units in 1965 to 33 units in 1976; cotton, from 42.6 units in 1965 to 49.8 units in 1976). The situation was particularly severe in 1976–77, when the supply of industrial goods faltered and their prices rose. The average tax included in the price of purchased industrial inputs involved was, even then, conservatively estimated by the Chinese at around 20 percent (Tang and Stone 1980). Surveys showing similar results were conducted in Guangdong, China's most prosperous southern prov-ince, and in advanced areas of the lower Yangzi Valley. Sichuan, China's most populous province, was perhaps the hardest hit.

The most direct explanation for this surprising state of affairs is that most of the gains from China's cumulatively large investment in technical change in agriculture were not realized until recently, due to insufficient application of the relatively small quantities of additional capital expenditures required to complement efficiently even this labor-intensive strategy.

The extreme capital scarcity in the Chinese agricultural transformation strategy showed up in a number of ways. First, almost complete lack of mechanization and insufficiently anaerobic storage facilities for organic manures meant that nitrogen volatilization losses were greater and fermentation gains for other nutrients lower than could have been achieved in this extremely labor-intensive fertilization process. Because most nitrogen was lost in collecting, mixing, transporting, and spreading organic manures, nitrogen was a constraining element in yield growth despite massive application of manures. Until the late 1970s, it was inadequately supplied by manufactured fertilizers: in the 1950s this was due to modest growth from a very small base; in the 1960s and most of the 1970s, the problem was concentration on highly volatile ammonium bicarbonate production based on a simple process that could rely heavily on local capital generation and local feedstock resources. Resolution of the nitrogen constraint did not rapidly improve until the late 1970s, with major increases in urea application (Stone 1986a; Tang and Stone 1980).

Other examples of counterproductive capital conservation in agriculture's labor-intensive strategy include insufficient mechanization to increase labor productivity and rural incomes (and occasionally even aggregate production) in the transition to higher cropping intensity in many areas (Ishikawa 1978; Ishikawa, Yamada, and Hirashima 1982). Another example would be the overreliance on local, poorly capitalized and supplied cement and steel facilities, leading to collapse of dams and other water-retaining structures. Another example would be insufficient mechanization in earthworks and reclamation projects. In each of these areas, relatively small amounts of additional properly expended capital would seem to promise high productivity payoffs, even within highly labor-intensive techniques and strategies. Partial resolution of the more critical of these constraints (nitrogen application and requisite mechanization for raising the returns to multiple cropping) have been instrumental in the rapid acceleration of Chinese food production since the late 1970s.

Second, the local self-sufficiency movement and the increasing direct controls over farmland allocation among crops and input allocations among farms and crops (all products of the failure to accelerate grain production enough by other means to boost the share marketed) brought about serious deterioration in the productivity of resources both among and within collective units (Tang and Stone 1980; Lardy 1983a).

Third, the deleterious impact on farm labor incentives of the chronically low prices and the arbitrary expansion of procurement quotas and of collective agriculture in general were criticized. The attempted solutions have been higher prices structured for growth incentives (1979–84); the substitution of a contract system for quotas (1985), and the replacement of collective farming by the production responsibility system (early 1980s), but the quantitative effects of each on grain production are difficult to estimate.

Another reason for poor profits for Chinese farmers was that relative prices for industrial goods were so high after World War II and the Chinese civil war and during the Korean War that even after a doubling in state grain prices and the claimed 50 percent decline in the price of industrial inputs to agriculture, mid-1970s relative prices for industrial goods were still generally higher in China than elsewhere (figs. 8.2 and 8.3). It turns out that the official price indices of industrial inputs to agriculture are flawed in several ways and considerably exaggerate the fall in prices for rural residents.[4] Furthermore, prices of industrial consumer goods had been increasing quite rapidly, deadening some incentive to sell additional quantities of grain.

These low relative farmgate prices were no accident. If purchase prices

---

4. This price scissors disfavoring agriculture was most pronounced in the 1950s, when purchases of industrial products were very low. Although official price indices show a considerable movement in favor of agriculture, there appear to be some ambiguities or inconsistencies among them. It is clear, for example, that the farmgate sale price of ammonium sulfate, the principal chemical fertilizer used over much of the period, remained high and constant while the ratio of the price of urea to that of grain, though declining considerably, was still high relative to most countries and became important to farmers only in the late 1970s. The price of ammonium bicarbonate, the most important fertilizer during the 1960s and 1970s, ranked second after urea in the 1980s, was generally high per unit of nutrient, and varied considerably depending on location; furthermore, the product itself was volatile and of inconsistent quality. How could the price of industrial inputs to agriculture have fallen by 48 percent between 1950 and 1979 when the price of the principal purchased input (manufactured nitrogen) had changed little? The answer seems to be that current year weights were used to form this price index so that it is dominated to an inappropriate extent by urea. Since 1957, urea's ex-factory price has fallen by two-thirds, but until the mid-1970s production was very minor and allocated primarily to industry.

At the same time, the state maintained high prices for both consumer and producer durables and achieved a near-monopoly on the production of cotton goods and sugar, which are the major nongrain processed consumption goods in rural areas. The prices of diesel fuel (until 1983) and electricity have been subsidized, but the quantities allocated to agriculture are extremely limited and supply is unstable, while the price ratios of kerosene and gasoline to grain remain high by international standards. Equally important, inter-rural exchange of grain and other farm goods was limited and, unlike urban sales, was conducted at prices which moved upward with the procurement price (Stone 1984b, tables V-1, VI-1, and VIII-2).

The increase in grain purchase refers to within-quota sales and has been approximately confirmed in a recent source which lists the index numbers for each year from 1966 to 1977 as between 220 and 223 with 1950 = 100 and as between 182 and 185 with 1952 = 100 (Zhongguo Guojia Tongjiju 1984). The above-quota index would fall between 252 and 290 for the period (1950 = 100) or between 209 and 241 (1952 = 100).

Figure 8.2 Nitrogen to paddy price ratios associated with preferred farm producers, 1952–85

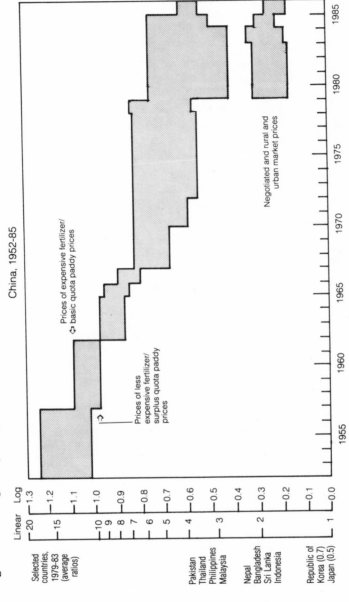

China, 1952-85

Prices of expensive fertilizer/ ↪ basic quota paddy prices

Prices of less expensive fertilizer/ surplus quota paddy prices

Negotiated and rural and urban market prices

Source: Stone 1986a; 1983–85 data have been added from official sources.
Notes: Nitrogen prices are for urea, ammonium sulfate, and ammonium nitrate. Ammonium bicarbonate, although very important in China, is not included since its price varies considerably among localities. Changes in the price ratios are due to changes in fertilizer or quota procurement prices or availability of surplus, negotiated, or market prices for paddy, or changes in the price increment for surplus quota delivery. This downward trend in the price ratio was curtailed in 1984 when urea prices were increased 13.3 percent and in 1985 with the establishment of a single price for all contractual purchases between basic and surplus quota purchase prices. Black market fertilizer prices (30–100 percent above preferred prices) and, since the mid-1980s, non-preferred market prices (up to 50 percent above preferred prices) are not represented here. Preferred farm-producer prices are generally those selling larger proportions of their output to the state.

Figure 8.3   Nitrogen to wheat price ratios associated with preferred farm producers, 1952–85

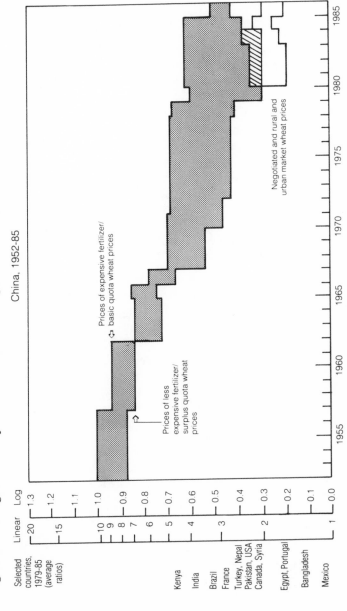

China, 1952–85

Prices of expensive fertilizer/
basic quota wheat prices

Prices of less
expensive fertilizer/
surplus quota wheat
prices

Negotiated and rural and
urban market wheat prices

Selected
countries,
1979–85
(average
ratios)

Linear	Log
20	1.3
	1.2
15	1.1
	1.0
10	
9	0.9
8	
7	0.8
6	
5	0.7
	0.6
4	
	0.5
3	
	0.4
2	0.3
	0.2
	0.1
1	0.0

Kenya

India

Brazil
France

Turkey, Nepal
Pakistan, USA
Canada, Syria

Egypt, Portugal

Bangladesh

Mexico

Source: Stone 1986a; 1983–85 data have been added from official sources.
Notes: Slashed area represents an overlap of ratios based on state sales and on rural and urban market prices; no market price averages are available for 1985. Nitrogen prices are for urea, ammonium sulfate, and ammonium nitrate. Ammonium bicarbonate, although very important in China, is not included since its price varies considerably among localities. Changes in the price ratios are due to changes in fertilizer or quota procurement prices or availability of surplus, negotiated, or market prices for wheat, or changes in the price increment for surplus quota delivery. This downward trend in the price ratio was curtailed in 1984 when urea prices were increased 13.3 percent and in 1985 with the establishment of a single price for all contractual purchases between basic and surplus quota purchase prices. Black market fertilizer prices (30–100 percent above preferred prices) and, since the mid-1980s, non-preferred market prices (up to 50 percent above preferred prices) are not represented here. Preferred farm-producer prices are generally those selling larger proportions of their output to the state.

could be kept low, then urban wages could also be kept low, facilitating high savings rates in industry and lower fiscal drag of the large and growing government service sector. Furthermore, cheap grain could be sold on a rationed basis to legal urban residents, increasing control over rural-urban migration. Yet planners were well aware that without acceleration in foodgrain production growth, marketed ratios would remain low. And without technical transformation of agriculture, there would be no prolonged acceleration in production. But, inevitably, technical transformation of agriculture would be expensive both for farmers and for the state. Was this transformation compatible with low relative foodgrain prices, given the state's complex of priorities? To answer this question, it is necessary to examine agriculture's expected contribution to Chinese economic development and the role of prices as a mechanism for realizing that contribution.

AGRICULTURE'S CONTRIBUTION TO ECONOMIC DEVELOPMENT: THE THEORETICAL CONTEXT

In the international literature on the development process, the agricultural sector is typically viewed as making four contributions to the process of economic development outside the sector: 1) furnishing food and labor to other developing sectors; 2) providing a domestic market for the goods and services of other sectors; 3) providing domestic savings for investment in other sectors; and 4) generating foreign exchange required for the development of the rest of the economy. The "other sectors" to be developed are usually abstracted as, or viewed literally to be, industry. Agriculture's own development, unlike that of industry, is rarely seen as an end in itself, but is valued principally for facilitating its contributions to the growth of other sectors.[5]

5. This view has been reflected in the postwar development strategies of many Third World countries, both in terms of government investment priorities and in pricing and other industrial protectionist policies that effectively bias the domestic terms of trade against agriculture in favor of industry and manufacturing. Consequences of those policies have often included a growing shortfall of domestic food production, increasing reliance on imports, and an increasing number of rural poor.

Hla Myint has made a useful distinction between agriculture's role seen in terms of its voluntary contributions, or spontaneous functions, reflecting its interrelationship with the rest of the economy during the long-term process of economic development, and agriculture's role seen in terms of the compulsory contributions that can be extracted from the agricultural sector, or the functions it can be made to perform by deliberate policy. While this dichotomy cannot be seen in its perfect form either in historical cases in this century or in any developing country today, much of the literature dealing empirically with agriculture's role leans toward experiences illustrating Myint's first interpretation, while development planners and their advisors naturally emphasize the second. Any inconsistencies among the components of agriculture's role are heightened, as the exigencies of immediate planning horizons cause planners to attempt to compress the stages of economic growth, and to accelerate the intricate long-term process of development, according to a simplified theoretical model which cuts corners (Stone 1984a, pp. 2–4; Myint 1975).

When conflicts develop among these expected roles for the sector, the generation and transfer of savings and provision of cheap urban food are usually seen as agriculture's indispensable contributions. But difficulties are generated when the country not only is relatively undeveloped in its nonagricultural sectors but is more or less stagnant in its agricultural sector as well. If savings are consistently invested in the nonagricultural sector, there will ultimately be an increase in the demand for agricultural products, especially food, which will not be cheaply satisfied without continuous technical change in agriculture. But bringing about rapid technological advance in agriculture, in many cases, requires considerable investment, and if the agricultural sector is indeed very poor and stagnant, its own surplus resources may be insufficient.

Here we come up against an inconsistency: agriculture's principal role is supposed to be to provide resource transfers out of the sector (to aid industrial development). Yet to do so, technical transformation is required which necessitates resource flows into the sector. Various tactics are recommended to manage this without doing violence to the original conceptualization. They amount to suggesting either that, with careful management, net transfers into agriculture can be kept low or negative, despite the investment requirements, through emphasis on demand linkages with other sectors tapping internal saving, and land tax applications or that, if the net flows are strong and positive, the situation is temporary and will be quickly followed by a subsequent stage in which they will turn negative (Stone 1984a). Let us review how the Chinese experience relates to this theoretical context.

AGRICULTURE'S CONTRIBUTION AND THE ROLE OF PRICES

It is clear that China, too, has tried to use agriculture as a source of investment funds and of cheap wage goods (food) for other sectors.[6] It is also inevitable that with the elimination of the private trading, banking, and landlord classes in China, government's role in providing mechanisms of transfer would be paramount. Any close examination of the economic history of the People's Republic reveals a scrupulous attempt to keep the flows of nonlabor resources into agriculture relatively low and the flows out

6. There are several factors which distinguish the Chinese case from the classic description of urban development bias (e.g., Lipton 1977). Several have been enumerated by Nolan and White (1984), who prefer the term "state bias" to describe the Chinese development disposition. There were, in fact, important substantive contributions in China in the areas of rural health and education, and pressure on incomes was not limited to the rural sector. Yet the balance of evidence suggests that the adopted development strategy, as executed in China, tended to disfavor rural labor and consumers to a greater extent than their suburban and urban counterparts during the first thirty years of the People's Republic and that the largest share of gross resource transfers into the rural sector was rather directly associated with agriculture's technical transformation, rather than more general rural welfare concerns.

of the sector relatively high. In fact, the flows almost ceased to have any spontaneous character at all and were increasingly controlled through central planning and administrative procedures. But this deliberate extraction of resources from the agricultural sector was not taken to the extent of completely ignoring the contradiction inherent in attempting to squeeze a stagnant agriculture. There was a clear sense that agricultural growth would require some investment geared toward technical change, and that an important portion of this investment would need to be mobilized on a governmental scale exceeding that of rural cooperative institutions. This effort at technical transformation of agriculture became quite significant in the later 1960s and 1970s, although it began in the 1950s (Tang and Stone 1980; Ishikawa 1983; Stone 1984a).

Substantial efforts at irrigation and other farmland capital construction were supplemented by accelerating and sequential adoption of domestically developed, higher-yielding seed varieties; considerable increases in the rural stock of farm machinery; and the most rapid growth rate of fertilizer application anywhere for a comparable historical period. On the other hand, clear efforts were made to keep to a minimum the flows of nonlabor resources into agriculture required for the transformation.

The use of organic manures, already the most extensive in the world, was considerably intensified prior to rapid growth in chemical fertilizer application. Total growth in yield through increased cropping intensity was emphasized, greatly raising farm labor requirements relative to capital expenditures. The farmland construction efforts at irrigation, drainage, and field improvement heavily emphasized labor from within the sector and involved very modest commitment of state capital resources. From 1950 to 1979, agriculture claimed only 11.2 percent of state investment funds. Growing slowly from a modest base were total state aid to agriculture (used to promote mechanization among rich farm areas and to promote production in various ways among poor areas) and agricultural loans featuring high interest rates (about half of which originated within rural areas). Between 1953 and 1971, the total of state funds allocated to agriculture was only 23.4 percent more than the modest farmland tax. While this percentage increased in the 1970s, most of the increase was provided through taxation of rural enterprises (Stone 1984a).

Meanwhile, efforts were made to raise resource flows out of the sector. Although farmland taxes were a minor and decreasing mechanism of savings extraction required to finance these flows, the price system was a major and increasing one. Compulsory procurement of farm products at low, state-dictated prices contrasted with the high prices for industrial consumer and producer goods purchased by farmers. But the commodity terms of trade turned almost monotonically in favor of the agricultural sector during the period from the 1960s until the mid-1980s. The price system became increasingly important as a transfer mechanism only because the absolute flows of real resources increased considerably while the land tax remained relatively constant.

What were the actual net flows of savings and real resources throughout the period? This calculation depends entirely upon the system of prices used. If one adopts the 1957 price structure, which heavily discriminated against farm goods, then net resource flows out of agriculture turned from decreasingly and slightly positive in the 1950s to (increasingly) negative during the 1960s and 1970s (Ishikawa 1967; Ishikawa 1987). If the price structure used is that of 1980 (disfavoring agriculture to a lesser extent), then the net resource flows out of agriculture did not turn negative until the 1970s. In either case, however, the long-term trend in the net flows is in the direction of imports into the sector. This contrasts with the hypothetical state in which technically transformed agriculture becomes an increasing source of net resources at a fairly early period. The actual result resembles the Ricardian growth trap, in which emerging dynamism in the industrialization process is constrained by slower progress in agriculture subject to diminishing returns in absence of sufficient technical change (Ishikawa 1987; Stone 1986c). The increasing flows *into* agriculture have been dominated by flows of agricultural producer goods from the industrial sector.

The behavioral model which emerges for the entire PRC period through the end of the 1970s is one in which every effort seems to have been made to maximize the savings at government's disposal. Investments, for this reason and a variety of others, were predominantly oriented toward heavy industry (Stone 1986c). Incomes in both agriculture and non-agriculture were kept at low levels, although increasing urban dominance and proximity to government over time allowed urban subsidies to increase much faster than those in the countryside (Lardy 1983b; Nolan and White 1984). When this pattern resulted in insufficient growth in food marketings or in generalized agricultural crises, investment was increased in agriculture, as well as in industrial subsectors which manufacture agricultural producer goods; and additional resources were directed to utilizing existing capacity more fully. This commitment simultaneously generates considerable pressure to sell available output.

When rural incomes are too low to accomplish such increased sales, despite political pressure exerted through collective institutions, a number of financing mechanisms are entertained, including: 1) twists in the terms of trade; 2) increases in loans and credit, particularly in association with input purchases and commitments to increased sales of farm products; 3) increased payment to collective institutions for rural labor in association with increased inventories of labor-intensive capital construction projects benefiting agriculture or with unskilled rural contract labor for industrial capacity expansion; 4) other rural subsidies. While each of these financing mechanisms has been regularly used, the third emerged as quite important during the 1960s and 1970s. The first and second were more dominant during the 1950s and the late 1970s and were proportionally less important in the intervening period. Finally, when these financing methods put too great a strain on other budgetary categories, deficit financing has been undertaken (Ishikawa 1987), especially via increased note issue by the People's Bank or by de facto expansion of credit by the Bank when such note issue is resisted.

In general, agricultural production has responded at least in some measure to these periodic initiatives (Tang and Stone 1980). When some of the marketing pressure is relieved, the easiest negative adjustment appears to have been in the third category, especially in terms of fewer rural capital construction starts, and has often been accompanied by emphasis on completion of existing projects. Although instances of terms-of-trade movements against agriculture have occurred, they have not been numerous and have generally encountered considerable resistance, although the problem has been partially mitigated by introduction of improved producer goods at substantially higher prices or additional (relatively high-priced) consumer goods. However, the particularly poor state of financial development in China (Ishikawa 1987), coupled with some degree of rural distrust of existing financial institutions and, most recently, the dissolution of the communes, has left China with an increasing problem of governmental mobilization of rural savings except in some association with deficit financing.

One aspect of intersectoral resource flows, the quantification of which is least clear, involves agriculture's investment in rural nonagricultural enterprises. The collective has been a remarkable instrument for mobilizing farm savings and labor resources for moderate development projects, and it is unclear what proportion has been invested in rural industry. But it *is* clear 1) that state investment in rural industry has been minor; 2) that state taxation of commune and brigade enterprises in the late 1970s was roughly 22 to 25 percent of profits; 3) that fees to local authorities accounted for 2.5 to 3.5 percent of *sales* of such enterprises (perhaps 12.5 to 17.5 percent of profits); and 4) that 35 to 40 percent of after-tax profit had to be turned over to local authorities for general construction funds, a portion of which was reinvested in agriculture. These funds represented 60 percent of the state's basic agricultural construction investment in 1978 (Stone 1984a; Ishikawa 1967; Ishikawa 1983).

The production mix of permissible rural industries was, for some time, constrained in a highly capital-intensive direction. Although they were more labor-intensive than their nonrural counterparts, choice of technique could do little to compensate for capital intensity in the mix of production, and the marginal product of labor in many rural enterprises was consequently close to zero. But since these enterprises were primarily owned by the county (or the commune or brigade), they provided, despite heavy taxation and restraints, an important savings and investment mechanism for local projects.

This all suggests not only low agricultural prices and strong financial discouragement of rural enterprises but low capital construction investment relative to the task of agricultural transformation, particularly in view of the implied constraints on the effectiveness of this investment. It may be illuminating to review the history of agriculture's share in state investment during technical transformation in the context of a low purchase price policy, and its relationship to output growth.

AGRICULTURE'S SHARE IN BASIC STATE INVESTMENT DURING TECHNICAL TRANSFORMATION

Despite scattered earlier efforts, China's comprehensive experiment with technical transformation of agriculture did not begin in earnest until September 1962. Through 1957, a development strategy emphasizing the concentration of resources on the expansion of industrial producer goods, a central focus of attention on national security, and preoccupation with organizational reform in both rural and urban sectors resulted in low priority for technical transformation. During this period real resources moved out of the agricultural sector. Industry absorbed the largest and an increasing share of the state's basic construction investment. Not only did agriculture's direct share of state investment decline from 5.0 to 2.9 percent, but its share of infrastructural investment in water control—the key to technical transformation—dropped from 8.9 to 5.0 percent of the total. These two components (plus investments for development of forestry and meteorology) averaged only 7.1 percent for the 1953–57 period. Despite the location of almost nine-tenths of the population in rural areas, agriculture's share of gross fixed investments (including modern and traditional farm implements, carts and livestock, land reclamation, peasant water control, and other imputed investments) declined rapidly from 31.8 to 23.5 percent, while industry's share rose from 22.0 to 36.5 percent (Tang and Stone 1980).

The unreliability of all of the statistics during and shortly after the Great Leap Forward (1958–59) makes estimation of agriculture's share unfruitful, but total fixed investments in all sectors over the 1960–62 period fell to around the 1953 level. And it should be noted that attempts to increase agricultural investment and production relied heavily on labor-intensive methods. Following the disastrous agricultural performance from 1959 to 1962, the 1963–65 period was marked by a particular concentration of scientific and technical efforts on the goal of agricultural transformation, as well as some increase in the sector's share in gross fixed investment (17.7 percent) and a twist in the terms of trade in agriculture's favor.

The first phase of the Cultural Revolution (1966–69) saw scattered industrial slowdowns, failures to deliver agricultural inputs, a drop in the farm-related state investment share (to 10.7 percent), an eclipse of scientific and technical manpower, and greater reliance on motivation through development of public-mindedness and patriotism as opposed to individual and small group self-interest, all leading to agricultural stagnation in 1968–69.

Chinese authorities became recommitted in the early 1970s to the goals of technical transformation and partially rectified the errors of the late 1960s, with resultant rapid agricultural recovery and growth through 1975. But improvement in the rural terms of trade evidently ground to a halt after 1972, far short of the degree of change necessary to ensure broad participation in technical transformation, and major infrastructural projects were increasingly financed through expropriation of rural savings and uncompensated manpower, as the farm-related share of state investment fell to 9.8 percent. At the very least there was no improvement in relative prices as a whole during the 1975–77 period, and according to some calculations the ratio dropped to the level of 1964–65.[7]

INCONSISTENCIES AMONG AGRICULTURE'S ECONOMIC DEVELOPMENT ROLES

While the method of extraction of agriculture's "surplus" was one which emphasized the short-term complementary role of furnishing cheap wage goods (food) and raw materials for the industrial and other sectors, short-term emphasis on the excessive fulfillment of these roles jeopardized their long-term fulfillment, as well as leading to the crippling of agriculture's performance of its other developmental functions. Mobilization of agriculture's savings and labor for its own technical transformation was certainly considerable for a land-poor traditional agriculture such as China's. But due to the inefficiency with which a large proportion of investments were inevitably undertaken, the amount of supplemental state investment, while sufficient to generate a reasonable growth rate in agricultural output, was not enough to bring about an increase in the marketed ratio of foodgrains, which formed the increasingly dominant complex of crops. Recognition of this failure by the early 1970s provided the impetus to pur-

---

7. Tang and Stone 1980, pp. 117–18. "Farm-related share" refers to state investment allocations to agriculture, forestry, water control, and meteorology, of which water control and agriculture represent the largest percentage. The statistics on farm-related share are from Zhongguo 1983, pp. 324, 325.

chase thirteen large-scale synthetic ammonia/urea complexes from abroad, a striking departure from Maoist foreign exchange parsimony, particularly vis-à-vis the agricultural and rural sectors. No single decision was more contributory to the startling agricultural productivity increases of the late 1970s and early 1980s (Stone 1985, 1986a).

In more market-oriented economies slow growth in food marketings might have led to a rise in the ratio of agricultural to industrial prices and to an eventual reversal of the net flow of resources out of agriculture. In China, this situation was prevented by state control of prices and rationing. But while the state-dictated ratio allowed some modest extraction of agricultural surplus without eliminating growth of the sector and its technical transformation, it did not permit a sufficient increase in rural per capita consumption. This led to decreasing rural cooperation and, coupled with bad weather and a failure in capital construction progress and the supply of industrial inputs, to farm output stagnation from 1975 to 1977.

What of agriculture's other roles? Capital-intensive emphasis in industry created a low demand for productive employment in the sector. Most of the remaining urban residents were absorbed in relatively low-productivity pursuits, generally organized by or within government, and the state retained the obligation to provide all legal urban residents with adequate foodgrain rations at low prices. Insufficient agricultural investment owing to excessive concentration on industry led to inadequate production and marketed ratios and to great difficulty in extracting sufficient food at low prices for the nonagricultural population.

Concern over this whole predicament caused the state to restrict migration out of agriculture and even to move urban residents back to the countryside. This isolation of the bulk of China's labor resources from the bulk of its capital investment virtually ensured low aggregate productivity of both capital and labor under the prevailing initial conditions of extreme capital scarcity. It also had serious equity implications, especially so because the methods of administrative control isolated rural areas not only from the cities but from each other as well. Thus agriculture fulfilled its role of supplying cheap labor for the development of the urban industrial sector to a lesser degree than it might otherwise have. Rural industrialization, China's well-publicized solution, was handicapped by the official and de facto financial policy of the central and local administrations (Stone 1984a).

Because of the excessively extractive price ratio, rural incomes were too low to provide much of a dynamic market for domestic industrial products, with the principal exception of chemical fertilizer sales. The concern over procurement of grains led the government not only to restrict inter-rural farmgoods trade and rural industrialization consistent with more rapid development of the agricultural sector but also to attempt to limit the allocation of farm labor for the production of handicrafts, farm subsidiary products, and even livestock goods which could have provided income to purchase industrial goods.

And finally, as is the case with many developing countries, agriculture's role in foreign exchange generation was primarily perceived in China in terms of import substitution of basic grains, that is, of being a source of cheap urban food rather than also becoming a dynamic or steady exporter of more highly valued farm products. With the extreme emphasis on grains, especially wheat, rice, and corn, China became a net importer of several traditional export farm commodities such as soybeans, oils, and sugar; exports of oilseeds decreased and those of tea, tobacco, and fruit stagnated at a low level until the recent policy changes. Inadequate investment, even for foodgrain and fiber development, ultimately resulted in massive foreign imports of grains, cotton, and, to a lesser extent, other fibers until the mid 1980s. Even within the context of a narrowly conceived emphasis on grain supplies, the degree of concentration on import substitution was undoubtedly misplaced. Although domestic wheat production provided the principal import substitute, greater emphasis on (more highly valued) rice and other exportables in the Yangzi Valley and the south, on cotton in North China, and on soybeans in the northeast, at the expense of wheat (and corn) which could be obtained cheaply on the international market, would have left China in a stronger position in terms of both grain supplies and foreign exchange.[8] Although such an internationally oriented strategy could not easily have been contemplated by the isolated China of the 1950s and 1960s, for which self-sufficiency was as much a strategy of national defense as of economic development, the failure to develop aggressively multiple trading relationships and a trading orientation ultimately left China in a more vulnerable position, since grain imports proved difficult to eliminate.

RURAL ORGANIZATION, PRICE, AND INVESTMENT REFORMS, 1979-84

The reforms required to alleviate this situation included a drastic shift in rural organization away from the cherished socialist goals for the sector and substantial rural price and investment increases. The rural incentive

8. Stone 1984a, p. 9. In 1982 total foodgrain and granulated sugar imports exceeded 16 million and 2 million tons, respectively. Cotton imports peaked at 897,600 tons in 1980 (Zhongguo 1983, pp. 437-38). It has been observed that China indeed engaged in a rice-wheat arbitrage, exporting rice to help finance larger wheat import volumes. Research at IFPRI has shown the international price of rice to be one of the important determinants of China's rice export volume. But rice exports did not increase commensurately with wheat imports, and pursuit of this activity was minor relative to what was potentially remunerative.

structure outlined by the Plenary Session in December 1978 and embodied in the 1979 National Economic Plan and Draft State Budget constituted the most extreme rural policy change since collectivization and was buttressed by long-term grain import agreements and a reform in the structure of state procurement of farm produce. Peasants were afforded considerably greater latitude in production decisions than in the previous two decades and received more pecuniary benefits from successful decisions than before.

Other changes were reflected in the government and party repudiation of "commandism"—a dictatorial tendency aimed at maintaining rural capital construction despite inadequate commitment of state resources. It often led to the application of production team labor and savings, without team approval, to projects that would benefit larger organizational units, had unacceptably long gestation periods, or were otherwise unpopular with the team. It also took the form of the frequent increase, contrary to national policy, in compulsory purchase quotas by ambitious local officials. Commandism, of course, not only alienated peasants from authorities but resulted in declines in labor productivity and in locally generated savings and investment.

The proportion of state-budgeted funds for capital construction to be devoted to agriculture was scheduled to increase from 10.7 percent in 1978 to 14 percent in 1979 to 18 percent in 1980–82. Operating expenses for agriculture and state outlay of aid to communes, brigades, and teams rose from 6.9 percent of the State's annual expenditures in 1978 and 6.3 percent in 1979 to 8 percent in 1980. Long-term, low-interest loans to rural people's communes from the Agricultural Bank of China and the rural credit cooperatives rose from 13 billion yuan in 1978 to 17 billion yuan in 1979. The total sum made available in 1980 was to be 20 billion yuan (35 billion yuan including exempted repayments), and the volume by 1985 was supposed to be "more than double" the 1978 level (Tang and Stone 1980).

Finally, in 1979 the terms of trade between agricultural and industrial products were made more favorable to agriculture and rural areas than in any previous year. They included a 20 percent increase in the government purchase price of within-quota grain; a 50 percent price premium for delivery of surplus grain; the decision not to raise the quotas of grain that must be delivered at the lower, within-quota price and the abolition of ceilings on collective grain distribution to commune members; a planned 10 to 15 percent decrease in the sales price of industrial inputs to agriculture; increased preferential input allocations to localities that increased output; and encouragement of rural fairs for inter-rural exchange and the sale of produce from private plots and sideline production and, now, from individually assigned collective plots (after tax, quota or contract, and collective cost obligations have been met). The rural fairs were ultimately allowed to grow into rural and urban markets where even foodgrains could be exchanged once tax, quota, and surplus quota responsibilities to the state were fulfilled. Thus, along with the procurement price rise discussed in previous sections, substantially higher rural and urban *market prices* for foodgrains became legal alternatives. Finally, since quotas were frozen, if the state needed to purchase additional foodgrains it could do so at a *negotiated price,* which tended to be only slightly lower than the market price, although there is evidence that quotas for delivery of negotiated purchases were established in some areas (table 8.1).

The estimated gross financial transfer to the countryside in 1979 brought about by the changes in state purchase prices of farm goods and sales prices of industrial goods, together with reduction and remission of rural taxes, was estimated at 9 billion yuan. For comparison, state aid to rural units was 2.06 billion yuan and for administrative expenses related to agriculture, water control, and forestry, 7.91 billion yuan, whereas state capital construction for the sector was 6.24 billion yuan in 1979. The gross

Table 8.1 PRC wheat and rice prices, 1980

	Wheat	Paddy
	(yuan per kilogram)	
Basic quota state purchase price	.3144	.2312
"Surplus" quota state purchase price	.4716	.3468
State negotiated purchase price	~.5940[a]	~.6200[a]
Rural market price	.5940	[b]
Urban market price		.6200
State retail price for rationed sales to "nonagricultural" population	[c]	[d]
State resale price to "agricultural" population	.3395	.2497
State resale price to low-income peasants and those suffering from natural disasters	.1997	.1469
Internal accounting price for in-kind distribution within production units	.2722	.1904

Sources: The 1980 basic quota prices and the surplus resale prices based on them are from China, People's Republic of, Nongye Jishu Jingji Shouce Bienweihui 1983, p. 742. The same table with somewhat different prices and interpretations appears in Lardy 1983b, p. 7. The milling rate data are from rural processing facilities cited in FAO 1979, pp. 17–28.

[a] Approximated at the market price.

[b] .780 yuan for milled rice. Milling rates in China run 68–78 percent. On the basis of weight equivalence, this would suggest a comparable paddy price of .5304–6084. But in most developing countries paddy rice prices are around half those of milled rice owing to processing costs.

[c] .370 yuan for rationed flour.

[d] .303 yuan for rationed milled rice. See n. *b* above. Comparable paddy prices would be in the range of .152 to .237 yuan.

financial transfer through the price mechanism for 1980-82 relative to 1979 would be substantially higher.[9]

The output response to these shifts was dramatic. From stagnation at 285 million tons during 1975-1977, foodgrain production vaulted to more than 407 million tons by 1984 (table 8.2). Available evidence suggests that this unprecedented growth was mostly real and not the product of statistical distortion. If the excellent weather year 1979 is compared with 1984, the implied growth is still very impressive. The impact on other agricultural production categories was generally even greater.

Of course it is virtually impossible to sort out the effect of the price changes *alone* in the presence of such sweeping reforms. It is quite possible

9. Tang and Stone 1980, pp. 118, 147; Zhongguo 1983, pp. 452-53. Whether there is any *net* transfer of resources depends upon the system of prices selected as "normal." If 1978 prices are used, there was a net transfer of resources into agriculture. Yet 1978 Chinese prices still discriminated against agriculture relative to the international price structure and from the point of view of average profit margins over production costs.

Table 8.2 Growth in foodgrain yields and chemical fertilizer application surrounding the 1979-85 policy reforms, 1975-86

Year	Foodgrain sown area	Foodgrain output	Average yields	Chemical fertilizer application
	(million hectares)	(million metric tons)	(metric tons per hectare of sown area)	(million tons of nutrients)
1975	121.062	284.515	2.35	5.369
1976	120.743	286.305	2.37	5.828
1977	120.400	282.725	2.35	6.480
1978	120.587	304.765	2.53	8.840
1979	119.263	332.115	2.78	10.863
1980	117.234	320.555	2.73	12.649
1981	114.958	325.020	2.83	13.349
1982	113.463	354.500	3.12	15.134
1983	114.047	387.275	3.40	16.598
1984	112.884	407.305	3.61	17.398
1985	108.845	379.108	3.48	17.758
1986	109.733	391.090	3.56	19.520

Sources: Zhongguo 1983; Zhongguo 1984, pp. 137, 141, 145, 175; Zhongguo 1986, pp. 149, 156, 174-80; Xinhua [New China News Agency] news bulletin, 8 February 1987; Zhao 1987, p. III; *Renmin Ribao,* 14 March 1987, p. 1; Zhongguo 1987, p. 3.
Note: Foodgrains include paddy rice, wheat, coarse grains, soybeans, pulses, and, valued at one-fifth natural weight, sweet potatoes and white potatoes. The chemical fertilizer figures include application to all crops, not just foodgrains. But foodgrain sown area was around 80 percent of total sown area throughout the period, and fertilizer application to foodgrains comprised a roughly equivalent proportion of chemical fertilizers used.

that they would not have been so effective without the other important changes in rural incentive structure allowing farmers to keep most of their increased output or to sell it profitably in the free markets. But it is also clear that without the price changes, the additional application of fertilizers indispensable to such a massive increase in yields might not have been possible. Without the price changes, the allocational distortion of inputs and labor away from unremunerative foodgrain fields (which, through administrative control, could not easily be reduced) would have been even more severe in the grain surplus areas. In such a case, the realized increase in foodgrain yields would not have been possible.

CONSEQUENCES OF THE REFORMS FOR AGRICULTURE'S ROLE

As should be obvious, there have been major consequences associated with the substantial shift in financial flows brought on by the reforms. In order to satisfy urban consumption while allowing farmers to keep most of the increased output, Chinese grain imports accelerated from 2 percent of the international grain market in 1976 to roughly 7–10 percent of a 40 percent larger international market in 1981–82 (Zhongguo 1983; FAO 1983b), so that the proportion of urban food supply furnished domestically became the smallest in PRC history (table 8.3). The government was ultimately able to reverse this increase in food imports as the reforms, as well as investment and price increases, took effect. But with a politically powerful urban population long dependent on cheap food, the price increases could not be passed on to citydwellers. This brought about an increase in the food subsidy cost to the government to more than one-quarter of the state budgetary expenditures at all levels, an immense drain on state resources. The subsidies benefited an already relatively well-off rural government and urban minority, with the exception of about 10 percent of the total, which went to disaster-stricken rural areas (table 8.4). Thus agriculture's contribution to investment in other sectors, never a very large proportion, became substantially smaller, or negative, depending upon the system of prices used.[10]

On the other hand, the markets for industrial consumer goods, as well as industrial inputs to agriculture, have blossomed, and, with more liber-

10. Stone 1984a, pp. 10–11. The subsidies represent 6.2–6.5 percent of Chinese national income (according to the Chinese method of calculation) or around 33 percent of the wage bill of state workers and employees (*Renmin Ribao*, 27 June 1983). By contrast, the Indian subsidies of rationed cereals were less than 2 percent of central and state government expenditures and were considerably less than 1 percent of net national product. Polish food subsidies rose to 17.6 percent of the wage fund in 1980, but they are distributed to well over half the nation's citizens, whereas Chinese subsidies are concentrated on around 16 percent of the total population, primarily in urban areas (Lardy 1983b, pp. 38–40).

Table 8.3 International trade in foodgrains, sugar, cotton, and chemical fertilizers, 1950–85

Years	Avg. annual total foodgrain exports	Avg. annual foodgrain imports Total	Wheat only	Avg. annual net imports	Ratio of net imports to domestic foodgrain production (percent)	Avg. annual fertilizer imports (thousand metric tons of standard weight)	Share of domestic application (percent)	Avg. annual granulated sugar imports (thousand metric tons)	Ratio of sugar imports to domestic production (percent)	Avg. annual raw cotton imports (thousand metric tons)	Ratio of cotton imports to domestic production (percent)
	(million metric tons)										
1950-54	1.65	0.03	0.02	−1.63	−1.23	306.4	—	73.9	17.9	65.1	7.6
1955-60	2.79	0.13	0.06	−2.66	−1.76	1,350.7	60.0	144.9	21.5	67.6	4.6
1961-65	1.62	5.93	4.89	4.31	2.96	1,889.8	42.3	797.2	162.9	113.6	8.1
1966-70	2.57	4.98	4.42	2.41	1.30	5,041.3	39.0	475.0	33.2	93.0	4.1
1971-76	2.94	5.05	4.09	2.10	0.94	5,679.1	24.7	535.8	32.1	255.3	11.0
1977-83	1.61	12.33	10.26	10.72	3.81	9,678.3	16.5	1,430.1	53.1	514.3	19.1
1984	3.57	10.45	10.00	6.88	1.69	18,356.2	21.1	1,228.7	32.3	39.8	0.6
1985	9.33	5.97	5.38	−3.36	−0.89	7,609.4	8.6	1,908.7	42.9	0.2	—

Sources: These figures appear in or were calculated from data appearing in Zhongguo 1984, pp. 141, 142, 145, 397, 410–12; China, People's Republic of, State Statistical Bureau 1985, pp. 255, 281, 336, 339, 510, 516, 517; China, People's Republic of, General Administration of Customs 1986, pp. 20–30; China, People's Republic of, State Statistical Bureau 1986.

Notes: Trade and domestic production of foodgrains includes milled rice, wheat, coarse grains, soybeans, and potatoes valued at one-fifth natural weight. "Standard weight" denotes 21 percent N in the case of nitrogen fertilizers, 18 percent P_2O_5 for phosphate fertilizers, and 25 percent K_2O for potash fertilizers.

Table 8.4 State budgetary revenues and expenditures and state food consumption subsidies and their recipients, 1974-81 (billion nominal yuan)

	1974-78 avg.	1979	1980	1981	1979-81 average
State food consumption subsidies					
Indirect subsidy of domestic grains and oils	*~4.1*	*>7.8*	*10.3*	*>12.8*	*10.2*
Indirect nonstaple food subsidy		*>0**	*>3*	*2.8*	*(~2)*
Direct nonstaple food subsidy	0	<1.0*	~1.6*	(13.4)	>5.33
Indirect subsidy on imported grain		*0-0.8*	*0-2.1*	*0.6-2.4*	*0.2-1.8*
Total		(9.0-10.5)	14.9-17.5	(29.7-31.5)	(17.7-19.5)
Total state budgetary revenues		*110.33*	*108.52*	*108.95*	*109.27*
Total state budgetary expenditures		*127.39*	*121.27*	*111.50*	*120.05*
Recipients of state food consumption subsidies					
"Non-agriculture" average population (millions)	(~143)	(~156)			
Urban		*124.28*	*131.375*	*136.415*	*130.69*
Suburban & rural nonagricultural		~19	25		
Amount received (billion yuan)		(8.1-8.9)	(17.5-19.6)	(20.8-22.6)	(15.5-17.1)
"Agricultural" average population (millions)	(~821)	*820.36*	~(811.1)		
Rural and suburban					
Urban contract labor			*9.3*		
Amount received (billion yuan)		<3*	*3.0*	~3*	(~3)

Sources: Renmin Ribao, 16 April 1982, 27 June 1983; *Hongqi* (Red Flag), no. 1, 1982; Lardy 1983b; China, People's Republic of, State Statistical Bureau 1984.

Note: Figures in italics are quoted from a Chinese source or are calculated directly from official figures. Figures in parentheses are derived. Asterisks indicate rough estimates.

alization, an active rural nonagricultural sector which supplies simple manufactured consumer goods and services and provides simple components to industry is becoming economically important. Agriculture, in fact, has been so successful and the budgetary drain of the food subsidy program has increased so significantly that the government reversed the rapid growth in net agricultural imports, and the full planned reduction in prices of industrial inputs to agriculture was never authorized.[11] Instead, the farmgate price of urea was raised 13 percent in 1984, and a market for fertilizers partially replaced the direct allocation system, although government restrictions of supplies in 1985 kept fertilizer market prices even higher. The bumper crops of the early 1980s hastened an overhaul of the procurement system, which had been totally unsuited to surplus conditions: government reversed its long-standing pledge to purchase all grain and cotton offered for sale. In 1985 a contract system was established combining the old quotas and "surplus" quotas and featuring a single price between the two. Above-contract deliveries, if purchased, would be subject to flexible prices reflecting supply and demand conditions but generally not above the fledgling market prices.

More ominously, the percentage of the state's capital construction budget allocated to agriculture never reached 18 percent. The total state construction budget declined by 21 percent in 1981, and the proportion allocated to agriculture, forestry, water control, and meteorology fell to 6.6 percent, then to 6.1 percent of a recovered budget in 1982, 6.0 percent in 1983, and 5.0 percent in 1984. Additions to fertilizer production capacity in 1983 and 1984 were at the lowest absolute levels since the 1950s, and future plans call for only partial aggregate recovery, though they purport to address nutrient imbalance.[12]

11. Actually, urban foodgrain consumption was already subsidized in the early 1960s (probably with the 1963 procurement price increase), but the subsidy was reduced in 1965. It is not clear whether the 1966 procurement price increases were reflected in retail prices, but by 1970 the domestic grain subsidy alone was almost 2.5 billion yuan, increasing to 4.3–5.2 billion yuan during 1975–77. The greatest increase in these subsidies occurred after 1978, however, and was financed partly through inflation and partly by reducing the total capital construction budget, national defense expenditures, bank loans to rural areas, expenditures on technical innovation and trial production in enterprises, and additions to circulating funds for enterprises (Zhongguo 1983, pp. 325, 448–49; *Beijing Review*, no. 48, 1982; Zhongguo Guojia Tongjiju 1984, p. 314; Zhongguo Shangyebu 1984, p. 521; China, People's Republic of, State Statistical Bureau 1985).

To make matters worse, commune dissolution, increased decisionmaking power of farmers, selectively reduced quotas, and higher surplus prices were creating a situation in which farmers were increasingly able to manipulate the system to raise average prices even above planned levels, a problem exacerbated by the unfamiliar bumper crop situation of the 1980s, to which the system was ill-suited. The accentuated incentive pricing has ultimately had excessive intersectoral and interregional distribution consequences, as well as having rewarded system manipulation and guideline evasion to a considerable extent.

12. Loans to rural communes and production brigades fell more than 4 billion yuan short of the 1984 plan of 20 billion yuan but continued to grow to 19.9 billion by 1983, then vaulted to 31 billion in 1984 and 35.25 billion in 1985, surpassing the plan to double the 1978 level,

All of this does not indicate a saturated demand for grains but is evidence of an administrative response to the short-range problems of budgetary crisis and suddenly unmanageable stocks in a system ill-suited to continued rapid growth in supply of agricultural goods, and within a context whose essential orientation toward urban and capital-intensive industrial development is still incompatible with sustained balanced growth. Although short-term incentives for several crops can indeed be rolled back to more maintainable levels, deterioration in long-term investment in agriculture's technical transformation may cause difficulties in future. A steady long-term program to underwrite the future basis for supply growth should involve considerably increased emphasis on labor-intensive nonagricultural development to boost effective farm product demand, along with heavy investment in infrastructure to facilitate rural growth in both farm and nonfarm sectors and in market development to link them (Stone 1985, 1986a, 1986b).

CONCLUSIONS

Unlike the countries depicted as successful models of economic development, which are reputed to have financed industrialization by squeezing agriculture, the People's Republic of China was unable to extract resources from the agricultural sector through deliberate policy without serious consequences for the rate of overall economic growth and the destruction of agriculture's other developmental functions.[13] This was the case despite very effective rural institutions for mobilizing savings, a substantial increase in labor application per hectare, and an active rural response to rural industrialization and technical transformation of agriculture.

---

though the real values are lower due to generalized price inflation. China is clearly relying on local investment in agriculture to make up for the drift in central expenditures. One of its primary mechanisms is a rebate to counties and townships for taxation of their industries, one-quarter of which is supposed to be spent in support of agricultural production. This could be an important source of agricultural development financing, but, like the loans to communes and brigades, it is not clear what proportion of these funds are actually spent to support growth in crop productivity. With the exception of a few large projects, state expenditures on water control have dropped substantially. Again, local efforts are supposed to take up the slack, financed by water fees imposed on farmers. This transition, however, is not likely to be easy (Zhongguo 1985, p. 526; Zhongguo 1986, p. 616; Stone 1986a; discussion with members of the Rural Development Research Center, Jiangsu, Shandong, and Beijing, April 1986; Ren 1987).

13. This conclusion is reminiscent of Ellman's (1975) findings for the Soviet Union in the 1930s and is of some relevance to a large number of developing countries whose attempts to squeeze agriculture have failed to extract a surplus of much quantitative importance to national capital formation in the short run while leading to disastrous implications for the longer run.

As in many other developing countries, an immediate policy emphasis on cheap urban food in the PRC, without sufficient state investment in all requisite aspects of agriculture's technical transformation, set up a contradiction between the short-term and long-term fulfillment of the sector's role as a source of savings and food for the development of other sectors. Increasing market control for various farm inputs and outputs and rural organizational efforts to resolve the contradiction also focused on short-term gains at the expense of long-term deterioration in resource allocative efficiency and perhaps in the quality and intensity of applied agricultural labor.

These are the elements that combined to depress the returns to Chinese agriculture's incomplete technical transformation. And thus relative prices, no longer far out of line internationally, still proved a critical limitation. But it is important to note that it was not price increases alone that resolved the problem. What did prove effective was the combination of massive provision of nitrogen, revival of gains from regional and occupational specialization, resolution of imbalanced allocational patterns limiting resource productivity within farming areas, and reestablishment of the link between effort and reward underwritten by the positive shock of price increases—all these added to a firm base, developed over decades, of improved seed technology, relative agronomic sophistication, and water control.

Finally, during the three decades in which an urban, capital-intensive strategy increasingly constrained agriculture's ability to provide food and savings for the dynamic development of other sectors, agriculture's other developmental functions—as a source of labor and foreign exchange and as a domestic market for goods and services of other sectors—were seriously curtailed. All in all, it is not yet evident how, in China's case, a sufficient state investment in agriculture to allow balanced growth would have been consistent with a sizable net outflow of resources from the sector for a large part of the People's Republic period.

Yet China is now at a crossroads. Substantial resolution of the constraints which have inhibited the acceleration of farm production of a considerably transformed agricultural sector now provides an unprecedented opportunity for agriculture to fulfill several of its theoretical functions as a pivotal sector in the rapid development of the entire economy. What remains to be determined is whether the struggle to deal with the short-term difficulties associated with the unfamiliar chaos of China's current economic revolution will lead the country to return to more familiar inertial states of urban and industrial orientation and restriction of growth in order to achieve a measure of control, or whether China will succeed in forging ahead with the second half of the program aimed at rebalancing the economy. This would call for an employment-intensive development of the rural nonagricultural sector, bolstered by infrastructural investment as a counterpart to sustained commitment to agricultural expansion and a link to the capital-intensive urban sector. In all of this, the role of price, as China's markets for food, inputs, and consumer goods are decreasingly controlled by government, may be neither the most critical instrument for achieving this development nor even an appropriate one, but rather an indicator of sectoral performance.

9

Determination of Administered Prices of Foodgrains in India

J. S. SARMA

Agricultural price policies and allied instruments evolved in India in the context of shortages and excess demand during World War II (India 1975). Procurement and distribution of major foodgrains were begun and statutory maximum prices were set, though not strictly enforced. Assurances were given to farmers that the state would purchase foodgrains at fixed prices if market prices fell precipitously; but till 1954 there was no sharp decline in food prices. Minimum prices were announced for wheat, jowar, rice, and maize in 1954–55 when prices started falling sharply (Chopra 1981). The recommendations of the Foodgrain Prices Committee, also known as the Jha Committee, in 1964 provided the foundation for a sound agricultural price policy and a systematic determination of producer prices of major foodgrains and maximum wholesale and retail prices (India 1965a). However, some believe that agricultural price policy in India was more oriented toward consumers' interests, at least until the mid-seventies.[1]

India's agricultural price policy includes three main types of administered prices: support, procurement, and issue. The support price is generally announced at sowing time, and the government agrees to buy all grain offered for sale at this price. These prices guarantee to the farmer that, in the event of excessive production leading to a glut in the market, prices of his produce will not be allowed to fall below the stated price. Support prices generally affect indirectly farmers' decisions regarding land allocation to crops. The areas to be sown, however, depend upon the actual prices farmers realized for the previous crop and their expectations for the coming season.

The procurement price is generally fixed and announced at the start of

---

1. This chapter focuses attention on the principles and procedures of determination of administered prices of foodgrains in India and does not attempt a rigorous evaluation of public intervention in foodgrain markets in the country.

the marketing season.[2] It represents the price at which the state agencies procure grain from producers directly or in the market, depending upon the system of procurement adopted, including compulsory levy. The quantity to be procured is determined by the government's needs for disbursements under the public distribution system. In recent years, however, the actual quantities procured have depended upon the grain offered for sale by farmers at prices fixed by the government. These prices are generally higher than the support prices but lower than the free market prices in normal years. In a good crop year, in surplus states, free market prices would have been lower but for government purchases; after the surplus is mopped up, market prices tend to run higher than procurement prices.

Issue prices are fixed by the government for releasing grain stocks from the "central pool" and are usually concessional or subsidized. Issue prices are invariably much higher than procurement prices. The subsidy arises from the fact that the total pooled expenditure, including storage costs, interest, transport, and handling charges in public distribution, are not fully recovered through sales at issue prices. These prices are designed to provide food to the vulnerable sections of the population at a rate cheaper than that prevailing in the market. In addition to the above, India has statutory minimum prices for jute and sugarcane and maximum control prices, which have sometimes been fixed for foodgrains to prevent profiteering.[3]

The government recognizes the importance of assuring reasonable prices to farmers to motivate them to adopt improved technology and to promote investment by them in farm enterprises for increasing agricultural production. The basic objective of agricultural price policy in India is, however, to evolve a balanced and integrated price structure to meet the overall needs of the economy while protecting, in particular, the interests of the producer and the consumer. The policy is designed to facilitate the attainment of growth and equity objectives of economic development plans.

AGRICULTURAL PRICES COMMISSION

The government of India is advised by the Agricultural Prices Commission (APC), set up in 1965 on the recommendation of the Jha Committee. In

2. By this time it is possible to estimate the size of the crop and also take into account any increases in input prices taking place after the sowing time. However, in response to persistent demand in Parliament and from farmers' organizations, the procurement/minimum support prices are now announced before the sowing season. The time schedule laid down by government for announcement of these prices is 15 April for kharif cereals and 15 August for rabi cereals.

3. Maximum control prices have not been fixed for cereals in the last few years. When prices rise exorbitantly high in any area, it is a signal to the government of developing scarcity conditions which need to be met by rushing larger supplies through the public distribution system to that area.

recommending price policy and structure, the Commission is specifically charged with keeping the following in view:

(a) the need to provide incentives to the producer for adopting improved technology and for maximizing production;

(b) the need to ensure rational utilization of land and other production resources; and

(c) the likely effect of price policy on the rest of the economy, particularly on the cost of living, level of wages, industrial cost structure, etc. (India 1965b).

The Commission is required to suggest non-price measures that will facilitate the achievement of the above objectives. An amendment in March 1980 required the Commission to take into account the changes in the terms of trade between the agricultural and nonagricultural sectors when recommending procurement/support prices (India 1980a). The commodities for which the Commission has responsibility include paddy/rice, wheat, jowar, bajra, maize, ragi, barley, gram, and other pulses among foodgrains and sugarcane, cotton, jute, groundnuts, soybean, sunflower seed, rapeseed, and mustard and tobacco among nonfood crops.

The Commission has four members and is headed by a distinguished professional economist. Two other members are economists, and the third has practical experience in farming. It is assisted by a small technical staff and advised by a panel of farmers.[4]

APC Criteria for Determination of Prices

The reports of the APC mention that, when recommending a price level for a commodity, its recommendations are influenced, among other factors, by the prices fixed in the previous year, trends in open-market prices reflecting overall shortages, the latest available estimates of cost of production and changes in the prices of inputs since the completion of the cost studies, the need for securing a balanced growth in the output of related crops, reduction in interstate price dispersion, the likely effect on cost of living, and the general price level and need for curtailing inflation.

The most important of these criteria is the cost of production; for unless prices cover costs there will be no incentive to increase production. But the main problem here is the concept of cost to be adopted and the items to be covered in the total cost. The APC is generally guided by the average cost (designated as Cost C) generated under the comprehensive scheme for studying the cost of cultivation of crops in the main states producing the commodity, as it is the level which would "induce the farmers to improve their efficiency and would discourage production in inefficient farming

---

4. The Agricultural Prices Commission was re-designated as the Commission for Agricultural Costs and Prices in 1985, and its membership was enlarged.

areas and on inefficient farms" (Kahlon and Tyagi 1983). Cost C covers items of expenses of cultivation and also imputed value of items such as rental value of owned land and interest on fixed capital and imputed value of family labor.[5] The principles of evaluation and allocation (in the case of joint costs) to be adopted in determining costs are also laid down uniformly.

Questions are often raised as to whether the managerial cost and costs of transportation to the market are to be included in the costs of production. A suggestion by a Special Expert Committee on Cost of Production Estimates (Sen Committee) that both items be included has been accepted (India 1982a). The APC preferred to take average rather than marginal cost into consideration in price fixation on the grounds that the latter would be much more unstable than the former and hence cannot be used meaningfully for achieving price stability objectives.[6] The Sen Committee also recommended against including risks arising out of asset losses or yield variability except for premiums for crop insurance covering such risks. Since cost data for the current year are not available when the APC recommends the support or procurement prices, the APC uses underlying trends in costs measured by the changes in input prices, which are computed through a system of index numbers.

The parity approach in India differs in several important respects from that adopted in developed countries such as the United States and Japan.[7] The APC is guided by several concepts of parity, such as intercommodity price parity, intersectoral price parity, input-output price parity, and parity between prices received and prices paid by farmers, though these different parities are not formally synthesized into a composite parity index.

Rational utilization of land and other production resources is one of the

5. The cost data are being collected under the comprehensive scheme for studying the cost of cultivation of crops, operated by the Directorate of Economics and Statistics. The scheme is working in sixteen states, where, for the most part, the agricultural universities plan and conduct field investigations on a continuous basis. Four types of cost of cultivation are used in India, defined as follows: Cost A_1: all paid-out costs or expenses incurred in cash and kind on material inputs, hired human labor, bullocks, and machine labor; Cost A_2: Cost A_1 + rent paid for leased-in land; Cost B: Cost A_2 + rental value of owned land and interest on owned fixed capital excluding land; and Cost C: Cost B + imputed value of family labor. In particular, Cost A_1 includes the value of hired human and bullock labor, hired machinery charges, owned bullock and machine labor, value of material inputs such as seeds (owned and purchased), fertilizers, and insecticides; manures (owned and purchased); depreciation on implements, machinery, and farm buildings; irrigation charges; land revenue; cesses and other taxes; interest paid on crop loans; interest on working capital (excluding crop loans); and miscellaneous expenses (artisans, etc.).

6. For a discussion of the wide variation in cost of production and the circumstances leading to the greater instability of marginal cost, see Kahlon and Tyagi 1983, pp. 174–75.

7. The price support level in this approach, as adopted in the United States, is related to a historical average price received for the commodity and the index of price paid by farmers, so that the purchasing power of the commodity remains more or less constant.

specific terms of reference of the APC. For ensuring this, intercrop price parities are examined. The intersectoral price parity arises when the prices of cash crops such as sugarcane, cotton, and jute are determined. In these cases, the effect of any possible changes in industrial raw material prices on the relationship between them and the prices of manufactured goods is also a factor considered by the APC. The input and output price parities reflect the changes in the overall cost of production of a crop and as such are a relevant factor in price determination. It is believed that any automatic linkage between the prices received by the farmer and the prices paid by him will only feed the vicious circle of cost-price inflation (India 1975).

The amended terms of the APC's mandate also require it to consider the terms of trade while fixing prices. The concept adopted is the ratio of indices of prices received and prices paid by the agricultural sector. An analysis of the domestic terms of trade recently done by Tyagi (1987) shows that during the period 1964-65 to 1974-75 the terms of trade have generally remained in favor of the agricultural sector compared to the late 1960s and early 1970s but moved against it during 1975-76. However, Kahlon and Tyagi (1983) expressed the view that "an effective approach for correcting the distortions resulting from terms of trade becoming adverse to the agricultural sector would seem to be in adopting all such measures which result in increases in productivity, although some improvements in terms of trade could be effected by adjusting the output prices."

After examining these various criteria and the Commission's recommendations, Krishna and Raychaudhuri (1980) observed that the record shows that "the various criteria listed above were applied and emphasized in an uncoordinated way. Some of them were stressed and used for some decisions and others on other occasions. They were never integrated into an objective model to compute the price to be recommended." George (1985) also came to the conclusion that there was no direct relationship between the prices recommended and any of the considerations listed above.

Agricultural commodity prices show large spatial, varietal, and quality differences as well as variations over time. Spatial differences can be explained partly by transport costs and partly by imperfections in the market. The approach to quality differences is to fix the price of a well-specified fair average quality with differentials for other qualities. A similar approach is used for varietal differences. Prices are determined for standard varieties, and prices for all others are indicated in terms of price differentials based on past relationships. The government of India fixes a single price for a specified variety of each cereal. However, state governments fix different prices for different varieties, particularly in the case of rice. For example, as compared to an all-India price of Rs 142 per quintal of common variety of paddy for the 1985-86 crop, the prices fixed by the states range from Rs 218 per quintal in Gujarat to 242 in Haryana for the same variety of rice, with a conversion ratio of two-thirds. The prices of fine variety of rice range from Rs 224 to 256 per quintal and those of the superfine variety from Rs 229 to 264 per quintal.

The APC generally submits its recommendations and the rationale behind them in reports. Prices recommended by the Commission are referred by the Central Department of Agriculture and Cooperation to the state governments and are ordinarily discussed with them at special conferences. The views of central departments and ministries such as Food, Commerce, Industry, Finance and Economic Affairs, and the Planning Commission are obtained by the Central Department of Agriculture and Cooperation. The policy developed in this procedure is then considered by the Cabinet Committee on Economic Affairs before decisions are announced.

Though the procurement prices recommended by the APC are generally accepted by the government, in some years the prices announced by them were higher, as is seen in table 9.1. For example, for wheat, the prices fixed exceeded those recommended by the APC by Rs 2.50 to Rs 5 per quintal in three out of eleven years. For crop year 1983–84, however, the price announced by the government was lower by Rs 3. In the case of paddy, higher prices ranging from Rs 2 to 5 were announced for four out of eleven years.

Table 9.1 All-India procurement prices of cereals recommended by the Agricultural Prices Commission and those announced by the government, 1975–76 to 1985–86

Crop year	Paddy, common variety		Wheat, fair average quality		Coarse cereals, fair average quality	
	Recommended by APC	Announced by govt.	Recommended by APC	Announced by govt.	Recommended by APC	Announced by govt.
	(rupees per quintal)					
1975–76	74	74	105	105	74	74
1976–77	74	74	105	110	74	74
1977–78	77	77	110	112.50	74	74
1978–79	82	85	115	115	78	85
1979–80	90	95	117	117	85	95
1980–81	100	105	127	130	97.50	105
1981–82	115	115	142	142	116	116
1982–83	122	122	151	151	118	118
1983–84	132	132	155	152	124	124
1984–85	137	137	157	157	130	130
1985–86	140	142	162	162	130	130

Source: India 1985b.

The differences between the two sets of prices were larger, at Rs 7 to 10 a quintal for coarse grains.

FOOD CORPORATION OF INDIA

The Food Corporation of India (FCI), created in 1965 as a public sector undertaking, is the principal agency through which food procurement and distribution policies are implemented. Its main aims are to ensure that the primary producer gets the minimum price set by the government and to protect the consumer from the vagaries of the speculative trade. It handles all purchase, storage, movement, and distribution and sale of foodgrains on behalf of the central government and some of the state governments as well. Through these operations FCI is expected to secure for itself a strategic and commanding position in the foodgrain trade in the country. Imports and exports of cereals (when given as loans or grants to countries in need) are also handled by FCI. In addition, some states have food and civil supplies corporations or cooperative marketing agencies which make purchases and sales on their behalf. FCI issues foodgrains to the public distribution system based on allocations made by the government of India. It also supplies grains to state governments for special schemes such as food-for-work, and for relief measures during floods and cyclones.

The total storage accommodation available to FCI at the end of October 1985 was 24.1 million tons, of which 9.2 million tons was owned by it, and 10.9 million tons was hired from various agencies. The balance represents covered and plinth storage (meaning a cement base under and plastic cover over the grain).

IMPLEMENTATION OF PRICE POLICY

The government relies on procurement, public distribution, and buffer stocks as its main instruments for the implementation of price policy.

Procurement

The volume of foodgrains procured in India increased substantially from 1.4 million tons in 1964 to 20.1 million tons in 1985, the latter figure comprising 10.3 million tons of wheat, 9.6 million tons of rice, and the balance of coarse grains. The overall quantity of cereals procured forms about 15 percent of the total production. The percentage of marketed surplus would be much higher. An analysis by states (table 9.2) shows that a little more than half of the total procurement of foodgrains was from Punjab, followed by Uttar Pradesh and Haryana, with about 15 percent each. With Andhra Pradesh, the four states shared around 90 percent of total procure-

Table 9.2 Procurement of foodgrains, 1985 (calendar year)

State	Rice	Wheat	Other cereals	Total cereals
		(thousand tons)		
Andhra Pradesh	1,704	—	—	1,704
Assam	15	—	—	15
Bihar	31	4	—	35
Gujarat	34	—	—	34
Haryana	973	1,961	—	2,934
Jammu and Kashmir	43	5	—	48
Karnataka	112	—	—	112
Kerala	Neg.	—	—	Neg.
Madhya Pradesh	383	14	9	406
Maharashtra	1	—	152	153
Orissa	111	—	—	111
Punjab	4,358	6,155	—	10,513
Rajasthan	40	37	—	77
Tamil Nadu	705	—	—	705
Uttar Pradesh	960	2,136	—	3,096
West Bengal	73	—	—	73
All-India[a]	9,564	10,354	161	20,079
Total production	58,636	44,229	31,164	134,029
Procurement as percentage of production	16.3	23.4	0.5	15.0

Source: India 1986.
[a] Includes other states and union territories.

ment in 1985. Again nearly 60 percent of the wheat and 45 percent of the rice procured in the country came from Punjab in that year.

In the early fifties, domestic procurement accounted for a little less than 50 percent of the total public distribution of foodgrains. Subsequently, except in good crop years, major reliance was placed on imports for meeting domestic requirements. During 1961–63, domestic procurement represented around one-eighth of the public distribution. Until 1964, procurement was confined to surplus states. It was extended to deficit states as well during the drought years and thereafter. In a situation of shortage or scarcity, unregulated purchase and movement of foodgrains by private trade may lead to indiscriminate and speculative rise in prices by movement of surpluses of the producing regions to areas of high purchasing power. Thus the objective of procurement till the mid-sixties was to redistribute the limited supplies from producers to consumers through government agencies within a crop year: its purpose was not to even out supplies between good and bad years. The situation began to change after 1967–68, as the output of foodgrains, particularly wheat, increased with the adoption of new technology based on high-yielding varieties of seeds. The proportion of procurement in total public distribution increased, and by 1978 imports were stopped. In most subsequent years requirements were met entirely from domestic procurement and stocks. In this sense the country achieved self-sufficiency, though the per capita consumption of the poorest sections of the population was far below the desired nutritional level.

The four main systems of procurement are monopoly procurement, graded levy on producers, levy on millers and traders, and preemptive/open market purchases (Saran 1971). The choice of a particular system depends upon the structure of production, the development of the infrastructure, including the marketing system, the nature of the food situation, and, above all, the administrative organization and experience of the state government. Imposition of interstate movement restrictions (referred to below) was a prerequisite to successful procurement operations.

The procurement system adopted also varied over time and by commodity. For example, procurement of wheat and coarse grains is done through preemptive/open market purchases (except in Maharashtra for jowar), which is facilitated by the existence of regulated markets for these commodities.[8] For paddy, which is traded in milled form, a levy on millers and traders is operationally more convenient. When the food situation was more acute during the sixties, monopoly procurement and graded levy (i.e., levy at progressive rates) were imposed in many of the rice-producing states, particularly those with a deficit. Currently, only Kerala State has a graded levy on producers of paddy. (The Annex to this chapter gives the systems of procurement of foodgrains in the states in 1981–82.) Cereals are procured mostly by the field staffs of the Food Corporation of India, the state civil supplies corporations or departments, cooperative marketing agencies, etc.

The public distribution system has to supply reasonable quantities of foodgrains at reasonable prices, particularly to vulnerable sections of the population. Procurement from domestic production must also be done at reasonable prices, which may have to be lower than the ruling market prices in some years, particularly years of food shortage. In such cases, the remainder of the marketable surplus is sold in the open market at prices higher than they would have been had there been no procurement. It is argued that the weighted average price received by the producer from the sale of the levy and the non-levy portions of marketable surplus may not be less than the price he would have received in the absence of the levy and

---

8. Preemptive purchases of wheat are made when procurement tends to be extremely low as a result of two or three successive years of low production. The general approach is that most procurement, particularly of wheat, is voluntary.

would be high enough to avoid any disincentive to farmers (India 1975; George 1983).[9]

Public Distribution

The public distribution system is an essential component of government's food management policy. The system operates through a network of ration shops and fair price shops. In the past, when food deficits were large, areas of high purchasing power such as big cities were cordoned off to prevent unduly large quantities of supplies being drawn off from the rural areas, and statutory rationing was introduced in those areas. The system also catered to the needs of working classes in the industrial areas and big cities. After the improvement in the food situation, statutory rationing was withdrawn, except in the Greater Calcutta-Asansol industrial belt.

Most of the country is covered by about three hundred thousand fair price shops, more than three-fourths of which are in or around rural areas. Reliable data on the quantities of foodgrains distributed in rural and urban areas are not available. However, George (1985) estimated that the offtake from the public distribution system in the urban areas was about 85 percent of the total. Under the informal rationing or fair price shops system, the vulnerable sections of the population are provided a minimum requirement of foodgrains at reasonable prices. People are free to purchase additional foodgrains in the open market (India 1966b).[10] Nearly 660 million persons had access to fair price shops or ration shops at the end of 1981. In 1982, 14.8 million tons of foodgrains were distributed under the public distribution system, an average of 1.2 million tons per month. This included sales to roller flour mills and quantities distributed under the Food for Work Program, since modified as the National Rural Employment Program. The direct sale of wheat to roller flour mills for conversion to flour prevented bulk purchases from the open market, which, it was thought, would raise prices excessively.

To facilitate procurement of foodgrains from surplus areas at reasonable prices, movement of grains from one zone to another was restricted until the late 1970s. Most often, each state formed a zone, but in some cases a zone was made up of a group of adjoining states or a few contiguous

9. Subbarao (1979) examined the issue on the basis of empirical evidence for paddy from coastal districts of Andhra Pradesh, and came to the conclusion that farmers were compensated for the lower procurement price through a rise in the open market price. This result is true, in the short run, when the price elasticity of aggregate supply remains absolutely smaller than the price elasticity of poor consumers' demand (Hayami, Subbarao, and Otsuka 1982).

10. The distinction between statutory rationing and informal rationing is that in the statutorily rationed areas, the open market is legally barred from purchasing, and the government undertakes the responsibility for supplying specific rationed quantities to consumers. On the other hand, in the informally rationed areas, the open market can legitimately function.

surplus districts. The zones were different for rice, wheat, and coarse grains. These restrictions, however, resulted in depressing prices in the surplus areas, thus increasing regional price differentials. By 1978-79, with the easing of the food situation, most zonal restrictions were withdrawn. Among the other measures taken to implement food policy are regulation of private trade and of bank advances against foodgrain stocks and a ban on forward trading in grains.

The issue prices at which foodgrain stocks are distributed to fair price shops are lower than the average cost of the grain to the government. The difference is treated as subsidy. Whenever procurement prices are raised, a question arises as to whether and to what extent the increase is to be passed on to consumers. Raising the issue price affects the cost of living of people in other sectors of the economy. Where wages are linked to cost of living, they also will have to be raised. If the issue prices are not raised, the implicit food subsidy to be borne by the public exchequer goes up. By 1980-81 the total budgetary burden of foodgrain operations in India had risen to a staggering Rs 6.6 billion (US$ 840 million), including consumer subsidy and cost of buffer stock operations. In that year foodgrain subsidy represented about 5 percent of the total revenue expenditure of the central government (George 1985).[11]

Buffer Stocks

Buffer stocks are maintained, built out of internally procured grain supplemented by imports in years of shortfall in production, to even out fluctuations in supplies and prices. A conceptual distinction needs to be drawn between buffer and operational stocks, though a physical distinction is neither necessary nor feasible. As there are two main crop seasons in most of the country, and three in some parts, market arrivals, government procurement, the offtake from the public distribution system, and levels of government stocks vary from month to month.

There are several arguments against building up large buffer stocks. First, large funds are locked up in stocks, large investments are needed for storage construction, operating costs are high, and stocks are likely to deteriorate unless there is adequate turnover. A technical group set up by the government of India in April 1981 recommended buffer stocks of 10 million tons, including 5 million tons of rice and 5 million tons of wheat, over and above the operational stocks needed for running the public distribution system, which may vary between 6.5 and 11.4 million tons at different times of the year. The total stocks with central and state governments on 1 July were 22.5 million tons in 1984 and 29.2 million tons in 1985 (India

11. The figures are exclusive of interest foregone because of concessional rates allowed to FCI by banks on foodgrain trade and on working capital provided by the government.

1985a). It is true that these stock levels are excessive and expensive to maintain, and concerted efforts are necessary to reduce them by utilizing them for food-for-work or other programs to raise the consumption level of the poor.[12]

PRICE POLICY FOR COMMODITIES OTHER THAN FOODGRAINS

The APC also advises the government on price policy for cotton, jute, sugarcane, tobacco, potatoes, onions, groundnuts, rapeseed, and mustard, soybean, and sunflower seed. These prices are often minimum support prices. The principles adopted for determining prices for these crops are similar to those for foodgrains. Additional considerations include the relationships between the prices of raw materials and manufactured products, price behavior in international markets, etc. The agencies for procurement of these commodities were not as effective as those for foodgrains. The Cotton Corporation of India and the Jute Corporation of India were established to ensure fair prices to producers. The proportion of the crops handled by the two was initially small, though it has increased in recent years. In the case of potatoes and onions also, government intervention has helped to bring a considerable degree of stability in prices at harvest time.

Statutory minimum prices are fixed for sugarcane. Actual prices payable by factories to farmers are higher than these minimum prices. Under the dual pricing arrangements for sugar, a certain proportion of the output is procured by public agencies, or agencies designated by the government, at prices linked to statutory minimum prices. The remaining supplies are disposed of by the factories at market prices. The supplies procured by the government are distributed at fixed prices through approved public distribution channels.

LESSONS FROM THE INDIAN EXPERIENCE

Incentive prices in the form of minimum support prices are essential to the success of agricultural production programs based on high-yielding-varieties technology. At the same time, undue reliance cannot be placed on high prices alone as an incentive for increasing production of foodgrains, especially when shortages are widespread. Effective implementation of price support policies requires adequate institutional arrangements for the purchase of quantities offered for sale at that price. At the same time, the

12. Alternatives to large buffer stocks such as foreign exchange buffer funds and/or option forward dealings are often suggested; these are not considered here, as the stocks now held by the government arise out of purchases under price support operations.

foodgrain consumption needs of the vulnerable sections of the population have to be met through appropriate public distribution systems. These supplies may have to be sold at prices below the economic cost. This implies subsidization.

Procurement and public distribution are in fact two sides of the same coin. A public distribution system can be effectively maintained through domestic procurement of grain at reasonable prices. Quantities procured through price support operations find an outlet through the public distribution system. To even out the supplies between good and bad years and ensure price stability, buffer stock policies are essential to prudent food management. Imports do not provide a complete answer in bad crop years, particularly in countries with severe foreign exchange constraints. Although large buffer stocks are expensive to operate, these costs must be weighed against the gains to society from mitigation of the hardships caused by supply and price instabilities.

In India, institutional support for implementation of price policy is provided by the Agricultural Prices Commission and the Food Corporation of India. The former plays an advisory role to the government in price determination. The latter assists in coordinated implementation of procurement, distribution, and buffer stock policies and functions in a manner somewhat similar to that of BULOG in Indonesia (see chapter 5). Both the Indian and Indonesian experiences suggest that public intervention in the foodgrains market requires considerable administrative resources and analytical support.

Annex: Systems of procurement of foodgrains, 1981–82

Rice/Paddy[a]

Andhra Pradesh
Levy on millers/dealers at 50 percent.
Levy on movement of paddy outside the state at 50 percent.

Assam
Levy on millers at 50 percent or 2,500 quintals in lump sum.
Levy on wholesalers at 35 percent or 1,000 quintals in lump sum.

Gujarat
Levy on millers/dealers at 50 percent.

Haryana
Levy on millers/dealers at the following rates:
    Common and fine variety at 90 percent
    Superfine variety at 75 percent

Karnataka
Levy on millers/dealers at 50 percent.
Levy on movement of paddy outside the state at 70 percent.

Kerala
Graded at levy on producers of paddy.

Madhya Pradesh
Levy on millers/dealers at 60 percent.
Levy on movement of paddy outside the state at 60 percent.

Punjab
Levy on millers/dealers at the following rates:
  Common variety at 90 percent
  Fine and superfine variety at 75 percent

Rajasthan
Levy on millers/dealers at 50 percent.

Tamil Nadu
Levy on wholesalers at 50 percent.

Uttar Pradesh
Levy on millers/dealers at 60 percent, 40 percent in certain districts.

West Bengal
Levy on millers/wholesalers at 60 percent.[b]

Chandigarh
Levy on millers/dealers at the following rates:
  Common variety at 90 percent
  Fine and superfine variety at 75 percent

Delhi
Levy on millers/dealers at 75 percent.

Wheat

Madhya Pradesh
Levy on traders of wheat at 50 percent.[c]
Persons intending to export wheat outside the state are required to deliver an equivalent quantity of wheat to the state government.

Delhi
Persons intending to export wheat outside the Union Territory are required to deliver an equivalent quantity of wheat to the Union Territory Administration.

Coarse Grains

In most of the producing states, coarse grains are procured under price support operations. However, during the year under report, the government of Madhya Pradesh imposed a 25 percent levy on the movement of maize and jowar out of the state. The levy, however, was withdrawn on 21 April 1982.

Source: India 1982b.
[a]In rice-producing states during Kharif Season, 1981–82.
[b]Levy reduced to 40 percent w.e.f. 1 April 1982.
[c]Levy withdrawn w.e.f. 7 August 1981.

III

PRODUCTION RESPONSE, TECHNOLOGY, AND COMMERCIALIZATION

10

Capital Accumulation, the Choice of Techniques, and Agricultural Output

YAIR MUNDLAK

Economic growth is achieved largely through capital accumulation and technical change. However, these two processes are not independent. Generation of technical change requires resources and in this sense can be considered to be an investment activity, as is recognized by calling cumulative investment in nonphysical capital "human capital." The implication is that the rate of growth of the economy depends, to a large degree, on the rate of capital accumulation. This chapter will discuss some aspects of the structure of this interdependence between capital accumulation and technical change. The emphasis will be on agriculture, but many of the propositions are of a general nature.

As a background for the discussion, reference is made to the green revolution. A recent empirical study by Bhalla, Alagh, and Sharme (1984) of foodgrains growth in India based on district data provides empirical evidence for some of the propositions developed here. In comparing production changes from the period 1962–65 (pre-green revolution) to 1970–73, a period when the new technology in Indian agriculture was well established, the authors conclude that the introduction of HYV has required capital inputs, that it is capital-intensive in the sense that it increases the share of capital inputs in total output, and that it represents technical change in that it increases yields and increases the productivities of all inputs including labor, whose factor share declines. Most important, it has taken a long time, and after twenty years it is far from being completed.

There is no comprehensive framework that can produce all these results. The reason is that most of the work on the production side of the economy is based on the concept of a production function. As such, the empirical evidence quoted above is dealt with under the rubric of labor-saving technical change. That is, the production function changes by factor augmentation to yield higher capital-labor ratios under given prices. Under such an analysis the production function changes, but at any time there is only one. Thus coexistence can be considered as a transitional phenomenon resulting from imperfect knowledge, but this explanation cannot account for the length of time required to introduce the modern techniques and for geographical variations. The green revolution is considered here as an example—indeed, a very important one. Another example would be the motorization of agriculture. Motorized agriculture represents a different technology from non-motorized and has also taken a long time to be implemented.

The point of departure is the recognition that at any time there are numerous production functions. Basically, a production function is a micro-concept; it describes the input-output relationship of what is referred to here as a technique. Thus, traditional agriculture and HYV agriculture are distinct techniques described by two distinct production functions. The production function that describes a technique relates changes in output to some changes in the inputs, holding some of the variables—such as plant variety or soil type—constant. The variables that are held constant are discrete.

The collection of all the available techniques at a particular time is referred to as technology. A change in the collection is referred to as technical change. Not all the techniques that are available are actually implemented at any time. It is, therefore, useful to distinguish between the available and the implemented technology. The foregoing comments on the relationships between technical change and capital accumulation refer to the effect of capital accumulation on the determination of the implemented technology. The framework of Danin and Mundlak (1979) is used for the choice of technique. It begins with the supply side of the economy, followed by the discussion of the choice under equilibrium of supply and demand.

For simplicity of exposition it is assumed that agricultural technology consists of two techniques, "traditional" and "modern," denoted as 1 and 2, respectively. They are represented by well-behaved production functions, displaying constant returns to scale in the inputs. For purpose of graphical illustration, we assume that there are only two factors, labor (L) and capital (K). Alternatively, this can be viewed as a presentation of the aggregate production function.[1] The unit isoquants of the two techniques are shown in figure 10.1. The curve denoted by $Y_1 = 1$ represents the various combinations of labor and capital that result in a unit output generated by the traditional technique. A similar interpretation applies for the modern technique, as represented by $Y_2 = 1$. Note that the curves are

1. In this connection we ignore the conceptual problem of input aggregation. The qualitative nature of the results is unaffected by the form of aggregation. Thus, capital is considered as an aggregate of all components including working capital. The generalization to more than two inputs is straightforward (Mundlak 1984).

Figure 10.1 A convex combination of two techniques

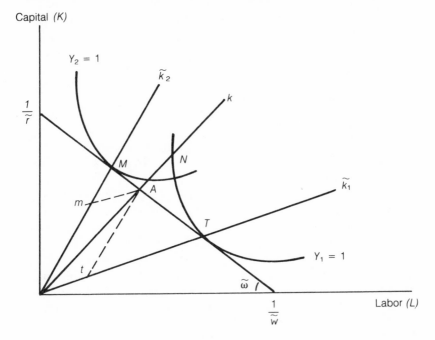

drawn in such a way that the modern technique is considered to be more capital-intensive.

The choice of techniques by an individual farmer in the situation described in figure 10.1 depends on the ratio of wage rate (w) to rental rate on capital (r). At a low wage-rental ratio, $\omega = w/r$, the labor-intensive traditional technique has a lower cost of production, and therefore the modern technique will not be employed. Conversely, for a relatively high wage-rental ratio, only the modern technique is used. Under a weak assumption with respect to the behavior of the isoquants, there exists a value $\tilde{\omega}$ for the wage rental ratio at which the cost of production of the two techniques is the same. This is shown in figure 10.1 by the isocost line with slope $\tilde{\omega}$ tangent to the two isoquants. Thus, at $\tilde{\omega}$ the two techniques are equally efficient. Consequently, the farmer is indifferent to the choice of technique. He can use the traditional technique with capital-labor ratio $\tilde{k}_1 = k_1(\tilde{\omega})$ or the modern technique with a capital-labor ratio $\tilde{k}_2 = k_2(\tilde{\omega})$ or a combination of the two techniques. The values $\tilde{k}_1$ and $\tilde{k}_2$ are the input ratios that correspond to $\tilde{\omega}$ of the traditional and modern techniques, respectively.

Turning from an individual farmer to agriculture at large, let figure

10.1 represent agricultural technology. The factor endowment is summarized by the capital-labor ratio, $k = K/L$, which is shown as the slope of the ray through A. The wage-rental ratio is now determined as the slope of the isoquant for the given k. The question is which is the relevant isoquant. For a sufficiently low capital-labor ratio, specifically $k < \tilde{k}_1$, only the traditional technique will be employed. In this case ω will be determined by the slope of the isoquant of the traditional technique evaluated at k, and by construction, for $k < \tilde{k}_1$ we have $\omega(k) < \bar{\omega}_1$. Conversely, for $k \geq \tilde{k}_2$, $\omega(k) \geq \bar{\omega}_2$. In those two cases agriculture specializes in one of the two techniques. Consequently, the two techniques coexist when $\tilde{k}_1 \leq k \leq \tilde{k}_2$. In this sense, $\tilde{k}_1$ and $\tilde{k}_2$ can be viewed as threshold values.

Under the assumption of full employment, the intensity of utilization of the individual techniques is determined by k, $\tilde{k}_1$, and $\tilde{k}_2$. This can be shown graphically by drawing a parallelogram. Thus, in terms of figure 10.1, when the economy produces at A, m represents the proportion of output generated by the modern technique, and the complement, $t = 1 - m$, comes from the traditional technique.[2]

While the threshold values ($\tilde{k}_1$, $\tilde{k}_2$) are determined solely by the technology, k reflects capital accumulation. Thus, as the choice of techniques depends on k, it will change with capital accumulation that leads to an increase in k. Given full employment in agriculture, the intensity of utilization of the modern technique increases with k at the expense of the traditional technique; that is, the proportions of labor and capital employed in the modern technique increase or, alternatively, the proportion of agricultural output generated by the modern technique increases. This can be shown graphically by moving point A to the left along the cost line and drawing a new parallelogram.[3]

This simple analysis has a very important implication. Capital accumulation leads to the employment of capital-intensive techniques. In general, we view the modern techniques to be capital-intensive. Consequently, their relative importance increases with capital accumulation. The converse is also true. It is impossible to increase the relative importance of the modern techniques without capital accumulation. This result is established here in a partial analysis of agriculture, considering only the supply side. This is also true when the whole economy is considered and demand is taken into consideration.

---

2. The assumption of full employment of K and L can be expressed as $k = lk_1 + (1 - l)k_2$, where $l = L_1/L$ is the proportion of the agricultural labor force allocated to the traditional technique.

3. Analytically, solve for l from the full employment conditions given in n. 2 above and note that we deal with the case of coexistence, so that $k_i = \tilde{k}_i$, $i = 1, 2$. $l = (\tilde{k}_2 - k)/(\tilde{k}_2 - \tilde{k}_1)$. Consequently, $dl/dk < 0$.

THE ECONOMY

To extend the analysis to the economy as a whole, it is necessary to show how techniques are selected along its equilibrium path. This is the path of points at which supply and demand are equated. A point on the equilibrium path is represented here by the intersection of the transformation curve and a properly defined demand curve. To simplify the analysis, nonagriculture is aggregated into one sector, and it is assumed that it uses only one technique. Also, without a loss in generality, it is assumed that nonagriculture is more capital-intensive, so that its capital-labor ratio (k_I) is larger than that of agriculture (k_A); specifically it is assumed that $k_I(\omega) > k_2(\omega) > k_1(\omega)$.

The resulting transformation curve is shown in figure 10.2, with points T, A, and M marked on it. The curve is divided into segments identified by the utilized techniques. At low levels of agricultural production, only the traditional technique is used, but at a high level of output only the modern technique is used. In between is the region where both techniques are used. Designate the price of the agricultural product in terms of the nonagricultural as p. Then, the segment representing coexistence of techniques corresponds to a constant price, $\bar{p}$. To show the relationship between agricultural output and the price p, the supply function is drawn in the lefthand panel of the figure. When the two techniques coexist, it is possible to increase agricultural output without increasing prices. This, however, re-

Figure 10.2   The appearance of a new technique and the transformation curve

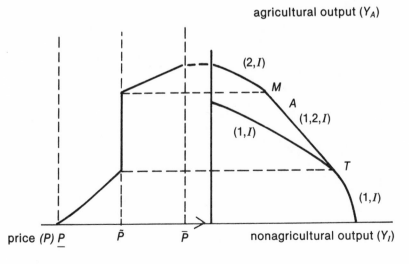

agricultural output (Y_A)

price *(P)* $\underline{P}$ $\tilde{P}$ $\bar{P}$ nonagricultural output (Y_I)

quires a shift of resources from non-agriculture to agriculture and therefore a decline in nonagricultural output (Y_I).

A transformation curve is drawn in figure 10.2 for the same economy without modern technology. Obviously, this is an inferior situation to an economy whose output plan is to the left of T.

The next step is to introduce demand functions. When there are only two products, the income consumption curve contains all the information on the demand in the economy. This curve is drawn in figure 10.3 for price $\bar{p}$ in such a way that the demand for the agricultural product x_A is expressed as a function of the demand for the nonagricultural product, x_I. When the two products are normal, the curve is ever-increasing with respect to the two axes. The economy is initially at point A where the two techniques coexist. With capital accumulation, the transformation curve shifts outward and the equilibrium point moves from A to E, where the price remains unchanged. Consequently, capital accumulation produces only income effect and no price effect. Therefore, the increase in sectoral outputs is proportional to the income elasticities. When the two products are normal, both increase with capital accumulation. Such a joint increase in production requires a decline in the relative importance of the traditional technique. To see this, we note that the price at A and E is the same, so the capital-labor ratios $\bar{k}_1$, $\bar{k}_2$, and $\bar{k}_I$ must also be the same. Then the only way to increase nonagricultural output with prices held constant is to

Figure 10.3   Product composition under capital accumulation and coexistence of techniques

agricultural
output (Y_A)

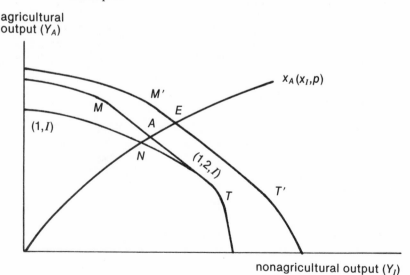

nonagricultural output (Y_I)

shift resources from agriculture to non-agriculture. But at the same time, it is required that agricultural output also increase. This can happen only if the traditional technique in agriculture is replaced by the modern technique. Such a shift will cause an increase in the agricultural capital-labor ratio. It can thus be concluded that capital accumulation which takes place when the two techniques coexist in agriculture generates a shift of resources away from the traditional technique. It should be noted that the result is achieved for an economy that is always in a short-run equilibrium and as such reflects both demand and supply conditions.[4]

RATE OF IMPLEMENTATION OF NEW TECHNIQUES

The main point of the foregoing discussion is that an introduction of new capital-intensive techniques is subject to capital constraint, and therefore its rate of adoption depends on the rate of capital accumulation. It is clear that the introduction of a new technique in an important sector of the economy may take time.

To relate this finding to other treatments of the adoption of new techniques, refer to figure 10.1. Assume that when the modern technique is introduced, the capital-labor ratio is k and the economy is initially located at point N. Obviously, after the introduction of the modern technique, the efficient production plan is changed from N to A.

The question generally asked is what determines the pace of movement from N to A, but our concern has been the movement from T to A. In other words, we have dealt with movements *along* a newly formed efficiency frontier, whereas the movements from N to A can be interpreted as a movement *toward* this frontier. The determinants of the pace of such a movement often given in the literature can be classified as those related to heterogeneity of capital and those related to uncertainty and imperfect knowledge.

In the foregoing discussion, it was implicitly assumed that capital goods are homogenous, so that horses and tractors are the same thing. Eliminating this simplification and recognizing that capital goods are heterogenous introduces another dimension into the discussion. If the two techniques in question require different forms of capital, the pace of movement from N to A will be determined by the ease of changing the composition of the capital stock. In general, the capital good associated with the traditional technique disappears through obsolescence or discard while the introduction of the capital good associated with new technique is determined by

4. There are other possibilities where, at the initial or the end equilibrium point, there is a specialization in a single technique. These are not interesting cases from the point of view of applications and therefore are not discussed here.

gross investment. Consequently, the rate of implementation of the new technique will be determined by the rate of *gross* investment, whereas the decline in the traditional technique will depend on the rate of disappearance of the capital good associated with it. Thus, the movement from N to A would imply a gradual reduction of the capital-labor ratio in the traditional technique from k to $\bar{k}_1$. In this process ω will gradually decline from its level at N, as determined by the traditional technique, to $\bar{\omega}$.

The essence of the argument on heterogeneity of capital is that the two techniques may require different compositions of the various capital goods. If this is the case, a change in the composition of the two techniques will result in a change in the composition of the various capital goods. If this process takes the economy off the efficiency frontier, the pace of the return to the frontier will depend on gross investment.

So far we have treated the modern technique as new and completely unrelated to the traditional one. In subsequent discussion, we comment on the economics of generating techniques. However, from a strictly formal point of view, once the new technique is available, it can be expressed as if it were obtained by some change of the traditional production function. Doing so may help us to utilize known results related to various forms of technical change. This, however, is of only limited value, as it does not explain the coexistence of techniques and the determinants of their implementation.

However, incorporating some known forms of technical change helps isolate the importance of the various determinants. Start by assuming that the modern technique is obtained simply by a Hicks neutral technical change in the traditional technique.[5] In this case, there is no difference in the threshold values, $\bar{k}_1 = \bar{k}_2$, the new technique completely dominates the old, and it is therefore disadvantageous to employ them simultaneously. Yet if the two techniques use different capital goods, there will be a transition period during which the two techniques will be used simultaneously. A special case of this is in the embodiment hypothesis developed by Solow (1963). Under this hypothesis, the new technique is embodied in a new capital good, say, a machine, which cannot be applied with the old machine. Consequently, the rate of introduction of the new technique will depend on the rate of *gross* investment rather than net investment. Thus, the traditional technique will disappear eventually, even if net investment is nil.

The situation is somewhat different when the modern technique is generated by a factor augmenting technical change in the traditional technique. In contrast to the previous case, such a change generates a difference in the threshold value so that $\bar{k}_2 > \bar{k}_1$. In this case, if $\bar{k}_2$ exceeds the

5. Technical change that does not affect factor shares at given factor prices.

available capital-labor ratio, the rate of implementation will eventually depend on net investment. Thus, if the economy does not accumulate capital, it will not discard the traditional technique.

Another reason for coexistence of techniques is uncertainty or lack of knowledge. The new technique may be superior, but firms do not know it and may require time to sample it. During this period, the various techniques will coexist. The search process requires resources. At the farm level, the resources devoted to the search depend on their cost (Kislev and Shchori-Bachrach 1973; Feder and Slade 1984). At the industry level, the cost depends on the availability of such resources. The result of a search by a farmer depends on the time that he allocates to the search and to his ability to digest it. The latter, as Schultz (1968) postulated, depends on the level of education. Hence, the speed of implementation which reflects imperfect knowledge is also positively related to capital in the form of human capital.

GENERATION OF NEW TECHNIQUES

Firms, private or public, which spend resources on research and development generally have choices of research strategy. For our discussion, the key variable is the capital intensity of the new techniques. The foregoing indicated that capital accumulation generates demand for capital-intensive techniques. Thus, the producers of techniques should aim at the development of capital-intensive rather than labor-intensive techniques. However, overshooting is counterproductive. Since the rate of implementation depends on the rate of capital accumulation, the threshold level of the new techniques should not be too high. Otherwise, the market for them will be very limited.

This story can be told by looking at the firm level. In the absence of a new capital-intensive technique, capital accumulation increases the capital-labor ratios, thus increasing real wages and decreasing the real rate on capital. Thus, the owners of capital will be interested in investing their capital in techniques that prevent the rate of return from falling. This generates the demand for the capital-intensive techniques.

By its very nature this process leads to a decline in the labor share (S_L) and as such can be considered as laborsaving. For a constant return to scale production function in K and L we can define the following function of labor share: $\Theta = \omega/k = wL/rK = S_L/1 - S_L$. Θ is monotonically increasing with S_L. Referring to figure 10.1, the movement from T to A increases k with ω held constant. Consequently Θ, and therefore S_L, decline. The transition from N to A implies a decline in ω under a constant k which again results in a decline of the labor share.

For the purpose of simplification, we have dealt with two techniques, traditional and modern. The appearance of additional techniques can be handled in a very similar fashion. One case, however, is worthy of examination, the case of Hicks neutral technical change in the modern technique. We have a purpose in selecting the modern technique to be the subject of the Hicks neutral technical change. It has been argued that the process of capital accumulation causes a shift in the direction of capital-intensive techniques. Then, other things being equal, the demand will call for the improvement of the modern techniques. In a more detailed framework, the cost of producing and changing techniques, as well as the required research time, should be introduced. If the required time is significant, by the time the research is completed the traditional technique may not be important. Therefore, efforts will be directed at increasing the productivity of the modern techniques. This consideration has a dynamic aspect. With time, the modern techniques become traditional, and, since the easy gains might have already been made, additional gains may be subject to increasing cost. Thus, both from the demand side and the supply side, it is likely that the effort to improve an existing technique will be aimed at the modern techniques.

An improvement in the productivity of a technique should increase its utilization. This is illustrated graphically in figure 10.4. The initial tech-

Figure 10.4   Choice of techniques under Hicks neutral technical change in the modern technique

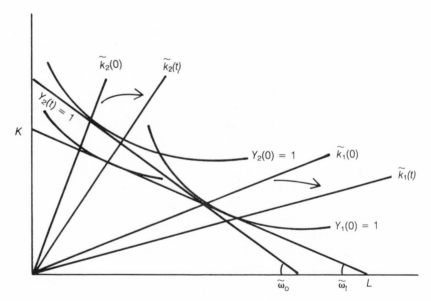

niques are represented by $Y_1(0)$ and $Y_2(0)$ with threshold values $\bar{k}_1(0)$ and $\bar{k}_2(0)$. Neutral technical change in the modern technique shifts its unit isoquant to $Y_2(t) = 1$. The threshold values decline accordingly to $\bar{k}_2(t)$ and $\bar{k}_1(t)$. For any value of k, the importance of the traditional variety declines.[6] The net effect of this change is again laborsaving. Thus, we have a situation where the net effect of a Hicks neutral technical change is laborsaving.

The foregoing discussion describes the changes in technology that are called for by the process of capital accumulation. They apply to all sectors of the economy. The reference to the work of Bhalla, Alagh, and Sharma (1984) at the beginning of this chapter illustrates their relevance to an understanding of the changes brought about by the green revolution.

EMPIRICAL IMPLICATIONS

The present framework has a variety of empirical implications. In discussing them it is helpful to represent the two techniques in terms of their input-output relationships rather than isoquants. Assuming constant returns to scale in terms of capital and labor, the average labor productivities are functions of the capital-labor ratios which are drawn in figure 10.5. The points on this figure correspond to those with the same designations in figure 10.1. Corresponding to figure 10.1, the envelope is identical with $f_1(k_1)$ for $k \leq \bar{k}_1$; it moves along the segment TM for $\bar{k}_1 \leq k \leq \bar{k}_2$; and thereafter, for $k \geq \bar{k}_2$ it becomes identical with $f_2(k_2)$.[7]

The scope for increasing average labor productivity in agriculture for such an economy consists of capital accumulation in agriculture and the introduction of new techniques which are not excessively demanding in terms of their capital requirements. To determine the role of prices it is necessary to distinguish between equilibrium and disequilibrium analysis. Both the foregoing and the following discussion are largely within the framework of equilibrium analysis. Introducing disequilibrium in the factor market will introduce additional complications but will not change the nature of the results.

The real factor prices (prices in terms of the product) are determined by the production function, and are shown in figure 10.5. Consequently, for agricultural technology which consists only of the traditional technique, the movement from T to N will imply an increase in the real wage w/p and

6. This can be shown analytically by writing the ratio of labor employed in the modern to that of the traditional technique as: $1 - l/l = k - \bar{k}_1/\bar{k}_2 - k$. This ratio is increased when both threshold values decline, as should be expected. In fact, it can be shown that, for a given k, this is the only way that $1 - l$ can increase.

7. In the literature on agricultural development, following Hayami and Ruttan (1971), the envelope production function is referred to as a meta production function.

Figure 10.5 Average labor productivity and the choice of techniques

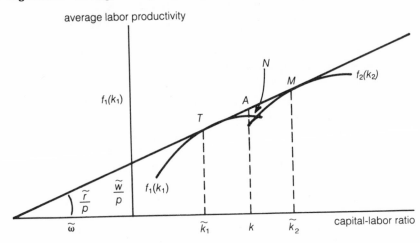

a decline in the real rate of return on capital, r/p. The introduction of the modern technique into agriculture facilitates the movement from N to A and thereby simultaneously increases average labor productivity and rental on capital and decreases the wage rate and the labor share. All this is basically a restatement of our previous isoquant analysis and is consistent with the empirical evidence set forth by Bhalla, Alagh, and Sharma (1984).

Once point A, or any other point on segment TM, is reached, average productivity increases only with capital accumulation, with constant factor prices. This process continues until the traditional technique is completely abandoned, as indicated by point M.

Capital accumulation in the economy at large reflects saving behavior and as such may be responsive to the rate of return on capital. In this discussion the interest is in sectoral analysis, and overall capital accumulation is taken as given. The intersectoral allocation of the capital stock is done mainly through new investment. It is assumed that the share of agriculture in total investment is positively related to the ratio of the rate of return in agriculture to that in the rest of the economy. Empirical support for this assumption can be found in the analysis of the Argentinian experience by Cavallo and Mundlak (1982). Similar results are obtained by the yet unpublished work of Coeymans and Mundlak for Chile and by Mundlak and Strauss (Mundlak 1979) for Japan, through the use of the flow of funds equation.

The introduction of the modern technique and the movement from point N to segment TM increases the rate of return in agriculture, and agricultural investment should increase accordingly. This then increases the rate of capital accumulation in agriculture and speeds up the implementation of the new technique.

This assumption is substantiated by the data for the Punjab, as demonstrated in figure 10.6, which shows the number of private tubewells and electricity and fertilizer consumption. It can be seen that these variables increased very rapidly from the mid-sixties once the opportunities of the high-yielding varieties were recognized.

The increase in the capital-labor ratio in agriculture is achieved not only by capital accumulation but also by the drain of labor from agriculture. The drain should be interpreted as a growth of the agricultural labor force at a rate lower than the increase in the total labor force. Thus, if the economy were in a steady state, where the overall capital-labor ratio remains constant, such a drain of labor from agriculture would increase the agricultural capital-labor ratio.

So far, the analysis has dealt only with the supply side of the economy.

Figure 10.6   Index of private tubewells, electricity consumption in agriculture, and fertilizer usage in Punjab, India, 1960–79

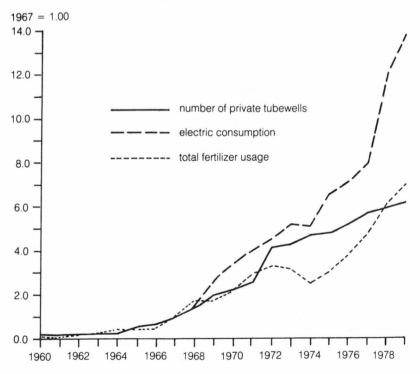

To complete the analysis, demand is now brought in. Again reference is made to figure 10.3 for an illustration of equilibrium determination in a closed economy. Prior to the introduction of the modern technique, the economy is located at N. After the introduction the economy moves in the direction of A merely by reallocating existing resources. Such a move involves an increase in agricultural and nonagricultural outputs and a decline in agricultural price. The decline in price is shown in two steps, first $P_N > P_T$, since they are both on the same transformation curve, and second, $P_T = P_A$ by construction. Therefore, $P_N > P_A$. Although this result may seem strange, it conforms to the data. For instance, taking the ratio of prices received by farmers to that of prices paid by farmers as an approximation of the agricultural price relative to the nonagricultural price, we find that in 1977 the ratio in the United States was 66 percent of the 1910–14 average, and in Australia it was at 56 percent of the 1961–63 average. A similar trend is observed for most other countries (FAO 1977).

Obviously a single-equation empirical analysis of supply with such data would show negative supply elasticities. This would be misleading in the sense that the movement from N to A is the net result of changes in supply and demand. The movement is initiated by the technical change, which has a direct effect on the agricultural supply. If the demand remained constant, such a change would have identified a demand rather than a supply function. However, the technical change increases income and as such, also causes a shift in the demand curve. Consequently, the curve connecting output and price is neither a supply nor a demand curve. This is an identification problem which requires a more detailed framework for empirical analysis.

The move from N to A was considered under the assumption of no capital accumulation. With capital accumulation the transformation curve moves, and, as indicated above, point E represents an equilibrium point achieved with the augmented capital. Note that the price at E is the same as in A. Consequently, a situation is generated where an increase in output is obtained with price held constant. This represents a perfectly elastic supply and this indeed is what figure 10.2 indicates. But such a situation is contrary to all the empirical evidence on supply response. Yet there is no inconsistency between this framework and the known empirical results.

To dramatize the situation, suppose that the economy in question is an open rather than a closed economy and is at point T where the price is $p_T = \tilde{p}$. Suppose that the international price increases to p. Under the new price, the economy should adjust to a new equilibrium point to the left of M. Such an adjustment requires a substantial shift of resources from nonagriculture to agriculture. Such a high mobilization of resources does not occur for the following reasons. As already discussed above, the intersectoral allocation of capital is done largely through gross investment. A dramatic change in the share of agriculture in the capital stock thus may require many years to accomplish. Similarly, as the empirical analysis of off-farm migration indicates, this process is also time-consuming (Mundlak 1979). Thus it may take a long time for the response to materialize. However, it will materialize provided the price remains at the new level. But will the price remain stable? The movement from T to M indicates a major change in supply. That could only be absorbed by a corresponding decline in price; therefore, the new price is not sustainable. In a narrow sense, this argument does not apply to a small, open economy. However, agricultural technology is, in general, a public good, and other countries having a similar technology are expected to respond in the same way. The best example is the HYV of grains which are used all over. The world is a closed economy, and therefore prices decline, as argued above. By this argument, point M will not be reached unless the demand justifies production at M. The mechanism of stopping short of M can either be rational expectation on the part of farmers or simply trial and error. Since the resource adjustment consistent with the movement from T to M is timeconsuming, somewhere in the adjustment process prices will start falling and the process will terminate. It is clear that the response of agriculture to annual variations in prices is going to be weak. This is postulated as a reason for the weak supply response often obtained in empirical analyses. Yet this framework suggests that when techniques coexist the response to expected long-run prices is rather strong.

The whole discussion was conducted under the simplifying assumption of a single agricultural product. In reality, any region can grow a variety of products. Some of these utilize the same resources, and the adjustment in such cases is easier and faster. Consequently, a stronger response is expected to price variations of short duration. This is consistent with empirical analyses which report stronger response for individual crops than for aggregate outputs.

Another simplifying assumption made above is that there are no intermediate products or raw materials. The introduction of such inputs into the analysis have several dimensions. In the case of a closed economy, an increase in the demand for such inputs requires adjustments in the nonagricultural sector of the same nature as those discussed above. For instance, the increase in the demand for fertilizers brought about by the green revolution required a shift of resources to augment the production capacity of the fertilizer industry. During such a process, fertilizer availability becomes a constraint to the increase of agricultural output. This point was discussed by Desai (1982). For an open economy, the adjustment may be faster if there are no foreign exchange constraints. But again, if the same technology is spreading all over the world and there is no excess capacity, a similar delay would be expected.

The case of energy is somewhat different in that there is no availability problem, only a price problem. Thus, when the price of energy increases, it affects more strongly the price of the techniques which are energy-intensive. In terms of our graphical analysis, this can be considered as a technical decline. In this case, instead of output, the figures should report value added. An increase in the price of energy (or any other raw material) decreases the value added. Thus, applying the results stated above with respect to Hicks neutral technical change, the intensity of the use of the energy-intensive technique will decline.

If we allow for the fact that agricultural production utilizes raw materials, and that those can be changed faster than capital and labor, we can expect some price response.

To conclude the argument on supply response to prices for aggregate output subject to demand constraints, we have distinguished three major cases: (1) technical change in the form of a new technique generating an increase in output and a decline in price; (2) an increase in capital with constant technology of coexisting techniques generating an increase in output under constant prices; (3) an increase in the price ratio of output to raw materials generating a positive supply response. (However, this last response reflects the importance of the raw materials in total cost and as such will not be very strong.) Empirical analyses which do not differentiate between these effects will result in some mixture. This mixture will also reflect the fact that the response is largely to expected rather than to observed prices.

Yet it has been suggested that with the technology under consideration, a strong supply response can be expected to result in permanent price changes, but that this may take a long time. Can this claim be substantiated? As indicated above, empirical analysis of the process of intersectoral resource allocation does indeed indicate that the *rate* of allocation is price-responsive in the anticipated direction. Integrating labor migration and investment allocation with the production structure will produce the output response.

There is, however, another way to derive some evidence on the supply response as well as on some of the considerations just mentioned. It is noted that technical change affects farm income in a way similar to prices. Consequently, a 1 percent increase in yield affects income almost to the same degree as a 1 percent change in price. The word "almost" is used because an increase in yield does increase harvest and handling cost. Thus the variable that farmers respond to should be the expected revenue ($AR = p \times$ yield $\times c$), where c is a fraction to adjust for the extra harvest cost (cf. Mundlak and McCorkle 1956). AR increases with technical change and, as such, has a permanent component which should guide farmers' decisions. Preliminary empirical results indicate that AR produces higher elasticities than prices in acreage response equations.

CONCLUSIONS, POLICY IMPLICATIONS, AND SCOPE

The discussion has centered on the role of capital accumulation in the introduction and implementation of technical change. It has been argued that in the event of capital accumulation there will be a tendency for technical change to take the form of capital-intensive techniques. A major outcome of the analysis is that such technical change cannot be implemented without capital accumulation.

Capital is broadly interpreted. It represents the resources that the economy diverts at any period from present consumption in order to increase its production in the future. The capital goods produced by such diverted resources include physical as well as nonphysical components such as education, research, extension, or, briefly, human capital. The conclusion, then, is that an increase in the rate of capital accumulation should foster growth.

The rate of capital accumulation depends on private saving behavior, on the behavior of the public sector (government saving), and on foreign saving (borrowing from abroad). A detailed discussion of these components is beyond the scope of this chapter. However, it is important to note that foreign borrowing may be helpful if it is properly used. Recent experiences of some countries indicate that it can be misused. In what follows, it is assumed that resources are used efficiently.

Taking the overall capital constraint of the country as given, agricultural growth will depend on the generation of new techniques and on the resources available for their implementation. Policies that extract resources from agriculture will have a negative effect on agricultural growth, and the opposite is true for policies which facilitate the flow of resources into agriculture. That of course, assumes that agriculture continues to have a flow of new techniques that can be implemented efficiently. We have used the HYV as an example of growth constrained by capital availability. In this case, capital takes the form of irrigation facilities, fertilizers, insecticides, roads, and nonphysical items such as domestic research, extension, and general level of schooling.

Some of the investment necessary for the expansion of agricultural output is generally performed by the public sector. These funds are mainly directed at investment in infrastructure. Investment on farms is largely private, although in part it might benefit from subsidized finance. Assuming rational behavior, the higher the profitability of new investment, the larger the investment will be. Therefore, the price system has an important role in influencing the rate of accumulation and therefore on technical change in agriculture. The response may be slow but it is there. Thus policies directed at the taxation of agriculture are likely to have a serious cost in terms of agricultural growth, as was the case in Argentina (Cavallo and Mundlak 1982).

In the foregoing analysis land was suppressed by assuming the agricultural production function to be constant returns to scale in capital and labor. The introduction of land would complicate the analysis without changing the main conclusion. However, the conclusion can now be extended. The size of a country is given, and that determines the size of the available land. Land varies by quality. The size of the cultivated land depends on the returns on land and on the cost of bringing more land under cultivation. These factors depend on prices and on capital availability. The return on the marginal land is zero; that is, output is absorbed by inputs other than land.

This has two repercussions. First, capital accumulation can be used for expanding the cultivated land. If, however, such an expansion becomes increasingly expensive, it can be expected that techniques will be developed to reduce land expansion. This leads to landsaving technical change, which is analogous to laborsaving technical change. Such an approach can explain the puzzling situation where on small farms the factor share of land is sometimes rather small.[8] The second repercussion is related to the taxation of rent. Sometimes it is claimed that taxing rent, as was the case in Japan, for instance, is neutral in the sense that it should not affect agricultural growth. This approach assumes, at least implicitly, that the size of land is unaffected and that there is only one technique. Obviously imposing a land tax on marginal land will cause it to go out of production. If the investment has already been made, cultivation may continue, but expansion of cultivated land will be affected. As to the choice of techniques, taxing rent will generate a demand for land-intensive techniques, so that the rent on land will decline. That means that the ratio of land to other inputs will increase or, to put it another way, will cause resources to move out of agriculture.

The foregoing conclusions assume that farmers are rational and do utilize changing opportunities. Sometimes this assumption is questioned as a result of failure of empirical analyses to detect supply response to prices. Analysis of the possible reasons for such empirical results indicates that the response should be observed at the level of intersectoral resource flow,

---

8. This question was discussed in Mundlak (1964) with respect to the low factor share of land in family farms in Israel. Such farms are mostly less than four hectares. The explanation given was that in order to overcome the area limitation, farmers moved to products which require little land but are capital-intensive.

and here the empirical evidence quoted above shows that such flows are indeed price-responsive.

The reason why the resource adjustment is not easily observed by direct measurements is that it is slow, whereas the prices vary, and that variations reflect mainly transitory components. To overcome this problem, it is argued that the supply response might be better measured with respect to changes in average revenue.

The discussion was conducted largely within the framework of equilibrium analysis. It also assumes implicitly that the relevant markets exist and function. The analysis is aggregate and deals with a simple world and as such does not answer specific micro questions. That fact, however, should not dilute the conclusions.

A possible extension of the analysis that was not included is related to disequilibrium in the factor markets. Such an extension would require some changes in the analytical framework but again would not change the nature of the conclusions.

From the analytic point of view, the special feature of the analysis is in the structure of production, where the technology is allowed to consist of more than one technique. The concept of a technique is very general indeed and can be used opportunistically according to need. It was indicated above that different products are identified with different techniques. Thus capital accumulation leads to an increase in output of capital-intensive techniques, and thus the process of product cycle known in the literature of international trade is produced.

Alternatively, each firm can be considered as a different technique. Each firm has embodied in it some specific factors which are summarized by the term "entrepreneurial capacity." Entrepreneurs that have a low level of human capital can be identified or represented by capital-extensive techniques. As such they lose ground in the process of capital accumulation. Consequently, the industry will realize a concentration of entrepreneurs with a higher level of human capital. If such entrepreneurs are also more productive, then the exit of firms will increase the productivity of the industry as a whole. Applying this process to agriculture, it is postulated to have contributed to the increase in agricultural productivity in the developed economies (Kislev and Rabiner 1979).

11

Technological Change, Production Costs, and Supply Response

C. G. RANADE, DAYANATHA JHA, and
CHRISTOPHER L. DELGADO

The economic argument for intervention in product or factor markets in the agricultural sector rests largely on the need to provide incentives to producers. A reduction in unit cost of production, made possible by technological change, provides another and perhaps more powerful incentive. Therefore, an understanding of the cost relationships under technological change is crucial for a realistic assessment of the need for market interventions.

The Punjab in India experienced rapid technological change after fertilizer-responsive modern wheat varieties were introduced in the mid-sixties. The gains in production were soon threatened by rising costs in addition to declining real wheat prices. The Punjab data provide some evidence of how farmers adjusted to these changes by adopting more innovations and by trying to maintain and augment returns to the most scarce factor—land. This example illustrates how a responsive research system keeps up the supply of relevant innovations and helps maintain an environment conducive to further productivity gains. Semiarid West Africa provides another example of the evolution of cost of production under technological change in a situation involving a scarcity of labor.

A related issue is the impact of technological change on the response of output to prices. It is argued that by improving productivity of the limiting resource, technological change leads to a more elastic output response which augments the potential effectiveness of producer price policies. Empirical evidence on this hypothesis is sketchy. However, we present some evidence on the impact of technological change on output response for wheat in the Punjab (India) and discuss issues related to output supply response for foodgrains in sub-Saharan Africa.

CHANGES IN COSTS IN THE PUNJAB

The impact of modern varieties of wheat introduced in the mid-sixties on yields and costs in the Punjab is shown in table 11.1. The yield of wheat rose from about 1.1 tons per hectare in the pre-modern-varieties period (1954–57) to nearly 2.7 tons in 1969–70.

Table 11.1 reveals a substantial increase in per hectare costs for almost all inputs except bullock labor from 1954–57 to 1969–70. Total costs in per hectare terms rose by about 73 percent. The cost of purchased inputs (that is, hired human and bullock labor, machines, seed, fertilizers, and irrigation) increased from 2.33 to 7.51 in terms of quintals of wheat per hectare.

Table 11.1 Costs and returns in wheat equivalents for wheat, Punjab (India)

	Output/costs			Share in total cost	
	1954–57	1969–70	1978–79	1969–70	1978–79
	(quintals per hectare)			(percent)	
A. Yield	11.07	26.75	27.49		
B. Costs[a]					
Human labor					
Hired	0.59	2.54	2.68	19.8	15.1
Family	2.08	1.98	1.18	15.4	6.6
Total	2.67	4.52	3.85	35.2	21.7
Bullock labor					
Hired	0.59	0.01	0.01	0.1	0.1
Family	2.22	2.00	1.21	15.6	6.8
Total	2.81	2.01	1.22	15.7	6.9
Machine labor	—	0.95	2.73	7.4	15.4
Seeds	0.64	1.11	1.17	8.6	6.6
Fertilizer, insecticides, and manure	0.15	2.06	4.43	16.0	24.9
Irrigation charges	0.36	0.84	0.85	6.5	4.8
Interest on working and fixed capital & depreciation	0.50	1.23	3.35	9.5	18.9
Miscellaneous	0.28	0.11	0.14	1.0	0.8
C. Total cost	7.41	12.83	17.76	100.0	100.0
	(66.94)[b]	(47.96)	(64.59)		
D. Operator's residual[c] (A − C)	3.66	13.92	9.73		
	(33.06)	(52.04)	(35.41)		

Sources: Data for 1954–57 are from India 1966a; data for 1969–70 are from Kahlon 1971; data for 1978–79 are from Kahlon and Tyagi 1983.

[a] Costs are the current costs per hectare divided by the price of wheat per quintal.

[b] Figures in parentheses represent the percentage share in yield.

[c] Operator's residual is the net return to land and management.

Yet because of higher proportional gain in output, costs per unit of output declined by about 30 percent and operator's residual per unit of land nearly quadrupled. It is clear that no reasonable increase in output price could have generated this kind of incentive environment.

Output increases since then have not been of comparable magnitude. At the same time, costs have increased significantly. Figures for 1978–79 suggest an almost 50 percent increase in costs and a 30 percent decline in operator's residual from 1969–70. Not surprisingly, this has generated considerable pressure for higher producer prices. One should note, however, that changes in the cost structure indicate that producers have attempted to hold on to their margins by input substitutions and by adopting innovations supplied by the research system. These have been largely in the form of savings in labor, both human and bullock. The relative share of these inputs in total costs declined from 51 percent in 1969–70 to 29 percent in 1979–80.

Other data for the Punjab illustrate this technological dynamism more clearly (table 11.2). Changes in costs and operator's residual (in terms of wheat equivalents) for the holding as a whole rather than just for wheat illustrate the point that options for technological adjustment are greater in a multi-enterprise farming system.

Table 11.2 reveals that operator's residual from the farming unit as a whole continued to increase despite the declining trend shown for wheat in table 11.1. Introduction of short-duration, high-yield rice varieties which meshed well with the wheat-based farming system was largely responsible

Table 11.2 Costs and returns per hectare of cropped area in wheat equivalents and changes in crop mix, Punjab (India)

	1969–70	1980–81
A. Gross income/ha[a]	30.79	46.32
B. Total costs/ha[a]	21.07	33.59
	(68.43)[b]	(72.51)
C. Operator's residual[a]	9.72	12.73
	(31.57)	(27.49)
D. Share in cropped area (%)		
Wheat	42	38
Rice	10	19
E. Share in gross output (%)		
Wheat	50	39
Rice	9	33

Source: Data from Punjab, India, 1980–81 (India 1981b). The samples in the two years are not strictly comparable, but the data do reflect the broad changes fairly well.

[a] Expressed in wheat equivalents (quintals per hectare).

[b] Figures in parentheses represent the percentage share in output.

for this increase. Rice acreage and output rose substantially between 1969–70 and 1980–81. The slight increase in unit costs and the decrease in operator's residual (both expressed in terms of shares in output) are significantly smaller than those for wheat in table 11.1. These data clearly show that a stream of technological innovations helps maintain productivity growth. Of course, these changes are influenced by price movements, and it is difficult to sort out individual effects. Yet had the research system not come up with suitable rice varieties, a large expansion in rice area in the Punjab would have been technically infeasible, regardless of price incentives.

Aggregate data for the state as a whole (India 1981a) support these trends. Between 1965–66 and 1980–81, cultivated area grew at only 0.7 percent per annum, while the total cropped area grew at the rate of 1.9 percent. This was mainly due to an increase in the area cropped more than once at the rate of 5.3 percent per annum. The resulting increase in cropping intensity (from 128 to 161) boosted the returns to land and management. The area and yields of paddy increased from 0.3 million hectares to 1.2 million hectares and from 1.2 tons per hectare to 2.7 tons per hectare, respectively. It is this growth in rice production that has substantially increased demand for labor in the Punjab, causing seasonal migration of labor from other parts of India. The wheat story was, on a lesser scale, repeated for rice. For crops like gram, for which yields remained stagnant, the area declined. These changes highlight the processes through which farmers search for alternatives to increase their incomes.

TECHNOLOGICAL CHANGE IN SEMIARID WEST AFRICA

Documented cases of the impact of sustained technological change on the cost of production are scarce in West African agriculture. Historically, agricultural research in the area concentrated on nonfood export crops. Attention to food crops is more recent and thus harder to assess. This may be the case for most of the continent. The notable success of high-yielding hybrid maize in eastern and southern Africa has been confined to high-potential highlands, which are not typical of most of the arable areas on the continent. For this reason, cases from more representative environments were selected for study. The first case was of rapid yield increases in smallholder cotton production in southwestern Burkina Faso, an area adjacent to southern Mali where cotton research and extension have a long and successful history. The second was a cross-sectional study of proposed packages of improved practices for increased sorghum production in southern Niger, based on improved varieties, increased purchased input use, and animal traction.

Cotton cultivation was of negligible importance in the colonial era in Burkina Faso. It was also limited by the fact that the most productive "black" soils—those most suited to cotton cultivation—are found only in the western part of the country. Nevertheless, cotton was intensively promoted after independence in 1960. Average farm yields per hectare increased 10 percent per annum over the 1961–64 to 1975–79 period (table 11.3). Measured in terms of purchasing power for the main foodgrain, sorghum, the value of the increase in per hectare cotton yields was about 6 percent per annum. The lower increase when measured in terms of sorghum equivalents was due to the fall of domestic cotton prices in the 1970s relative to sorghum prices. Nevertheless, on a per hectare basis cotton producers were still doing very well indeed, since the growth in yields far outstripped the decline in relative cotton prices and the growth in purchased input costs taken together. As shown in table 11.3, the returns to primary factors nearly tripled on a per hectare basis, even though the share of purchased inputs in gross revenue increased.

The main technological innovation was increased use of purchased inputs in conjunction with increasing use of animal traction. Financial costs to the farmer were equivalent to 0.4 quintals of sorghum per hectare in 1961–64 and to 2.17 quintals in 1975–79, due mainly to increased inputs

Table 11.3 Relative costs and returns per hectare in sorghum equivalents for cotton cultivation, western Burkina Faso, 1961–64 to 1975–79

	1961–64	1965–69	1970–74	1975–79
A. Physical yield (quintals of seed cotton per hectare)	1.63	3.18	4.10	7.60
B. Gross revenue per hectare in sorghum equivalent (A × G)	2.71	5.06	5.34	8.36
C. Purchased inputs per hectare	0.40	0.96	1.74	2.17
D. Percentage share of purchased inputs in gross revenue (C/B)	15	19	33	26
E. Returns to primary factors (B − C)	2.31	4.10	3.60	6.19
F. Average national sorghum yields per hectare (under low purchased input use)	4.63	5.36	5.08	5.91
G. Ratio of official cotton producer price to official sorghum consumer price	1.67	1.59	1.34	1.12
H. Percentage of national area harvested under cotton	1.9	2.9	3.2	3.0

Source: Calculated from unpublished data generated by the Burkina Faso cotton company SOFITEX and reported in various World Bank sector evaluation documents. Items are expressed in terms of quintals of grain sorghum per hectare by dividing cash values by the official sorghum consumer price.

use. Since cotton land is still abundantly available in southwest Burkina Faso and most labor is family-provided, it may be inferred that the increase in returns to primary factors are primarily to family labor. This, of course, is a major difference from the situation in India and parts of eastern and southern Africa, where land is scarce, alienable, and returns to land are an important consideration.

In the case of Burkina Faso cotton, reliable field data are not available on changes in labor input over the period. While it is clear that labor per hectare has increased, Indian experience suggests that it has not come close to doubling. Thus real returns per unit of labor input have increased significantly over the 1961–64 to 1975–79 period. Furthermore, table 11.3 shows that the value of purchased inputs per unit of cotton output (in terms of sorghum) first rose and then dropped back to a level not much higher than in 1961–64, when overall use of purchased inputs was low.

The cotton story in western Burkina Faso provides five related insights. First, technological change based on increased input use was associated with decreased real costs per unit of output. This was true for labor and also to some extent true for purchased inputs, after an initial period of rising costs. Second, success in raising cotton yields benefited from twenty years of prior work under similar ecological conditions in neighboring Mali. Third, despite a decreasing real price of cotton (in terms of foodgrain), the profitability of cotton cultivation improved dramatically, relative both to labor, the scarce input, and to sorghum, a major competing activity. Fourth, despite declining output price incentives, yields continued to increase and production expanded rapidly from a small base. This led to a more than 50 percent increase in the share of cotton in national cropped acreage. Fifth, evidence from the zone, as well as from neighboring cotton projects in Mali and northern Ivory Coast, suggests that foodgrain output in the cotton villages may have increased as well. This is because the new crop (cotton) has a different labor profile from the predominant grains, permitting the aggregate expansion of cropped areas, and because of residual effects of cotton fertilizer use on grain yields (Vallaeys et al. 1987). The effect of the "cotton roads" on facilitating market outlets for grain should not be neglected either. Thus investment in technological change in this case may have encouraged an aggregate response of both cotton and grain production.

The second case study in semiarid West Africa concerns contemporary attempts to increase sorghum output on small farms in the southern part of Niamey Department, Niger. Millet is the predominant crop, and sorghum currently accounts for about 10 percent of cropped area (Ithaca International Limited 1984). Currently, farmers use few purchased inputs and land is relatively abundant. Proposed technical packages include a "partial" approach, involving use of improved local varieties, fertilizer, other purchased inputs, and improved manual cultivation practices. The "full" package incorporates further changes made possible by use of a pair of bullocks and various cultivation tools.

The data in table 11.4 represents the careful, educated guesses of an evaluation team rather than the results of intensive field surveys. They include figures using prevailing ("financial") prices and figures using border prices as a measure of opportunity costs ("economic" prices). Four main conclusions may be drawn.

First, given the underlying assumptions, the highest net return per hectare across technologies does not generate the highest return per labor unit. Financial returns to primary factors under the partial package dominate the corresponding returns to both traditional technology and the full package. It is worth noting that this situation is primarily the result of heavy subsidies on the import price of fertilizer. Without it, the economic returns to primary factors per hectare are hardly better for the partial package than for traditional technology.

Second, the highest returns per labor unit, the scarce resource in Niger, are obtained with the full package because of the assumed laborsaving aspects of animal traction technology. Given this and the high subsidies on traction equipment and credit, it is to be assumed that adoption will be rapid. In fact, evidence elsewhere suggests that the proposed technology is more laborshifting than laborsaving and that these projections are overly rosy (Delgado and McIntire 1982).

Third, despite favorable assumptions, economic returns to all technologies are negative if family labor is costed at wage rates corresponding to casual employment in towns. The least negative return at economic prices is for the full package.

Fourth, if fertilizer and other purchased inputs are costed at the heavily subsidized "financial prices," the full package of technology provides returns to labor that are more than competitive with nonagricultural wage labor opportunities. Even if labor is costed at its urban opportunity cost, a substantial residual profit per hectare remains.

The second case study illustrates that laborsaving technology is the key to the economic and financial profitability of agriculture in semiarid West Africa. Consequently, output price or input subsidies may be necessary to support agriculture, in view of the radical effect of high differentials to returns to labor between agriculture and non-agriculture. This might be thought of as a "second best" policy in response to the inevitable effects of the rapidly increasing contacts of many African economies with the outside world, including the effect of large-scale foreign aid in driving up urban wage levels. However, not enough is known about the true impact on labor use of proposed technologies. Therefore the appropriate way to support agriculture through technological change is not always clear.

Table 11.4 Financial and economic returns to smallholder sorghum cultivation, Niger, 1982/83

	Traditional technology		Partial package technology		Full package technology	
	Financial	Economic[a]	Financial	Economic[a]	Financial	Economic[a]
			(CFAF per hectare[b])			
Total receipts (sales, own-use, by-products)	53,950	53,950	88,025	87,525	99,100	97,600
Fertilizer	0	0	7,250	26,100	7,250	26,100
Other cash expenses	3,675	3,675	5,470	9,562	16,746	26,303
Capital recovery and 18% interest on equity	0	0	0	0	6,760	14,179
Total expenses	3,675	3,675	12,720	35,662	30,756	66,582
Returns to primary factors	50,275	50,275	75,305	51,903	68,344	31,018
Average product of labor per person day (APL)	474	474	607	418	1,367	620
APL in kg. of sorghum at harvest prices	5.9	5.9	7.6	5.2	17	7.8
Returns costing family labor at 750 CFAF/man/day[a]	(29,225)[b]	(29,225)	(17,695)	(41,097)	30,844	(6,482)

Source: Ithaca International Limited 1984, vol. 1, annex B.

Note: Figures are based on a three-hectare farm with five inhabitants (two full-time-worker equivalents) in the 400- to 600-mm.-rainfall belt of Niamey Department. Partial package includes no animal traction; full package includes use of one pair of bullocks.

[a] At resource opportunity costs. U.S.$1 = CFAF 360.

[b] Figures in parentheses are negative numbers.

TECHNOLOGICAL CHANGE AND OUTPUT RESPONSE

Technological change has been recognized as one of the shifter variables in supply response, and a large number of empirical studies have shown this effect. The models used have almost always been concerned with intercept shifts and have not investigated how technological change affects output response to price.

Economic theory indicates that changes in elasticity of output supply would depend upon the nature of the shift in the production function as well as supply conditions for inputs. On both scores, land-augmenting (seed-fertilizer-based) technological change in a land-scarce situation would be expected to lead to higher output response. It has been argued (Krishna and Raychaudhuri 1980) that in periods of rapid yield growth (induced by yield-augmenting technical changes like irrigation, modern varieties, and fertilizers), both the determinants of output, area and yield, would respond to price changes and output response would be higher. In contrast, when yields are inherently stagnant due to the lack of an ongoing process of technological change, area changes are the only source of output growth (Lipton 1985).

In West Africa, labor—especially seasonal labor—rather than land may be the primary constraint to increased agricultural output. Arable land is still abundant in most areas of the region. Furthermore, some preliminary results of work at IFPRI suggest that constant returns to scale is a reasonable assumption (Mellor and Ranade forthcoming). Agricultural wage labor typically accounts for a very small share of total farm labor, except in the tree crop zones. All of this strongly suggests that returns to labor and capital are the key factors in agricultural incentives in West Africa, rather than returns to land. Thus the impact of price incentives on aggregate agricultural output needs to be assessed in terms of impact on the average product of labor, and the same applies to technological change promoted by other means.

Land and wage labor may account for a larger factor share in eastern and southern Africa (Delgado and Ranade 1987). Furthermore, in future they are likely to account for an increasing share. Thus long-term policies, especially for research, will need to incorporate intensification strategies (Lipton 1985, 1987). In this respect, the higher-potential agricultural areas of eastern and southern Africa may be structurally more similar to the high-potential cereals areas of Asia than they are to West Africa.

A few empirical studies have attempted to compare output supply or acreage response elasticities between modern and traditional technologies. Table 11.5 summarizes these studies for Asia. It shows that statistically significant evidence suggesting higher production elasticities in the post-green-revolution period is not available. The Philippines case study, how-

Table 11.5 Impact of technological change on supply elasticities

Country	Crop	Period of study	Production[a] Ia	IIa	Area I	II
Philippines	Rice	1949/50–1973/74	0.07	0.11	—	—
Ajmer (India)	Aggr. output	1955/56–1976/77	0.27[b]	0.29[b]	—	—
Madhya Pradesh India	Wheat	1956/57–1971/72	—	—	0.10	0.15[b]
Punjab (India)	Wheat	1914/45–1957/70	—	0.82[b]	0.08[b]	0.28[b]

Sources: For the Philippines, data are from Ryan 1978, p. 53; for Ajmer, data are from Bapna 1981, p. 98; for Madhya Pradesh, data are from Gour 1975, p. 115; for the Punjab, data are from Krishna and Raychaudhuri 1980, pp. 35, 41.

[a] Except for the Punjab, I and II refer to pre- and post-green-revolution periods, respectively. For the Punjab, I refers to the preindependence period 1914–45 and II to the post-independence period 1957–70.

[b] Statistically significant.

ever, suggests that output response to fertilizer prices and irrigation is stronger in the period after technological change. The study by Krishna and Raychaudhuri for the Indian Punjab estimated area, yield, and output response functions of wheat for the postindependence period 1957–70, when yields grew at the rate of 3.08 percent per annum. Compared with the acreage response elasticity for wheat for the preindependence period 1919–45 estimated by Krishna in an earlier study, the evidence suggests a marked increase in the elasticity in the postindependence period.

These studies are based on data for the early seventies. We report below the results of an empirical exercise for wheat in the Indian Punjab, covering the period 1952/53 to 1979/80. Results based on production, area, and yield response functions are shown in table 11.6. The table supports the hypothesis that production became more responsive to prices of both outputs and inputs in the post-green-revolution period. It also shows that productivity increase is the dominant response and that wheat acreage is now determined almost exclusively by expansion of irrigation. These results are consistent with Krishna and Raychaudhuri's conclusions.

These results need to be tested more rigorously because of their important policy implications. They confirm that production incentives assume greater significance in a technologically dynamic setting, an apparently noncontroversial finding that appears nevertheless to be ignored in some of the more ideological stances on price policy, especially for West Africa.

Work on aggregate agricultural price response for Africa is even less well developed than for Asia. It has long been established that the supply

Table 11.6 Response of output, area, and yield to changes in price of wheat, Punjab (India), 1952–53 to 1979–80

| | Elasticity with respect to | | | | | |
| | Wheat price[a] | | Fertilizer price[a] | | Irrigation[a] | |
Dependent variable	I	II	I	II	I	II
Production	0.08	0.52[b]	—	−0.29[b]	2.55[b]	1.69[b]
Area	0.03	0.02	—	−0.06	−0.10	0.68[b]
Yield	0.05	0.50[b]	—	−0.23[b]	2.66[b]	1.00[b]

Source: Estimation done by the author.
[a] I and II refer to pre- and post-green-revolution periods, respectively.
[b] Statistically significant at 5 percent.

response of individual crops to relative prices is high in smallholder agriculture, where resources can be reallocated among competing activities (Bond 1983). However, virtually no work has been done on aggregate supply response because of lack of suitable field data. Methodologies are frequently deficient, and it is difficult to conclude much from this literature one way or another. Yet even in this sparse "pro-price-response" literature there is little to support the view of high aggregate price responsiveness.

Bond's attempt to show aggregate responsiveness to price over roughly fifteen years with national level data for nine sub-Saharan countries shows little significant response. Out of nine cases considered, the price response parameter is statistically different from zero only in Ghana and Kenya. In the Kenyan case, short- and long-run price elasticities of 0.1 and 0.16 are estimated by Bond. Even if the figures are taken at face value, aggregate responsiveness appears low; the only significant positive response was established in the one country of the sample in which significant prior technological change had occurred in food as well as export crop production. This is fully consistent with empirical data for Asia and with the conceptual framework set forth in chapter 10 above.

The main reason for taking a pessimistic view of aggregate supply response to price in most of Africa is the inelasticity of labor supply in agriculture. Table 11.7 suggests that agricultural wages in the West African savanna in the late 1970s were at least as high as the average product of labor estimated for smallholder agriculture in Niger in the early 1980s (table 11.4), and probably higher. To the extent that this finding is typical of the region, it could help explain the very low incidence of the use of hired labor in Niger agriculture. Hired agricultural labor in West Africa on a sustained basis and on a large scale is primarily used only in the highest-value cash-cropping activities, such as the perennial beverage crops in the humid zone. It is reasonable to assume that it is competition from these

Table 11.7 Commodity agricultural wages in West Africa compared to India

Location	Agricultural potential	Cropping season	Cash wage per man day		Grain equivalent in sorghum at harvest prices
West Africa					
Dori, Burkina Faso	Low	1980/81	CFAF	550	6.9
Segou, Mali	Medium	1977/78	FM	450	6.0
Gusau, Nigeria	Medium	1977/78	N	1.44	6.0
Gombe, Nigeria	Medium	1977/78	N	1.76	7.3
Gombe, Nigeria	Medium	1978/79	N	2.24	9.5
Agboville, Ivory Coast	High	1980/81	CFAF	872	9.7
Ibadan, Nigeria	High	1980/81	N	4.00	11.4
India					
Dryland Gujarat	Low	1978/79	Rs.	5.0	4.6
Dryland Andhra Pradesh	Medium	1978/79	Rs.	5.5	5.0
Punjab	High	1978/79	Rs.	8.9	7.9
Punjab	High	1980/81	Rs.	11.5	8.8

Sources: For Burkina Faso, data are from McIntire 1982; for Mali, data are from personal communication from John McIntire, 1981; for Nigeria to 1979, data are from personal communication from Roger H. Slade; for Nigeria in 1981, data are based on the author's visits to Ibadan and Zaria; for the Ivory Coast, data are from Ivory Coast 1980; for Gujarat, data are from India 1979; for Andhra Pradesh, data are from Kahlon and Tyagi 1983; for the Punjab, data are from India 1981a.

uses and from the nonagricultural sector that has served to increase labor costs above viable levels for smallholders on average land in the savanna. The implication is that either cereals output prices or yields would have to increase substantially before cereal farmers on average land would be in a position to compete for available labor supplies.

Table 11.7 also suggests, as a hypothesis, that agricultural wages in terms of grain are higher in West Africa than in those areas of India outside the highest potential zones.

All of the above is consistent with the view that because of land abundance the marginal product of labor in semiarid West African agriculture is close to average product, and it is higher than the marginal product of labor in semiarid Indian agriculture. This is despite the fact that because of improved technology the average product of labor in the Indian case is probably higher than in the African case (Mellor and Ranade forthcoming).

The view that the agricultural labor supply is inelastic is also supported by a brief glance at the history of the past decade in the region. Sub-Saharan African GNP attributable to the industry and service sectors grew 5 percent per annum during the 1970s, compared to about 1 percent per annum in agricultural GNP (World Bank 1981). This indicates a major disequilibrium between rural and urban areas that marginal price changes are not likely to eliminate. High overall nonagricultural growth may have occurred in response to deliberate policy or exogenous capital inflows from foreign assistance or mineral rents, or simply as a result of the rapid opening of Africa to world trade. In any event, incentives to labor in African agriculture are frequently a small fraction of incentives to unskilled nonagricultural work. In Kenya, for example, the ratio of real agricultural wages to real nonagricultural wages for unskilled workers fluctuated between one-fifth and one-quarter (ILO 1977; ILO 1983). Similar ratios for the Ivory Coast and Burkina Faso were about 40 to 50 percent over the same period (Delgado 1981). Furthermore, the ratios are even smaller if returns to family labor are compared to those of unskilled and casual nonagricultural employment. The rule of thumb of 4 : 1 to 9 : 1 has been advanced for the 1970s (World Bank 1981).

Whatever the cause, migration to cities during the 1970s was at an annual rate of 6.5 percent per annum (8.5 percent for 35 capital cities). In some areas of the West African hinterland, the very young and the very old are the only members of the male population left on the farm.

The policy problem is twofold. First, surveys show that prices for starchy staple foodstuffs have been increasing over the last decade in many countries relative to both domestic nonagricultural prices and world cereal prices, even when adjusted for overvalued exchange rates. Food in Burkina Faso is an example: the urban food price index appreciated 35 percent relative to the consumer price index during the 1970s (Ghai and Smith 1987). Furthermore, domestic food prices in West Africa appear to be increasingly "protected," in that world cereal prices have fallen considerably relative to West African domestic prices at market exchange rates (World Bank 1986b). The starchy staples still account for the bulk of sub-Saharan agricultural production outside the forest belt. Thus, short of greatly increasing protection of the food sector, policymakers have relatively little latitude to raise food prices further without incurring severe social costs. Second, and a related point, food and export crop price increases that it might be reasonable to bring about do not fundamentally alter the pattern of change of the structure of agricultural incentives relative to a small but rapidly growing non-agriculture. Therefore, to have a major impact on incentives, price policies must be linked with technological change that significantly raises returns to labor. The potential that price rises alone can induce this change appears somewhat limited in much of sub-Saharan Africa. This is primarily because the overall opportunity costs of labor in dual economies are subject to continuing large inflows of outside resources that create multiplier effects on service sector and other nonagricultural incomes.

POLICY CONCLUSIONS

Our analysis of Asian and African examples suggests that production costs per unit of output decline under technological change. The more detailed Asian data also show that rising costs for specific inputs over time lead to substitution of cheaper inputs, involving substantial technological restructuring of production. The Punjab data, in particular, suggest that output becomes more responsive to product and factor price changes under technologically dynamic regimes. Furthermore, yield rather than area accounts for the additional output. In contrast, the West African examples suggest that the key issue in technological change there is returns to labor, particularly seasonal bottleneck labor. To the extent that high differentials exist between returns to nonagricultural and agricultural labor, labor-productivity-increasing technological change may be expected to increase marginal responses to both output and input price incentives. This is because agriculture in much of West Africa, at least, is not generally competitive with non-agriculture for increased input use, given the continued rapid expansion of labor and capital demands in the nonagricultural sector of economies that are only now becoming integrated into the world system. If this analysis is correct, technological change in crop production becomes a precursor (or at least a concomitant) rather than a result of successful price policies.

Two immediate implications for pricing policies follow. First, technological change is an important policy instrument for inducing output shifts in its own right. Second, the fact that output and scarce input cost reduction are keys to furthering technological changes suggests the need for continuous monitoring and evaluation of agricultural production cost structures.

12

Policy for Rapid Growth in Use of Modern Agricultural Inputs

GUNVANT M. DESAI

Accelerated growth in agricultural production of developing countries depends on exploiting more fully the existing production potential and continuously raising that potential through technological change. This requires sustained rapid growth in the use of inputs such as seeds of better quality, fertilizers, pesticides, farm implements, and machinery. Price policy issues dominate in discussions on how to increase the use of these inputs, often without sufficient attention to certain non-price factors and policies. Such an approach is lopsided and could mislead us as to the role and limitations of price policy in the use of modern agricultural inputs in developing countries.

Growth in the use of modern agricultural inputs in the developing world has become significant only in the last three decades. There is still a sizeable untapped potential for further growth. The gap between actual and potential levels implies that the pace of growth is governed by the workings of such systems as agricultural research, extension, credit, input supply, and distribution. Together, they work to convert that potential into farmers' effective demand for inputs and to satisfy this demand at a growing number of locations. Because of the many deficiencies of these systems in developing countries, it seems rather simpleminded to let price policy issues dominate discussions on how to achieve rapid growth in the use of inputs. This is especially so because the development and working of these systems are more strongly influenced by such factors as public expenditure on agricultural research and extension, investment in relevant physical infrastructure, institutional setup, and administrative arrangements for supply and distribution of inputs than they are by prices of crops or inputs. All this suggests that the growth path of the use of modern agricultural inputs, usually delineated by a logistic curve, is determined by a variety of factors. Understanding their relative importance at different stages in the movement of actual levels of use of inputs toward their potential levels becomes crucial to formulation of the most appropriate policies.

This chapter will review briefly past growth of fertilizer use in developing countries. It then presents a heuristic framework which brings out the policy requirements for future sustained rapid growth of fertilizer use. The usefulness of the framework is demonstrated by focusing on the Indian experience. Fertilizer is chosen as an example because it is dominant among modern inputs and because a substantial proportion of further growth in agricultural production is expected from raising fertilizer use. In addition, fertilizer subsidies are a growing budgetary burden in many developing countries.

Fertilizer use in India has increased from less than 1 kilogram per hectare to more than 40 kilograms per hectare over three and a half decades. Growth within this range is typical of many developing countries. The Indian scene is characterized by persistent geographical concentration in fertilizer use and wide variations in the growth in use on different crops. These also are common features in the developing world. Other major similarities between India and many developing countries are the impact of high-yielding varieties (HYVs) on growth in fertilizer use, circumstances affecting the development of distribution and supply systems, and a growing burden of fertilizer subsidies in recent years. For these reasons, India is a useful case to illustrate and analyze the policy requirements to sustain rapid growth in fertilizer use.

PAST GROWTH AND FUTURE NEEDS

Chemically manufactured fertilizers first came into use about 140 years ago, with the establishment of a factory in Rothamstead, England (Lamer 1957). A century later, annual world fertilizer consumption had grown to about 10 million metric tons (mmts) of nutrients (FAO 1951). Appreciable fertilizer use was, however, confined to some countries of Europe, the United States, and Japan. The developing countries of Asia, Africa, and Latin America accounted for less than 5 percent of the world total.

Fertilizer consumption in the developing world really began after World War II and reached 43 mmts in 1983/84.[1] The share of developing countries in world fertilizer consumption increased from about 7 percent in the early 1950s to about 12 percent in the early 1960s, about 22 percent in the early 1970s, and about 35 percent in the early 1980s. The levels of fertilizer consumption and the pace of its growth have varied widely among developing countries. However, its importance has been recognized even in coun-

1. The terms "developing world" and "developing countries" include countries classified as "developing market economies" and "Asian centrally planned economies" by the Food and Agriculture Organization of the United Nations in its statistical literature. Estimates of fertilizer consumption used in this paragraph are based on various issues of the FAO *Fertilizer Yearbook*.

tries with low rates of application and poor growth in consumption. China, India, and Brazil are now among the top ten countries of the world as consumers and producers of fertilizers. None was in this category, not even as a consumer, until the 1960s.

Fertilizer consumption in the developing world increased substantially during the last decade characterized by oil crises, rising from 18.5 mmts in 1973/74 to 43.2 mmts in 1983/84. This increment accounted for about 60 percent of the growth in total world consumption during the ten-year period and was more than twice the growth in the entire world consumption during the first century of fertilizer use. The vast growth in fertilizer use, however, has been accompanied by a mounting burden of fertilizer subsidies in many developing countries.

Despite such impressive growth, fertilizer use in the developing world is still quite low—about 54 kilograms of nutrients per hectare of arable land. A majority of developing countries use less than 25 kilograms per hectare. In contrast, use per hectare averages 225 kilograms for western Europe, 122 for eastern Europe and the U.S.S.R., and 94 for North America. The growing pressure of population on land, persistent food deficits, depleted soil fertility, and the dependence of proven yield-increasing technologies on high levels of fertilizer application all point to the urgent need to raise fertilizer use in the developing world.

The magnitude of the task is illustrated by data from India. India was using less than 50,000 metric tons of nutrients in the late 1940s. This grew to about 800,000 metric tons by 1965/66, 2.8 mmts by 1973/74, and 7.7 mmts by 1983/84 (Fertiliser Association of India 1985). Fertilizer consumption must grow to about 20 mmts by the year 2000—by about 750,000 tons annually—to raise agricultural production to the desired level. This is imperative because about four-fifths of the additional foodgrain production required by the year 2000 will depend on increased use of fertilizers (India 1976; UNIDO 1976). So far, the annual increment has exceeded 500,000 tons only five times. It is, therefore, pertinent to ask what policies are required to accomplish the task.

A HEURISTIC FRAMEWORK

One approach to the above question is to view growth in fertilizer consumption as an outcome of growth in farmers' demand for fertilizers due to *changes* in variables which affect their returns on its use. This approach underlies a number of empirical studies which consider fertilizer consumption as a function of such agroeconomic variables as irrigation, area sown to fertilizer-responsive crop varieties, cropping patterns, and prices of crops as well as fertilizers. The estimated growth parameters of different explanatory variables are then used to draw policy conclusions.

This approach raises three questions. What are the magnitudes of changes required *every year* in the variables that shift fertilizer response functions upward or in the relative prices of fertilizers to increase fertilizer consumption by the desired amount? Which policies will produce these changes? Are these policies sustainable? The last question is no less relevant than the other two because every change in fertilizer consumption is treated as causally determined only by changes in variables behind fertilizer response functions and prices of fertilizers and crops.

Important as fertilizer response functions and prices are, it is absurd to say that continuous changes in them are necessary to sustain growth in fertilizer use under all circumstances. Both a priori reasoning and the experience of many countries (including India, as discussed later) clearly suggest that such a mechanistic interpretation of growth in fertilizer consumption within the framework of comparative statics is inappropriate. More important, it could lead to imprudent—if not altogether unrealistic—price policy prescriptions if the possibilities of continuous upward shifts on response functions are limited in the short run. To discuss policy requirements for a sustained growth in fertilizer use, it is therefore crucial to go beyond changes in response functions and relative price of crops and fertilizers. This is especially true of developing countries which have an untapped potential of fertilizer use and in which processes generating growth in actual fertilizer use are generally weak (Desai 1988).

The agronomic potential of fertilizer use in a country is determined by factors like soil quality, climatic environment, cropping patterns, genetic characteristics of crops, and use of inputs other than fertilizers. Together, these factors determine physical responses of crops to fertilizer use and thus the maximum amount of fertilizer which can be used to increase agricultural production. The *economic* potential of fertilizer use is determined by the above factors behind fertilizer response functions and prices of crops, as well as inputs including fertilizers. These determinants of economic potential we shall call agroeconomic variables. Each set of these variables determines the maximum amount of fertilizer which could be used most profitably. The economic potential is less than the agronomic potential because fertilizer is not a free input.

Actual fertilizer use is an outcome of both the conversion of the economic potential into farmers' effective demand for fertilizers and the fulfilment of this demand through fertilizer supply and distribution systems. Besides agroeconomic variables, three processes and their interactions influence the level of actual fertilizer use. These processes are the conversion of the economic potential into farmers' effective demand for fertilizers, the timely delivery of fertilizers to farmers at geographically dispersed locations, and the creation of an adequate aggregate supply of fertilizers through domestic production and imports.

Empirical evidence consistently indicates that in each country fertilizer use has begun with a few farmers applying it on selected crops at limited locations. There was less than complete diffusion of fertilizer use on land where it was potentially profitable, and rates of application on fertilized land were suboptimal. This fact implies a vast untapped economic potential of use under prevailing response functions and prices. Actual fertilizer consumption has grown over time as a result of the spread of use on unfertilized land and increase in rates of application on fertilized land.

The evidence also shows that the pace and the pattern of growth in fertilizer use were influenced more decisively by the development of the agricultural research, extension, credit, and fertilizer distribution systems plus supply systems than by marginal changes in prices of either crops or fertilizers. This is not surprising because farmers, though rational, are not omniscient. They need location-specific information on the responses of crops to fertilizer use in order to judge which crops could be profitably fertilized and to work out details of fertilizer practices. Agricultural research systems which generate such information and the extension system which delivers it to farmers influence these decisions. Similarly, sufficient credit is often necessary to convert farmers' perceptions of profitability of fertilizer use into their *effective* demand for fertilizer. But even this is not enough. Actual use of fertilizers will still depend on whether adequate fertilizers are available at the right place and time. This depends on the level of development and efficiency of fertilizer distribution, production, and import systems.

Development of the above systems has influenced growth in fertilizer consumption not only by tapping unexploited potential but also by raising the profitability and economic potential of fertilizer use. Agricultural research and extension systems have been behind upward shifts in response functions by developing and spreading new technologies in crop production and by educating farmers in the efficient use of fertilizers. Reductions in farmers' fertilizer cost have resulted from technological breakthroughs and operational efficiencies in supply and distribution systems coupled with higher prices of crops resulting from expansion in demand due to rapid economic growth. Propping up prices of crops or lowering fertilizer prices through subsidies are not effective substitutes. Instead, such measures usually distract the attention of policymakers from the more demanding task of developing the systems which will generate sustained growth in fertilizer consumption.

The above framework is especially relevant for developing countries for three reasons. First, aggregate fertilizer consumption in most of them is below the potential as determined by prevailing response functions-price environment. Second, systems which influence growth in fertilizer use are inadequately developed and inefficient. And third, interactions between these systems are usually not governed by the price mechanism. Hence price policy interventions are at best a poor substitute for the real tasks of adequately developing such systems.

The policy requirements of further growth in fertilizer consumption cannot be correctly identified without interpreting the past growth in fertilizer consumption in the framework outlined.

THE INDIAN EXPERIENCE

Fertilizer use began in India on tea plantations in the 1920s. It spread little outside the plantation sector until 1943, when the government launched the Grow More Food Campaign in the wake of the Japanese occupation of Burma, the source of rice imports to India, and the Bengal famine. Efforts to promote fertilizer use in the nonplantation sector to raise food production rapidly gathered momentum after India became independent in 1947. The major aims were: (1) to create farmers' demand by generating and spreading knowledge about responses of crops to fertilizer use through thousands of trials on farmers' fields; (2) to improve the response function environment through development of irrigation and spread of high-yielding varieties (this effort began in the mid-1960s); (3) to develop a fertilizer distribution system linked with the agricultural credit system; (4) to enlarge fertilizer supplies by developing domestic fertilizer industry and imports; and (5) to control fertilizer prices.

The major features of the fertilizer price policy were establishment of uniform prices throughout the country, the virtual absence of subsidies until the mid-1970s, and the growing fiscal burden of these subsidies in recent years (Desai 1984). Incidentally, the real price of fertilizer in India (that is, its price relative to the prices of crops) has been generally higher than in many other countries during the last three decades.

Because of the above efforts and the vast untapped potential, fertilizer use in India grew from 0.5 kilograms of nutrients per hectare in the late 1940s to more than 40 kilograms in the early 1980s. India now ranks fourth in total fertilizer consumption after the United States, the U.S.S.R., and China.[2]

Despite such impressive growth, total fertilizer consumption has been

2. India's fourth rank is of course due to its large size, but the same applies to the United States, the U.S.S.R., and China. All rank much lower on a per hectare basis. India's record in raising its fertilizer consumption from less than 1 kilogram per hectare in the late 1940s to more than 40 kilograms per hectare by 1983/84 is impressive compared with the time taken by many other developing and developed countries to achieve similar increases. On the other hand, it is much less impressive than that of China. It is important to note that farmers' real price of fertilizer has been higher in China than in India throughout the last three decades.

below the potential indicated by the response functions-price environment.[3] That there was sufficient scope for faster growth is indicated by less
than complete diffusion of fertilizer use on all crops, even on irrigated
areas, until at least the mid-1970s (Desai 1982). Similarly, fertilizer use
under unirrigated conditions, even on traditional varieties, grew steadily
but slowly. The diffusion of fertilizer use was under way on both large and
small farms. In fact, rates of application on fertilized land were often
higher on small than on large farms, and there were no major differences
between the two categories with respect to crops not fertilized. The reasons
why growth in fertilizer use was not faster thus lie in the various deficiencies in fertilizer promotion, distribution, and supply systems. These include inadequate efforts to convert the potential into farmers' demand for
fertilizers through meaningful extension activities, slow expansion of and
various inefficiencies in the fertilizer distribution system, repeated shortfalls in planned domestic fertilizer production, and wide annual fluctuations in fertilizer imports.

Fertilizer diffusion has been most rapid on crops and varieties which
respond to fertilizer use dramatically, even though they do not have the
best price environment. Concentration of fertilizer use on irrigated areas
and HYVs also indicates the strong influence of fertilizer response functions
on growth of fertilizer use. Growth in fertilizer use on oilseeds and pulses
has been slower than on rice and wheat despite a better price environment,
relative to international prices, for the former. Also, diffusion of fertilizer
use has been faster in irrigated areas than on the same crops in unirrigated
areas, further confirming the assumption that changes in variables behind
fertilizer response functions have been more important than changes in
prices.

Although fertilizer use was more profitable on irrigated areas, it was not
confined to them. More important, fertilizer use on unirrigated areas under virtually all crops grew steadily even where there was scope for further
diffusion on irrigated areas. For instance, by 1976/77 use had spread to
about 18 percent of total unirrigated areas, even though about one-third of
the irrigated areas was still not fertilized. The explanation for this is that
the systems influencing growth in fertilizer consumption in certain regions
with low irrigation were relatively better than in those with high levels of
irrigation, as is clearly shown in the experience of Gujarat State.

With less than 20 percent of its area irrigated and relatively poor rainfall, Gujarat in 1981/82 had the highest level of fertilizer consumption per
hectare of all states and union territories in which up to 40 percent of ara-

3. For instance, under the fertilizer response functions-cum-price environment of the
early 1960s, Panse estimated that 3.57 million tons of nitrogen could be used in India (Panse
1964). Actual consumption at that time was only about 300,000 tons.

ble land was irrigated. Fertilizer use on unirrigated areas accounted for more than half of total fertilizer consumption in the state in the mid-1970s. This was double the share of unirrigated areas for the country as a whole. Relatively faster growth on unirrigated areas of Gujarat was mainly due to certain strengths of the fertilizer distribution system and to pressure from the supply side, especially from the fertilizer factories in the state (India 1983).

Wide variations in the rates of growth in fertilizer consumption among different districts within states have commonly been attributed to interdistrict variations in irrigation, cropping patterns, and spread of HYVS. In addition, differences among districts in the development of fertilizer distribution systems and the supply of agricultural credit have also been responsible. Recognition of these variations is obviously useful in evolving policies to broaden the geographical base of growth in fertilizer use.

Both fertilizer diffusion and rates of use have reached fairly high levels in regions which have accounted for the bulk of the past growth in fertilizer use.[4] This being so, continued dependence of the government and fertilizer industry on these regions for further growth in fertilizer consumption has started to generate pressures for higher prices of crops and lower prices of fertilizers because of diminishing marginal production from additional fertilizer use. These pressures can be effectively countered only if promotion and distribution systems are developed in other regions and fertilizer response functions are shifted upward in regions where fertilizer use is concentrated. In this context, improving efficiency of fertilizer use on both irrigated and unirrigated land is no less important than further development of irrigation and fertilizer-responsive varieties.

POLICY REQUIREMENTS OF FERTILIZER CONSUMPTION GROWTH

India is a useful case not only to illustrate the relative importance of different factors in the past growth of fertilizer use but also to identify policies required for sustaining further rapid growth. These policies should simultaneously aim at exploiting the remaining untapped potential and raising the economic potential of fertilizer use through improving the response function environment.

4. Thus, for instance, districts accounting for about one-fifth of the country's cultivated area have been dominant in the past growth of fertilizer consumption, with a share of about 55 percent. Average rates of fertilizer application in these districts had reached more than 50 kilograms per hectare by the late 1970s. In one-fourth of these districts, rates exceeded 100 kilograms per hectare. Since all cultivated land in a district seldom comes under fertilizer use, rates of application on *fertilized* land in these districts must have reached considerably higher levels than these figures indicate.

Most of the unexploited potential is on the more than 70 percent of cultivated land which is unirrigated.[5] This land accounts for more than 80 percent of the production of jowar, bajra, pulses, and oilseeds, about 67 percent of the cotton production, and 30 to 40 percent of the production of rice and wheat. Therefore, at this stage raising productivity of unirrigated areas is crucial to sustaining yield-based growth in agricultural production and to increasing production of pulses and oilseeds, which are in short supply. Among the constraints on efforts to raise productivity of unirrigated areas, low soil fertility is as severe as any other. Unless concerted efforts are made to raise soil fertility through judicious use of fertilizers, farmers will have little incentive to invest in other dryland technologies.

Since agroclimatic environments of unirrigated areas differ, location-specific knowledge of fertilizer response functions, fertilizer practices, and other agronomic matters (like sowing time, plant population, etc.) needs to be generated through strengthened, decentralized research. Improved coordination among agricultural research and extension systems is also needed so that research information can be effectively spread among farmers.[6] These efforts should be simultaneously supplemented by an adequate and timely flow of credit to farmers and development of efficient fertilizer distribution systems. Small increases in distribution margins (a price policy measure) may not suffice to accelerate expansion of fertilizer distribution systems in rainfed areas, especially if vigorous efforts to promote fertilizer use are absent and fertilizer turnover remains low.

Neither promotional efforts nor expansion of distribution systems in unirrigated regions will sustain growth unless the aggregate fertilizer supply stays ahead of the growth in the market for fertilizers in current and newly irrigated areas. For quite some time to come, supply will depend on fertilizer import policy. More often than not, this policy has been governed by the desire to protect the domestic fertilizer industry, to clear inventories, and to realize savings in foreign exchange. Such attitudes must be replaced by an understanding of the role of the supply side in converting untapped

5. The problem of raising fertilizer consumption under unirrigated conditions should not be viewed as occurring only with low rainfall. A study based on the fertilizer growth performance of districts during the 1960s clearly showed that districts with low irrigation located in *high* rainfall regions, particularly in eastern India (including parts of Madhya Pradesh), performed the worst among all districts with little irrigation (Desai and Singh 1973). Scrutiny of fertilizer consumption trends of districts during the 1970s suggests a similar pattern. Available evidence also reveals that districts in eastern India have the least developed fertilizer distribution and agricultural credit systems.

6. This cannot be overemphasized because additional production due to fertilizer use depends on such things as timing and method of application, balance among nutrients, sowing time, choice of variety, and plant population. What makes these considerations critical in rainfed areas is that without appropriate agronomic practices, returns to fertilizer use are considerably lower and more uncertain than in irrigated areas. On the other hand, available research clearly indicates that with appropriate practices, returns to fertilizer use in rainfed areas could be considerably enhanced (Desai 1983).

potential into actual fertilizer use. The experience of Gujarat State clearly demonstrates how sustained pressure from the supply side opens up fertilizer markets in rainfed regions.

A policy of "liberal" imports of fertilizers will most likely be resented by the domestic fertilizer industry and may also lead to an increase in inventories in the short run. Effective mechanisms to resolve conflicts of interest among different segments of the fertilizer system must be developed. The highest priority must be given to providing adequate credit to fertilizer distribution systems and strengthening the physical infrastructure for transportation and storage.

Raising rates of application on fertilized land to optimum levels is another way to generate growth in consumption. To tap this component of unexploited potential, farmers must be educated in efficient fertilizer practices such as balanced use of nutrients, correct timing and placement of fertilizers, and, wherever necessary, use of micronutrients and soil amendments. There is ample evidence of deficiencies in these practices, even in regions with high levels of fertilizer use. Adoption of correct practices will increase the efficiency of fertilizer use and thus raise returns on it. Clearly, such efforts are preferable to using price policy to raise rates of fertilizer application.

The economic potential of fertilizer use must be increased if sizeable growth in fertilizer consumption is to be sustained. Diffusion of fertilizer and currently available high-yielding varieties on presently irrigated land is virtually complete. Rates of application are also fairly high. While they could be raised still further, efforts to do so should be accompanied by improvements in fertilizer and other agronomic practices and in water management. Without such gains, the attempt to increase fertilizer use on land which is already fertilized at fairly high rates will lead to pressures for lower fertilizer prices and higher support prices of crops.

To increase the economic potential of fertilizer use, accelerated development and utilization of irrigation are imperative. In addition, the agricultural research system must be strengthened to improve response to fertilizers in both irrigated and unirrigated areas. In order to exploit the economic potential of these policies, however, deficiencies in agricultural extension and credit as well as in fertilizer supply and distribution systems must be remedied. Therefore, it seems necessary to distinguish between policies which aim at increasing the economic potential of fertilizer use and those which aim at rapidly converting potential into actuality. Inadequate appreciation of the complementarity of these sets of policies results in long delays in fully exploiting the potential.

The discussion thus far has focused on non-price policies for three reasons. First, past growth in fertilizer consumption was determined more by non-price factors and processes than by changes in prices of either crops or fertilizers. Second, further development of these systems and continuing technological change which raises the fertilizer potential are crucial to rapid growth in consumption. Third, India cannot continue to lower prices of fertilizers relative to those of crops through price policy interventions, at least not in the short run.

Since 1943, the Government of India has controlled fertilizer prices at factory, port, and farmgate levels (Desai 1984). Major features of fertilizer price policy have been insulation of domestic farmgate prices from fluctuations in the world market, equalization of the cost of domestic and imported fertilizers for farmers, and uniformity in prices all over the country. Until the early 1970s, there was no major budgetary subsidy on fertilizers; in fact, there was a surplus in all but a few years, setting India apart from many other developing countries.

The situation has changed since 1973/74; fertilizer subsidies in the 1983/84 budget of the central government exceeded Rs 10,000 million. Initially subsidies were necessitated by the dramatic impact of the oil crisis on the cost of imported fertilizers. After 1975/76, however, both imported and domestic fertilizers were subsidized. The subsidies on domestic fertilizers rose rapidly after the introduction of the Retention Price Scheme in 1977. In 1983/84 domestic fertilizer accounted for 86 percent of total fertilizer subsidies.

The Retention Price Scheme originated in the enhanced cost of fertilizer production after the oil crisis of the early 1970s and the policy to encourage the growth of the domestic fertilizer industry. The scheme assures a manufacturer 12 percent post-tax returns on net worth provided certain norms with respect to capacity utilization and consumption of raw materials are achieved. The average cost of supplying domestic fertilizer has been higher than the prices fixed for farmers. The difference between the two has also grown over time due to the high investment cost of new fertilizer factories, escalation in the administered prices of virtually everything which goes into fertilizer production, and the increased cost of fertilizer distribution.

The targeted growth in fertilizer consumption is expected to cause fertilizer subsidies to rise substantially by 1990, perhaps to as high as Rs 70,000 million (*Economic Times* [Bombay] 1984). It must, however, be noted that these estimates do not represent the *economic* subsidy on fertilizers. The cost of production of domestic fertilizers is very largely governed by administered prices, and some of these prices are much higher than in other countries. There is scope to contain the growth in the budgetary burden of fertilizer subsidies through rationalization in the pricing and fiscal policies for fertilizer raw materials, feedstocks, and capital equipment (Jain and Nand 1980; Venkitramanan 1983). On the other hand, the average cost of fertilizers supplied by the domestic industry is likely to rise over time because the investment cost of newer plants is higher.

It is beyond the scope of this paper to discuss the relative merits of domestic production vis-à-vis imports of fertilizers. The issue is complex, involving the technology capability and experience gained in fertilizer production (Fertiliser Association of India 1980), the place of the fertilizer industry in the development strategy, and the foreign exchange requirements of large-scale imports every year. At present, India ranks either first or second to China in net imports of fertilizers among all countries (FAO 1983a). Thus India's presence in the world fertilizer market influences prices. Moreover, prices do not always reflect the real cost of production in the countries exporting fertilizers, nor can they be directly compared with the cost of domestic production because the latter is governed by administered prices of fuel and feedstocks which are higher in India than in other countries. One thing, however, seems clear: given the strategy of meeting fertilizer requirements through growth in domestic production, the mounting burden of fertilizer subsidies on the nation's budget clearly suggests that there is hardly any scope to lower the prices of fertilizer charged to farmers and thus raise the profitability of its use, at least in the near future.

Since the mid-1960s, the price policy for crops has played a key role in generating growth of fertilizer use through accelerating the spread of HYVs. Due to their superior response functions, fertilizer use is more profitable on HYVs than on traditional varieties. In the absence of public procurement operations, a large marketable surplus might have lowered the prices of foodgrains, and thus slowed down the diffusion of HYVs with a consequent adverse impact on the growth of fertilizer use. But the time when agricultural price policy could have such an impact on the growth of fertilizer use is virtually over. Currently available HYVs are widely diffused. While there is scope to raise rates of fertilizer application on land sown with HYVs, what is needed to exploit this potential are various non-price measures because the "low" rates are due to deficiencies in fertilizer and agronomic practices. Another constraint on the policy of supporting prices of crops at higher and higher levels is the relatively slow growth in domestic demand for foodgrains and the inability of surplus production to compete in world markets without export subsidies. This has resulted in large procurement and stockholding by the government and an ever-growing burden of food subsidies. Removal of the domestic demand constraints depends on rapid growth in employment, and this calls for containing upward pressures on agricultural prices.

Because of these constraints on lowering *real* prices of fertilizers, non-price policies will be more crucial than ever before in determining the pace of future growth in India's fertilizer consumption. However, there is no need for pessimism about the future growth of fertilizer consumption or for failing to develop the policies required for this purpose. The relative prices of fertilizers and crops are still reasonable. They need not become more favorable to farmers in order for further growth in fertilizer consumption to occur unless we assume that in the prevailing price environment there is neither untapped potential of fertilizer use nor scope to raise profitability of fertilizer use through improving the response functions environment. Clearly, such assumptions are not valid.

SUMMING UP

Eight major propositions emerge from the discussion of the role and limitations of price policy in generating sustained rapid growth of fertilizer consumption in developing countries. Although largely an interpretation of Indian experience within a heuristic framework, these propositions are relevant to many developing countries.

First, while the economic potential of fertilizer use is determined by fertilizer response functions and prices of crops and fertilizers, actual fertilizer use is also affected by agricultural research, extension, credit, fertilizer supply, and distribution systems. These systems convert the potential into farmers' demand for fertilizers and satisfy this demand under a given response functions-price environment.

Second, until fertilizer consumption reaches its full potential, there will be a disequilibrium between actual consumption and the variables behind the response functions-price environment. The rate of growth in actual consumption (that is, the speed at which the disequilibrium is corrected) will be determined not only by changes in the variables behind the response functions-price environment but also, and often more important, by development of the systems mentioned above.

Third, the second proposition is especially relevant to developing countries where actual consumption is below the potential and the various systems which influence its growth are inadequately developed. Thus it is a fundamental error to judge the influence of changes in prices on fertilizer consumption growth from fertilizer demand models. These models usually specify fertilizer consumption as a function of variables behind response functions and prices of crops and fertilizers. In other words, they leave out many other variables which influence the development and workings of the systems which convert potential into actual consumption.

Fourth, besides prices of crops and fertilizers, the development and working of agricultural research, extension, credit, fertilizer supply, and distribution systems are governed by many factors such as physical infrastructure, various institutional and administrative arrangements, and development policies.

Fifth, the pace of growth in fertilizer consumption and its geographical distribution by crop are more powerfully influenced by variables behind fertilizer response functions such as irrigation, cropping pattern, and crop varieties than by prices of crops or fertilizers. Nevertheless, various deficiencies in the systems influencing consumption often prevent rapid utilization of full potential even in areas characterized by superior response functions. Conversely, better development of these systems in regions with only fair response functions often induces rapid exploitation of fertilizer potential.

Sixth, geographical pockets of concentration in consumption develop as fertilizer consumption grows toward its potential. These are mainly areas with a superior response function environment or better development of systems facilitating growth in consumption, or both. Continued dependence on these areas for further growth in aggregate fertilizer consumption generates pressure for a more favorable price environment due to the diminishing marginal productivity of fertilizer use. Price policies which respond to these pressures may be effective in raising total fertilizer consumption in the short run, but they do not sustain the growth for long because they do not generate commensurate growth in agricultural production. Nor do they broaden the geographical base of growth in fertilizer consumption, since it is constrained by inadequate development of systems which facilitate growth in fertilizer use.

Seventh, the keys to widening the base of growth in fertilizer use are geographical expansion of fertilizer distribution and agricultural credit systems and removal of various inefficiencies in them, location-specific research on the response function environment, and the spread of knowledge about efficient fertilizer practices among farmers through agricultural extension and commercial promotion systems. Critical to the success of these efforts, however, is that growth in total fertilizer supply keep ahead of growth in demand in regions of high consumption. This may necessitate public expenditure on carrying larger fertilizer inventories. But such expenditure will have a more favorable impact on sustaining growth in fertilizer consumption and increments in agricultural production than the budgetary burden of price policies which aim at raising fertilizer use in regions which have already reached fairly high levels.

Eighth, as growth in fertilizer consumption approaches its economic potential it can only be sustained by expanding that potential. This calls for accelerated development of irrigation and other technologies which improve the response function environment.

The above propositions indicate that there is a wide range of public policy issues relevant to generating sustained growth of fertilizer consumption in developing countries. These issues cannot be realistically tackled through price policy interventions such as high fertilizer subsidies and crop support prices. This is not to argue that prices of crops or fertilizers do not matter in the process of growth of fertilizer use. Obviously, these prices and response functions determine farmers' returns on fertilizer use. Other things remaining the same, therefore, the better the price environment, the faster the growth in fertilizer use. Similarly, as actual consumption approaches the economic potential, further growth in use becomes increasingly sensitive to changes in prices, as the experience of many developed countries during the 1970s clearly illustrates. But this should be distinguished from the role of price policy in generating sustained growth of fertilizer consumption in developing countries with a large, unexploited fertilizer potential.

By definition, unexploited potential implies scope for growth in fertilizer consumption under the prevailing price environment. Hence the thrust of our argument has been that acceleration in the growth of actual consumption should be achieved through policies which develop the systems facilitating growth in consumption, rather than through price policy interventions which constrain availability of public resources to develop these systems.

13

Government Credit Programs: Justification, Benefits, and Costs

MARK W. ROSEGRANT and AMMAR SIAMWALLA

Subsidized credit programs for agricultural producers have often been used to boost production in less developed countries. The "traditional" views in support of this policy instrument, as summarized by von Pischke, Adams, and Donald (1983), are that credit programs are easier to implement than such policies as land reform or infrastructure development, that subsidized credit can offset the negative impact on farm income and disincentives of government policies such as overvalued exchange rates and price controls, and that credit programs are necessary to provide capital for adoption of new technology. The informal credit market moneylenders are considered monopolistic, exploitive, and antidevelopmental, and incapable of providing the necessary credit.

Considerable opposition to the traditional view has developed. Critics claim that credit programs are not essential to adoption of new technology because most innovations can be adopted piecemeal rather than all at once, that informal moneylenders perform legitimate economic functions, that high interest rates are primarily caused by high opportunity and risk costs, and that subsidized formal market interest rates cause rationing of credit to rich farmers, discourage mobilization of rural savings, and cause a misallocation of funds to lower-payoff investments.

Based on this critique, von Pischke, Adams, and Donald recommend a shift from subsidized supply-oriented credit programs to efforts oriented toward market integration and savings mobilization with interest rates determined by market forces.

In this chapter, the determination of interest rates and the supply of funds in informal agricultural credit markets is explored in order to assess the conditions which might justify supply-oriented credit programs. The benefits and costs of a Philippine government credit program are then examined as an illustrative case study. The chapter concludes with general observations on the possible role of government in agricultural credit markets.

INTEREST RATE DETERMINATION

Interest rates in informal rural credit markets are typically much higher than those in institutional markets. In the Philippines, for example, informal money interest rates vary from 30 percent to more than 100 percent, with median rates of 45 to 50 percent. Institutional rates in the agriculture sector range from 16 percent to 20 percent. Analyses of interest rate determination in informal markets have concluded that risk premiums, opportunity costs, and high costs of administration account for much of the high interest rates, but generally some degree of monopoly rent has been found. Monopoly power has been variously attributed to institutional factors, such as the social and economic power exercised by landlords over tenants, and market imperfections, such as the domination of local markets by monopolists.

An interpretation of the source of monopoly rent in informal market interest rates which is more fruitful in assessing the likelihood of success of government intervention in agricultural credit markets has been presented by Virmani (1982). In competitive equilibrium, the interest rate on loans must be such that the expected returns to the lender are equal to the total cost of the loanable funds:

(1) $E(L) = (1 + r)(1 - p)L + pC = (1 + i + t)L$

or

(2) $r = (i + t + p - pC/L)/(1 - p)$,

where $E(L)$ is expected returns to the lender, L is loan size, r is loan interest rate, p is probability of default of borrower, i is opportunity cost of funds to lender, t is transaction costs of lending, and C is collateral on loan.

The competitive equilibrium interest rate is a function of the opportunity cost of funds to the lender, the transaction cost, the probability of repayment of the loan, and the amount of collateral on the loan. If loans are made with collateral, the equilibrium interest rate is less. From the standpoint of the expected return to the lender, interest and collateral are substitutes. It is possible to obtain a given expected return on a loan by different combinations of interest rate and collateral (Binswanger and Rosenzweig 1982; Stiglitz and Weiss 1981; Virmani 1982).

This framework is useful for identifying the source of monopoly power in informal credit markets. Assume initially that borrowers intend to pay back loans, so that any default is involuntary, caused, for example, by crop failure. In a competitive environment with perfect information, each lender's estimate of p (the probability of default) for any given borrower should be identical. However, it is reasonable to expect that each lender, or potential lender, will have different subjective estimates of the probabilities of default due to differential access to information regarding the borrower; the less information the lender has about the borrower, the higher his subjective estimate of the probability of default. From equation (2), the higher the estimate of the probability of default p, the higher is the interest rate which must be charged. (See Virmani for a formal presentation of these axioms.)

The lender with the most information can charge the lowest interest rate. He need not charge the rate which equalizes his own marginal costs and returns, but rather can charge just under the rate which would be charged by the lender with the next-best information. Information thus serves as a barrier to entry of other lenders. One major source of monopoly power of the traditional moneylenders is the information generated from long-term personal, social, and economic contacts with local borrowers.

The second, closely related source of monopoly power is that the moneylender will have lower transaction costs for both delivery and collection of loans than do potential competitors because of long-term experience with borrowers in his locality. However, he can charge a rate that exceeds his transaction costs because of the higher transaction costs of potential new lenders in the locality.

DISCRETIONARY DEFAULT

The preceding assumes that default occurs only when the borrower is unable to pay due to crop failure or other adverse circumstances. However, borrowers may choose not to repay even though it is feasible. Binswanger and Rosenzweig (1982) point out that borrowers seeking to maximize utility will default if the penalty from default, arising from loss of future earnings and collateral, is less than the value of repayment plus interest.

The possibility of discretionary default strengthens the ability of the lender with the closest information links to the borrower to extract monopoly profits through high interest rates. In addition to a better subjective estimate of the probability of nondiscretionary default, this lender, through his relationship with the borrower, can enforce a lower rate of discretionary default. Consequently, he can charge an interest rate with a premium for both higher subjective probabilities of nondiscretionary default and higher rates of discretionary default facing potential competition. The implications for government credit programs are discussed below.

SUPPLY OF FUNDS IN INFORMAL CREDIT MARKETS

Empirical evidence on the supply of credit from informal sources in rural areas is limited. Available evidence, however, indicates that it is probably almost adequate for static traditional production technology but inadequate to finance optimal levels of input and production following introduction of new production technology (Rosegrant and Herdt 1981). The conceptual framework in chapter 10 above supports this view by emphasizing the role of capital constraints in slowing the rate of growth that can be achieved from technological change.

Figure 13.1 shows the impact of the informal market loan constraint on borrowings following the introduction of new technology. Let $S_0 S_0$ be the supply curve for credit to a farm from the informal credit market as a function of the interest rate. Although the shape of this curve is not well established in the empirical literature, it is generally agreed that the curve is rather sharply upward-sloping, with the interest rate offered increasing with the amount of the loan. A number of factors may contribute to this relationship. First, following the simple model of discretionary default, the probability of default (in the absence of collateral) will increase for any borrower as the amount of the loan increases because of the increase in the benefits of default. Second, the proportion of potential defaulters in the mix of borrowers tends to increase as the amount of the loan goes up. They tend to seek larger loans and to consider riskier investments. Conse-

Figure 13.1   Credit supply and demand as a function of interest rates in informal and institutional markets, with and without modern production technology

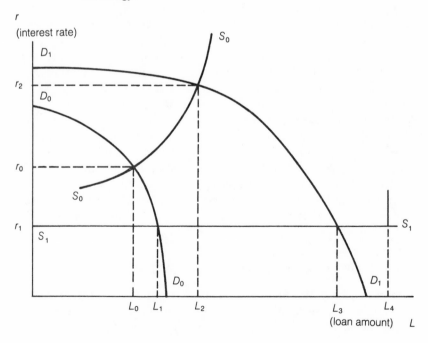

quently, the interest rate to all borrowers increases to compensate for a higher proportion of risky loans. Third, as loan size increases the opportunity costs of funds to the moneylenders will tend to increase.

Assume that the government institutes a credit program (or subsidizes private banks) which will provide credit up to the amount L_4 at the interest rate r_1. The supply schedule for institutional credit is thus given by S_1S_1. The impact of this credit program on the amount borrowed, and therefore on input use and production, is highly dependent on whether or not there is modern productive technology available.

Figure 13.1 shows two different demand schedules for credit, D_0D_0, which represents the demand for credit for traditional technology (such as traditional rice varieties), and D_1D_1, which is the demand for credit to be utilized for modern technologies (such as fertilizer-responsive rice varieties). The curve D_0D_0 is assumed to be highly inelastic because the response of credit demand to changes in interest rates is limited by the low productivity of inputs to be financed with the credit.

Introduction of new technology, which has inputs of much higher marginal productivity, shifts the credit demand curve to the right. At any interest rate, more credit will be demanded relative to the traditional technology case. The demand curve for credit for new technology is shown as first having a fairly elastic segment, then becoming progressively more inelastic, with a quite inelastic segment around the interest rate offered under the government credit program. This representation of the demand curve is derived from the simulation analysis for the Philippines presented below.

The figure shows that if only traditional technology is available the impact of the credit program on loan amount (and therefore on production) is small (the shift from L_0 to L_1). The main effect of the program is to transfer income to borrowers due to the reduction in the interest rate from r_0 to r_1. Following the introduction of new technology, the government credit program can have a substantial impact on the amount borrowed, as shown by the shift from L_2 in the informal market to L_3 in the credit program, and therefore on input use and production.

Figure 13.1 indicates that a shift to the right of the supply curve in the informal market (S_0S_0) after the introduction of new technology would increase the income of lenders in this market. This shift does not occur or occurs very slowly, primarily because lenders in the informal market generally lend out of their own equity and do not acquire deposits from outside sources. Therefore, the supply curve can shift only with increases in lender equity. Such increases may occur over time with increases in income from the loan business (and other enterprises of informal lenders such as rice milling and input supply) due to the new technology. But the response will be slower and smaller than if lenders also generated loans from deposits.

Binswanger and Rosenzweig point out two reasons for the dependence on equity in informal credit markets. The first is the seasonality and timing of the loan/production process. With both depositors and lenders involved in agricultural production, withdrawal of depositor funds for production purposes will coincide with borrowing. Therefore, the lender cannot utilize the deposits to finance loans. Second, yield covariance causes covariance of default risks and covariance of incomes among depositors and borrowers. Crop failure can result in depositors' withdrawing deposits because of low incomes at the same time that borrowers are unable to repay loans. A lender who lends out of deposits may be unable to reschedule loans, and instead may have to liquidate loans at a loss to cover deposit withdrawals.

Little or no empirical research has been done on the source of funds for moneylenders, but the broad picture presented above is generally accepted. However, it is possible that lenders may be able to expand their operations by drawing on funds from the national banking system (and thus avoid the covariation problem). Proposals for governments to provide funds for informal lenders have been made but not adopted. The Philippine Masagana 99 program, in which the government injects funds directly into the rural bank system, is a variant of these policies.

IMPLICATIONS FOR GOVERNMENT CREDIT PROGRAMS

The way in which informal agricultural credit markets set interest rates and supply funds has a number of implications for government credit programs which attempt to reduce interest rates and increase the supply of credit in these markets.

The availability of productive technology is essential for a credit program to have a significant impact on borrowing, input use, and production. Subsidized credit will have little impact on production characterized by static traditional technology because the quantity of credit supplied by informal sources is adequate, or nearly so. With static technology, the only justification for subsidized credit is to eliminate the monopoly rent (if any) in interest charged by moneylenders and thus to increase the incomes of farmers. Even in this case, the subsidies required to induce institutional lending in agriculture may be too high to be justified. The benefits will exceed the costs only if modern production technology is available and utilized.

The belief that physical fragmentation of rural credit markets is the source of monopoly rent has often led to an underestimation of the costs of intervening and to simplistic assumptions that introduction of institutional credit will provide the competition to reduce interest rates. The alternative framework here indicates that interest rates are a function of the opportunity costs of funds, the probability of default, transaction costs, and collateral. The sources of monopoly rent are differential access to information and different transaction costs among lenders. The lender with the best information links and the most efficient delivery and collection can charge an interest that just covers the higher estimated probability of default and higher transaction cost of the next-best lender. This prevents other lenders from entering the market.

Compared to informal lenders, institutional lenders (either government agencies or banks) typically have much poorer access to information and higher transaction costs in the agriculture sector. In urban areas, institutional lenders have better information access and lower transaction costs than in rural areas. Yet most government agricultural credit programs have sought to induce institutional lending to farmers at interest rates at or below urban rates. To accomplish this, the government must compensate the institutional lender for its high probability of default and transaction costs by reducing the opportunity cost of funds below the opportunity cost in the urban market. This can be done, for example, by permitting rediscounting of agricultural market loans at the central bank at preferential rates.

A further cost of effective government intervention into the rural credit market is discretionary default. Government lending programs often result in making default attractive to borrowers. To some extent this is unavoidable, since most programs attempt to reach small farmers with no collateral, so the probability of default will be higher than for loans to farmers with collateral. The lack of information and high transaction costs in collections further increase the probability of default. Attempts at sanctions against default are usually ineffective because farmers often assume that they will be permitted back into the program after a brief lapse of time or that the program will be discontinued. In each case, the expected loss of future earnings due to default is much reduced.

Because of these problems, institutional development should be a major component of any government credit program. Government subsidies on lending to rural markets are probably necessary in the early stages of intervention into the market, even to maintain interest rates at the same level as urban rates. This is because new lenders in the rural market lack information collection and processing capability and have high transaction costs. However, these subsidies tend to substitute for institutional development unless efforts are made to develop the information collection and processing and general management abilities of the institutional lenders and to reduce default probabilities and transaction costs. In the long run, such development can reduce rural interest rates, and subsidies relative to urban rates can be phased out.

SUBSIDIZED AGRICULTURAL CREDIT IN THE PHILIPPINES

Assessment of the benefits and costs of the Masagana 99 credit program reinforces the points made above. The impact of the program, begun in the Philippines in 1973, on farmer input use, yield, and income is examined using a multi-season farm decisionmaking model incorporating stochastic production technology, risk-neutral and risk-averse decision rules, short-term savings/consumption behavior, and a dual financial market (Rosegrant and Herdt 1981).

Prior to 1973/74, few Philippine rice farmers had access to institutional credit, primarily because of high collateral requirements of private banks (Sacay 1973). A series of typhoons in 1972 reduced the rice crop 16 percent from the previous three-year average, and during the same year the entire country was brought under a land reform program that was expected to restrict severely the credit traditionally provided by landlords to share tenants. Attempting to boost rice production, the government increased the flow of low-cost credit to rice farmers in 1973/74 through a program called Masagana 99.

During Masagana 99's initial year, farmers were allowed to borrow up to 900 pesos per hectare (P/ha) per six-month season. In 1974/75 the loan limit was increased to P 1,200/ha (P 7.30 = US$1 between 1973 and 1979). These production loans were available at an effective interest rate, including service charges and discounting, of approximately 16 percent per year in money terms. In 1974/75, over 40 percent of the national rice area was financed under Masagana 99. Financing declined to about 10 percent in 1977/78, mainly because frequent defaults disqualified farmers from further borrowing under the program.

Table 13.1 shows the declines in total loans granted and number of borrowers. The repayment rate also has generally declined, largely because late repayments increased the totals of the early years. Collections as of the due date are much lower. Due date collections of rural banks for Phases IV–XI were 67.5 percent, compared to 80 percent as of April 1979 (Esguerra n.d.).

The primary alternative source of production loans is the informal financial market. Credit availability in this sector varies, but surveys conducted by the International Rice Research Institute indicate a range of effective credit ceilings of P 300–P 600/ha in central Luzon. Informal market interest rates vary from 30 percent to 100 percent and average 45 percent to 50 percent (Rosegrant 1978; Manto and Torres 1974).

The Philippine government also established a two-tier fertilizer pricing system in 1973, when supplies in the international market were becoming tight and world prices were increasing rapidly. A subsidized price was established for rice and other food crops. A higher price for export crops

Table 13.1 Masagana 99 total country program, phases I–XI, Philippines, 1973–79

Phase	Year/season	Total loans granted	Area financed	Farmers served	Average loan granted		Repayments	
		(million pesos)	(hectares)		(P/ha)	(P/borrower)	(million pesos)	(%)
I	1973/wet	369.5	620,928	401,461	595	920	347.4	94
II	1974/dry	230.7	355,397	236,116	649	977	216.9	94
III	1974/wet	716.2	866,552	429,161	826	1,353	601.6	84
IV	1975/dry	572.3	593,624	354,901	964	1,612	469.1	82
V	1975/wet	573.0	558,335	301,828	1,026	1,898	435.4	76
VI	1976/dry	255.6	255,884	150,464	999	1,699	207.3	81
VII	1976/wet	275.1	244,467	144,265	1,125	1,907	219.4	80
VIII	1977/dry	164.4	148,801	89,623	1,105	1,834	133.1	81
IX	1977/wet	251.8	221,522	131,590	1,136	1,914	185.2	74
X	1978/dry	175.1	155,095	92,476	1,130	1,903	140.1	80
XI	1979/wet	236.9	202,606	116,624	1,167	2,025	161.0	68
Total		3,820.6	4,223,211	2,448,509	905	1,499	3,116.5	82

Sources: Computed from basic data from the National Food and Agriculture Council, Ministry of Agriculture, Diliman, Quezon City, Philippines; Esguerra n.d.

reflected import and marketing costs. This system continued until 1975/ 76, after which a uniform, subsidized price applied to all crops (table 13.1).

THE MODEL OF FARMER DECISIONMAKING

Figure 13.2 outlines the model. Initially, output and input prices and initial savings are set and farm characteristics specified to determine a yield distribution for any set of inputs. The yield distributions were computed from a production function incorporating random environmental variables and their estimated frequency distributions (Rosegrant and Herdt 1981). The financial market in which the farmer borrows determines his interest rate and credit ceiling. The net income distribution for any input level can then be computed and optimal input levels chosen by the specified decision rule, subject to the credit ceiling.

The actual yield is generated by random sampling from the yield distribution corresponding to the optimal input level, and actual net income is computed. If net income plus nonfarm income exceeds subsistence requirements, savings are carried forward to the next season to begin another iteration. If total income is less than subsistence, the farm defaults on its loan and, if necessary, borrows from the informal credit market to cover subsistence requirements. Savings are computed, and the next iteration begins with the farm denied access to the institutional market because of default. If total income exceeds subsistence requirements, the farm remains in the institutional market and begins the next iteration.

For any set of specified prices, interest rates, loan ceilings, and farm characteristics, the model can be solved for mean input use, yield, and income over several seasons.

Impact of Credit and Fertilizer Policy

A subsidized credit program with increased loan ceilings, similar to those under Masagana 99, and a fertilizer subsidy comparable to that of the Philippine government were evaluated for crop years 1973/74 (the first year of Masagana 99) through 1977/78. Model parameters such as farm size, nonfarm income, wages, rents, herbicide and insecticide prices, and sharing rates were set at representative values for central Luzon. Farm prices of rice were set at the prevailing annual level.

Fertilizer prices were set for successive runs of the model at the annual subsidized and unsubsidized rates derived from table 13.2. Financial market variables were set to simulate the presence or absence of a Masagana-type credit program. For model runs simulating a credit program, all farms were assumed to begin in the institutional market, with a loan ceiling of P 1,200/ha and an interest rate of 16 percent per year. The farms

Figure 13.2   Flow chart of farm decisionmaking model

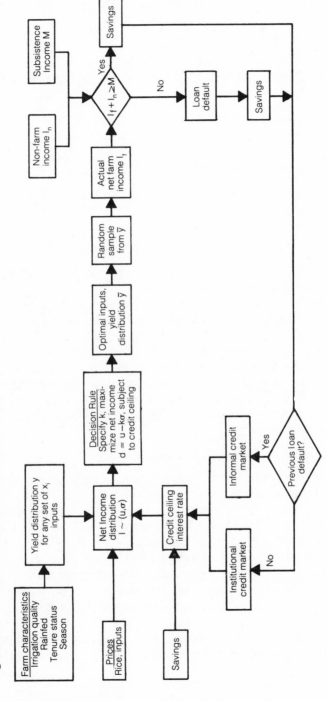

Table 13.2 Prices of nitrogen and phosphorus fertilizer (p/kg) for rice and export crops and subsidies, Philippines

Crop year	Price for rice production		Price for export crops		Rice production subsidy[a]	
	Nitrogen	Phosphorus	Nitrogen	Phosphorus	Nitrogen	Phosphorus
1973/74	2.15	2.56	3.82	4.22	1.67	1.66
1974/75	4.38	3.83	7.07	6.48	2.69	2.65
1975/76	3.97	3.84	6.24	6.34	2.27	2.50
1976/77	3.68	4.09	3.68	4.09	0.72	1.21
1977/78	3.68	4.09	3.68	4.09	0.22	0.51

Source: Rosegrant and Herdt 1981, data from Fertilizer and Pesticide Authority, Republic of the Philippines.

[a] This figure represents the difference between the price for rice production and for export crops for 1973/74 to 1975/76; it represents import plus marketing costs less sale price for 1976/77 and 1977/78.

continue to borrow in the institutional market until default, after which they enter the informal market.

Interest rates in the informal market were set at 48 percent per year, with maximum loan limits at P 300/ha and P 600/ha for alternative runs. For model runs simulating the absence of a subsidized credit program, all farms were assumed to borrow only from the informal market.

Three policies were evaluated: the credit program with the fertilizer subsidy, the credit program with no fertilizer subsidy, and the fertilizer subsidy with no credit program. In each case, the estimated impact of the policies is compared with the case of no government credit program and no fertilizer price subsidy.

Combined Credit Program with Fertilizer Subsidy

The combined impact of the credit program and fertilizer subsidy is large with either informal credit market loan limit (table 13.3). With a P 300/ha loan limit in the informal market, the combined credit program and fertilizer subsidy is estimated to increase the average nitrogen use on irrigated and rainfed farms by 43 kg/ha, other input use by P 129/ha, yields by 510 kg/ha (30 percent), and income by P 131/ha (29 percent). For the P 600/ha informal market loan ceiling, the estimated combined impact is reduced but still impressive: average increases of 38 kg/ha in nitrogen use, P 90/ha in other inputs, 393 kg/ha (21 percent) in yields, and P 118/ha (25 percent) in income.

Irrigated farms are considerably more responsive to combined credit and fertilizer policies than rainfed farms. They also gain higher benefits.

Table 13.3 Estimated increases in input use, yield, and income due to credit program and fertilizer subsidy, 1973/74 and 1977/78

Policy	Farm type	Nitrogen	Other inputs	Yield	Income
		(kg/ha)	(P/ha)	(kg/ha)	(P/ha)
		Informal market loan limit of P 300/ha[a]			
Credit program, fertilizer	Irrigated	49	162	619	158
subsidy	Rainfed	30	69	308	81
	Average[b]	43	129	510	131
Credit program, no	Irrigated	22	127	397	67
fertilizer subsidy	Rainfed	7	41	114	34
	Average[b]	17	103	298	56
Fertilizer subsidy, no	Irrigated	14	−13	106	55
credit program	Rainfed	14	−5	102	38
	Average[b]	14	−10	105	49
		Informal market loan limit of P 600/ha[a]			
Credit program, fertilizer	Irrigated	42	115	466	142
subsidy	Rainfed	30	45	257	74
	Average[b]	38	90	393	118
Credit program, no	Irrigated	13	78	221	49
fertilizer subsidy	Rainfed	6	12	50	28
	Average[b]	10	54	127	35
Fertilizer subsidy, no	Irrigated	30	47	311	85
credit program	Rainfed	6	33	207	39
	Average[b]	27	35	274	69

Source: Rosegrant and Herdt 1981.

[a] Estimated increases are computed relative to the case of no credit program and no fertilizer subsidy.

[b] The average taken of irrigated and rainfed farms, weighted by the area harvested in central Luzon.

The reasons for their higher responsiveness are to be seen in the separate effects of the credit program and fertilizer subsidy.

Credit Policy

The credit program alone produces substantial gains for irrigated farms but considerably lower benefits for rainfed farms. For the P 300/ha case, for example, irrigated farms increase yields by 22 percent and income by 14 percent due to implementation of a credit program without fertilizer subsidy, while the yield and income benefits for rainfed farms are 7 percent and 9 percent, respectively.

Irrigated farms gain higher benefits from a credit program that releases a binding credit constraint because they can utilize higher input levels more profitably. This is due to lower moisture stress in both seasons, high solar radiation, and lack of typhoons in the dry season, which increase the marginal productivity and optimal level of nitrogen and other inputs, leading to larger benefits than on rainfed farms.

Additional runs were made to estimate the impact of reducing interest rates from 48 percent to 16 percent without increasing the availability of credit. The independent impact of such a reduction in interest rate is relatively modest: an average increase, for irrigated and rainfed farms, of 5 kg/ha in nitrogen, 3 percent in yields, and 6 percent in income with the P 600/ha loan limit, and 3 kg/ha nitrogen, 2 percent in yield, and 3 percent in income with the P 300/ha loan limit.

The maximum interest rate impact occurs when credit is not constraining, so farmers can respond fully to price. Sensitivity tests using the model with no credit constraint show a maximum increase in yields of 5 percent and in incomes of 10 percent caused by a reduction in the interest rate from 48 percent to 16 percent. When the credit ceiling is binding, price changes are not effective. Instead, an interest rate reduction works by increasing the amounts of inputs which can be financed for a given amount of credit by increasing income and savings available to finance inputs. This effect is smaller than the price impact, and causes a reduced interest rate effect when a binding loan constraint holds for some or all farms.

Default Rates

The model predicts average annual default rates on institutional market loans of 9.7 percent with the fertilizer subsidy and 10.6 percent without subsidy. This is lower than the total repayment rate (table 13.1) because the model simulates only nondiscretionary default, and does not include discretionary default. As of the 1977/78 crop year in the simulated credit program, only 66 percent of farmers were eligible for institutional credit in the subsidized fertilizer case and 63 percent in the unsubsidized fertilizer case. With a P 300/ha informal market loan limit, the average yield loss due to default in 1977/78 was 8 percent with income reduction 6 percent. For the P 600/ha informal loan limit case, the reductions in benefits due to default were approximately half as large.

Fertilizer Subsidy

The impact of a fertilizer subsidy with no credit program is highly dependent on the availability of credit in the informal market. With the P 300/ha loan limit (which is binding on most farms), the decrease in the price of fertilizer (due to the subsidy) permits 14 kg/ha more fertilizer to be financed within the loan limit. Other input use decreases by P 10/ha because a small amount of the other inputs are replaced by fertilizer, which, because of the subsidy, becomes relatively more profitable. The net yield benefit of the fertilizer subsidy is 6 percent, with incomes increasing 11 percent. Irrigated and rainfed farms get approximately the same benefits.

With the P 600/ha informal credit limit (which is nonbinding on many farms), the fertilizer subsidy boosts fertilizer use through the price impact, increasing marginal returns and optimal fertilizer levels. It also permits more fertilizer to be financed through loans. The impact of the subsidy on fertilizer use is nearly double that of the P 300/ha loan limit case. With the higher loan limit, irrigated farms get 50 percent higher yield benefits and double the income benefits of rainfed farms due to the higher productivity of fertilizer.

GOVERNMENT FINANCIAL COSTS AND SUBSIDIES FOR MASAGANA 99

The production and income benefits of the Masagana 99 credit program should be compared with the cost to the government and the total subsidy to financial institutions and farmers. Two sources of costs can be identified: interest rate subsidies due to provision of capital to banks and farmers at less than the cost to the government and losses on defaulted loans guaranteed by the government. In order to estimate these costs we must understand the method of financing the program. (The descriptive material which follows is drawn largely from Esguerra [1981 and undated]. Esguerra used a similar framework for analysis of program subsidies, but an incorrect definition of the opportunity cost of capital inflated his subsidy estimates.)

Masagana 99 subsidized credit was channeled to farmers through rural banks, the Philippine National Bank (PNB) and other commercial banks, and the Agricultural Credit Administration (ACA, a cooperative organization). The first two sources accounted for nearly 48 percent, respectively, of the total loans to farmers in 1973-79; ACA accounted for less than 5 percent. Over 99 percent of the total provided by commercial banks was supplied by PNB. In the following discussion, PNB refers to the other commercial banks as well.

At the beginning of each phase, seed money for Masagana 99 farmer loans was provided by the central bank to the rural banks and PNB through Special Time Deposits (STDs) with interest rates of 3 percent per annum, payable in sixty days. However, the full portfolio of loans to Masagana farmers was eventually funded by rediscounting of farmer-borrowers' loan papers to the central bank. First, farmer-borrowers' loan papers whose financing needs were initially covered by funds from STD releases were rediscounted to the central bank, providing funds for additional lending. The loan papers from the succeeding set of lending transactions were in turn rediscounted to repay the STDs from the central bank. The rediscounting process continued until the lending institutions were able to cover all loan requirements and pay back the STDs. ACA did not have access to STD and rediscounting arrangements. It utilized internal funds which came from the national government budget for Masagana lending operations.

The total financial cost to the government of the interest rate subsidy under the program can be computed as $R(r_c - r_p)m$, where R is the total amount of loans rediscounted to the central bank, r_c is the cost to the government of obtaining the funds for rediscounting, r_p is the preferential rediscount rate to the rural banks and PNB, and m is the maturity of the loan expressed as a fraction of a year (0.50 for six-month loans).

Masagana 99 loans rediscounted to the central bank during 1973–79 totaled more than P 3.5 billion (table 13.4). The preferential rediscount rate was 1 percent to rural banks, 3 percent to PNB during phases I–VII, and 1 percent to PNB thereafter. The funds provided by the central bank to finance the rediscounting came from the proceeds of Central Bank Certifi-

Table 13.4 Total financial cost to the government and total subsidies to financial institutions and farmers, Masagana 99, phases I–XI, Philippines, 1973–79

	Rural banks	PNB	ACA[a]	Total
	(million pesos)			
(1) Total loans rediscounted to central bank	2,405.2	1,121.8	—	3,527.0
(2) Financial cost to government of interest rate subsidy	134.1	54.2	—	188.3
(3) Total interest rate subsidy	204.4	95.4	—	299.8
(4) Total loans granted to farmers	1,817.5	1,821.9	181.2	3,820.6
(5) Interest rate subsidy to farmers	18.2	18.2	—	36.4
(6) Interest rate subsidy to financial institutions: (3) − (5)	186.2	77.2	—	263.4
(7) Total loans in default	258.5	386.7	59.1	704.3
(8) Financial cost to government of default	193.9	290.0	44.3	528.2
(9) Total financial cost to government: (2) + (8)	328.0	344.2	44.3	716.5

Source: See table 13.1.

[a] Subsidy not computed on ACA loans because internal funds were utilized. At market interest rates, the total interest rate subsidy would be P 14.5 million.

cates of Indebtedness (CBCIS), on which the government paid a 9 percent rate of interest. However, CBCIS are not subject to the usual 35 percent tax on interest income, so the gross cost (r_c) to the government of the loanable funds for Masagana 99 was 12.15 percent per annum. The net cost of the interest rate subsidy was therefore 11.15 percent per annum (9.15 percent for PNB, phases I–VII) for every peso channeled through the rural banks and PNB to farmer-borrowers. The total financial cost of this subsidy was about P 188.3 million through 1979, or about P 45/ha averaged over the area financed by the program (table 13.4).

This amount, however, understates the total subsidy channeled through rural banks and PNB. To compute the total subsidy, the interest rate used should be the opportunity cost of capital. Estimates of the true opportunity cost of capital during this period range from 14 percent to 20 percent (Bautista et al. 1979). A rate of 18 percent per annum is used here.

The distribution of this subsidy between financial institutions and farmer-borrowers is an important issue, since boosting farm income was a major goal of the program. The interest rate subsidy to farmers can be computed as $L(r_o - r_f)m$, where L is the loan amount received by farmers, r_o is the opportunity cost of capital, and r_f is the effective interest rate to farmers on Masagana 99 loans (16 percent). As shown in table 13.4, the total interest rate subsidy to farmer-borrowers in 1973–79 was P 36.2 million, leaving a total interest rate subsidy to the rural banks and PNB of P 263.4 million. In other words, 88 percent of the total interest rate subsidy provided under the Masagana 99 program was retained by the financial institutions, with farmer-borrowers receiving only 12 percent. Additional service charges were imposed on some farmers which could increase the effective interest rate on Masagana loans to 30 percent. Farmers charged these rates were actually taxed relative to the opportunity cost of capital.

The rural banks retained a particularly high proportion (91 percent) of the interest rate subsidy channeled through them. This high retention rate is due to the fact that almost P 600 million of rediscounted funds did not reach farmers under the Masagana 99 program (table 13.4). Almost one-fourth of the funds acquired by rural banks at the Masagana 99 preferential rediscounting rate were apparently diverted to other investments.

In addition to the financial costs to the government of providing the interest rate subsidy, losses were incurred due to the default of Masagana 99 farmer-borrowers. The government guaranteed 75 percent of each loan, thereby absorbing three-fourths of the losses due to default. As shown in table 13.4, these losses totaled P 528.2 million during phases I–XI, bringing total government financial costs to P 716.5 million, or an average over the total area financed of P 170/ha. The total financial costs to the government are thus higher than the farmer income benefits estimated for the program.

CONCLUSIONS AND IMPLICATIONS

Following the very poor harvest of 1972/73, the Philippine government instituted subsidized credit and fertilizer policies. Between 1972/73 and 1977/78, Philippine rice production increased by 56 percent and rice yields increased by 38 percent. This outstanding achievement could not be attributed only to government credit and fertilizer policies. The analysis, using a dynamic model of farmer decisionmaking, shows that credit and fertilizer policies could have induced a yield increase of 21 to 30 percent for a set of farms representative of those in central Luzon.

The analysis of program benefits confirms that the provision of institutional credit to farmers when the supply of credit from informal sources is limited and inelastic and productive technology is available can generate large gains in input use, yield, and farmer income. The importance of the availability of appropriate production technology is underscored by the failure of the Philippine government credit programs for corn production due to the lack of profitable technology adapted to farm conditions.

Provision of credit also increases the impact of subsidies on other inputs such as fertilizer. Where the availability of loan funds from informal sources is limited, the credit program makes its greatest impact on the effectiveness of fertilizer price subsidies by releasing the credit constraint through institutional lending. The independent effect of interest rate reductions is relatively small. Even when productive technology is available, the demand for credit and inputs purchased with this credit is relatively inelastic with respect to the interest. Significantly higher interest rates than those prevailing in the Masagana 99 program could be charged without substantially reducing yield increases and farmer income benefits.

The estimated financial costs of the program to the government were even higher than the large estimated farmer income benefits. Furthermore, nearly all of the interest rate subsidy financed by the government was captured by the financial institutions rather than by the farmers. Few of the resources captured by financial institutions were reinvested in institution-strengthening activities. Although new institutional lenders will tend to have poor information links, high default risks, and high transaction costs in lending when entering the agricultural market, the level of subsidy provided to compensate the institutions (a 15 percent spread between the cost of funds to the banks and their lending rate) appears excessive by any standards. With an 18 percent default rate on Masagana 99 loans and only 25 percent exposure of the banks on defaults, the total loss through defaulted loans would be only 4.5 percent, leaving a very large interest spread to cover all other costs of administering the loans.

The large interest rate subsidies and high level of government guarantee of loans reduced incentives for the banks to pursue collections aggressively. The farm decisionmaking model predicts average annual default rates of around 10 percent, based only on nondiscretionary default. The actual 18 percent rate of default thus includes a large amount of discretionary default which could have been reduced by active collection. The increasing rates of default over time show that the collection performance of banks declined, significant evidence of lack of institutional development.

The low cost of funds (1 percent) for the Masagana 99 program discouraged banks from seeking alternative sources of funding. With an interest rate on customer deposits of 6 percent, there was little incentive to seek such deposits. A study by the Technical Board for Agricultural Credit showed that short-term obligations to the central bank constituted an average of over 50 percent of the assets of rural banks in 1979.

In general, the financial institutions substituted the high level of subsidies for the development of management capabilities. The banks were unable to compete effectively in the agricultural credit market without such subsidies. The failure to develop the banks as viable competitive institutions by linking subsidies to institutional development locked the government into continuing high-cost subsidies.

A number of lessons can be drawn from the Masagana 99 program. Subsidies to farmers on agricultural credit relative to informal market interest rates are justified when there is a monopoly profit element in these interest rates arising from differential access to information and differential transaction costs. If profitable technology is available and the supply of credit from informal sources is limited, institutional credit can provide large production and income benefits. Even if new technologies such as modern rice varieties can be adopted on a step-by-step basis, adequate credit can be essential to achieving full benefits from its adoption.

Subsidizing interest rates at levels below the opportunity cost of capital, or below market-determined rates in the urban sector, do not appear justified. For example, raising interest rates on Masagana 99 loans to the opportunity cost of capital (or even higher) would have had little effect on loan demand and program benefits. Moreover, an increase in interest rate would permit a reduction in the subsidy required to induce financial institutions to enter the agricultural credit market.

Subsidies to financial institutions on the costs of funds for agricultural loans in the early stages of their penetration of the agricultural market appear to be justified. However, the government should emphasize developments which will increase their access to information and reduce transaction costs. This would permit a phased reduction in subsidies to the banks.

This is the fundamental dilemma facing governments in devising a policy to develop a viable agricultural credit delivery system. In the early stages of development of new production technology, it is important to channel loanable funds to farmers. During this period, subsidies will be required to induce institutions to lend. In the medium to long term, however, the main constraint to development of a viable agricultural credit sector is not the cost or availability of loanable funds but the development of human capital within financial institutions. How the government manages the transition from short-term subsidies to long-term financial stability through institutional development will determine the success of government credit policy.

Criticism of the traditional rationale for government credit programs has been useful in pointing out the importance of institution-building in rural financial markets and the allocative problems caused by subsidized interest rates in the agricultural sector. However, it has been too quick to dismiss the possible role for subsidies during the early stages of institutional development of agencies entering agricultural credit markets. More important, the critique has failed to recognize the potential benefits from supply-oriented credit programs when the supply of credit from informal moneylenders is inelastic and insufficiently responsive to the development and introduction of new technologies.

IV

CONSUMERS' WELFARE

14

Food Subsidies: Consumer Welfare and Producer Incentives

PER PINSTRUP-ANDERSEN

Policies to strengthen incentives to expand food production through higher food prices are likely to result in short-run reductions in real incomes of food consumers. Since a large share of the income of the poor is generally spent on food, higher food prices may cause severe hardships to those who do not derive their incomes from food production either directly as producers or farm workers or indirectly as providers of inputs and consumption goods to farmers.[1]

But not only the poor will be adversely affected. Food expenditures of the better-off consumers also will rise as food prices increase. Although the poor will have a larger loss relative to current incomes, their absolute loss will be smaller.

Although increased food prices may contribute to long-run economic growth and food self-sufficiency goals, the short-run economic, welfare, and political implications may be untenable. Reactions by urban consumers to recent attempts to increase food prices in a number of countries have clearly demonstrated the political implications. Furthermore, a number of studies have shown that food price increases may cause serious hardships for the poor, including deterioration of an already precarious nutritional situation.

There is no easy solution or general policy that would be applicable to all countries. The choice and design of policies for each country must be based on its particular mix of economic, social, and political considerations, including the characteristics of low-income population groups. Options available to governments for dealing with food price issues based on the experience from various countries and the results from studies are presented below.

1. Gray (1982) estimated that the poorest 30 percent of the Brazilian population spent 59 percent of total income on food, as compared to 16 percent for the 20 percent with the highest incomes. Mellor (1978) found that the poorest 20 percent of the Indian population spent 54 percent of income on foodgrains alone, as compared to 15 percent for the richest 5 percent.

GENERAL FOOD POLICIES AND SUBSIDIES

Many countries follow cheap food policies enforced through various combinations of exchange rate manipulations, domestic price fixing, forced food procurement, export taxes, and government monopolies in foreign and/or domestic food trade. Combined with similar measures for nonfood agricultural commodities, these policies have resulted in the extraction of economic surplus from agriculture for use in promoting growth in nonagricultural public and private sectors, thereby reducing investment and production incentives in agriculture.

The impact of cheap food policies on the real income of the poor cannot be measured easily. Different groups may be affected differently. The most obvious distinction is whether a group depends on food production for its income. Furthermore, the immediate impact may be quite different than the intermediate and longer-run effects.

The immediate impact of an increase in food prices on poor wage-earners who do not derive their income from food production would be negative. The longer-run impact depends on whether higher food prices lead to higher wages and whether upward adjustment in food prices improves the efficiency of resource allocation and utilization and thus generates economic growth and increased employment. In a study of Argentina, Cavallo and Mundlak (1982) found that trade liberalization and exchange rate management would accelerate economic growth while causing agricultural prices to increase faster than nonagricultural wage rates, thus reducing real wages in terms of food. They further demonstrated that compensation could be paid to consumers in the form of subsidies which would keep food wages constant, at an economic cost considerably less than the economic gains resulting from trade liberalization and exchange rate management. Thus, although, under the assumptions of their model, the rate of economic growth would be lower if food wages were kept constant, it was shown that policies reflecting long-term economic efficiency goals would be feasible without adverse effects on food wages.

The extent to which benefits from food price subsidies are captured by consumers rather than passed on in the form of lower wages varies among countries, and empirical evidence is scarce. The period of adjustment of wage rates is also likely to vary depending on institutional and other aspects. Pending additional empirical evidence, it may be concluded only that while the effect of food price increases on real incomes of poor wage-earners who do not derive their income from food production is likely to be negative in the short run, it may eventually become positive in the longer run. However, long-run effects may be of little or no interest to the poor who are adversely affected in the short run. The subjective discount rate for the poor is likely to be very high, and uncertain future gains may be insufficient to compensate for immediate losses. Thus food price increases may be politically difficult or impossible unless compensation is made for short-run losses.

The impact of food price increases on the poor who derive their incomes from food production would be expected to be positive provided that the price increase is reflected in farmgate prices. Higher prices would add to revenues from marketable surpluses, and labor demand in food production would be expected to increase. However, total demand for rural labor need not increase if the food price increases cause substitution of less labor-intensive for more labor-intensive commodities, for example, substitution of rice for jute in Bangladesh (Ahmed 1981).

Food price increases often may be much less favorable for the rural poor than expected. Many of the rural poor derive only a small share of their incomes from wage labor in food production or from the sale of food. Results from a study of the implications of increasing domestic rice prices in Thailand show that the rural poor would not benefit greatly from such increases (Trairatvorakul 1984). Even though many of the poor are rice producers, the marketable surplus is often small, and a large proportion are net buyers of rice. Although these findings may not have general application, it is clear that food price increases will create short-run hardships among many rural poor, particularly those in the informal sector. Thus compensatory measures may be needed in both urban and rural areas. In the somewhat longer run, increasing demand for rural services is likely to result in increased incomes among the same groups of rural poor.

A variety of compensatory measures are available, including increases in wages in the public sector and in minimum wages in the private sector. While the poor nonwageearners—for example, the large number of people working in the informal sectors—would be affected in roughly the same way as wageearners, compensation through wage manipulations would obviously not be possible. Other compensatory measures are discussed later.

EXPLICIT GENERAL SUBSIDIES

Some countries have used subsidies to shield consumers from the effects of increasing food prices (whether the increase is in real or nominal terms) in order to maintain political stability, avoid negative impact on the poor, and maintain low wages. The fiscal costs of a publicly financed wedge between consumer and producer or import prices can be very high, depending on the size of the subsidy, the marketing costs if borne by the public sector, and the amount of food to which the subsidy is applied. The size of the subsidy depends on the source and price of the food available to governments and the desired consumer price levels. The wedge may be large, as illustrated by domestic consumer prices fixed by the government for wheat, sugar, and beans in Egypt, which were 28, 29, and 35 percent, respectively, of the international prices in 1980 (von Braun and de Haen 1983).

The size of the subsidy may change considerably over time, either to insulate domestic consumers from price fluctuations in the international markets or because of a widening gap between international and domestic price trends. Because of its traditionally large price fluctuations, the sugar market provides a good illustration of the former. Domestic sugar prices to Egyptian consumers varied from 22 percent of the international prices in 1974, to approximately parity in 1977, to 144 percent in 1978, and back to 29 percent in 1980 (von Braun and de Haen 1983). One of the principal reasons for a widening gap between international and domestic price trends in some countries is a desire to maintain constant or near-constant nominal prices for basic food staples in the face of increasing general price levels. Alderman, von Braun, and Sakr (1982) report that consumer prices of wheat and rationed sugar, rice, and lentils in Egypt were virtually unchanged in nominal terms during 1971–81. Since international prices increased in nominal terms and the value of the Egyptian currency fell, the price wedge increased. In the case of wheat, von Braun and de Haen report that the subsidy rose from 44 percent of international prices in 1971 to 71 percent in 1980.

Unless the subsidized quantity is reduced, a larger publicly financed price wedge results in higher fiscal costs. If no targeting or rationing is attempted, costs may be high. The fiscal costs of the wheat subsidies in Egypt, which are neither targeted nor rationed, increased from E£ 21 million in 1970/71 to E£ 511 million in 1980/81, or the equivalent of 0.05 to 3.5 percent of GDP (Alderman, von Braun, and Sakr [1982]). Rationing of the quantities subsidized without targeting does not assure low fiscal costs. Although smaller than those of the wheat subsidies, which are not rationed, the fiscal cost of subsidies on rationed foods in Egypt is high.

Large public expenditures on food subsidies may have significant macroeconomic effects, as illustrated by Scobie in a study for Egypt (Scobie 1983). On the assumption that the explicit Egyptian food subsidy program is financed through deficit spending at the margin, that is, that changes in the fiscal costs of subsidies would be reflected in similar changes in deficit spending, it was estimated that a 10 percent change in subsidy expenditures would result in a change in the rate of inflation of 5 percent in the same direction. In other words, increasing subsidy costs would fuel inflation. They would also cause an increase in foreign liabilities and a devaluation of the free market exchange rate for Egyptian currency.

Import demand for food in Egypt was found to be very inelastic. This is in large measure caused by the subsidy program, the high priority on maintaining stable and relatively low food prices for Egyptian consumers, and the government monopoly on food imports, which makes it easier for government to control imports. As a consequence, changes in either the price of imported food or the supply of foreign exchange are likely to be reflected primarily in the importation of industrial goods. It was estimated that a fall of one dollar in foreign exchange would reduce imports of food and other consumer goods by only sixteen cents, while imports of industrial raw material, fuel, and chemicals would fall by forty cents and capital goods by thirty-four cents. This has important implications for real output and investment in the industrial sector. The study estimates that a fall of 10 percent in foreign exchange supplies reduces real industrial output by 4 percent and investment by 6 percent. Similarly, a 10 percent rise in the cost of imported food will result in a fall of 1 to 2 percent in industrial output, as imports of raw materials are reduced to provide more foreign exchange for food imports.

Rapidly increasing fiscal costs occurred for the Sri Lankan food ration shop scheme through the first half of the 1970s, reaching Rs 1,000 million in 1975, or around 15 percent of total government expenditures (Gavan and Chandrasekera 1979). Changes in the subsidy program during the second half of the 1970s, including a shift to food stamps with a fixed nominal value, rapidly increasing food prices, and exclusion of about one-half of the population from the program reduced the fiscal costs of the Sri Lankan food subsidies dramatically to the current level of about 3.5 percent of total government expenditures (Edirisinghe 1987). These reductions have been attained by targeting as well as drastic reduction in the real value of the subsidy to the poor target groups.

TARGETED FOOD PRICE SUBSIDIES

Because of the high fiscal costs of maintaining general food price subsidies, efforts have been and are currently being made to target food subsidies to groups of households expected to be particularly vulnerable to high and increasing food prices and to limit the subsidies to specific foods or rations. If the sole goal of food subsidies is to increase or sustain the ability of the poor to purchase enough food to meet nutritional requirements and other basic necessities, the goal could be reached and cost reduced by targeting, provided that it is politically and logistically feasible.

The cost-effectiveness of explicit subsidies, that is, the cost to government of improving the ability of food-deficient households to acquire a certain amount of food, is positively correlated with the degree of targeting up to a certain level. This is because targeting excludes some or all nondeficit households from the benefits of the subsidies. However, the administrative costs of operating a food price subsidy program go up as the degree of targeting increases. Thus there is a point beyond which increases in administrative costs exceed savings from further reducing benefit leakages to nondeficit households.

Targeting implies restriction of eligibility or participation. It may imply rationing of the quantity of food that can be obtained under the subsidy program or it may limit subsidies to particular periods of the year, for example, to the months when seasonal fluctuations in food supplies or purchasing power are a major cause of malnutrition. Targeting may be based on other criteria, the most obvious of which would be household income, whether total or per person. While this is used as a criterion in certain programs, for example, Sri Lankan food stamp scheme, it is usually difficult to obtain a reasonably accurate estimate of individual household incomes. Another criterion relates to the location of outlets for subsidized foods: they may be placed in neighborhoods with a high proportion of poor households. A third approach used in a number of integrated health and nutrition programs—for example, the rural health clinics in Costa Rica and the recently terminated food stamp program in Colombia—is to select malnourished individuals at existing health clinics. Targeting may also result in cases where the customers desiring to purchase subsidized foods must wait in line for a long time. Whether intentional or merely a result of inefficient operation, a long wait may discourage participation by higher-income groups. Of course, if the subsidy is sufficiently large, those with higher incomes may hire persons to wait in line for them.

Targeting can also be accomplished by offering lower-quality products that are considered undesirable by higher-income groups. Distribution of subsidized wheat flour perceived to be of low quality (atta) in ration shops in Pakistan is a case in point. In a study of wheat flour consumption in Rawalpindi City, Khan (1982) found that poor households purchased more than 30 kg/month of subsidized wheat flour from ration shops, compared with around 20 kg/month for the highest-income households. Purchases of nonsubsidized wheat flour from the open market was about 16 kg/month for the poor and 58 kg/month for the highest-income group. A study for Bangladesh concluded that distribution of sorghum through the ration shops in Bangladesh would be more cost-effective than the distribution of rice and wheat because sorghum would be acquired almost exclusively by the poor (Karim, Majid, and Levinson 1980).

Targeted or rationed food price subsidy programs may be implemented in various ways. Food may be distributed in public ration shops, as in India, Bangladesh, and Pakistan, through private shops, or through a combination of the two, as in Egypt. Target households may be issued ration cards that specify the amount of food that can be obtained under subsidy.

Although food price subsidy policies have been implemented with reasonable success in many urban areas, their success has been limited in rural areas except for Egypt, Sri Lanka, and parts of India. Limited success in rural areas may be due to lack of rural infrastructure or government priorities.

Implementation of targeted food price subsidy programs may be difficult. Correctly identifying target groups and assuring that subsidized food is obtained by them may be a much greater and more costly task than was envisaged prior to initiating the program. As a result, a large proportion of the subsidized food may actually go to nontargeted households while administrative costs run high.

Obtaining food for a subsidy program presents difficult problems. These include the most appropriate way of procuring food domestically to avoid disincentives in production and negative effects on incomes of poor producers and the proper combination of foreign food aid, commercial imports, and domestic procurement. Frequently, certain commodities are available on concessional terms under foreign food aid programs. Use of these commodities would greatly reduce government costs of a subsidy program. Furthermore, it might reduce the need for procurement from domestic producers at prices below the market. However, great care should be taken to avoid extensive use of food aid commodities that are not readily produced within the country. Consumer preferences may be generated that may be difficult to meet out of domestic production at a later time. The implications of heavy dependence on foreign food aid should be carefully considered in view of the uncertainty of future supplies of food under concessional terms (see chapter 15 below).

Procurement schemes that include producer prices below market prices may be hard to enforce and may involve not only large administrative costs but also large economic costs and disincentives for the agricultural sector. Rice subsidies in Egypt provide an illustration. The greater part of the difference between consumer and producer/import prices for most foods is financed by the government, that is, the subsidy is mostly *explicit*. However, the rice subsidy is borne by the producers through depressed prices and is basically *implicit*. The low prices are enforced by a combination of forced procurement and export taxes. The procurement price varied from 11 percent of international prices in 1974, to 50 percent in 1972, to 42 percent in 1980. These variations reflected a relatively constant and low procurement price in the face of wide fluctuations in the international market. Losses to the producer sector were equal to about 20 percent of explicit food subsidies. However "because it is financed mainly by the farmers it does not appear in the government's accounts and the public awareness of it is small" (von Braun and de Haen 1983). Insufficient recognition by the government of the costs of implicit subsidies is a common problem, even when the cost is borne by the public sector. Unfortunately, it appears that revenues foregone by government generally receive much less attention than government expenditures in the deliberations about fiscal budgets and deficit spending.

EFFECTIVENESS OF SUBSIDY PROGRAMS IN REACHING THE POOR

According to a number of studies, food subsidies have increased incomes and improved the nutritional status among the poor, particularly the urban poor. A study of the past Sri Lankan food ration shop scheme "indicates that the scheme contributed to a better standard of living among low-income groups and a more even pattern of consumption throughout the society. . . . At its peak, the ration subsidy contributed the equivalent of 16 percent of the purchasing power of low-income families in Sri Lanka" (Gavan and Chandrasekera 1979). Research on food ration shops in Kerala, India, shows that about one-half of the total income of low-income families was accounted for by ration income. The researcher concludes that "the removal of rationing would have a very serious impact on these low-income consumers" (George 1979). Kumar (1979) found that rations supplied the bulk of rice eaten by low-income groups and that the subsidy scheme "greatly improved the distribution of income." She further concludes that the "subsidy program was effective in raising nutrition and consumption levels of the poorest households and was more effective than other forms of direct resource transfers."

In a study of the food ration shop scheme in Bangladesh, Ahmed (1979) concludes that "rationing has aided the urban poor quite successfully since without it the consumption levels of the poorest 15 percent of the urban population would have been 15 to 25 percent lower in 1973–74 than they were. A strong urban bias was found in food subsidies in Bangladesh. Most of the poor people reside in rural areas, but two-thirds of the subsidized grain were distributed to urban areas." Yet the study concludes that expanding the rationing program in rural areas would be extremely expensive and would, if based on external food aid, cause strong downward pressures on domestic food prices and disincentives to domestic producers.

The Egyptian food subsidy policies account for 6 to 7 percent of average consumer incomes (Alderman and von Braun 1984). Since the absolute value of the subsidy is virtually constant among income groups, the poor receive a much larger percentage of total income from subsidies than the rich. Food subsidies account for about 16 percent of the incomes of the poorest quartile of the population but only about 3 percent of that of the richest. Contrary to common belief prior to the study, no urban bias was found for the food price policies as a whole. However, due to higher consumption of wheat bread in the urban areas, some urban bias was found in the explicit wheat subsidy. This bias was offset by a higher rural consumption of explicitly and implicitly subsidized wheat flour. The relative bias was less than the difference between rural and urban incomes, with the subsidies contributing 7 percent of rural and 6 percent of urban incomes. If other agricultural price distortions, such as the protection of animal production, are included, the rural sector received considerably larger net benefits.

Further insights into the short-run welfare and nutritional implications of food subsidies were provided by studies for Brazil, Sudan, and Mexico. In the Brazil study, it was found that a shift of existing explicit subsidies on wheat to rice would greatly enhance the impact on calorie consumption by calorie-deficient population groups without changing government outlays (Gray 1982). Similar analyses aimed at the estimation of the short-run nutritional effects of reducing or removing existing wheat subsidies among urban households in Sudan found that poor and calorie-deficient households would make relatively large adjustments in calorie consumption in response to changes in bread prices (Pinstrup-Andersen et al. 1983). Thus, a 50 percent increase in the bread price would increase calorie deficiencies among the poorest 12.5 percent of the population by about one-third. The decrease in real incomes would be positively correlated with income level if measured in absolute terms, and negatively if expressed in percent of current income level.

While the above studies used household food consumption as a proxy for nutritional impact, a study of the Mexican milk subsidies analyzed the impact of a subsidy program on individual household members (Kennedy 1983). Preliminary results indicate that, while the subsidy caused an increase in milk consumption by preschool children, their total calorie consumption did not increase. Thus it appears that the program caused commodity substitution in the diet of the children. Their protein intakes increased and their calorie intakes held constant. Furthermore, calorie intakes by other household members increased.

ALTERNATIVE MEASURES

In addition to food price subsidies, tied or untied cash transfers and food transfers provide another set of policy measures by which governments may increase the purchasing power of the poor and compensate for losses in real incomes caused by higher general food prices. Untied cash transfers tend to be less palatable politically than transfers linked to food such as food stamps, targeted food price subsidies, or food supplementation schemes. Political resistance to programs directly aimed at reducing starvation and malnutrition is likely to be much less than to cash transfers, even when the former results in transfer of real income that is partially or fully interchangeable, as in most food stamp programs. Cash transfer programs are very difficult to implement, and the cost of control measures to avoid excessive leakage to nontarget groups and fraud is likely to be high. Self-targeting, which may be possible if food subsidies are aimed at less desired foods, is not possible in cash transfers.

Another argument in favor of food-related transfers is that they contribute to substitution of food for nonfoods by reducing food prices relative to other commodity prices. However, food price subsidies and direct feeding schemes are frequently limited to quantities of food that are less than what would be purchased in the absence of subsidies. Thus food does not become cheaper at the margin.

There is some evidence that the marginal propensity to consume food is higher for real income originating from food subsidy programs or direct feeding schemes than from cash (Kumar 1978). The reason is probably to be found in differences in preferences of household members and the relationship between source of income and intrahousehold control of budget.

Finally, in comparing the pros and cons of cash vs. food transfer schemes, it should be recognized that food may be available from foreign aid at a cost to governments considerably below its market value, thus making food-related transfer less expensive. If food aid donors permit monitizing of the food aid, this advantage disappears.

Some countries have attempted to reduce leakages to nontarget households and to focus more sharply on improved nutrition by supplementation of food or direct feeding of individuals deficient in calories and protein. These usually are children and pregnant and lactating women. School lunch programs and feeding of preschool children in health and nutrition clinics are examples of direct feeding. Such programs may assure that leakages to nontargeted households are small. However, intrahousehold leakages will still occur through adjustments in the allocation of food to target individuals. Households also may reduce food acquisition from other sources.

In a review of over two-hundred reports of past food distribution programs for young children, Beaton and Ghassemi (1979) found that the net increase in food intake by the target recipients was 45–70 percent of the food distributed. Thus, leakage varied between one-half and one-third of the food provided. But such leakage benefited other household members through added real household income and possibly improved nutrition. The leakage merely reflects household preferences regarding expenditure and consumption patterns. These programs have generally not improved the nutritional status of target individuals over and above the effect operating through transfer of real income to households except in cases where they were effectively integrated with nutrition education or primary health care. Furthermore, administrative costs tend to be large relative to other income transfer programs.

Other policy measures are available for increasing the ability of the poor to acquire food, such as food-for-work programs and policies aimed at reducing unit costs in food production and marketing.

CONCLUDING COMMENTS

Efforts to develop the most appropriate food price policies for a given country involve complex economic, social, and political considerations. Considerations of their impact on consumers were the focus of this chapter.[2] Highlights include the following:

(1) Changes in food prices have important implications for low-income urban and certain groups of rural consumers. Failure to consider these in efforts to provide incentive pricing to farmers may result in severe hardships for the poor, at least in the short run. The political reactions may be untenable for the government unless compensatory measures are introduced.

(2) Before such measures are designed it is important to clarify which consumer groups the government wishes to compensate and whether such compensation will meet welfare goals as well as dissipate political opposition. Opposition to food price increases may not be most effectively expressed by those most adversely affected.

(3) Depending on the extent to which food price changes are reflected in wages, the benefits of consumer food price subsidies may be passed on to employers in the form of lower wage rates. In some cases, food price subsidies are closely linked with public sector wage levels, and removal of the subsidies is likely to result in equal or close to equal wage increases.

(4) General food price subsidies may be very costly either for the government, in the case of explicit subsidies, or for the agricultural sector, in the case of implicit subsidies. Irrespective of the source of financing, food subsidies are likely to have implications for economic growth.

(5) A move away from general to targeted food price subsidies may greatly reduce both fiscal and economic costs without reducing the effectiveness of the subsidy to reach welfare goals, provided the target households can be identified.

(6) Identifying households below a specified income level is one of the most challenging and difficult tasks facing governments in efforts to improve the cost-effectiveness of subsidy programs.

2. A more complete discussion of these considerations is provided in Pinstrup-Andersen forthcoming.

(7) In addition to targeted food price subsidies, a number of alternative measures are available to governments for alleviating hardships experienced by poor consumers due to high or increased food prices. These measures include tied or untied cash transfers as well as food transfers and food-for-work programs.

(8) The focus on subsidies and transfer programs in this chapter should not be interpreted to imply that they are necessarily the most effective way of dealing with the conflict between high producer and low consumer prices of food. Long-term self-sustaining solutions should be sought in policies and development strategies which generate and expand the income-earning capacities of the poor while improving the efficiency and reducing the unit costs of food production and marketing. However, for a long time to come, consumer subsidies and/or transfer programs will be needed in many developing countries to achieve welfare goals.

15

Implications of Food Aid for Price Policy in Recipient Countries

JOACHIM VON BRAUN and BARBARA HUDDLESTON

Although it is widely believed that food aid distorts incentives to increase agricultural production, detailed empirical country studies conducted in recent years suggest that the disincentive effect of food aid has been overemphasized. An analysis of sixteen developing countries that achieved particularly high growth rates in food production of 3.9 percent during 1961–76 shows that they also received about 80 percent more food aid per capita than the average food aid recipient country.[1] Six of these countries were receiving an especially high amount of food aid over an extended period.[2] While there is no clear-cut negative or positive relationship between food aid and growth in food production, they are not mutually exclusive. Government policy plays a crucial role in this regard.[3]

Overemphasis on the disincentive effect of food aid can be attributed to simplistic theoretical reasoning, for example, neglect of the dual structure of markets in most recipient countries. Von Plocki's in-depth analysis of the Indian case (1979) shows the shortcomings of much of the earlier work. He concluded that an additional 100 tons of food aid to India reduced domestic production by only 15 tons. Food aid in the Brazilian case had a positive effect on government-administered wheat support prices and production, according to Hall (1978). This effect was mostly due to the use of government revenues from wheat imports to support prices to wheat producers. A similar conclusion was reached by Stevens (1978) for Tunisia. For *Egypt,* von Braun (1982) estimated that food aid (wheat) reduced domestic wheat production by an amount equivalent to 4 to 9 percent of total food aid. In this case, the change in wheat production was not equal to

1. The countries included in the analysis mentioned here are Brazil, Colombia, El Salvador, Ghana, Iran, Ivory Coast, Malaysia, Mexico, Morocco, Pakistan, Paraguay, the Philippines, Sri Lanka, Sudan, Thailand, and Tunisia. Bachman and Paulino (1979) studied their agricultural growth and development.
2. These countries were Brazil, Morocco, Pakistan, Paraguay, Sri Lanka, and Tunisia.
3. This chapter deals with cereal aid only. For the specifics of dairy aid see Clay 1987.

reduced farm output because the decrease in production was mainly from changes in acreage allocation toward other competing crops. In Bangladesh, preliminary results of a normative model by Norton and Hazell (1984) yielded a price elasticity of staple food with respect to food aid of only −0.013. This result indicates that food aid had relatively little effect on domestic prices.

Maxwell and Singer (1979) concluded that in most cases the combination of more rapid economic growth and government price supports seems to have led to the maintenance of both relative prices and production. This is supported by the fact that a number of countries which had absorbed large amounts of food aid during rapid growth in food production received significantly less food aid in the 1980s. These included Taiwan, Korea, India, Paraguay, Colombia, and Brazil. Such cases demonstrate that food aid need not lead to long-term dependence.

Taiwan is a particularly interesting case in terms of the relationship between the "disincentive effect" of food aid for a single crop and overall agricultural growth (Lu 1973). The country received high amounts of food aid (wheat) during the 1950s and 1960s, and agricultural output grew at the exceptional rates of 4.6 and 5.9 percent per annum, respectively, in the two decades. However, wheat production increased rapidly during the 1950s but fell back to its earlier levels during the 1960s, when more profitable winter crops replaced wheat. Food aid's disincentive effect may be only part of the reason why wheat lost its comparative advantage. Furthermore, the cheap import supply of wheat (food aid) contributed to high growth in rice exports. Consequently, the country and the agricultural sector obtained substantial benefits from food aid through the resource transfer and reallocation of domestic agricultural resources. The lesson is that "disincentive effects" must not be assessed through a single crop perspective. Production and trade effects for competing crops must be assessed as well. The effects of food aid on demand for foreign exchange and the exchange rate must also be kept in perspective, given the direct effects of exchange rate changes for the structure of incentives.

SPECIAL CHARACTERISTICS OF FOOD AID

To a certain extent, food aid may be understood as a supply of imports to developing countries at a reduced price. In this perspective, it is simply a practical case of what was comprehensively discussed in chapter 4 on the implications of domestic price setting and in chapter 7 on trade and exchange rates. However, some special characteristics of food aid and their particular implications for food price policy deserve consideration here. First, a number of regulations for the disposal of food aid imply that it has repercussions on the commercial food and nonfood trade of the recipient countries. Second, a considerable share of food aid is not provided on a grant basis but rather as long-term soft loans with related long-term foreign exchange and fiscal implications. Third, concern about the developmental impact of food aid supplies seems to be increasing. Fourth, food aid, as we show below, is an unstable and insecure source of supply. Food aid tends to have an opportunity cost to the donor countries not only in the sense that it results from misallocated agricultural resources but also in the sense that it partly replaces capital aid, which may be used more effectively in development.

In view of these aspects of food aid, recipient countries are continually facing policy dilemmas as to how to optimize the use of available food aid in both the short and the long run and how to adjust domestic price policies, given their economic, and possibly political, costs. This discussion is largely based on the current food aid disposal policies of donor countries. We do not imply that suppliers should not explore policy improvements. Numerous efforts have been made to persuade donor countries to adjust food aid supplies to enhance the potential growth, employment, and nutritional effects in recipient countries. In particular, these adjustments include policies to assure a continuous flow of food aid, viewed as a resource transfer under multi-year commitments, and to provide food aid to stabilize domestic food availability in less developed countries with short domestic production and depleted foreign exchange reserves. However, various exogenous factors, such as protection of agriculture in the United States and Europe and fluctuating international price levels, continue to determine the availability of food aid to low-income countries.

THE SHORT-TERM RELIEF AND LONG-TERM BURDEN OF FOOD AID/CONCESSIONAL IMPORTS

The "market" in which food aid transactions are negotiated is highly regulated and segregated. Complex bargaining among suppliers as well as between demanders and suppliers finally determines the quantity flowing to a particular country in a particular year. It also should be pointed out that political considerations of costs and benefits continue to play a major role in equating supply and demand of food aid (Hopkins 1980).

There are two types of food aid: project aid provided by donors on a grant basis, a large share of which is funneled through the World Food Programme, and program aid on a grant basis or funded by long-term soft loans for which no specific project use is identified. The economic value and costs of the two types to recipient countries are quite different. Huddleston (1984) attempted to compute the "true cost" of cereal imports, which is comprised of the c.i.f. value of commercial cereal imports plus the c.i.f. value of the non-grant component of concessional imports.

According to calculations for 1976–78, food aid reduced the total cost of cereals imports by about one-third for low-income countries but only 2 to 5 percent in other developing countries.

Total grain imports, though growing, are equivalent to only about 6 percent of total export earnings of low-income countries as a group. But Bangladesh and an increasing number of African countries are important exceptions. These countries usually receive a high proportion of food aid on a grant basis, and the share of food aid in total imports is high. Consequently, the reduction in the "true cost" of grain imports is also high.

To the extent that the cost of grain imports is significantly reduced by food aid, it may be misinterpreted by policymakers in recipient countries as secure and everlasting and also viewed as an effective reduction of the opportunity costs of domestic production. Yet the costs of a unit of food aid do not usually represent the marginal import price, which actually determines the opportunity cost of domestic production.

A particular problem arises from the long-term repayment schedules of food aid provided on a soft-loan basis, which usually starts with a ten-year grace period. It seems fair to assume that a period of ten years is far beyond the food supply planning horizons of most governments in low-income, food-deficit countries. Nor is it likely that import planners use a social discounting rate, however constructed, in formulating the demand for concessional imports. In the case of a continuous inflow of this type of food aid, the repayment burden grows exponentially after the grace period is over (Srivastava et al. 1975). Egypt, for example, is currently shifting into this phase, since it has been receiving food aid under P.L. 480 Title I continuously since the early 1970s.[4] A shrinking value of the domestic currency compared to the dollar may further reduce the ex-post perceived benefit of food aid received a decade before if repayments are due in hard currency. This is increasingly the case. Consequently, debate on rescheduling "food aid debts" may become an issue in a number of recipient countries in the 1990s.

IMPORTANCE AND DRAWBACKS OF FOOD AID

Low-income, food-deficit countries (LFDCs)[5] have received about 7.6 million tons of food aid in recent years. This was about 15 to 17 percent of

4. A common agreement on food aid supplied under U.S. P.L. 480 Title I during the 1970s and 1980s has the following terms: initial payment of 5 percent; 31 installments of equal annual amounts; ten-year grace period; initial interest rate of 2 percent; continuing interest rate of 3 percent.

5. Includes all food-deficit countries with per capita income below the level used by the World Bank to determine eligibility for IDA assistance, which, in accordance with the guidelines and criteria agreed to by the CFA, should be given priority in the allocation of food aid. This definition differs from the one used by Huddleston (1984) in the study mentioned in the text above.

total cereal imports. During 1976–78, food aid exceeded 20 percent of total grain imports in one-half of the LFDCs receiving food aid and in one-third of all recipient countries. Although food aid was not very important in some developing countries, it certainly mattered to a number of the poorest. During 1976–78, food aid covered between 6 and 16 percent of total grain consumption in nine low-income countries. It was even more important for the poor in some of these countries because their special food subsidy schemes depended on food aid.

Research at IFPRI has shown that, in the aggregate, food aid supplies are not very responsive to short-term fluctuations in LDCs' import requirements. However, if allocated appropriately over time and countries, the same quantities could significantly contribute to increased food security (Huddleston 1981).

Except for 1974, the year of the grain price crisis, total annual food aid ranged between about 7 and 12 million tons of grain (most of which was wheat) during 1970–83. However, the drop from 10.1 to 5.7 million tons in 1973–74 suggests that food aid can hardly be relied upon to provide food security in severe crisis situations. As long as the food aid commitments of major donors are made largely in terms of fiscal allocations rather than actual quantities, prices will significantly influence food aid supplies.

The instability of food aid becomes even more evident in a country-by-country analysis. During 1962–78, the average coefficient of variation of food aid was 1.25 in LFDCs in which food aid averaged more than 10 percent of grain imports. Clearly, that means that the quantities of food aid received fluctuated substantially from year to year over the time period.[6] Frequently, countries that have been important recipients for some time suddenly face a "blackout" of food aid. Twenty-seven countries confronted this situation between 1965 and 1978.[7] Frequently, domestic and foreign policy events cause the interruptions of the food aid inflow. The time series on food aid shows no diminishing trend in these "blackouts." Food aid remains an insecure and risky source of supply.

RESPONDING TO UNSTABLE FOOD AID SUPPLIES

During 1964–78 only one-half to two-thirds of all countries facing a cutback in food aid fully replaced the aid with commercial imports in the short run (fig. 15.1). The difference was particularly wide when cuts in

6. The coefficient of variation is the standard deviation divided by the mean value for each country. The 1.25 represents the average over the sample of countries. The individual values for countries ranged from 0.43 (Pakistan) to 2.08 (Mozambique) (computed from IFPRI data bank on food aid by country).

7. Food aid, which had exceeded 15 percent of imports over three years, dropped below 3 percent in the next year in these cases (computed from IFPRI data bank on food aid by country).

Figure 15.1   Fluctuations in food aid and response in commercial imports, 89
countries, 1964–78

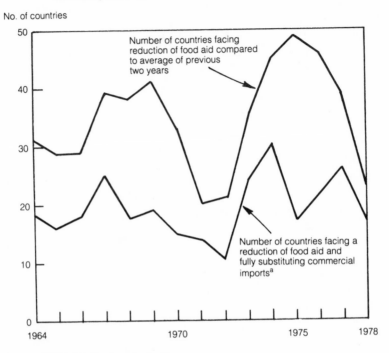

No. of countries

Number of countries facing
reduction of food aid compared
to average of previous
two years

Number of countries facing a
reduction of food aid and
fully substituting commercial
imports[a]

1964   1970   1975   1978

Source: IFPRI data bank on food aid.
[a]This group is a subset of those depicted by the upper line in the graph.

food aid coincided with high world prices and related foreign exchange
constraints that prevented imports from staying at normal levels. Increase
in domestic supplies, which are not accounted for in the data, were insufficient to compensate fully for the incomplete substitution of commercial
imports for food aid.

The incomplete substitution between trade and aid is further indicated
by the following analysis. We estimated the following simple regression for
the 32 biggest food aid recipients: $CIM_t = a + b\,AID_t + \Sigma_t$, where CIM
is the deviation from trend of commercial imports; AID is the deviation
from trend of food aid; Σ is an error term; and t is 1962–78 (two-year averages).

For 13 of the 32 countries a negative significant b is estimated, indicat-
ing substitution. The average is -0.8 for the significant bs.[8] This means

8. The test for significance was performed for b being different from 0. Most of the other
countries showed nonsignificant, though negative, parameters.

that a reduction of food aid by one ton from trend levels increases commercial imports by 0.8 tons in these countries. Obviously, the response is not uniform. Given the simplistic approach, the parameters should not be interpreted with too much emphasis on numerical results. Of course, this is not a monocausal relationship. Commercial grain imports in the medium run are determined by import prices, foreign exchange availability, domestic supplies, stocks, etc., which are not taken into account sufficiently by a trend variable. The estimation results suggest that substitution occurs to a certain extent but that food aid cannot be viewed as either a simple balance of payments support, which would be the case if it substituted completely for commercial imports, or as fully additional. This has direct implications for the price effects of food aid in recipient countries.

Among factors which determine the incomplete substitution between trade and aid, the following seem important. First, it is clear that food aid represents a resource transfer which may allow further expansion of demand for food and other goods and services. To the extent that food aid is channeled into employment- and demand-creating programs, the additional demand requires continuation of at least a fraction of earlier commercial imports to avoid domestic food price inflation. Second, and probably more important, donors regulate provision of food aid so as to avoid reducing commercial imports by food aid. The "usual marketing requirements regulation" (UMR) in the food aid convention is intended to serve this purpose. Although not always enforced, this regulation has at least some relevance for major food aid recipients who also are major commercial importers and reduces the ability of food aid to contribute to balance of payments support. Third, when food aid is used to build up domestic stocks and therefore is received only erratically, its relation to normal imports should be small, and its price effects largely depend upon releases of grain from stocks.

Because of the instability of food aid and the numerous forms of its regulation, trade and price policy must be extremely flexible to avoid its undesirable side effects or even to use it as an incentive. The domestic price effects of food aid depend to a large extent on the degree to which it substitutes for, or is in addition to, trade. An improvement in capacity of recipient country institutions, including physical facilities (ports, storage, transportation, etc.) and less rigid food aid disposal rules such as UMRs, would certainly increase the ability of such countries to use food aid as a source of foreign exchange savings and fiscal support with no disincentive effects on domestic production. However, using food aid just as a general resource transfer conflicts with the concern for its equity effects through raising food consumption levels of the poor (Mellor 1980). As a means of achieving the latter objectives, food aid must be at least partly additive to normal supplies, as is generally the case. The general problem of food aid for price policy stems from attempts to achieve these conflicting objectives simultaneously with the same instrument. The compromise appropriate for a specific country depends on its ability to channel additional food to the poor and at the same time generate demand-creating employment.

Food aid appears to be inherently unstable and insufficiently tuned to meet shortfalls in domestic food production or to supplement foreign exchange needs. The general instability of food aid matters very much to countries confronted with high levels of instability in food production and severe short-term constraints in foreign exchange reserves and storage capacities. This situation is familiar in many sub-Saharan African countries. To provide effective food security to such countries, it is necessary to eliminate the insecurity associated with the supply of food aid. Donor coordination and improved planning and managerial capacities in recipient countries are required for this purpose. The potential of the IMF cereal import financing scheme can be exploited fully if some of its regulations can be reformed further to provide easier access to low-income countries with emergency need for food supply (IMF 1981).

ENHANCING INCENTIVE EFFECTS OF FOOD AID: AN ISSUE OF THE DOMESTIC MARKET AND PRICE POLICY

Whether food aid has disincentive effects is mainly a question of the market and price policies in a recipient country and its response to changes in food aid supplies. What follows is a broad classification of the circumstances in which disincentive effects may arise and how they may be transformed into incentives. To avoid a distorted perspective other objectives of food aid such as consumption, nutrition, and foreign exchange also are discussed. Three typical cases serve as points of departure (table 15.1).

The first deals with a situation in which food aid substitutes for commercial imports and is not additional to normal supplies (column 1, table 15.1). This would have no effect or minimal effect on domestic prices. In a completely open economy, savings in foreign exchange would tend to increase the value of domestic currency compared to foreign currency, for example, the U.S. dollar, and thus would somewhat decrease domestic prices. Food consumption would hardly change, at least in the short run. Over a longer period, saving foreign exchange may lead to growth if it increases the supply of investment goods. The capacity of the government to increase public investment would result from fiscal resources which are generated when food aid is released domestically at prices above its actual procurement cost to the government. Through such growth effects, the total per capita demand for food would increase over time and would be met by increased supply in an open economy, even though food aid was not additional to food supply initially. The extent to which this process would

Table 15.1 Implications of food aid for selected variables under different price and market policies

Variables	Food aid *not* additional to normal imports (open economy)	Food aid additional to normal imports	
		Sales on open markets at prevailing prices	Rationed sales below prevailing prices; support of farm prices
Disincentive effect	0	+	0 or −
Food consumption	0	+	+
Foreign exchange saving	+	0 or −	0 or −
Fiscal resources	+	+	+ or 0

Note: 0, no or small effect; +, increasing effect; −, decreasing effect.

actually occur would depend on the use of the fiscal resources and foreign exchange provided indirectly by food aid.

In the second case (columns 2 and 3 of the table), food aid does not replace commercial imports but is additional. The underlying forces which lead to this widespread situation were discussed above (for example, UMR, the concern of both donors and recipients for increased consumption). Foreign exchange is not saved in this case. To the extent that food aid is provided on the basis of long-term soft loans or that the recipient covers costs of shipment, an additional drain on foreign exchange may occur. Food consumption does increase, depending on the extent to which food aid is additional to normal imports, on the one hand, and, on the other, its disincentive effect for domestic production—that is, the induced price depression and consequent supply response. The disincentive effect depends mainly on how food aid supplies are marketed and how the fiscal resources generated from food aid are used.

If food aid is simply injected into the domestic market at prevailing prices (column 2, table 15.1), the negative impact on domestic production may be significant. This case was intensively argued in the earlier debates on the disincentive effects of food aid, but with little empirical evidence. Economic costs result from the induced misallocations of resources within agriculture and among the sectors of the economy (Schultz 1960).

Thus disincentive effects should be broadly interpreted. They are not established just by reduced intensity of agricultural production or diversion of acreage to crops which produce higher private profits yet have lower economic profitability in the long run. Disincentives may also include longer-term costs of induced factor mobility, for example, out of agriculture, and related costs of rapid urbanization, misallocation of long-term investment, and constraints on institutional innovations. However, such extreme disincentive effects of food aid seem rare. They are not strongly supported by empirical evidence to date.[9]

In most recipient countries, dual structures for grain markets are prevalent. Such structures exist largely independent of food aid. On the consumer side, low-price, quantity-controlled sales occur, and on the producer side procurement policies at fixed prices are quite common. The open market is cleared by the prices determined through total supply and demand, to some extent affected by the factors determining the size of the remaining marketed surplus of domestic producers (column 3, table 15.1). Although such market structures do not assure that disincentive effects are excluded, they provide the potential to reduce them considerably or even transform them into incentive effects. Total demand may be increased by channeling low-price food (aid) to poorer consumers who have a high marginal propensity to consume basic food. On the producer side, existing procurement systems can be used to introduce price support schemes at least partly financed out of fiscal revenues generated from food aid sales.

POTENTIAL ROLES OF FOOD AID FOR DEVELOPMENT

Food aid can play a crucial role in supporting increased employment in the early stages of growth. Mobilization of labor out of low productivity requires an increased supply of food. When labor receives a higher income and spends it largely on food, increased supplies are needed to prevent inflation of food prices and rising wages that would then reduce the demand for labor (Mellor 1983). Food aid can supply a basic wage good needed to back a rapid growth in employment when agricultural growth initially lags and foreign exchange is too scarce to maintain a labor-intensive growth strategy.

Food aid may also play a favorable role in maintaining basic food consumption in the wake of policy reforms for restructuring the economy, which may require drastic measures be taken to cope with debt servicing and foreign exchange problems. A careful connection of food aid to strategies for structural adjustment may make them more acceptable at an earlier stage, thus contributing to their efficiency.

Food aid may relieve the tax burden on agriculture by providing an additional source of government revenues. This may occur in countries which tax agriculture heavily through forced procurement at low prices and export taxes and trade restrictions. Such situations are fairly common in de-

9. Maxwell and Singer (1979), in their survey of nine non-India studies of food aid, cite two countries in which a significant disincentive effect can be identified (Colombia and Pakistan). However, these countries achieved particularly rapid growth in food production during the 1960s and 1970s (Pakistan, 4.7 percent; Colombia, 4.2 percent).

veloping countries. Although farm prices may not rise at the margin if food aid is additional, average farm prices could rise due to increased prices for government procurement quotas, which, in the absence of food aid, are frequently kept low by the fiscal situation. This could improve the overall terms of trade between agriculture and the rest of the economy. Such a relationship between the implicit tax burden on agriculture and availability of government revenues is evident in Egypt, a major food aid recipient (von Braun and de Haen 1983).

Funds generated through domestic sales of food aid in the recipient country may also be used for public investment to decrease costs of food production. Through contractual arrangements with recipients, donor countries try to impose such a use of fiscal resources in order to tie food aid to enhanced food production. The results of these attempts, however, appear to be, at best, mixed.

CONCLUSIONS

Optimal use of food aid to improve agricultural growth and overall incentive structures can only be achieved if effective instruments for channeling additional food to demand-creating employment and for producer price supports are in place. Both require a reasonable institutionalization of dual market channels. These are not free of charge. Once established, bureaucracies managing procurement and distribution cannot easily be dismantled. Setting up such systems for this purpose alone may not be desirable because of the high degree of instability and insecurity of food aid. But in many developing countries such systems are already established, so their costs to the economy are not part of food aid costs. In these circumstances, food aid can provide the means for a more efficient use of dual market systems that will provide price incentives for producers through price support schemes and food for consumers oriented toward employment and equity.

Increasingly donors are attempting to include food aid as an important component of a package program of cooperation (USAID 1982). Given the nature of food aid and current rules for its disposal, some interaction between the parties is certainly required. In order to improve the incentive effects of food aid, recipient countries should focus on efficient systems of dual markets, while donors should emphasize more stable flows of food aid under long-term commitments which do not preclude an effective variable emergency component.

16

CONCLUSIONS
Agricultural Price Policy
for Accelerating Growth

JOHN W. MELLOR and RAISUDDIN AHMED

INTRODUCTION

The public expects a responsible government to foster growth to provide greater income and well-being in the future, equity to provide a fair society and social cohesion, and stability to reduce the tensions of uncertainty and the likelihood of a sharp reduction in consumption or destruction of the means of livelihood. Growth, equity, and stability are themselves interrelated, and agricultural price policy has a potentially major and often conflicting effect on each.

This concluding chapter focuses on the relation of agricultural price policy to growth. In low-income countries, the resources generated by a high rate of growth can contribute markedly to increased equity and stability. Indeed, it may be only through growth that a low-income country can marshal the resources necessary to improve conditions for the large proportion of its population in absolute poverty or to reduce the instability that results when a large proportion of national income is subject to the vagaries of weather and wildly fluctuating international commodity prices.

A short-run emphasis on equity and stability may impede growth and lead to an unmanageable problem in providing equity and stability in the future. Conversely, the tensions accompanying inequity and instability may inhibit growth. Thus long-term considerations must involve short-term balances between policies for growth and those for equity and stability. Agricultural price policy, with its profound income-distributional effects and political overtones, is particularly subject to this stricture.

The extent to which growth meets equity and stability objectives depends not only on the pace of growth but its pattern as well. To meet equity needs in low-income countries, growth must be associated with a rapid increase in the supply of food and demand for labor. Since the poor are substantially deficient in food, their marginal propensity to spend for it is high. And it is only through increased demand for labor that they can earn

265

additional income to purchase it. Although these truths are self-evident, development policies commonly neglect the food sector and provide a low rate of growth in demand for labor.

In low-income countries, agriculture accounts for a major share of all productive activity and food is a dominant share of total consumption. In such circumstances, it is not surprising that fluctuations in relative agricultural prices are the dominant source of fluctuations in income for a substantial proportion of agricultural producers and for most consumers. A change in relative agricultural prices causes a major change in the relative distribution of income not only between agricultural producers and consumers but among income classes as well, according to the relative weight of agricultural commodities in their income and expenditure. Future agricultural production and employment and their distribution among regions and classes will be affected by relative agricultural prices through changes in relative costs and returns.

Despite its great economic and political importance, agricultural price policy is circumscribed by the fact that price policies favorable to some groups or objectives tend to be unfavorable to others. Thus price policy may change sharply from time to time according to the changing political weight of various interests. Further, because of the immense weight in the economy of agricultural supply and demand forces, public price policy can be inconsistent with those forces to only a limited extent and period of time, and even then the efficiency losses may be immense. Governments can and do have a major influence on those underlying supply and demand forces and thus indirectly determine relative prices.

The most obvious conflict in agricultural price policy is between prosperous producers who sell much of what they produce and low-income consumers who purchase the bulk of the food they consume. In the early years of political independence and of economic growth it is common for urban consumers to dominate agricultural price policy in favor of cheap food. As the political system and development progress, the vast number of farmers may achieve greater political weight and legislate farm support prices that transfer income to themselves. The relative political weight of these groups varies among countries and over time and is the cause for quite different agricultural price policies.

But the price policy conflicts go well beyond simple producer-consumer differences. For example, price stabilization schemes (constraining price increases in poor crop years and price decreases in good crop years) will be income-stabilizing for richer farmers who sell most of what they produce, but income-destabilizing for small farmers who sell only a small proportion of output (Mellor 1968b). For the latter, poor weather years are the low-income years, compensated in part by higher prices. For big farmers the low-income years are the good production years when prices decline more than enough to offset the larger crop. The extent to which price stabilization destabilizes income depends on the price elasticities of demand and the proportion of production marketed. Since demand for food in developing countries is more elastic than in developed countries and marketable surpluses are much lower, stabilizing prices may cause increased instability of income for a majority of the farmers in developing countries (Mellor and Ponteves 1964; Lipton 1970).

As governments focus on the immense political pressures to change relative prices, they may underestimate the strength of underlying demand and supply forces that may work against their policy objectives. Food prices are so politically sensitive precisely because they are the product of powerful economic forces with conflicting consequences to various groups. Through exchange rate manipulation, trade policy, and domestic supply management, governments can and usually do insulate domestic prices from international prices in the short run. However, the resources required for governments to stand in the way of long-term cumulation of imbalances between supply and demand are formidable.

In many African countries in the 1970s and early 1980s, for example, the attempt to maintain an overvalued exchange rate depressed food prices, policies for improved agricultural technology were neglected, and rapid growth in urban incomes resulted in an excess demand for food which overtaxed domestic food production and foreign exchange to import food. Large-scale foreign aid or massive oil revenues allowed a prolonged imbalance. But eventually unofficial markets became increasingly important and food prices rose well above international prices at the overvalued exchange rate (Mellor, Delgado, and Blackie 1987). This pulled resources from export commodity production and probably slowed growth in urban food demand. Decline in agricultural exports and consequent scarcity of foreign exchange depressed food production due to shortages of such key imports as fertilizer and transport services (Lele 1985). Eventually the resultant inefficiencies, retarded growth, and rapid increase in food prices required major adjustments in public policy.

Because agricultural export commodities usually represent a smaller proportion of a low-income economy than food, and because domestic price policy with respect to exports only affects the supply side, the opportunity to discriminate against export agriculture is greater than for food crops and may continue longer. This is, of course, deleterious to economic efficiency and growth, shifting resources to less productive sectors and depriving the economy generally and the food sector specifically of vital foreign exchange (Lele 1985).

Governments can, of course, maintain depressed food prices in the face of only slowly increasing supply if they tightly constrain demand at the same time. That is essentially what the government of India succeeded in doing in the late 1950s and early 1960s. Food production grew very slowly, but the government followed investment policies that favored capital-intensive industries and hence slow growth in employment and in effective demand for food. Policies toward agricultural production and demand for food were roughly consistent and in equilibrium. Even that consistency broke down in the mid 1960s, even before the drought of 1965-67, when domestic food prices rose rapidly despite rapidly rising food imports as effective demand for food accelerated with faster nonagricultural growth (Mellor 1968a, 1976).

While control of food prices for more than short periods may be beyond the power of governments in developing countries, changes in prices are strong signals to governments of underlying problems. It is vital that governments read those signals promptly and correctly and take appropriate longer-term action. Rising food prices indicate that the supply of food is increasing less rapidly than demand. Meeting that problem by slowing growth in demand for labor and hence in demand for food has unfavorable growth and equity effects. The correct response is for more effective effort to increase the food supply, ideally through accelerated domestic production but also through increased imports.

Similarly, for a developing country dominated by agricultural production and food consumption, the appropriate answer to falling food prices is to accelerate employment growth rather than to reduce the food production growth rate by, for example, less investment in irrigation or research. Of course, in reading price signals, short-term changes due to transitory forces such as weather need to be distinguished from longer-term forces to which policy should respond. That distinction is itself difficult to make.

Rising and falling domestic prices stimulated by global changes of a long-term nature offer similar opportunities. Lower world food prices should stimulate more active domestic demand policies and higher prices more active production policies—not the converse.

Disequilibrium may be dealt with on both the supply and the demand sides (Mellor and Johnston 1984). But growth and equity are generally better pursued in developing countries by bringing up the laggard side of the equation rather than reducing the forward side. Governments must understand that the lags in accelerating growth in either demand or supply are long and that policy needs must be anticipated far in advance. Waiting for the right price signals may tempt governments to policies that retard the forward-moving element. What is needed in both cases is structural changes in demand and supply that deal with the underlying problems causing substantial price changes. For both sets of structural relations, government policy is important and influential. Unfortunately, slowing either demand or supply occurs with much less lag than accelerating them.

In summary, there are two problems in relying on the market to solve agricultural price problems. First, the market may equate the wrong side of the supply-demand equation. Second, the lags between action and its effect may be too long to be acceptable. Thus the task of agricultural price policy is much more than that of determining appropriate prices in the short run; it is also one of diagnosing well ahead of time what development policies are most needed and appropriate in anticipation of the price regimes that would prevail without those actions.

Severe disequilibrium between food supply and demand tempts governments to regulate prices rather than dealing with the underlying problem—which may be difficult and will certainly take considerable time. The mechanism of price regulation through public sector trading and the consequent growth of illegal markets increases transaction costs with large losses to both producers and consumers. The effect of such action is also to delay basic supply and demand corrections until a crisis is reached. The very act of price manipulation conceals the underlying imbalances and assists governments in deluding themselves that other actions are unnecessary.

We can see, then, that agricultural price policy is complex and fraught with conflicts and that, to be effective, it must be forward-looking. In such circumstances it is essential that governments develop the analytic capacity to monitor, evaluate, and recommend policy with respect to agricultural prices. The highly technical economic relationships require sophisticated analysis and measurement and include political as well as micro- and macroeconomic issues. When the various publics demand protection from the major growth, equity, and stability effects of changes in agricultural prices, governments must respond intelligently if they are to meet short-term political needs and still avoid serious longer-term problems. An institutional capacity to develop the necessary data base and to carry out the analysis is fundamental (Lele 1977).

AGRICULTURAL PRICES AND ECONOMIC GROWTH

Agricultural prices play a conflicting role even in the context of growth. Growth in agriculture and the demand for labor (and hence food) are close complements. Much of the increased demand for labor to complement accelerated growth in agriculture must occur in the nonagricultural, although still rural, sector (Mellor 1976). Rising food prices raise the cost of labor and hence slow the growth in demand for labor. The general resolution of this conflict lies with increasing production incentives to agriculture, not by high prices but by cost-reducing technological change.

The key role of improved technology in agricultural growth is enhanced by two factors. First, in the absence of technological change, which generally increases commercialization in farming, aggregate agricultural production is particularly unresponsive to prices. Chapters 10 and 11 explain and elaborate this point. Second, productivity-enhancing technological change is generally the most powerful engine of accelerated economic growth. When agriculture is the dominant sector, it is logical that technological change should have its greatest aggregate impact on agriculture. Improved agricultural technology directly accelerates growth and makes agriculture more responsive to price changes.

Labor Markets

Rising agricultural prices slow growth in demand for labor because food comprises a high proportion of the expenditures of laborers and a change in food prices has an immediate, inverse, and nearly proportionate effect on the real wage of labor. Of course, as incomes rise and food becomes less important in consumption, this relation weakens.

In a neoclassical world of equilibrium in all markets, higher food prices raise the price of labor in terms of what labor produces and reduces the returns to capital. This results in both a lower rate of capital formation and substitution of capital for labor, thereby reducing the demand for labor. The consequent equilibrium includes a lower real wage of laborers in terms of the goods they consume, lower employment, and lower output. In a dynamic context, growth rate slows.

In a neoclassical framework, the favorable effect of lower food prices on demand for labor is most rigorously demonstrated by treating the employment and wage relations as functions of two separate but interacting markets, a labor market and a food market (Lele and Mellor 1981). An increase in food supplies, in final equilibrium, would result in a decline in the real price of food, a decline in the capital-labor ratio, an increase in real income of the laboring class (from either higher wages or more employment, or both), and an increase in capital formation (Lele and Mellor 1981). The less elastic the offer curve for family labor and the more elastic the substitution rates of capital for labor, the greater the depressing effect of a rise in food prices on employment and wages.

In practice, rising food prices reduce demand for labor through a variety of mechanisms. Government may respond to inflation by contracting fiscal and monetary policies, thus reducing demand for labor. The labor class, including potential migrants, may offer less labor at the previous nominal wage in response to lower real wages induced by higher food prices. Entrepreneurs may hire less labor in response to higher wages relative to their output prices.

It is noted that many developing countries concentrate the bulk of their capital in large-scale, capital-intensive industries. In those industries the marginal product of labor, and hence wages, is high, and so food prices are relatively less important determinants of real wages, returns to capital, and rates of capital formation. The capital-oriented Fel'dman-Mahalanobis strategies of the Soviet Union, India, and China epitomize such a situation (Mellor 1976). The import-substitution strategies soon gravitate in that direction (Mellor and Johnston 1984; Mellor 1976). Consumer food prices may still be very important to political stability in such regimes because of the lack of growth in employment in the modern sector, the stagnation in the traditional sector, and generally slow overall growth. In fact, it is in such economies that public policy attempts to depress urban food prices while giving scant attention to facilitating technological change in agriculture (Mellor 1976).

In the real world, capital and labor markets are necessarily at least somewhat dualistic. Fixed, capital-intensive factor proportions are characteristic of some essential, nonimportable goods and services industries (for example, power generation). But if agricultural growth and low food prices are to foster overall growth, emphasis must be on minimizing the extent of dualism through international trade and through the structure of domestic consumption. That is, in effect, deploying capital to maximize the growth in demand for labor. As that is done, the labor market becomes increasingly sensitive to food prices, the food market becomes increasingly important to growth in demand for labor, and rising food prices become increasingly deleterious to growth in employment. Eventually, of course, rising incomes decrease the importance of food in laborers' expenditure patterns, and food prices lose this central place in influencing demand for labor and overall growth.

A change in agricultural prices redistributes income between the urban and rural sectors, which in turn affects consumption patterns and hence the labor intensity of production. However, the stimulus to growth in rural nonagricultural sectors from rising agricultural prices is balanced financially by a decline in purchases by nonfarm consumers. The net effect is favorable to growth if, as tends to be the case, goods consumed by rural people have a higher domestic employment content than those consumed by urban people (Mellor 1976; Mellor and Lele 1973). But the net effect is likely to be small and cannot be cumulative over a long period. Technological change in agriculture, by providing a net increase in national product, has a potentially larger net effect on consumption and has a clear potential to compound over time.

Agricultural Production: Aggregate

The effect of prices on agricultural production is conceptually simpler than the effect on the demand for labor. The short-run response of supply to price derives from movement along a production function with a given technology. Empirically, for an agriculture using traditional inputs, the aggregate supply response to price is quite inelastic—typically no more than a 0.1 to 0.2 percent increase in supply for a 1 percent increase in price (chapters 10 and 11; Herdt 1970).

Given such inelastic supply, increased prices represent a generally inefficient means of increasing agricultural production. The inelasticity of supply is the result of the diminishing returns or increasing costs that normally arise in agriculture with a fixed land area (for example, Asia). Inelasticity of supply also may result when very low labor productivity causes very low marginal utility of a given amount of work, as in Africa (Mellor and Ranade forthcoming). Thus, as agricultural prices rise, each successive unit of increased production requires successively larger quantities of resources and hence greater cost.

With technological change, agricultural supply becomes more price-responsive (chapter 11). The supply of purchased inputs tends to be elastic and a substitute for resources in inelastic supply. As response to price increases with technological change, the conflict between employment policy and agricultural production policy sharpens. Fortunately, technological change decreases the cost of production, and when full equilibrium is reached with respect to new agricultural technology, agricultural prices will tend to be lower than before (Lele and Mellor 1981).

Efforts to measure long-run supply response tend to show much more elastic response to price than indicated above. This is due largely to the effect of changes in technology and related capital investment. Chapter 10 places long-term capital accumulation and technological change in a supply response context. In this discussion we prefer to emphasize the planning needs and lags associated with technological change and therefore consider them apart from price response.

Finally, we must note the circumstances in which governments have grossly distorted agricultural prices through exchange rates, domestic demand control, and market interference. Reversing such action may provide scope for a radical increase in farm prices and a sharp increase in production on a once-and-for-all basis. But it is notable that removing restrictions on food prices may not bring major increases in food production unless associated with other actions such as increased input supply which have probably also been unfavorable to agriculture. The discussion of China in chapter 8 makes this point clearly.

Increased food prices may greatly increase official marketings and bring more production under the influence of other government policies. They may also reduce consumption somewhat. In the labor supply and demand conditions of Africa, they may cause some net change in migration patterns from urban toward rural areas, reducing demand and increasing supply.

Agricultural Production: Commodity Composition

While aggregate agricultural production is inelastic with respect to relative prices, the supply of individual commodities may well be highly elastic as farmers transfer the same resources from one commodity to another. Of course such transfers take time, and, given the volatility of international prices, governments may smooth the fluctuations to reduce the inefficient movement of resources. Chapter 10 makes clear the inappropriateness of resource transfers in response to short-term, weather-induced price changes.

Governments often distort prices by levying commodity taxes. Particularly in the case of export commodities, that may be inefficient, if not carefully formulated. Export commodities, in Africa, for example, often provide high rates of return to resources relative to their use in production for domestic consumption, and yet they frequently face inelastic foreign demand. The latter may be the case even for quite small countries, as they often have a significant share of the market for any one commodity. In such circumstances it is appealing to governments to raise revenues by driving a tax wedge between the world price and the domestic price. Two cautions are needed.

First, it is important that production be kept competitive by effective research, the returns to which may, in any case, be very high. Second, too large a tax wedge may shift resources massively out of the export commodity, with a consequent reduction in national output. Such excessive distortion most frequently occurs through major overvaluation of the currency. That has been a frequent problem in Africa. Once returns to export crops have been driven down to the level of returns in other crops, they may prove particularly responsive to price changes. This is because they often use only a small proportion of area and because even perennial crops offer an opportunity for a substantial change in labor use which can affect output markedly.

It is notable that it is only after a long period of development and economic transformation that agricultural commodities lose their dominant role as earners of foreign exchange. Even Taiwan earned 60 percent of its foreign exchange from agricultural exports as recently as 1960. By 1983 this figure had declined to 10 percent (Fei, Ranis, and Kuo 1979; ADB 1983). Thus it is important that developing countries allocate adequate resources to vigorous technological change (cost reduction) in export commodity production.

If export crops are to be taxed for government revenues it is particularly important that exchange rates not be overvalued. The latter means of taxation does not directly provide government revenues, and the additional price-depressing effect may drive returns below alternative uses of resources and cause a major supply effect.

The Ivory Coast has successfully expanded export commodity production, taxed export commodities on the order of 30 percent, and used the proceeds effectively to foster technological change in agriculture. At the other extreme, a number of countries have taxed the export sector by 60 to 70 percent and have not reinvested in rural development, with resultant gradual destruction of the export industries and major loss to overall development (Lele 1985). Thus price policy must be seen as interacting with other policies.

As economic growth accelerates, a major change occurs in relative demand for various agricultural commodities. It is important that price policy not interfere with the price signals that will encourage shifts in production in response to the dynamics of growth. Indeed, shifts in demand offer major opportunities to accelerate growth. High-income-elastic agricultural commodities tend to require more labor in production and to use it productively. Thus rising incomes favor increased utilization of resources, which favors increased national income and distributes it substantially to labor. It is particularly important that price policy not support the prices of commodities experiencing rapid technological change at the cost of commodities favored by rising incomes. The political pressures for such support are immense. In this context two non-price forces are particularly important: investment in technological change for livestock and horticultural commodities and investment in marketing and transport infrastructure for these and other income-elastic agricultural commodities. Without such investment increased demand will be met by rising prices and consumption will switch to other commodities—which may well have less labor-intensive production techniques.

AGRICULTURAL PRICE POLICY AND
TECHNOLOGICAL CHANGE

Farmers are economically motivated and respond to changing incentives. The basic case for technological change is that it provides incentives to farmers by reducing the cost of production via increased factor productivity and thereby makes a net addition to national income. The expenditure of that income adds a further stimulus to growth (Mellor 1976; Mellor and Lele 1973).

Increased prices may provide a net addition to national income by inducing the transfer of resources to more efficient activities or inducing the mobilization of underused resources. However, prices largely transfer income and resources from one activity to another, with the gains from one activity being substantially offset by the losses in another. This fact is often lost sight of when price analysis focuses entirely on one sector, such as agriculture. Nevertheless, prices have an important complementary role to play in technological change in agriculture. In particular, price policy must face five major public policy issues associated with technological change.

Instability

Increased instability in agricultural production, prices, and incomes tend to accompany accelerated technological change in agriculture and places growing pressures on political systems to respond. The consequent public financial costs are apt to be high and to conflict with financial requirements for continued support of technological progress.

Chapters 2 and 3 document the large increases in instability in international prices and in global and national production that have occurred in recent decades. Chapter 3 further notes the association of increased production instability with new technology. Some of the causal elements, such as inadequate and unreliable fertilizer distribution policies or electricity supply policies for water pumping and other production needs, should be rectified on pure production grounds. The part of the instability arising directly from the technologies themselves may eventually be reduced by increased expenditure on scientific development. Nevertheless, given the social and political costs, governments demand policies for reducing instability. The challenge is to meet that demand with minimum net costs to the processes of growth and development.

Technological change is likely to occur at a very uneven pace, both over time and across regions. Thus, while acceleration of the long-term growth rate in agricultural production over a large area by as much as one percentage point is impressive, the acceleration in a small area for a few years may be as much as five percentage points or even more. The latter is difficult to absorb through local consumption or even, given the realities of marketing systems, through distribution outside the region. The result may well be a collapse of prices at the farm level, at least for a short period of time. This problem is particularly severe for commodities with highly inelastic demand, as is the case for major food crops including cassava, millet, and sorghum in West Africa and in areas in which marketings are a small proportion of production.

The Punjab story in chapter 10 illustrates this well. For India, the green revolution accelerated the food production growth rate only a fraction of a percentage point above the population growth rate. But for a few years in the Punjab food production accelerated on an order of three times the all-India average population growth rate. With marketings highly elastic with respect to output, the burden of such an output increase on the marketing system was massive. Despite a highly developed private trade, major government intervention was probably necessary to prevent a far greater collapse in local prices than would be predicted by the all-India magnitude.

Such market failure results when the transport and storage systems became overloaded and the private trade has taken as much risk in purchasing and storing as it considers prudent. Chapter 5 describes public systems designed to prevent such a collapse. Market failure is even more likely when the marketing channels are poorly developed. Indeed, this has frequently occurred in response to weather (D'Silva and Raza 1980). It is for these reasons that developing country governments find it necessary to construct systems in which they can at least serve as buyer of last resort, with consequent establishment of regional purchasing and storage agencies.

At the same time that production instability and potential for market failure may be increasing, farmers are becoming more vulnerable to price instability as they purchase more inputs and sell a higher proportion of output.

The effect of price instability on production is difficult to judge. Fluctuations in producer prices are normal in well-operating markets and are not necessarily deleterious. Farmers are averse to risk, but they generally have little opportunity to avoid it by making adjustments to aggregate agricultural production. They will, of course, favor, in relation to average returns, individual commodities which demonstrate less risk. Thus stabilization policies for one commodity may draw large resources to that commodity.

In the face of large fluctuations in income, farmers may well invest more in profitable periods than they disinvest in unprofitable ones—a view consistent with the permanent income hypothesis of expenditure patterns. But market failure can drop prices sufficiently to wipe out returns to purchased inputs and impose a tight capital constraint by lowering income of farmers and increasing risk to lenders. In any case, whether it affects aggregate production levels or not, farmers and consumers will both expect governments to ensure some degree of stability. Thus the political case for stability-oriented market intervention through at least minimum floor prices is very strong.

From a producer point of view, the principal means of introducing protection from major fluctuations in production and prices is through the agricultural credit system. And one of the principal problems for the credit system is how to prevent the flexibility which permits stabilization through rescheduling loans from becoming a general license for nonpayment of loans. Thus use of the credit system for dealing with instability must be done in the context of a clearly understood set of rules and tight discipline. Crop insurance schemes are widely discussed, broadly utilized, and usually very expensive due to problems of controlling risk and, at least in a generalized form, are not a preferred means of controlling risk (Hazell, Pomareda, and Valdés 1986).

Governments may also enter into stocking arrangements to assure both producer and consumer stability. The cost of stocking policies tend to be very high, as pointed out in chapter 5, and can be greatly reduced by use of international trade. Chapter 5 shows that a consistent importer (or exporter) can operate a domestic price stabilization policy at low cost to the public treasury. Such policies benefit from a coordinated system of food aid and well-operating commercial food trade. An improved International Monetary Fund cereal financing facility could further assist such policies.

The costs of operating a price support policy to maintain stable prices under conditions of self-sufficiency are on average likely to be immense. Doing so through storage alone has very high costs because of the randomness of need. However, even if a country trades, the costs of transport, including international shipping, port costs, and transport within the country will cause large differentials between the export and import costs, which determine the band within which domestic prices can fluctuate. Koester (1986) shows, for the countries of southern Africa, that the upper level of the price band for which domestic stabilization efforts would be needed is over 100 percent of the lower level. The government is itself subject to the dangers of market failure when its costs are high. That a collapse of markets is likely to be particularly severe if government intervention fails suggests that governments should be conservative in estimating the levels at which they offer price stabilization guarantees.

Two conclusions on stabilization: (1) consistent exporters and importers have an advantage, they may need stabilization less, and it will be less costly; (2) wide bands should be set for price stabilization and only narrowed when the capacity to maintain them is proven.

Downward Price Trends

Prices may also trend downward over several years in response to major technological innovation in agriculture. It is doubtful whether governments should attempt to prevent such declines.

In the pure theory of an open economy, improved technology in one country would not depress prices in that country because increased production would not have a significant effect on global supply and imports or exports would prevent significant price change. However, in the real world, even of open economies, substantial transaction costs and wide swings in real exchange rates may allow domestic agricultural prices to fluctuate over a range that may be equal to 100 percent or more of base period prices.

In a closed economy, technological change in the agricultural sector will have a depressing effect on relative agricultural prices, even if employment expands sufficiently to use all the incremental food as wage goods (Lele and Mellor 1981). However, more usually, in addition to growth in demand from the direct and indirect employment effects of agricultural growth, there is further growth in demand from autonomous expansion of the nonagricultural sector. In that case, domestic food prices may rise and imports increase. That is the norm for contemporary developing countries, as chapter 2 documents.

Contrary to the developing country norm, some countries have been unsuccessful in expanding food consumption at the same pace as accelerated food production. For example, in India in the early to middle 1980s accelerated growth in foodgrain production resulted in reduced imports. Per capita food consumption rose relatively little, and stocks increased to a level as much as four times the level an optimal stocking policy would suggest. In those circumstances, lack of a purchase program for foodgrain would have resulted in a sharp decline in relative foodgrain prices, at least in the short run. A similar case occurred in the Philippines, where rapid growth in domestic food output would have resulted in a major decline in domestic food prices if imports had not been limited and exports subsidized. However, these are both cases of unfavorable policies for employment growth, largely due to inefficient allocation of capital. Improved capital allocations and faster growth of employment would have been preferable to subsidized stocks and exports.

At the global level, technological change in developed countries in the face of saturated domestic demand for food results in a rapidly growing exportable surplus that may depress international prices. Developing countries must decide whether these changes are long-term or short-term, whether they wish to shift agricultural resources if they are long-term, and whether they find the national income distribution effects acceptable. In such circumstances it is only prudent for developing countries to have a strategy and institutional structure for influencing domestic food prices.

In analyzing the implications of declining international prices for agricultural commodities, it is important to keep in mind two major points. First, because of capital scarcity it is unlikely that a low-income country will cease to have a comparative advantage within its existing large food production sector. Put in layman's terms, what else are all those people to do? Thus the problem of secular decline in international prices of food is more one of income distribution than production mix. Second, technological change in the large agricultural sector is still the most likely engine of growth and is probably profitable to pursue even in a low international price context.

In developing price policy in the context of an apparent downward trend in agricultural prices due to domestic technological advance, it is important to understand the relation between technological change and the cost of production. Chapter 11 discusses that issue and the implications for price policy. At least in major technological breakthroughs, the added inputs initially result in a sharp increase in total cost per unit of land, but as output increases the result is a sharp decline in unit cost of production.

The consequent large increase in supply will initially depress prices but probably not sufficiently to depress incomes to the pre-new-technology level. However, the decline in prices and incomes from their previous level induces farmers to increase efficiency in application of technological improvements. Then, as supply growth slackens and demand growth continues, prices tend to rise, encouraging a higher level of input use than would have been profitable previously. The result is a modest rise in cost of production. That tends to provide justification, through cost-of-production studies, for support of prices at higher levels. Technological breakthroughs in agriculture are likely to be associated with increased strength of farmer lobbies. That is because the institutional requirements for technological change in agriculture depend upon political support, which is most likely to arise in the context of increased political representation of farmers. That, in its turn, is likely to favor price polices that are pro-farmer.

Finally, it is important to recognize that lower costs of production for basic food staples for which demand is relatively inelastic may properly send a price signal to shift resources to commodities for which demand is more elastic. Price supports are deleterious to overall growth and employment growth in such circumstances.

In summary, in the context of cost-reducing technological change, prices can drift downward significantly without resulting in a disincentive to produce. Areas not benefiting from improved technology may then need to shift to other commodities. Thus, while a government may correctly choose to reduce price fluctuations, it needs sound analysis to distinguish that step from efforts to prevent longer-term changes in price relationships.

Purchased Inputs

A third problem for price policy associated with accelerated technological change arises from increased dependence of farmers on purchased inputs. Attention is drawn in chapter 6 to the increased risk and uncertainty associated with a large increase in the use of purchased inputs. A more basic problem lies in their availability and financing. It is clear from chapters 12 and 13 that availability, not price, is the key issue, at least for a broad range around international prices. Chapter 12 describes the pattern by which innovation and fertilizer use spread from commodity to commodity and region to region as a basis for prescribing effective institutions for input supply.

As nations increase attention to their agriculture, recognize the close association between technological change and increased use of purchased inputs, and encounter the many obstacles to spreading input use, they are apt to turn to input subsidies as means of accelerating growth in input use.

Cost of input subsidies is initially insignificant when usage is low. It soars with success. Fertilizer alone took 13 percent of public sector development expenditure for agriculture in Bangladesh in 1983/84.

Input subsidies are certainly not progressive in their distributional impact and may be mildly regressive. While macroeconomic relations favor somewhat more intensive application of inputs by small farmers, the larger farmers use more in total. In any case, the poorest rural people are the landless, who do not benefit directly from input subsidies. In practice, governments may restrict availability of crucial inputs to contain costs when subsidies are rising rapidly. The consequent rationing by political influence is bound to be even more unfavorable to the poor than rationing by economic power.

As input use spreads from region to region, costs per unit of sales of input distribution facilities are initially high in new areas. Thus, while usage is low, there is a strong argument for public financing of the institutional distribution structure. This will, in effect, involve subsidies while volume is low, but these will decline as volume increases—a politically desirable outcome. The opposite occurs when the inputs are subsidized directly through lower prices. The input pricing problem is a transitional one which is associated with expanding distribution networks. The same argument can be applied to credit. The point applies even more dramatically to improved seed, for which a complex distribution system may also be needed.

Thus comes to two conclusions on input subsidies: (1) that the distribution channels to achieve rapid expansion should be subsidized, not the inputs themselves; (2) that a public sector investment in storage and distribution itself is probably implied by (1), with all the attendant problems of trying to extricate government from those activities once the private sector is able to be self-sustaining.

Public Resource Scarcity

Public policy with respect to price stabilization, price support, and input subsidies must all be driven in the final analysis by the fact that government expenditure in agriculture must grow immensely to support accelerated technological change. Each of the four chapters dealing with technological change emphasizes the need for public expenditure if rapid progress is to be made. Chapter 10 makes the broad case for capital formation. Chapter 11 documents the large increase in expenditure associated with new technology. Chapter 12 emphasizes the need for research to increase the returns to inputs and for investment in institutions for fertilizer supply and distribution, at least in early stages of growth. Chapter 13 makes a similar point for credit.

Thus a critical issue for public, technology-related agricultural price policy is the competing claims for funds for (a) public sector expenditure for fostering technological change in agriculture; (b) support for agricultural prices when they decline secularly or cyclically; (c) subsidy for inputs or the distribution channels for inputs; and (d) encouragement of growth in employment. The first and the fourth tasks require massive infrastructural development. They leave few resources for price supports and subsidies. Given the immense growth and equity benefits of accelerated growth in agricultural production, use of public resources for input subsidies and price supports should take a back seat to expenditure on the structural requisites of growth in food production and employment. Chapter 5 is particularly valuable in emphasizing price targets for government policy and suggesting how they may be met at small public sector expenditure in an open trading regime. Unfortunately, that is not the usual story of public price interventions.

Equity

While technological change in agriculture reduces the cost of producing food and hence is generally desirable for the poor, it may tend to have a deleterious effect on some of the poor through its effects on nonparticipating regions and through increased instability.

Technological change occurs unevenly across geographical areas and is most likely to succeed where yields are already good. Therefore, farmers in more prosperous regions are more likely to be favored. Second, the disparities are likely to be further increased by strong multiplier effects of the new technology on the local economy. Third, if food prices decline as a result of increased production, regions not using the new technology will suffer absolute as well as relative income declines.

The standard means of reducing these disparities is through migration, with all of the resulting social problems of changing age distribution and depletion of human capital in the backward regions. Attempts to deal with the problem of absolute decline in income in an area through price supports are common, as farmers in all areas will favor such efforts. But this is likely to exacerbate the problem further, since added income in the progressive area will attract further investment, resulting in even more rapid growth. Thus, to the maximum extent that political forces will allow, the recommendation here is not price supports but rather further investment in other activities of natural advantage and in education in the less-favored area, which would facilitate migration. That is a policy which is pro-employment and hence strengthens effective demand for food.

Of course, if a region lags despite basic resource potential, the reasons should be diagnosed and dealt with. Inadequate investment in research, education, and infrastructure is a common cause of such preventable regional disparities.

The increased instability of production commonly associated with technological change bears particularly harshly on the poor. Analysis of time series for rural poverty in India shows that the proportion of the population below the poverty line swings between 40 percent and 60 percent of the rural population (Mellor and Desai 1985). Per capita food production (which affects employment) and food prices (which affect the purchasing power of income) are the two single most powerful forces determining the proportion of the population in poverty. In urban areas, food prices and poverty are even more directly linked. Even in the middle rank of the civil service in countries in the income class of Bangladesh, food accounts for over half of budget expenditures. No wonder food prices are a politically volatile issue.

Low-income consumers are extraordinarily vulnerable to sharp increases in food prices. Because high-income consumers have a highly inelastic demand for food, lower supplies and higher prices cause them to reduce consumption of other goods and services, with a consequent decline in employment. Thus the bulk of adjustment to a smaller food supply is made by low-income people, either as a result of higher prices or decreased employment. The extent to which either factor is dominant depends on complex forces (Mellor 1978). Thus variations in food supply sharply change the distribution of income. For a society in which the normal distribution of income is barely acceptable, it is essential to protect the poor from major fluctuations in poverty and in their share of societal income.

Soaring domestic food prices often are due to domestic crop failure. The inevitable result is extreme privation of low-income rural people, either small farmers with little reserves or the landless. In such cases, measures are needed to move food into rural areas and to preserve the purchasing power of the poor. For most rural people, a rural public works program will be effective. Because of long lead times for developing such systems, it is prudent to have them in operation at a low level in normal times so that they can be increased rapidly in time of need. Food aid can play a major role in mitigating the effect of fluctuations in domestic food production.

The rural poverty problem resulting from production variability in Africa has different dimensions than in Asia, where there is a very poor landless class which loses its employment when agricultural production declines and hence cannot buy food even if it is available. In Asia, the landless are in particular need of relief. In Africa, it is the small farmer who suffers most when production drops below the margin. Food supplies may be so low and consequent nutritional status so poor that planting in the next year may be reduced. Thus relief supplies of food are likely to have greater impact on future output in Africa than in labor-surplus Asia. Also, in Africa the lowest incomes are in the rural areas. All this argues for a major effort to meet rural food shortfalls in rural Africa. Again, food aid can play a major positive role.

As in the case of agricultural price supports for farmers, food subsidies for poor consumers run a great risk of becoming permanent, with escalating costs and consequent siphoning of funds away from the investments in agricultural growth and employment that represent the long-run solution to poverty.

Technological change also affects seasonal price fluctuations, increasing or decreasing them depending on the cropping pattern and the state of infrastructure investment. Over the longer run, the full set of forces of rural development should reduce seasonal fluctuations by decreasing marketing costs.

The price and income elasticities suggest that the poor make very major seasonal adjustments in food consumption. Chapter 5 suggests that a minimal seasonal fluctuation in prices of 40 percent is not unusual under free market conditions. In such circumstances, a seasonal reduction by one-third of food consumption by the poor would not be surprising. Even if this did not have major deleterious biological effects, it would at least be unpleasant. High priority should be given to reducing these fluctuations. Chapter 5 discusses how this may be done at modest cost in an open trading regime. Both chapters 4 and 5 suggest ways of avoiding a major escalation in costs of reducing seasonal fluctuations.

MANAGEMENT OF AGRICULTURAL PRICES

Virtually all governments, whether of high-income or low-income countries, intervene in agricultural markets. The clear message from the policy-makers at the IFPRI price policy seminar from which this book derives was that "agricultural price policy is far too vital to a wide range of national interests to allow determination by purely external forces such as international markets." The corollary is that domestic political forces inevitably intrude into agricultural price determination. A broad survey of its members by the International Federation of Agricultural Producers (IFAP) revealed that they rejected the free market as the final arbiter of the prices they received (IFAP 1984).

When governments interfere in the market, what devices should they use for interfering, what base should interference be measured from, and how great should that interference be? The preceding discussion provided broad guidelines for answering these questions from a growth perspective leavened by concern for equity and stability. The following provides a brief set of policy guidelines consistent with that discussion.

Mechanisms of Price Policy

The clearly preferred position for price policy is higher prices for producers to stimulate production and lower prices for consumers to improve income distribution and to increase employment by lowering the cost of labor. But before proceeding to comment on the means by which governments may drive a wedge between producer prices and consumer prices, it should be emphasized that improved agricultural production technology achieves the effect of higher producer prices by lowering cost of production while facilitating concurrently lower prices for consumers. Hence in viewing each mechanism for achieving a price wedge, its effect on the pace of technological change should be analyzed.

Financing a food subsidy by fixed compulsory procurement from farmers at below-market prices in combination with low-price sales to the poor serves as a tax on high-income consumers to benefit low-income consumers. The market supply is reduced and total demand is increased, since the procured supplies are directed to the poor, whose demand is relatively elastic. As a result, the market price will rise enough to more than offset the losses on procurement, thus taxing the well-to-do and reimbursing the producers who initially finance the subsidy (Mellor and Ponteves 1964). However, such low price procurement involves administrative costs and the distinct danger of drifting into displacing private trade by an inefficient public sector marketing agency. Such programs may well be politically unpopular, since the effect of higher market prices may go unnoticed by farmers who have initially sold a portion of their output at lower prices.

It is more common to pay for consumer food subsidies from general public revenues. Chapter 14 discusses various aspects of the costs and benefits of such programs. The immense magnitude of poverty in a low-income country makes the aggregate cost of even an efficient subsidy program very high. If governments are to foster low-priced food to the poor and to avoid spending 15 to 20 percent of public expenditure on such subsidies, as has happened in Sri Lanka, Egypt, or Bangladesh at various times, a significant effort at targeting to low-income people is essential.

Narrow targeting to a small set of the very poor tends to have illusory savings, in that the administrative costs tend to be high and much of the saving comes simply by reducing the proportion of the poor covered. Note that food stamps in Sri Lanka proved to be no more efficient in the proportion of expenditure reaching the poor than broad food price subsidies, although when introduced the overall coverage and cost was greatly reduced (Edirisinghe 1987).

A more effective approach to targeting is to select commodities that comprise a high budget share for the poor and, preferably, a low share for the more well-to-do. Particularly appropriate are the poorer grades of widely consumed foods. New high-yielding crop varieties have often had this characteristic, with major advantages to the poor. Locating low-price shops in areas of concentrated poverty has similar advantages.

For each targeting device, the greater the price wedge between consumer and producer prices, the larger the leakage to higher-income people. A spread of perhaps 10 to 15 percent is perhaps all that can be managed within an acceptable total budget constraint. That would be equivalent to an increase of 8 to 12 percent in income to the very poor, who spend over 80 percent of income on basic food staples. Such an increase would be significant to the well-being of the poor, given the initial low level of their consumption.

Many of the poorest people are in rural areas. Food subsidies in Egypt, Kerala, and Sri Lanka have effectively reached the rural poor. But the distribution costs are high and the total costs escalate enormously because of the high proportion of low-income population in rural areas. Food-for-work programs or, more generally, rural employment programs are a logical means of containing costs of income transfers in rural areas. Given the need for rural infrastructure and its labor-intensive methods, development objectives are well pursued in this manner.

Rural employment schemes have much in common with food subsidies, since the poor spend a high proportion of income on food. Thus a rural employment scheme with an aggregate impact must ensure that added food reaches the rural area. Direct payment of food for work can be effective if appropriately designed and implemented (IFPRI-BIDS 1985). But there should be no illusion that food for work with aggregate impact will be less expensive than a broadly targeted food subsidy. The advantage lies with built-in targeting and the creation of a well-planned infrastructure. These, however, also require substantial supplemental expenditures for such items as culverts and paving.

Rural employment schemes have the disadvantage of not reaching the incapacitated and possibly female heads of households, who are among the poorest in rural areas. A rural employment or guaranteed employment scheme has the advantage of providing a continuing administrative structure that can be rapidly expanded in time of crop failure, as well as providing constant monitoring of the food status of the rural poor.

Foreign assistance in the form of food aid in effect relieves the domestic economy and public revenues of the costs of food subsidies. Chapter 15 discusses the role of food aid in both food and employment subsidies and shows that it need not be a disincentive to agricultural production. The argument against food and employment subsidies is largely one of fiscal policy. It is claimed that excessive taxes incident to such subsidies result in disincentives to production and that government revenues are diverted from the essentials for production growth. Food aid may fill such a budgetary gap.

Many countries that successfully achieved rapid growth in agriculture were once major food aid recipients. This observation suggests that there is potential for food aid in the transition period when food production is growing slowly, employment has a potential to grow rapidly, and food imports are needed to keep food prices from escalating rapidly and cutting off employment growth. To ensure that food aid does not have a price-disincentive effect, it should be managed in the context of an explicit national price policy.

Subsidized employment has favorable effects on human capital and employment, both key growth factors, and thus should be looked at in the context of a high employment policy rather than as a purely welfare measure.

A common device for maintaining a low consumer price is an overvalued exchange rate. Chapter 7 shows how important the foreign exchange rate is in determining the relation between real domestic and international prices. As a device for distorting prices, it has little to recommend it. As is elaborated in chapter 7 and an earlier section of this chapter, agriculture in developing countries is severely penalized by an overvalued exchange rate. Export crops suffer the most from an overvalued exchange rate, as it converts the world price at which sales are made into a relatively low domestic price. In addition, the agricultural export industries usually sustain high direct taxes.

A pro-agriculture policy requires devaluation of overvalued currencies. However, since the exchange rate may be less a reflection of conscious discrimination against agriculture than it is a product of economy-wide forces, much more than devaluation may be required. This is dramatically illustrated by the experience of the United States in the 1980s, when exchange rate policy, with its immense impact on agricultural prices, was the inadvertent product of national defense and tax policies. Major oil exporters, Nigeria, for example, saw the value of their currencies grossly appreciated by the sudden increase in oil revenues. This was prejudicial to almost all other production, including agriculture. On the other hand, Indonesia successfully followed offsetting policies that allowed an acceptable growth record in agriculture. Other developing countries have used foreign aid in the same manner as oil revenue to inflate demand for government services initially and, indirectly, for a wide range of commodities, with the result that inflation is accelerated, currency overvaluation is encouraged, and government procrastinates in devaluing the currency in response to inflation for fear that the consequent higher import prices will further exacerbate inflation. The result has often been continued large overvaluation of the currency.

Rapid growth in money supply, perhaps driven by large development expenditures and weak tax systems, with a fixed exchange rate, has the same effect. The basic point is that policies made in the ministry of finance or the central bank, often with little thought to agriculture, have a profound effect on farming. Thus agricultural price policy must take into account these macro policies.

It is important to recognize that an overvalued exchange rate may be the inevitable byproduct of policies that favor capital-intensive urban industry, for example, financing such development through deficit financing and channeling foreign exchange through licenses to imported capital goods. In such cases the underlying development strategy must change, otherwise devaluation will simply be followed by renewed inflation and the need for further devaluation. Exchange rate misalignment is often the symptom of underlying policies unfavorable to agriculture rather than the cause.

For the same reasons, palliatives in the form of import subsidies or price supports for agriculture will be of little help in the face of the dynamics of basic monetary, fiscal, and trade policies that constantly shift prices against agriculture. Thus a pro-agriculture price policy should be established in the context of public expenditure policies that emphasize the essentials of agricultural technology development and application and broad participation of people in most regions through massive public investment in infrastructure and education. With those tasks undertaken, other public expenditures will have to be tightly constrained.

While the exchange rate should not become overvalued, large fluctuations are also deleterious. A crude but pragmatic approach to monitoring the real rate of exchange is to evaluate the domestic inflation rate and the inflation rates of trading partners continually and to operate exchange rate policies consonant with the differential movements of the relative inflation rates. Even that is a rough rule, at best roughly administered.

The Level of Prices

As is clear from chapters 4 and 7, a departure from international prices has major development costs. Therefore, the use of international price as a guide for domestic price has a strong logical base. In fact, because of the virtual necessity of trade to development, the connection of each price with all other prices, and the great economic influence of agricultural supply and demand forces, it is doubtful that governments of developing countries can for long maintain prices that differ widely from international prices. Although simply stated in theory, relating domestic to international prices is, in practice, difficult.

The most important problem in using international prices as benchmarks is the wide spread between what developing country consumers must pay for imports, especially in interior markets, and what their producers receive for export of the same products. Thus, even accepting in principle the use of international prices as benchmarks leaves a wide band within which internal supply and demand factors reign and within which governments may manipulate prices. Indeed, this band is typically so wide as to accommodate much of what is referred to as price distortion. Chapter 4 cites specific examples.

Ideally, international prices reflect underlying global supply and demand balances and hence serve as a basis for determining the comparative advantage for agriculture in individual countries. In practice, while the developed countries produce about one-half of the world's food and 80 percent of the food which enters international trade, food is a small proportion of their national incomes. Thus, unlike developing countries, they are able to impose major distortions on international prices. However, as long as developed countries maintain their policies, and there is little sign of change, a developing country has the opportunity of exchanging at those prices. If it can use its resources to produce something to exchange for more food than it gets from using those resources domestically for food, it gains by doing so, no matter how inefficient that may be for the sellers. In addition, the more a government policy departs from international prices, the greater the difficulty it will have in preventing leakages and distortion in other sectors. Thus, at the very least, a government must be aware of international prices, the extent to which domestic prices depart from them, the reasons for those departures, and the problems to be dealt with in maintaining that differential. It should not add to the costs of such a departure the inefficiencies from widespread black markets.

Three further problems interfere with the use of international prices as a benchmark for domestic agricultural price policy: (1) the wide fluctuations in international prices; (2) uncertainty as to their trend; and (3) the gross imprecision in calculations of real exchange rates and the departure of nominal rates from real rates, discussed in the previous section.

Chapters 3 and 7 document the problem of the large and increasing magnitude of fluctuations in international prices. Virtually all developing countries act to prevent domestic prices from fluctuating as much as international prices. Because of the unpredictable nature of international price fluctuations, it is difficult to determine trends in international prices of food. The trend over a very long term (for example, 1810–1980) has been for little change in relative price of coarse grains, with preferred cereals reducing their price premium (Martin and Brokken 1983). But in intermediate periods of five to ten years relative food rices have fluctuated 50 percent or more. The fluctuation is even more in the short run.

In view of the large changes and rather unpredictable behavior of international prices, chapter 4 suggests use of a moving average. Such rule-of-thumb measures seem to indicate greater stability in prices than "more scientific" projections. For example, Siamwalla shows that successive World Bank rice price projections have in effect been closely related to the previous year's price and tend to be much more volatile than those based on a longer-term average (Siamwalla and Haykin 1983).

In addition to the unpredictability in international prices, there is a second factor related to comparable quality that must carefully be assessed before setting domestic prices at world levels. The commodity consumed in domestic markets may differ in quality rather substantially from the commodity bought and sold in world markets. This difference occurs due to varietal difference and the difference in the degree of processing and packaging involved in products for domestic and for international markets. For example, the price differential between Thai 20 percent broken rice and U.S. no. 2 rice is about 100 percent. In general, food grains consumed in home markets of developing countries are generally appraised by the market as inferior to the products exchanged in international markets.

The average national price that is related to average international price must be translated into various levels of price consistent with a country's spatial and intertemporal diversities in markets. It is here that transportation and marketing costs influence farm and consumer-level prices. A major reason for low producer prices in developing countries is excessively large marketing margins and, in particular, high costs of transportation. There is no question that high transport costs cause far greater departures in farm-level prices from international prices than government manipulation of prices. This point is made vividly in chapter 4 by comparing marketing margins in Africa and Asia. Four recommendations for raising farm prices in a stable manner follow.

First, and in keeping with rural production and employment needs, governments must invest massively in rural infrastructure. Second, governments must invest in facilities and provide regulation to improve competitiveness in markets. Third, government monopoly in markets must be ended and efficiency of government agencies increased. A major factor reducing farm prices is inefficient public monopoly. The inevitable result is illegal private trade with very high costs forced by small-scale bribery and risk of illegal status. Particularly in Africa, these measures can create far greater increases in producer prices than can manipulation of exchange rates and regulation of prices.

Finally, when stabilization in intertemporal and spatial prices becomes essential for economic and political reasons, such programs should operate with a targeted price band, as explained in chapters 4 and 5. Without a clear-cut price target and operational rules, such programs become fiscally burdensome and provide little price support to either producers or consumers. When the price band is very narrow, it requires a large public effort and, at the same time, a substitution of public for private trade. On both these counts, such a narrow band is undesirable. On the other hand, if the price band is very wide, the program may lose its effectiveness in price stabilization. An optimal band can theoretically be worked on the basis of benefit and cost relations with various levels of stabilization. A pragmatic way to select the price band is to estimate the politically tolerable limit of price fluctuation and then gear the program to implement it at a minimum cost.

Given that institutional factors and availability of modern inputs and credit at the right time and place play a more dominant role in their diffusion than relative input prices, one should apply the same principles of relation to international prices of tradeable inputs as of product prices.

However, the problem of instability of fertilizer supplies and price in international markets is even more serious than that for cereals. This creates a serious setback to technological progress in agriculture and instability in production, particularly in countries where fertilizer is an important factor of production. In order to avoid this uncertainty, pricing of fertilizer should follow a smooth path whereby the domestic price would be above the international prices when the international price is low and below the international price when it is high. Such a stabilization policy in fertilizer implies that the developing countries maintain a security stock of fertilizers or foreign exchange beyond the requirement indicated by trend growth in demand. The international financial institutions could play a useful role in support of such policy.

Pricing of water is an especially controversial issue which requires a brief note. While water is often misallocated, that can rarely be rectified by price policy. Rather, engineering and management changes are needed to allow farmers to use water optimally.

Thus water pricing, and the financing of infrastructure generally, is primarily a matter of fiscal policy. Massive expenditures are needed which can be provided more rapidly if users can be charged. Payment is facilitated if the rate of return is high, which, in turn, requires a high level of technical and economic efficiency.

The extreme politicization of agricultural price policy needs to be recognized because of the danger that interference in markets will rise step by step to unmanageable proportions, requiring rapid, difficult adjustments in programs that can no longer be financed. And a change in political systems may bring a major destabilizing change in agricultural policies. Particularly striking is the gradual rise in developing countries of farmer lobbies that swing fiscal policy from subsidies to reduce consumer prices to subsidies to raise producer prices.

INTERNATIONAL COOPERATION AND
INSTITUTIONAL DEVELOPMENT

Agricultural price policy bulks particularly large in a development strategy that plays to the normal comparative advantage of a low-income country in fostering technological change in its agriculture and rapid growth in demand for its labor force. Choice of such a strategy benefits farmers and low-income consumers, and hence they may tend to be incorporated more fully in the political process, thereby further politicizing agricultural price policy.

Concurrently, the instability of national and international influences on agricultural prices is increasing. In that context, international structures that stabilize access to food will become more and more important. Greater stability of bilateral food aid programs can help. Even more important, a reliable International Monetary Fund financing facility such as an improved cereals facility would be timely and encouraging to the price and supply stability needed by an agriculture- and employment-oriented development strategy. International cooperation, by relieving pressures in times of shortage, would also facilitate maintaining the open trade regimes which are so important to such a strategy.

Each country's price policy objectives, means, and institutional structure differ from others so much that appropriate price policy cannot be drawn from general nostrums or from the pronouncements of passing expatriates. Within a broad framework of action, specific policies must be developed, monitored, and modified by national institutions. Thus the first requisite of good agricultural price policy is the development of a national research, analytical, and policy formulation capacity.

Deriving coherent policy conclusions by integrating diverse relations is a task that can be performed only by professionally skilled people operating in an institutional structure suited to the conditions of the country. The usefulness of general guidelines will depend on a country's ability to identify its unique problems and modify guidelines to suit its own conditions.

Price policy is not the basic engine of economic development, but it is of great political importance and can be a major drag on development if not properly articulated. As such, a substantial allocation of the scarce intellectual and institutional resources of developing countries to price policy is justified. We hope that unfolding the complexities of agricultural price policy and a general outline for managing such policies in developing countries will contribute to the effectiveness of such national efforts.

References

Adams, Richard. 1983. The role of research in policy development: The creation of the IMF Cereal Import Facility. *World Development* 11 (July).

ADB (Asian Development Bank). 1983. *Key indicators of developing member countries of ADB.* Manila: ADB.

Ahmed, Raisuddin. 1979. *Foodgrain supply, distribution, and consumption policies within a dual pricing mechanism: A case study of Bangladesh.* Research Report 8. Washington, D.C.: International Food Policy Research Institute.

————. 1981. *Agricultural price policies under complex socio economic and natural constraints: The case of Bangladesh.* Research Report 27. Washington, D.C.: International Food Policy Research Institute.

Ahmed, Raisuddin, and Andrew Bernard. Forthcoming. *Seasonality of rice prices, effect of new technology, and an approach to rice price stabilization in Bangladesh.* Washington, D.C.: International Food Policy Research Institute.

Ahmed, Raisuddin, and Mahabub Hossain. Forthcoming. *Role of rural infrastructures in income, consumption, savings, investment, and employment among rural households in Bangladesh.* Washington, D.C.: International Food Policy Research Institute.

Ahmed, Raisuddin, and Narendra Rustagi. 1985. *Marketing and agricultural price policies in selected countries of Asia and Africa: A comparative study.* IFPRI-FAO Study. Washington, D.C.: International Food Policy Research Institute.

Alderman, Harold, and Joachim von Braun. 1984. *The effects of the Egyptian food ration and subsidy system on income distribution and welfare.* Research Report 45. Washington, D.C.: International Food Policy Research Institute.

Alderman, Harold; Joachim von Braun; and Sakr Ahmed Sakr. 1982. *Egypt's food subsidy and rationing system: A description.* Research Report 34. Washington, D.C.: International Food Policy Research Institute.

Arrow, Kenneth J. 1971. *Essays in the theory of risk-bearing.* Chicago: Markham Publishing Co.

Bachman, Kenneth L., and Paulino, Leonardo A. 1979. *Rapid food production growth in selected developing countries: A comparative analysis of underlying trends, 1961–76.* Research Report 11. Washington, D.C.: International Food Policy Research Institute.

Bangladesh, Ministry of Agriculture. 1985. *Fertilizer pricing policies and food-grain production strategy.* International Food Policy Research Institute and Bangladesh Institute of Development Studies Joint Report. Dhaka: IFPRI and IDS.

Bapna, S. L. 1981. *Aggregate supply response of crops in a developing region.* New Delhi: Sultan Chand & Sons.

Barker, R.; E. C. Gabler; and D. Winklemann. 1981. Long-term consequences of technological change on crop yield stability. In *Food security for developing countries.* Edited by Alberto Valdés. Boulder, Col.: Westview Press.

Bautista, Romeo M., et al. 1979. *Industrial promotion policies in the Philippines.* Manila: Philippine Institute for Development Studies.

Beaton, G. H., and H. Ghassemi. 1979. Supplementary feeding programmes for young children in developing countries. Report prepared for UNICEF and the ACC Subcommittee on Nutrition of the United Nations. Mimeo.

Bennegan, Eugenia C. 1982. *Staple food consumption in the Philippines.* Working Paper 5. Washington, D.C.: International Food Policy Research Institute.

Bhalla, G. S.; Y. K. Alagh; and R. K. Sharma. 1984. Foodgrains growth—A districtwise study. Report on the second phase of the Jawaharlal Nehru University and the Planning Commission. Centre for the Study of Regional Development, Jawaharlal Nehru University, New Delhi. Mimeo.

Binswanger, Hans P. 1980. Attitudes toward risk: Experimental measurement in rural India. *American Journal of Agricultural Economics* 62.

Binswanger, Hans P., and M. Rosenzweig. 1982. *Production relations in agriculture.* Discussion Paper 105. Princeton, N.J.: Research Program in Development Studies, Woodrow Wilson School, Princeton University.

Blandford, D., and Schwartz, N. E. 1983. Is the variability of world wheat prices increasing? *Food Policy* 11.

Bohrnstedt, G. W., and A. S. Goldberger. 1969. On the exact covariance of products of random variables. *Journal of the American Statistical Association* 65.

Bond, Marian E. 1983. Agricultural response to prices in sub-Saharan African countries. *IMF Staff Papers* 30, No. 4.

Bouis, Howarth. 1983. Seasonal rice price variation in the Philippines: Measuring the effects of government intervention. *Food Research Institute Studies* 19.

Brainard, William C., and Richard N. Cooper. 1968. Uncertainty and diversification in international trade. *Food Research Institute Studies* 8.

Burniaux, Jean-Marc, and Jean Waelbroeck. 1985. The impact of the CAP on developing countries: A general equilibrium analysis. In *Pressure groups, policies and development.* Edited by Christopher Stevens and Joan Verloren van Themaat. London: Hodder and Stoughton.

Carter, T., and M. Parry. 1985. Climatic change and changes in crop yield variability. Paper presented at IFPRI and German Foundation for Agricultural Development workshop on Sources of Increased Variability in Cereal Yields, at Feldafing/Munich.

Cavallo, Domingo, and Yair Mundlak. 1982. *Agriculture and economic growth in an open economy: The case of Argentina.* Research Report 36. Washington, D.C.: International Food Policy Research Institute.

China, People's Republic of. *See* He Kang et al.; *and entries under* Zhongguo; Zhongguo Guojia Tongjiju; Zhongguo Shangyebu.

———. General Administration of Customs. 1986. *China customs statistics.* Hong Kong: Economic Information and Agency.

———. Nongye Jishu Jingji Shouce Bienweihui (Agro-Technical Economic Handbook Editorial Committee). 1983. *Nongye jishu jingji shouce* (Agro-technical and economic handbook). Beijing: Nongye Chubanshe (Agricultural Publishing House).

———. State Statistical Bureau. 1985a. *China: A statistical survey in 1985.* Beijing: New World Press and China Statistical Information and Consultancy Service Centre.

———. 1985b. *Statistical Yearbook of China—1985.* Hong Kong and Beijing: Economic Information Agency and China Statistical Information and Consultancy Service.

———. 1986. Communique of the State Statistical Bureau of the People's Republic of China concerning fulfillment of the 1985 economic and social development plan. Xinhua (New China News Agency) news bulletin, 28 February 1986.

China (Taiwan Executive Yuan). 1983. *Statistical Yearbook of the Republic of China, 1982.* Taipei: Executive Yuan.

Chopra, R. N. 1981. *Evolution of food policy in India.* New Delhi: MacMillan India Ltd.

———. 1984. The changing balance between private and public sector trading in Indian food system. Paper prepared for the fourth agriculture sector symposium, at New Delhi.

Clay, Eward. 1987. Dairy aid to developing countries, development and nutritional issues. Paper presented at International Food Policy Research Institute workshop on market development in selected countries, January, at Copenhagen.

Coffman, W. R., and T. R. Hargrove. Forthcoming. Modern rice varieties as a possible factor in production variability. In *Variability in cereal yields and implications for agricultural research and policy.* Edited by J. R. Anderson and P. B. R. Hazell.

Commission of the European Communities. 1981. *Toward a plan of action to combat world hunger.* COM (81) 560. Brussels: Commission of the European Communities.

Corden, W. M. 1981. *Inflation, exchange rates and the world economy.* 2d ed. Chicago: University of Chicago Press.

Cummings, R. W., Jr. 1967. *Pricing efficiency in Indian wheat market.* New Delhi: Implex India.

Danin, Yigal, and Yair Mundlak. 1979. *The introduction of a new technique and capital accumulation.* Working Paper 7909. Rehovot, Israel: Centre for Agricultural Economic Research.

Dantwala, M. L. 1967. Incentives and disincentives in Indian agriculture. *Indian Journal of Agricultural Economics* 22.

Delgado, Christopher L. 1981. Price policy, returns to labor, and accelerated foodgrain production in the West African savannah. In *Food policy issues and concerns in sub-Saharan Africa.* Washington, D.C.: International Food Policy Research Institute.

————. 1986. A variance component approach to food grain market integration in northern Nigeria. *American Journal of Agricultural Economics* 68.

Delgado, Christopher L., and John McIntire. 1982. Constraints on oxen cultivation in the Sahel. *American Journal of Agricultural Economics* 64 (May).

Delgado, Christopher L., and C. G. Ranade. 1987. Technological change and agricultural labor use. In *Accelerating food production in sub-saharan Africa.* Edited by John W. Mellor, Christopher L. Delgado, and Malcolm J. Blackie. Baltimore: Johns Hopkins University Press.

Dervis, K.; J. de Melo; and S. Robinson. 1982. *General equilibrium models for development policy.* Washington, D.C.: World Bank.

Desai, Gunvant M. 1982. *Sustaining rapid growth in India's fertilizer consumption: A perspective based on composition of use.* Research Report 31. Washington, D.C.: International Food Policy Research Institute.

————. 1983. Fertilizer use on India's unirrigated areas: A perspective based on past record and future needs. Paper presented at International Crops Research Institute for the Semi-Arid Tropics and Indian Society of Agricultural Economics seminar on technology options for dryland agriculture, August 22–24, at Hyderabad.

————. 1984. Growth in fertilizer consumption: Price and non-price policies. Paper presented at World Bank international seminar on fertilizer pricing, at the World Bank, Washington, D.C.

————. 1988. *Understanding the process of growth in fertilizer consumption: A conceptualization.* Washington, D.C.: International Food Policy Research Institute.

Desai, Gunvant M., and Gurdev Singh. 1973. *Growth of fertilizer use in districts of India, performance and policy implications.* Ahmedabad: Centre for Management in Agriculture, Indian Institute of Management.

Dixon, John A. 1982. *Food consumption patterns and related demand parameters in Indonesia: A review of available evidence.* Working Paper 6. Washington, D.C.: International Food Policy Research Institute.

Donnithorne, Audrey. 1970. *China's grain: Output, procurement, transfers and trade.* Hong Kong: Economic Research Centre, Chinese University.

Dornbusch, R. 1974. Tariffs and non-traded goods. *Journal of International Economics* 4.

D'Silva, B., and N. R. Raza. 1980. Integrated rural development in Nigeria: The Funtua project. *Food Policy* 5.

Duvick, D. N. Forthcoming. Possible genetic causes of increased variability in U.S. maize yields. In *Variability in cereal yields and implications for agricultural research and policy.* Edited by J. R. Anderson and P. B. R. Hazell.

Economic Times (Bombay). 1984. Subsidizing fertilizer.

Edirisinghe, Neville. 1987. *The food stamp scheme in Sri Lanka: Costs, benefits, and options for modification.* Research Report 58. Washington, D.C.: International Food Policy Research Institute.

Ellman, Michael. 1975. Did the agricultural surplus provide the resource for the increase in investment in the USSR during the First Five Year Plan? *Economic Journal* 85.

Esguerra, Emmanuel F. N.d. Who pays and who benefits from the Masagana 99 subsidy: Preliminary findings. Mimeo.

———. 1981. An assessment of the Masagana 99 credit subsidy as an equity measure. *Philippine Review of Business and Economics* 18.

FAO (Food and Agricultural Organization of the United Nations). 1951. *Fertilizers, a world report on production and consumption.* Rome: FAO.

———. 1961-70. *Agriculture producer prices.* Rome: FAO.

———. Production tapes, 1975, 1977, 1979, 1980, 1983. Rome: FAO.

———. 1977. *Production yearbook.* Rome: FAO.

———. 1979. *China: Rural processing technology.* Rome: FAO.

———. 1982a. *Producer yearbook.* Rome: FAO.

———. 1982b. *Statistics on prices received by farmers.* Rome: FAO.

———. 1983a. *Fertilizer yearbook.* Rome: FAO.

———. 1983b. *FAO trade yearbook 1982.* Rome: FAO.

———. 1985. *Agricultural supply utilization accounts tape, 1984.* Rome: FAO.

Farouk, Muhammad Osman. 1970. *The structure and performance of the rice marketing system in East Pakistan.* Occasional Paper 31. Ithaca, N.Y.: Department of Agricultural Economics, Cornell University.

Feder, Gershon, and Roger Slade. 1984. The acquisition of information and the adoption of new technology. *American Journal of Agricultural Economics* 66.

Fei, C. H. John; Gustav Ranis; and Shirley W. Y. Kuo. 1979. *Growth with equity: The Taiwan case.* New York: Oxford University Press for the World Bank.

Fertiliser Association of India. 1980. *Development of fertilisers in India.* New Delhi: FAI.

———. 1985. *Fertiliser statistics 1984-85.* New Delhi: FAI.

Fischbeck, G. Forthcoming. Change in the variability of winter wheat and spring barley yields in Bavaria: 1950-84. In *Variability in cereal yields and implications for agricultural research and policy.* Edited by J. R. Anderson and P. B. R. Hazell.

Flinn, J. C., and D. P. Garrity. Forthcoming. Yield stability and modern rice technology. In *Variability in cereal yields and implications for agricultural research and policy.* Edited by J. R. Anderson and P. B. R. Hazell.

Garcia, Jorge Garcia. 1981. *The effects of exchange rates and commercial policy on agricultural incentives in Colombia: 1953-1978.* Research Report 24. Washington, D.C.: International Food Policy Research Institute.

Gardner, Bruce L. 1979. *Optimal stockpiling of grains.* Lexington, MA: D. C. Heath.

Gavan, James D., and Indrani Sri Chandrasekera. 1979. *The impact of public foodgrain distribution on food consumption and welfare in Sri Lanka.* Research Report 13. Washington, D.C.: International Food Policy Research Institute.

George, P. S. 1979. *Public distribution of foodgrains in Kerala—income distribution implications and effectiveness.* Research Report 7. Washington, D.C.: International Food Policy Research Institute.

———. 1983. *Government interventions in foodgrains markets 1985.* Ahmedabad: Indian Institute of Management.

———. 1985. *Some aspects of procurement and distribution of foodgrains in In-*

dia. Working Paper on Food Subsidies 1. Washington, D.C.: International Food Policy Research Institute.

Ghai, D., and L. Smith. 1987. Food price policy and equity. In *Accelerating food production in sub-Saharan Africa.* Edited by John W. Mellor, Christopher L. Delgado, and Malcolm J. Blackie. Baltimore: Johns Hopkins University Press.

Goldman, Richard H. 1974. Seasonal rice prices in Indonesia, 1953–1969: An anticipatory price analysis. *Food Research Institute Studies* 13.

Gour, S. S. 1975. Impact of technological change and uncertainty on supply response of wheat in Madhya Pradesh. Ph.D. diss., Indian Agricultural Research Institute, New Delhi.

Gray, Cheryl Williamson. 1982. *Food consumption parameters for Brazil and their application to food policy.* Research Report 32. Washington, D.C.: International Food Policy Research Institute.

Gruen, Fred H. 1965. Welfare economics, the theory of the second best, and Australian agricultural policy. Monash University, Clayton, Australia. Mimeo.

Gulbrandsen, Odd, and A. Lindbeck. 1973. *The economics of the agricultural sector.* Stockholm: Almquist and Wiksell.

Hall, Lana L. 1978. Food aid and agricultural development: The case of P.L. 480 wheat in Latin America. Ph.D. diss., University of California, Berkeley.

Hayami, Yujiro, and Vernon Ruttan. 1971. *Agricultural Development: An International Perspective.* Baltimore: Johns Hopkins University Press.

Hayami, Yujiro; K. Subbarao; and K. Otsuka. 1982. Efficiency and equity in producer levy in India. *American Journal of Agricultural Economics* 64.

Hayashi, Nobumichi. 1977. *Fund Procurement Structure in China.* IDE Special Paper 6. Tokyo: Institute of Developing Economies.

Hazell, P. B. R. 1982. *Instability in Indian foodgrain production.* Research Report 30. Washington, D.C.: International Food Policy Research Institute.

———. 1984. Sources of increased instability in Indian and U.S. cereal production. *American Journal of Agricultural Economics* 66.

Hazell, P. B. R., and P. L. Scandizzo. 1977. Farmers' expectations, risk aversion and market equilibrium under risk. *American Journal of Agricultural Economics* 59.

Hazell, P. B. R.; C. Pomareda; and Alberto Valdés. 1986. *Crop insurance for agricultural development: Issues and experience.* Baltimore: Johns Hopkins University Press.

He Kang et al., eds. 1980. *Zhongguo Nongye Nianjian, 1980* (Agricultural yearbook of China, 1980). Beijing: Nongye Chubanshe (Agricultural Publishing House).

Herdt, Robert W. 1970. Disaggregate Approach to Aggregate Supply. *American Journal of Agricultural Economics* 50.

Herdt, Robert W., and Mark W. Rosegrant. 1978. The impact of price and income support policies on small rice farmers in the Philippines. *Philippine Review of Business and Economics,* No. 4.

Hirschleifer, J., and John G. Riley. 1979. The analytics of uncertainty and information—An expository survey. *Journal of Economic Literature* 17.

Holden, J. H. 1985. Genetic aspects of yield variability. Paper presented at IFPRI and German Foundation for International Development workshop on Sources of Increased Variability in Cereal Yields, at Feldafing/Munich.

Hopkins, Raymond. 1980. Food aid: The political economy of international policy formation. Report to U.S. Agency for International Development, Washington, D.C.

Hossain, Mahabub. 1984. *Food strategy review: Increasing food availability in Bangladesh—Constraints and possibilities.* Dhaka: Ministry of Agriculture and International Labor Organization.

Hsu, Robert C. 1982. Agricultural financial policies in China, 1949–80. *Asian Survey* 12.

Huddleston, Barbara. 1981. Responsiveness of food aid to variable import requirements. In *Food security for developing countries.* Edited by Alberto Valdés. Boulder, Col.: Westview Press.

———. 1984. *Closing the cereals gap with trade and food aid.* Research Report 43. Washington, D.C.: International Food Policy Research Institute.

IFAP (International Federation of Agricultural Producers). 1984. *National agricultural pricing policies for developing countries: A basic strategy.* Paris: IFAP.

IFPRI-BIDS (International Food Policy Research Institute-Bangladesh Institute of Development Studies). 1985. *Development impact of the food-for-work program in Bangladesh.* Submitted to the World Food Programme. Washington, D.C.: IFPRI-BIDS.

ILO (International Labor Organization). 1977. *Yearbook of labour statistics.* Geneva: ILO.

———. 1983. *Yearbook of labour statistics.* Geneva: ILO.

IMF (International Monetary Fund). 1981. *Annual report.* Washington, D.C.: IMF.

India, Government of. 1961–68. Economic and Statistical Advisor, Ministry of Agriculture. *Agricultural prices in India.*

———. 1965a. Department of Agriculture. *Report of the Jha Committee on foodgrain prices for 1964–65.* New Delhi.

———. 1965b. Ministry of Food and Agriculture, Department of Agriculture. *Report of the Agricultural Prices Commission on price policy for kharif cereals for 1965–66 season.* New Delhi.

———. 1966a. Directorate of Economics and Statistics, Department of Agriculture, Ministry of Food, Agriculture, and Community Development. *Farm management in India: A study based on recent investigation.* New Delhi.

———. 1966b. Department of Food. *Report of the Foodgrains Policy Committee.* New Delhi.

———. 1975. National Commission on Agriculture. *Interim report on agricultural price policy.* New Delhi.

———. 1976. Ministry of Agriculture and Irrigation. *Report of the National Commission on Agriculture.* New Delhi.

———. 1979. Ministry of Agriculture. *Agricultural situation in India.* New Delhi.

———. 1980a. Ministry of Agriculture, Department of Agriculture and Cooperation. *Annual report, 1979–80.* New Delhi.

———. 1980b. *Report of the Special Expert Committee on cost of production estimates.* New Delhi.

————. 1981a. Punjab, Government of. *Statistical abstract of Punjab, 1981.* Chandigarh, Punjab.

————. 1981b. Punjab, Government of. *Farm accounts in Punjab. Economic and Statistical Organization reports for 1969-70 and 1980-81.* Chandigarh, Punjab.

————. 1982a. *Annual report 1981-82.* New Delhi.

————. 1982b. Ministry of Agriculture, Directorate of Economics and Statistics. *Bulletin on food statistics 1981-82.* New Delhi.

————. 1983. Gujarat, Government of, Agriculture and Forest Department. *Report of the working group on fertilizer distribution system in Gujarat.*

————. 1985a. Ministry of Agriculture. *Agricultural situation in India.* Vol. 40, no. 5. New Delhi.

————. 1985b. Ministry of Agriculture. *Indian agriculture in brief, 20th edition.* New Delhi.

————. 1986. Ministry of Agriculture, Directorate of Economics and Statistics. *Bulletin on food statistics, 1985.* New Delhi.

International Road Federation. 1980. *World road statistics.* Geneva: IRO.

International Wheat Council. 1983. *Long-term grain outlook.* Secretariat Paper 14. London: IWC.

Ishikawa, Shigeru. 1965. *National income and capital formation in mainland China—An examination of official statistics.* Tokyo: Institute of Asian Economic Affairs.

————. 1967. Resource flows between agriculture and industry: The Chinese experience. *The Developing Economies* 5 (March).

————. 1977. China's food and agriculture: A turning point. *Food Policy* 2.

————. 1978. *Labour absorption in Asian agriculture: An issues paper.* Bangkok: International Labor Organization Asian Regional Team for Employment Promotion.

————. 1980. "Mo Shu ika" no saiken o mezasite (Examining "Post Mao-Chou" reconstruction). In *1980 nendai no tyuugoku keizai* (China's economy in the 1980s). Edited by Shigeru Ishikawa. Tokyo: Nihon Kokusai Mondai Menkyuujo (Japanese Research Institute for International Issues).

————. 1983. China's economic growth in the PRC period—An assessment. *China Quarterly,* No. 94.

————. 1987. Patterns and processes of intersectoral resource flows: Comparison of cases in Asia. In *Current state of development economics: Progress and perspective.* Edited by Gustav Ranis and T. Paul Schultz. New York: Basil Blackwell.

Ishikawa, Shigeru; Saburo Yamada; and Shigemochi Hirashima. 1982. *Labour absorption and growth in agriculture: China and Japan.* Bankok: International Labor Organization Asian Regional Team for Employment Promotion.

Ithaca International Limited. 1984. *An evaluation of the agricultural technical package for the Republic of Niger.* Report to U.S. Agency for International Development, December 1983. Ithaca, N.Y.: Ithaca International Limited.

Ivory Coast. Ministere de l'Agriculture. 1980. *Statistiques agricoles.*

Jabara, Cathy L., and Robert L. Thompson. 1980. Agricultural comparative advantage under international price uncertainty: The case of Senegal. *American Journal of Agricultural Economics* 62.

Jain, B. K., and Satya Nand. 1980. Productivity in the Indian fertilizer industry. *Fertiliser News* (December).

Jain, H. K.; M. Dagg; and T. A. Taylor. 1985. Yield variability and the transition to the new technology. Paper presented at IFPRI and German Foundation for International Development workshop on Sources of Increased Variability in Cereal Yields, at Feldafing/Munich.

Jansen, Doris J. 1980. *Agricultural pricing policies in sub-Saharan Africa in the 1970s.* Washington, D.C.: World Bank.

Ji, Long, and Nan Lu. 1980. A discussion of the scissors differential between industrial and agricultural products. *Honggi* (Red flag), No. 6.

Johnson, D. Gale. 1981. Food and agriculture of the centrally planned economies: Implications for the world food system. In *Essays in contemporary economic problems: Demand, productivity and population.* Edited by William Fellner. Washington, D.C.: American Enterprise Institute for Policy Analysis.

Johnston, Bruce F., and Peter Kilby. 1975. *Agriculture and structural transformation.* New York: Oxford University Press.

Jones, W. O. 1970. Measuring the effectiveness of agricultural marketing in contributing to economic development: Some African examples. *Food Research Institute Studies* 9.

Josling, T. 1980. *Developed country agricultural policies and developing-country supplies: The case of wheat.* Research Report 14. Washington, D.C.: International Food Policy Research Institute.

JPRS (Joint Publications Research Service). 1985a. Adjustment of cotton policies announced. *China report: Agriculture.* (Originally published in Chinese in *Jaingji Ribao,* 7 November 1984.) JPRS-CAG-85-001. Washington, D.C.: JPRS. Mimeo.

————. 1985b. Grain and cotton procurement policies discussed. *China report: Agriculture.* (Originally published in Chinese in *Jaingji Ribao,* 3 April 1985.) JPRS-CAG-85-018. Washington, D.C.: JPRS. Mimeo.

————. 1985c. Questions on cotton procurement policy clarified. *China report: Agriculture.* (Originally published in Chinese in *Zhongguo Nongmin Bao,* 18 September 1985.) JPRS-CAG-85-014. Washington, D.C.: JPRS. Mimeo.

Kaberuka, D. P. 1984. Evaluating performance of food marketing parastatals. *Development Policy Review* 2.

Kahlon, A. S. 1971. *Studies in economics of farm management, Ferozepur District (Punjab): Report for the year 1969–70.* Department of Agricultural Economics, Punjab Agricultural University, Ludhiana.

Kahlon, A. S., and D. S. Tyagi. 1983. *Agricultural price policy in India.* New Delhi: Allied Publishers.

Karim, Rezaul; Manjur Majid; and F. James Levinson. 1980. The Bangladesh sorghum experiment. *Food Policy* 5.

Kemp, M. C., and T. Negishi. 1969. Domestic distortions, tariffs, and the theory of optimum subsidy. *Journal of Political Economy* 77.

Kennedy, Eileen T. 1983. Determinants of family and preschooler food consumption. *Food and Nutrition Bulletin* 5.

Kenya, Republic of. 1982. Working Party on Government Expenditure. *Report and recommendations of the Working Party to His Excellency the President.* Nairobi: Government Printer.

Khan, Riaz Ahmad. 1982. *Issues of food distribution in Pakistan.* Staff Paper AE-101. Dacca: Pakistan Agricultural Research Council.

Kislev, Yoav, and U. Rabiner. 1979. Economic aspects of selection. *Australian Journal of Agricultural Economics* 23.

Kislev, Yoav, and Nira Shchori-Bachrach. 1973. The process of innovation cycle. *American Journal of Agricultural Economics* 55.

Knight, Henry. 1954. *Food administration in India 1937–47.* Stanford, CA: Stanford University Press.

Knudsen, Odin, and A. Parnes. 1975. *Trade instability and economic development.* Lexington, MA: D. C. Heath.

Koester, Ulrich. 1982. *Policy options for the grain economy of the European Community: Implications for developing countries.* Research Report 35. Washington, D.C.: International Food Policy Research Institute.

――――. 1986. *Regional cooperation to improve food security in southern and eastern African countries.* Research Report 53. Washington, D.C.: International Food Policy Research Institute.

Krishna, Raj. 1963. Farm supply response in India-Pakistan: A case study of the Punjab region. *Economic Journal* 73.

――――. 1982. Some aspects of agricultural growth, price policy and equity in developing countries. *Food Research Institute Studies* 18.

Krishna, Raj, and Ajay Chibber. 1983. *Policy modelling of a dual grain market: The case of wheat in India.* Research Report 38. Washington, D.C.: International Food Policy Research Institute.

Krishna, Raj, and G. S. Raychaudhuri. 1980. *Some aspects of wheat and rice price policy in India.* Staff Working Paper 381. Washington, D.C.: World Bank.

Krueger, Anne O.; Hal B. Lary; Terry Monson; and Narongchai Akrasanee. 1981. *Trade and employment in developing countries.* Chicago: University of Chicago Press for National Bureau of Economic Research.

Krueger, Anne O.; Maurice Schiff; and Alberto Valdés. Forthcoming. *A comparative study of the political economy of agricultural pricing policy.* Washington, D.C.: World Bank.

Kumar, Shubh K. 1978. *Impact of subsidized rice on food consumption and nutrition in Kerala.* Research Report 5. Washington, D.C.: International Food Policy Research Institute.

Kydd, Jonathan, and Robert Christiansen. 1982. Structural change in Malawi since independence: Consequence of a development strategy based on large-scale agriculture. *World Development* 10.

Lamer, Mirko. 1957. *The world fertilizer economy.* Stanford, CA: Stanford University Press.

Lardy, Nicholas R. 1978. *Economic growth and distribution in China.* Cambridge: Cambridge University Press.

――――. 1983a. *Agriculture in China's modern economic development.* Cambridge: Cambridge University Press.

――――. 1983b. *Agricultural prices in China.* Staff Working Paper 606. Washington, D.C.: World Bank.

Lele, Uma. 1971. *Foodgrain marketing in India.* Ithaca, N.Y.: Cornell University Press.

————. 1975. *The design of rural development: Lessons from Africa*. Baltimore: Johns Hopkins University Press.

————. 1977. Considerations related to optimum pricing and marketing strategies in rural development. In *Decision-making and agriculture*. Edited by Theodor Dams and Kenneth E. Hunt. Oxford: Oxford Agricultural Economics Institute.

————. 1984a. Tanzania: Phoenix or Icarus? In *World economic growth*. Edited by Arnold Harberger. San Francisco: Institute of Contemporary Studies.

————. 1984b. The role of risk in an agriculturally led strategy in sub-Saharan Africa. *American Journal of Agricultural Economics* 66.

————. 1985. Terms of trade, agricultural growth and rural poverty in Africa. In *Agricultural change and rural poverty*. Edited by John W. Mellor and Gunvant M. Desai. Baltimore: Johns Hopkins University Press.

————. 1987. Comparative advantage and structural transformation: A review of Africa's economic development experience. In *Current state of development economics: Progress and perspective*. Edited by Gustav Ranis and T. Paul Schultz. New York: Basil Blackwell.

Lele, Uma, and John W. Mellor. 1981. Technological change, distributive bias and labor transfer in a two-sector economy. *Oxford Economic Papers* 33.

Lipton, Michael. 1970. Farm price stabilization in under-developed agricultures: Some effects on income stability and income distribution. In *Unfashionable economies*. Edited by Paul Streeten. Oxford: Oxford University.

————. 1977. *Why poor people stay poor: Urban bias in world development*. Cambridge, MA: Harvard University Press and Temple Smith.

————. 1985. *The place of agricultural research in the development of sub-Saharan Africa*. Brighton, Sussex: Institute of Development Studies.

————. 1987. Personal communication to Christopher L. Delgado.

Lipton, Michael, and Richard Longhurst. 1985. *Modern varieties, international agricultural research, and the poor*. CGIAR Study Paper 2. Washington, D.C.: World Bank.

Little, I. M. D.; T. Scitovsky; and M. Scott. 1970. *Industry and trade in some developing countries: A comparative study*. London: Oxford University Press.

Lu, Chung-Chi. 1973. The role of food aid, agricultural development and capital formation in economic development: A case study of Taiwan. Ph.D diss., Iowa State University.

MacBean, Alasdair. 1966. *Export instability and economic development*. Cambridge, MA: Harvard University Press.

McIntire, John. 1981. *Food security in the Sahel: Variable import levy, grain reserves, and foreign exchange assistance*. Research Report 26. Washington, D.C.: International Food Policy Research Institute.

————. 1982. Reconnaissance socioeconomic surveys in north and west Upper Volta. International Crops Research Institute for the Semi-Arid Tropics Economic Program Progress Report 3. Ouagadougou: ICRISAT.

McIntire, John, and Christopher L. Delgado. 1983. *Variability and statistical significance of indicators of efficiency and incentives in semi-arid African agriculture*. Washington, D.C.: International Food Policy Research Institute.

Manto, J. M., and R. D. Torres. 1974. *Sources and costs of credit to rice farmers in central Luzon*. Paper 74-17. Quezon City, Philippines: National Food and

Agricultural Council, Department of Agriculture and Natural Resources Marketing Research Unit.

Martin, Michael V., and Ray F. Brokken. 1983. The scarcity syndrome: Comment. *American Journal of Agricultural Economics* 65.

Maxwell, S. J., and H. W. Singer. 1979. Food aid for developing countries: A survey. *World Development* 7.

Mears, Leon A. 1981. *The new rice economy of Indonesia.* Yogyakarta: Gadjah Mada University Press.

Mears, Leon A., and Teresa L. Anden. 1972. Who benefits from the post-harvest rice price rise? *Tonan Ajia Kenkyu* 9.

Mehra, S. 1981. *Instability in Indian agriculture in the context of the new technology.* Research Report 25. Washington, D.C.: International Food Policy Research Institute.

Mellor, John W. 1966. *The economics of agricultural development.* Ithaca, N.Y.: Cornell University Press.

———. 1968a. *Developing rural India: Plan and practice* (with Thomas F. Weaver, Uma J. Lele, and Sheldon R. Simon). Ithaca, N.Y.: Cornell University Press.

———. 1968b. Functions of agricultural prices in economic development. *Indian Journal of Agricultural Economics* 23.

———. 1969. Role of government and new agricultural technology. Paper presented at U.S. Agency for International Development spring review, 13–15 May, Washington, D.C.

———. 1973. Accelerated growth in agricultural production and the intersectoral transfer of resources. *Economic Development and Cultural Change* 22.

———. 1976. *The new economics of growth: A strategy for India and the developing world.* Ithaca, N.Y.: Cornell University Press.

———. 1978. Food price policy and income distribution in low-income countries. *Economic Development and Cultural Change* 27.

———. 1980. Food aid and nutrition. *American Journal of Agricultural Economics* 62.

———. 1983. The utilization of food aid for equitable growth. Presented at the World Food Programme—Government of the Netherlands. Seminar on food aid. The Hague, Netherlands, 3–5 October 1983.

Mellor, John W., and Gunvant M. Desai, eds. 1985. *Agricultural change and rural poverty.* Baltimore: Johns Hopkins University Press.

Mellor, John W., and Sarah Gavian. 1987. Famine: Causes, prevention, and relief. *Science* 235.

Mellor, John W., and Bruce F. Johnston. 1984. The world food equation: Interrelations among development, employment, and food consumption. *Journal of Economic Literature* 22.

Mellor, John W., and Uma Lele. 1973. Growth linkages of the new foodgrain technologies. *Indian Journal of Agricultural Economics* 28.

Mellor, John W., and Bruno de Ponteves. 1964. Estimates and projections of milk production and use of concentrate feeds: India 1951–1976. *Cornell International Agricultural Development Bulletin* 6.

Mellor, John W., and C. G. Ranade. Forthcoming. *Technological change in a low labor productivity, land surplus economy: The African development problem.*

Mellor, John W.; Christopher L. Delgado; and Malcolm J. Blackie, eds. 1987. *Accelerating food production in sub-Saharan Africa.* Baltimore: Johns Hopkins University Press.

Montgomery, Roger. 1983. *Open-market grain sales as a public policy instrument for moderating food price fluctuation in Bangladesh.* Dacca: U.S. Agency for International Development.

Mruthyunjaya, M., and D. Jha. 1985. A note on the impact of varietal improvement and intercropping on variability of cereal yields. Paper presented at IFPRI and German Foundation for Agricultural Development workshop on Sources of Increased Variability in Cereal Yields, at Feldafing/Munich.

Mundlak, Yair. 1964. *An economic analysis of established family farms in Israel: 1953-1958.* Falk Project for Economic Research in Israel. Jerusalem: Haomamim Press.

————. 1979. *Intersectoral factor mobility and agricultural growth.* Research Report 6. Washington, D.C.: International Food Policy Research Institute.

————. 1981. On the concept of non-significant functions and its implications for regression analysis. *Journal of Econometrics* 16.

————. 1983. Agriculture and economic growth, theory and measurement. Lecture notes, University of Chicago. Mimeo.

————. 1984. Endogenous technology and the measurement of productivity. Centre for Agricultural Economic Research, Rehoveth, Israel. Mimeo.

Mundlak, Yair, and Chester O. McCorkle, Jr. 1956. Statistical analysis of supply response in late spring potatoes in California. *Journal of Farm Economics* 38.

Myers, R. J., and C. F. Runge. 1985. The relative contribution of supply and demand to instability in the U.S. corn market. *North Central Journal of Agricultural Economics* 7.

Myint, Hla. 1975. Agriculture and economic development in the open economy. In *Agriculture in development theory.* Edited by Lloyd G. Reynolds. New Haven: Yale University Press.

Newbery, D. M. G., and J. E. Stiglitz. 1981. *The theory of commodity price stabilization: A study in the economics of risk.* Oxford: Oxford University Press.

Ng, Gek-boo. 1979. Incentive policy in Chinese collective agriculture. *Food Policy* 4.

Nolan, P., and G. White. 1984. Urban bias, rural bias or state bias? Urban-rural relations in post-revolutionary China. *Journal of Development Studies* 20.

Norton, Roger D., and Peter B. R. Hazell. 1984. A model for evaluating the economic impact of food aid. Paper prepared for IFPRI workshop, Washington, D.C.

Owen, Wyn F. 1966. The double development squeeze in agriculture. *American Economic Review* 56.

Oyejide, T. Ademola. 1986. *The effects of trade and exchange rate policies on agriculture in Nigeria.* Research Report 55. Washington, D.C.: International Food Policy Research Institute.

Panse, V. G. 1964. *Technical and economic possibilities of the use of nitrogen fertilizer in India.* New Delhi: Indian Agricultural Research Institute.

Parhusip, Uben. 1984. Intra-year movement of rice prices in Indonesia. Paper presented at workshop on rice policy in Indonesia, January 25–28, Jakarta.

Pasour, E. C., Jr. 1980. Cost of production: A defensible basis for agricultural price supports. *American Journal of Agricultural Economics* 62. (See also other references in this issue.)

Paulino, Leonardo A. 1986. *Food in the Third World: Past trends and projections to 2000.* Research Report 52. Washington, D.C.: International Food Policy Research Institute.

Peterson, C. J.; V. A. Johnson; J. W. Schmidt; and R. F. Mumm. Forthcoming. Contributions of genetic improvement to increases in wheat yields and variance of productivity in the Great Plains. In *Variability in Cereal Yields and Implications for Agricultural Research and Policy.* Edited by J. R. Anderson and P. B. R. Hazell.

Pfeiffer, W. H., and H. J. Braun. 1985. Yield stability in bread wheat. Paper presented at IFPRI and German Foundation for International Development workshop on Sources of Increased Variability in Cereal Yields, at Feldafing/Munich.

Pham, H. N.; S. R. Waddington; and J. Crossa. 1985. Yield stability of improved germplasm developed and distributed by the CIMMYT maize program. Paper presented at IFPRI and German Foundation for International Development workshop on Sources of Increased Variability in Cereal Yields, at Feldafing/Munich.

Pinstrup-Andersen, Per. 1988. *Food subsidies in developing countries: Costs, benefits, and policy options.* Baltimore: Johns Hopkins University Press.

Pinstrup-Andersen, Per, et al. 1983. *Impact of changes in incomes and food prices on food consumption by low-income households in urban Khartoum, Sudan, with emphasis on the effect of changes in wheat bread prices.* Report to Sigma One Corporation. Washington, D.C.: International Food Policy Research Institute.

Prabha, T. 1982. Public distribution and rice procurement in Tamil Nadu. Ph.D. diss. Center for Development Studies, Trivandrum, India.

Prebisch, Raúl. 1959. Commercial policy in the underdeveloped countries. *American Economic Review* 5.

Rachman, Anas; Sakrani; and Yogana. 1984. Inter-island location of reserves. Paper presented at the workshop on rice policy in Indonesia, January 25–28, Jakarta.

Renmin Ribao [People's daily], various issues.

Ren, Hongzun. 1987. North China plain irrigation and water management issues: An examination of Yucheng County. Unpublished paper. Washington, D.C.: International Food Policy Research Institute.

Reutlinger, Shlomo, and David Bigman. 1981. Feasibility, effectiveness, and costs of food security alternatives in developing countries. In *Food security for developing countries.* Edited by Alberto Valdés. Boulder, Col.: Westview Press.

Rosegrant, Mark W. 1976. *The impact of irrigation on the yield of modern varieties.* Paper 76-28. Los Banos, Phillipines: Department of Agricultural Economics, International Rice Research Institute.

————. 1978. Choice of technology, production, and income for Philippine rice farmers: Agricultural policy and farmer decision making. Ph.D. diss., University of Michigan.

Rosegrant, Mark W., and Robert W. Herdt. 1981. Simulating the impacts of credit policy and fertilizer subsidy on central Luzon rice farms, the Philippines. *American Journal of Agricultural Economics* 63.

Ryan, J. G. 1978. Comments on "Structural changes in rice supply relations: Philippines and Thailand." In *Economic consequences of the new rice technology*. Edited by Yujiro Hayami and Randolph Barker. Los Banos, Philippines: International Rice Research Institute.

Sacay, Orlando. 1973. Credit and small farmer development in the Philippines. *Spring Review of Small Farmer Credit: Small Farmer Credit in the Philippines*, vol. 23. Washington, D.C.: U.S. Agency for International Development.

Sahn, D., and Joachim von Braun. 1985. Yield variability and income, consumption and food security. Paper presented at IFPRI and German Foundation for International Development workshop on Sources of Increased Variability in Cereal Yields, at Feldafing/Munich.

Saran, Ram. 1971. Recent changes in food policy. *Agricultural Situation in India* 17.

Scandizzo, Pasquale. 1984. *The consequences of price stabilization policies: Theoretical problems and empirical measurements*. Rome: Food and Agricultural Organization.

Scandizzo, Pasquale, and Colin Bruce. 1980. *Methodologies for measuring agricultural price intervention effects*. Staff Working Paper 394. Washington, D.C.: World Bank.

Scandizzo, P. L.; P. B. R. Hazell; and J. R. Anderson. 1983. Producers' price expectations and the size of the welfare gains from price stabilization. *Review of Marketing and Agricultural Economics* 51.

————. 1984. *Risky agricultural markets: Expectations, welfare and intervention*. Boulder, Col.: Westview Press.

Schmidt, Guenter. 1979. *Maize and beans marketing in Kenya*. Nairobi: Institute of Development Studies.

Schultz, Theodore W. 1960. Value of US farm surpluses to underdeveloped countries. *Journal of Farm Economics* 42.

————. 1968. *Transforming traditional agriculture*. New Haven: Yale University Press.

Scobie, Grant. 1981. *Government policy and food imports: The case of wheat in Egypt*. Research Report 29. Washington, D.C.: International Food Policy Research Institute.

————. 1983. *Food subsidies: Their impact on foreign exchange in trade in Egypt*. Research Report 40. Washington, D.C.: International Food Policy Research Institute.

Scobie, Grant, and Rafael Posada. 1978. The impact of technical change on income distribution: The case of rice in Colombia. *American Journal of Agricultural Economics* 60.

Shalit, Haim, and Hans P. Binswanger. 1984. *Fertilizer subsidy: A review of policy issues with special emphasis on West Africa*. Washington, D.C.: World Bank.

Siamwalla, Ammar. 1986. Approaches to price insurance for farmers. In *Crop insurance for agricultural development: Issues and experience.* Edited by P. B. R. Hazell, C. Pomareda, and Alberto Valdés. Baltimore: Johns Hopkins University Press.

Siamwalla, Ammar, and Stephen Haykin. 1983. *The world rice market: Structure, conduct and performance.* Research Report 39. Washington, D.C.: International Food Policy Research Institute.

Sjaastad, Larry A., and K. W. Clements. 1981. The incidence of protection: Theory and measurement. Hamburg: Conference on the Free Trade Movement in Latin America. Mimeo.

Solow, Robert M. 1963. *Capital theory and the rate of return.* Amsterdam: North Holland.

Squire, Lyn; I. M. D. Little; and Mete Durdag. 1979. *Application of shadow pricing to country economic analysis with an illustration from Pakistan.* Staff Working Paper 330. Washington, D.C.: World Bank.

Srivastava, Uma; Earl O. Heady; Keith D. Rogers; and Leo V. Mayer. 1975. *Food aid and international economic growth.* Ames: Iowa State University Press.

Stevens, Christopher. 1978. The use of food aid in Tunisia. Overseas Development Institute (London) Working Paper 6. Mimeo.

Stiglitz, J. E., and A. Weiss. 1981. Credit rationing with imperfect information. *American Economic Review* 71.

Stolper, W., and P. A. Samuelson. 1941. Protection and real wages. *Review of Economic Studies* 9.

Stone, Bruce. 1979. Agricultural price policy in the People's Republic of China Paper presented at the International Food Policy Research Institute, Washington, D.C.

―――. 1983. The use of agricultural statistics: Some national aggregate examples and current state of the art. In *The Chinese Agricultural Economy.* Edited by Randolph Barker, Radha Sinha, and Beth Rose. Boulder, Col.: Westview Press.

―――. 1984a. Long-term intersectoral resource flows among countries undergoing technical transformation of agriculture: With special reference to the People's Republic of China. Paper prepared for the 31st International Congress of Human Sciences in Asia and North Africa, 1–3 September 1983, at Tokyo. (Abstract in proceedings volume edited by Tatsuro Yamomoto [Tokyo: Toho Gakkai (Institute of Eastern Culture)].)

―――. 1984b. An examination of the prospects for demand for chemical fertilizer, in the People's Republic of China. Paper presented at the World Bank, Washington, D.C.

―――. 1985. The basis for Chinese agricultural growth in the 1980s and 1990s: A comment on document no. 1, 1984. *China Quarterly* (March).

―――. 1986a. Chinese fertilizer application in the 1980s and 1990s: Issues of growth, balance, allocation, efficiency and response. In *China's economy looks to the year 2000: The four modernizations.* Edited by U.S., Congress, Joint Economic Committee. Washington, D.C.: U.S. Government Printing Office.

―――. 1986b. Food and agriculture in the context of rural employment generation problems of China and other developing countries: Emerging constraints and required research. Paper prepared for the International Rural Employment Promotion Strategies Seminar, April 6-13, Beijing.

————. 1986c. Chinese socialism's record on food and agriculture. *Problems of Communism* (September-October).

————. 1987. Foodgrain production and consumption performance in China and India. Paper prepared for the annual meeting of the American Association for the Advancement of Science, Chicago.

Subbarao, K. 1979. Producer levy, evasion and income loss: Empirical evidence from coastal districts of Andhra Pradesh. *Economic and Political Weekly* 14.

————. 1984. *Incentive policies and India's agricultural development: Some aspects of regional and social equity.* New Delhi: Institute of Economic Growth.

Suzuki, Yuriko, and Andrew Bernard. 1987. *Effects of panterritorial pricing policy for maize in Tanzania.* Washington, D.C.: International Food Policy Research Institute.

Tang, Anthony M., and Bruce Stone. 1980. *Food production in the People's Republic of China.* Research Report 15. Washington, D.C.: International Food Policy Research Institute.

Te, Amanda. 1982. An economic analysis of a reserve stock program for rice in the Philippines. Rice Policies in Southeast Asia Project, Working Paper 7. Washington, D.C.: International Food Policy Research Institute.

Technical Board of Agricultural Credit. 1983. A study on selected rural banks participating in the supervised credit programs. Mimeo.

Timmer, Peter C. 1976. A model of rice marketing margins in Indonesia. *Food Research Institute Studies* 13.

Trairatvorakul, Prasarn. 1984. *Rice price policy and equity considerations in Thailand: Distributional and nutritional effects.* Research Report 46. Washington, D.C.: International Food Policy Research Institute.

Tubpun, Somnuk. 1974. The price analysis and the rate of return on holding rice and paddy in Thailand. M.A. thesis, Thammasat University, Bankok.

Tyagi, D. S. 1987. Domestic terms of trade and their effect on supply and demand of agricultural sector. *Economic and Political Weekly* (Bombay) 22.

UNIDO (United Nations Industrial Development Organization). 1976. *Draft worldwide study of the fertilizer industry: 1975-2000.* Vienna: UNIDO.

Unnevehr, Laurian J. 1983. *The effect and cost of Philippine government intervention in rice markets.* Rice Policies in Southeast Asia Project, Working Paper 9. Washington, D.C.: International Food Policy Research Institute.

————. 1984. *World market demand for grain quality and Philippine export potential.* Manila: Asian Development Bank.

USAID (U.S. Agency for International Development). 1982. Approaches to the policy dialogue. AID Policy Paper. Washington, D.C.: USAID.

USDA (U.S. Department of Agriculture). 1986. *World grains situation and outlook.* Foreign Agriculture Circular (Grains), March. Washington, D.C.: USDA.

Valdés, Alberto. 1973. Trade policy and its effect on the external agricultural trade of Chile, 1945-1965. *American Journal of Agricultural Economics* 55.

————. 1986. Exchange rate and trade policy: Help or hindrance to agricultural growth? In *Agriculture in a turbulent world economy: Proceedings of the nine-*

teenth international conference of agricultural economists, Malaga, Spain. August 26–September 4, 1985. Edited by Allen Maunder and Ulf Renborg. Aldershot: Gower.

Valdés, Alberto, and P. Konandreas. 1981. Assessing food insecurity based on national aggregates in developing countries. In *Food security for developing countries.* Edited by Alberto Valdés. Boulder, Col.: Westview Press.

Valdés, Alberto, and Joachim Zietz. 1980. *Agricultural protection in OECD countries: Its cost to less-developed countries.* Research Report 21. Washington, D.C.: International Food Policy Research Institute.

Vallaeys, P.; M. Silvestre; Malcolm I. Blackie; and Christopher L. Delgado. 1987. Development and extension of agricultural production technology. In *Accelerating food production in sub-Saharan Africa.* Edited by John W. Mellor, Christopher L. Delgado, and Malcolm J. Blackie. Baltimore: Johns Hopkins University Press.

Van Wijnberger, Sweder. Forthcoming. Oil price shocks and the current account: An analysis of short-run adjustment measures. *Kyklos.*

Venkitramanan, S. 1983. Government policy issues and implications on fertilizer plant costs. *Fertiliser News* (May).

Virmani, A. 1982. The nature of credit markets in less developed countries: A framework for policy analyses. Working Paper 524. Washington, D.C.: World Bank.

Von Braun, Joachim. 1982. Effects of food aid in recipient countries, Egypt and Bangladesh, a comparative study. *Economics* (Institute for Scientific Cooperation, Tübingen) 26.

Von Braun, Joachim, and Hartwig de Haen. 1983. *The effects of food price and subsidy policies on Egyptian agriculture.* Research Report 42. Washington, D.C.: International Food Policy Research Institute.

Von Pischke, J. D.; Dale W. Adams; and Gordon Donald. 1983. *Rural financial markets in developing countries.* Baltimore: Johns Hopkins University Press.

Von Plocki, Joachim. 1979. *Auswirkungen der Nahrungsmittelhilfe unter P.L. 480 auf den Agrarsektor der Entwicklungslaender.* Wiesbaden: Steiner Verlag.

Walker, T. Forthcoming a. High-yield varieties and variability in sorghum and pearl millet production in India. In *Variability in cereal yields and implications for agricultural research and policy.* Edited by J. R. Anderson and P. B. R. Hazell.

————. Forthcoming b. Yield and household income variability in India's semi-arid tropics. In *Variability in cereal yields and implications for agricultural research and policy.* Edited by J. R. Anderson and P. B. R. Hazell.

Wang Tong-eng. 1980. *Economic policies and price stability in China.* China Research Monograph 16. Berkeley, CA: Institute for Chinese Studies.

Whetham, E. 1972. *Agricultural marketing in Africa.* London: Oxford University Press.

World Bank. 1976. *The Philippines: Priorities and prospects for development.* Washington, D.C.: World Bank.

————. 1980. *Price prospects for major primary commodities.* Washington, D.C.: World Bank.

————. 1981. *Accelerated development in sub-Saharan Africa: An agenda for action.* Washington, D.C.: World Bank.

————. 1983a. *Malawi agricultural sector report.* Washington, D.C.: World Bank.

————. 1983b. *Tanzania agricultural sector report.* Washington, D.C.: World Bank.

————. 1984a. *The outlook for primary commodities, 1984 to 1995.* Staff Commodity Working Paper 11. Washington, D.C.: World Bank.

————. 1984b. *Price prospects for major primary commodities.* Washington, D.C.: World Bank.

————. 1985. *Commodity Trade and Price Trends.* Washington, D.C.: World Bank.

————. 1986a. *Poverty and hunger: Issues and options for food security in developing countries.* Washington, D.C.: World Bank.

————. 1986b. *The world development report.* Washington, D.C.: World Bank.

Xiao, Shuping. 1983. Xin Zhongguo chengli yilaide liangshi jiage ji qi guanli (Grain prices and their management since the founding of New China). *Jiage Lilun Yu Shijian* (Price theory and practice) 5.

Zhao, Ziyang. 1987. Report on work of government. Address to the Fifth Session of the Sixth National People's Congress. *Beijing Review* 30 (April).

Zhongguo (Zhongguo Guojia Tongjiju [State Statistical Bureau of China]). 1983. *Zhongguo tongji nianjian—1983* (Statistical yearbook of China—1983). Xianggang: Xianggang Jingji Daobao Shechuban (Hong Kong Economic Reporter Publishing House).

————. 1984. *Zhongguo tongji nianjian—1984* (Statistical yearbook of China—1984). Xianggang: Xianggang Jingji Daobao Shechuban (Hong Kong Economic Reporter Publishing House).

————. 1985. *Zhongguo tongji nianjian—1985* (Statistical yearbook of China—1985). Xianggang: Xianggang Jingji Daobao Shechuban (Hong Kong Economic Reporter Publishing House).

————. 1986. *Zhongguo tongji nianjian—1986* (Statistical yearbook of China—1986). Beijing: Zhongguo Tongji Chubanshe (Statistical Publishing House of China).

————. 1987. Guanyu yijiubaliunian guomin jingji he shehui fazhan de tongji baogao (Statistical report of national economic and social development in 1986). *Renmin Ribao,* 22 February 1987.

Zhongguo Guojia Tongjiju (Zhongguo Guojia Tongjiju Maoyi Wujia Tongjisi [State Statistical Bureau, Department of Trade and Price Statistics]), eds. 1984. *Zhongguo maoyi wujia tongji ziliao, 1952-1983* (Statistical data on Chinese trade and prices, 1952-1983). Beijing: Zhongguo Tongji Chubanshe (Statistical Publishing House of China).

Zhongguo Shangyebu (Zhongguo Shangyebu Shangye Jingji Yanjiusuo [Ministry of Commerce of China, Commercial Economic Research Institute]). 1984. *Xin Zhongguo shangye shigao* (A brief commercial history of New China). Beijing: Zhongguo Caizheng Jingji Chubanshe (Financial and Economic Publishing House of China).

Appendix

Non-IFPRI Participants, IFPRI Workshop on Food and Agricultural Price Policy
Belmont Estate, Elkridge, Maryland, 29 April–2 May, 1984

T. Adlington, Senior Economist
Policy Analysis Division
Food and Agriculture Organiza-
tion, United Nations
Rome

Soegeng Amat
Badan Urusan Logistik
Jakarta, Indonesia

G. S. Bhalla, Chairman
Agricultural Prices Commission
Government of India
New Delhi, India

Marco Ferroni
Swiss Development Cooperation
Berne, Switzerland

Ahmed Goueli, Head
Agricultural Economics Depart-
ment
Zagazig University
Cairo-Giza, Egypt

Romulo Grados Fuentes, Principal
Advisor
Ministerio de Agricultura y Ali-
mentacion
Lima, Peru

Roberto Junguito, Ambassador of
Colombia
European Economic Community
Brussels, Belgium

A. M. A. Muhith, Visiting Fellow
The Woodrow Wilson School of
Public and International Affairs
Princeton University
Princeton, N.J.

I. K. Mutuku, Chief Planning
Officer
Ministry of Finance and Planning
Nairobi, Kenya

D. N. Namu, Permanent Secretary
Ministry of Agriculture and Live-
stock Development
Nairobi, Kenya

Vincente Valdepenas, Jr., Director-General
National Economic and Development Authority (NEDA)
Manila, Philippines

M. Syeduzzaman, Principal Secretary and Advisor

Ministry of Finance and Planning
Dhaka, Bangladesh

Miguel Urrutia, Vice Rector
Development Studies Division
The United Nations University
Tokyo, Japan

Contributors

RAISUDDIN AHMED is director of the Food Production Policy Program at the International Food Policy Research Institute. He has done research on food distribution and agricultural price policies in Bangladesh, food marketing and pricing policies in Asia and Africa, and the role of the rural infrastructure in agricultural productivity, rural employment, and rural income distribution. He formerly served as deputy chief of the Agriculture and Water Resources Division of the Planning Commission of the Government of Bangladesh and as chief agricultural economist in the Ministry of Agriculture.

JOACHIM VON BRAUN is a research fellow at the International Food Policy Research Institute and a coordinator of research on poverty alleviation. He was previously a research associate at the Institute of Agricultural Economics, University of Göttingen, Federal Republic of Germany. His work focuses on food and agricultural pricing policies, policies related to external assistance to the food sector, and the relationship between agricultural production and food consumption in the Third World.

CHRISTOPHER L. DELGADO is a research fellow and a coordinator for African research at the International Food Policy Research Institute. He has written on West African farming and pastoral systems, agricultural price policy, foodgrain marketing issues, the political economy of West Africa, and long-run policies to support African production.

GUNVANT M. DESAI is a research fellow and a coordinator of research on technology policy at the International Food Policy Research Institute. Earlier he was a professor at the Indian Institute of Management in Ahmedabad and chairman of IIM's Centre for Regional Management Studies. He is currently working on policy issues of agricultural inputs, particularly fertilizers. He has been a member of several advisory bodies, including the Government of India's High Powered Committee on Fertiliser Prices.

PETER B. R. HAZELL is an economist with the World Bank. Previously, he was director of the Agricultural Growth Linkages Program at the International Food Policy Research Institute. Apart from his current research on employment and income effects of increases in agricultural productivity and crop insurance, he is studying the increased instability in world cereal production.

BARBARA HUDDLESTON is chief of the Food Security and Information Service in the Commodities and Trade Division of the Food and Agriculture Organization of the United Nations. She was formerly a research fellow at the International Food Policy Research Institute. Before that she was an economist with the Africa Division of the U.S. Department of Commerce and director of the Trade Negotiations Division in the U.S. Department of Agriculture. She currently supervises FAO's Global Information and Early Warning System and services the organization's Committee on World Food Security.

DAYANATHA JHA is a research fellow at the International Food Policy Research Institute. He was formerly a professor of agricultural economics at the Indian Agricultural Research Institute in New Delhi and a visiting scientist at the International Crops Research Institute for the Semi-Arid Tropics in India. He is currently working on the generation and diffusion of agricultural technology, with particular reference to Africa.

JOHN W. MELLOR is director of the International Food Policy Research Institute. He was formerly chief economist for the U.S. Agency for International Development. Before that he was a professor of agricultural economics, economics, and Asian studies at Cornell University. In 1985 he received the Wihuri Foundation International Prize. The American Agricultural Economics Association honored him in 1986 for "The role of agriculture in economic development" (with Bruce F. Johnston). He was honored twice previously by that association for quality of research. He was a recipient of the 1987 U.S. Presidential End Hunger Awards. He is also a fellow of the American Academy of Arts and Sciences and the American Agricultural Economics Association.

YAIR MUNDLAK is Ruth Ochberg Professor of Agricultural Economics at Hebrew University of Jerusalem, F. H. Prince Professor of Economics at the University of Chicago, and a research fellow at the International Food Policy Research Institute. Formerly, he was head of the Department of Agricultural Economics, dean of the faculty, and director of research of the Center for Agricultural Economic Research at Hebrew University. He has written several books and numerous articles on micro and macro aspects of agricultural economics, with an emphasis on empirical analysis, as well as methodological articles on economics and econometrics. He has received several awards from the American Agricultural Economics Association and the Bareli and the Rothschild prizes.

LEONARDO A. PAULINO is director of the Food Data Evaluation Program at the International Food Policy Research Institute. He has served as director of the Bureau of Agricultural Economics of the Department of Agriculture in the Philippines, as a member of the governing board of the Southeast Asia Regional Center for Graduate Study and Research in Agriculture, and as a member of the task force of the Second Asian Agricultural Survey conducted by the Asian Development Bank. He has also been a visiting professor at the University of the Philippines at Los Baños.

PER PINSTRUP-ANDERSEN is a professor of food economics at Cornell University and director of the Cornell Nutrition Surveillance Program. He was formerly director of the Food Consumption and Nutrition Policy Program at the International Food Policy Research Institute. Before that he was a senior research fellow and associate professor at the Economic Institute, The Royal Veterinary and Agricultural University, Copenhagen, and director of the Agro-Economic Division of the International Fertilizer Development Center in Alabama. He has undertaken extensive research on the effect of public policy on income distribution, food consumption, and nutrition.

C. G. RANADE is an economist at the World Bank on the Managing Agricultural Development in Africa (MADIA) project. Previously he was a research fellow at the International Food Policy Research Institute and prior to that was an associate professor at the Indian Institute of Management in Ahmedabad.

MARK W. ROSEGRANT is a research fellow at the International Food Policy Research Institute and a coordinator of its research on technology policy.

Previously, he was a policy analyst with the Ministry of Agriculture of the Philippines and taught at the University of the Philippines. He has done research on the equity and productivity of alternative irrigation systems and water management methods, long-term irrigation investment strategies in Southeast Asia, the impact of risk on input use and production, biological technology in rice production, and agricultural credit policy.

J. S. SARMA is a staff member of the International Food Policy Research Institute. He previously held several posts in the Government of India, including chief executive officer of the National Sample Survey Organisations, member secretary of the National Commission on Agriculture, and economic and statistical adviser of the Ministry of Food and Agriculture. He has been president of the Indian Society of Agricultural Economics, vice-president of the Indian Society of Agricultural Statistics, and a member of the FAO Statistics Advisory Committee. His interests are growth with equity, agricultural development policies and strategies, and food production and consumption trends, particularly of livestock products and feedgrains.

AMMAR SIAMWALLA is program director for agriculture and rural development at the Thailand Development Research Institute. He was formerly a research fellow at the International Food Policy Research Institute, where his work included a study of the world rice market and an examination of pricing and marketing policies of the major commodities in Thailand, done for the National Economic and Social Development Board of Thailand and the World Bank. His present research interests are in various aspects of the Thai rural sector, such as credit, production growth, and pricing policies.

BRUCE STONE is a research fellow at the International Food Policy Research Institute. He recently completed a study of the Chinese fertilizer sector for the World Bank, a similar study for the Joint Economic Committee of the U.S. Congress, and a study of the Bangladesh fertilizer economy for the Bangladesh Ministry of Agriculture. He has written numerous articles on Chinese agricultural statistics and is coauthor of a report on food production in the People's Republic of China.

ALBERTO VALDÉS is director of the International Food Trade and Food Security Program at the International Food Policy Research Institute. He was previously an economist at the International Center for Tropical Agriculture in Colombia and served as director of the postgraduate program in economics and dean of the faculty of agriculture at the Universidad Católica de Chile. He has published extensively on trade policy and food security.

Index

Adams, Dale, 219
Adams, Richard, 83
ADBS. *See* Agricultural development banks
Africa, 256, 282. *See also specific countries*
Agricultural Bank of China, 145
Agricultural Credit Administration (ACA), 233
Agricultural development banks (ADBS), 95
Agricultural prices: and economic growth, 7, 269-74; and income distribution, 1-2, 271; management of, 283-90; and resource allocation, 2. *See also* Price policy
Agricultural Prices Commission (APC), 77-78, 167; established, 156-57; price determination criteria of, 157-61; procurement prices, 160 (table)
Agriculture: aggregate production, 271-72; commodity composition of, 273-74; comparative advantage for, 288; constant returns to scale in, 198; developmental functions of, 25, 142-44, 153; economic surplus from, 242; export-oriented, 117; to finance industrialization, 152; government expenditure on, 280-81; growth in, 204; home goods role in, 112; and industrial protection, 108, 110-12; instability in, 275-277; and investment, 8, 137-38, 145; in low-income countries, 266; modernization of, 2; motorization of, 172; relative profitability of, 63; research for, 8, 99; taxation of, 188, 262; during technical transformation, 141-42; technology, 107, 172-73, 185; terms of trade, 145, 263; and tradables, 114, 122
Ahmed, Raisuddin, 57, 70, 74, 75, 76, 77, 78, 248
Alagh, Y. K., 181, 182
Anderson, J. R., 99, 100

APC. *See* Agricultural Prices Commission
Argentina, 114
Arrow, Kenneth, 118
Average cost pricing, 157-58

Balance of payments, 115
Bangladesh, 284; and devaluations, 76; fertilizer subsidy in, 57; food aid to, 254, 256; food expenditures in, 282; food procurement in, 69, 70; price fluctuations in, 74; ration shops in, 246, 248; rice exports, 60
Beaton, G. H., 250
Bernard, A., 67, 76
Bhalla, G. S., 181, 182
Bigman, David, 82
Binswanger, Hans, 57, 94, 220, 221, 224
Blackie, Malcolm, 267
Black market, 71
Blandford, D., 27
Bond, Marian, 200
Brainard, William, 118, 119
Braun, H. J., 50
Brazil: fertilizer use in, 206; food aid to, 253; food subsidy programs, 249
Brokken, Ray, 288
Bruce, Colin, 56
Burkina Faso: agricultural wages in, 202; costs/returns for cotton, 194 (table); cotton production in, 193, 194
BULOG. *See* Indonesian National Logistics Agency

Capital: in Chinese agriculture, 132; defined, 187; gross investment rate, 178; heterogeneous, 177-78; intersectoral allocation of, 184; investment inefficiency, 142; and real exchange rates, 114-15; returns to, 182, 270; rural